Lyman Stowe

What is coming

A wonderful exposition of the prophecies and comparison with ancient and

modern historical and political events

Lyman Stowe

What is coming
A wonderful exposition of the prophecies and comparison with ancient and modern historical and political events

ISBN/EAN: 9783337134358

Printed in Europe, USA, Canada, Australia, Japan

Cover: Foto ©ninafisch / pixelio.de

More available books at **www.hansebooks.com**

What is Coming

IS

A WONDERFUL EXPOSITION
OF THE PROPHECIES AND
COMPARISON WITH ANCIENT
AND MODERN HISTORICAL
AND POLITICAL EVENTS,
TOGETHER WITH AN AMPLE,
THOUGH CONCISE HISTORY
OF MONEY FROM KING SOLO-
MON'S TIME TO THE PRESENT

By

LYMAN E. STOWE

Author of: "Poetical Drifts of Thought
or Problems of Progress," "Dynamite
and The Torch," "The Agnostic's
Lament," "My Wife Nellie
and I," Etc Etc. Etc.

DETROIT, MICHIGAN:
1896.

To the person who purchases a copy of this book and assists in abolishing interest on money to the invidual, thereby destroying the curse of the world, this book is dedicated.

Entered according to act of Congress in the year 1896

By LYMAN E. STOWE,

in the office of the Librarian of Congress at Washington, D. C.

FINANCIAL PHILOSOPHY.

INDEX.

	PAGE.
Why do we have hard times?	1
Are men mean enough to make it?	1
What is money?	1
Evidence that money is a creation of law	2
What is a pound?	2
What is a foot?	2
What is a bushel?	2
What is a gallon?	2
What is a dollar?	2
Should commodities of a high intrinsic or quality value be used as money?	2
What is intrinsic value?	2
Where can intrinsic value be found?	2
What constitutes utility value?	2
What is commercial value?	2
Where did the term dollar originate?	9
Laws on coinage	9-11
Making foreign coins	11
When was the first coin struck in this country?	11
Coinage laws continued	12
How many governments use the term dollar?	14
Extract from Ingall's speech	15
Life of paper money	17
A dollar abroad	17
United States Silver Commission	19
Value of gold in old Peru	20
Table of fluctuation of gold during the war	21
Jevons on gold	22
Adam Smith on gold	23
Colwell on gold	23
Conspiracy against gold	24
Value of gold and silver compared	25
Evidence of conspiracy	25
Interest on money	26
Where does interest differ from usury	27
Biblical quotations on usury	28 29
Murray on usury	29
The Pope becomes a usurer	31
The Pope defines usury	32
What interest means	33
Peter Cooper on interest	34
Would it destroy commerce to change our system of money	35
Can interest be governed by law?	37
Volume	37
Volume and civilized countries compared	38

Would prices settle to a small volume? 42
Money in history............... 43
Hebrews or Israelites............... 43
Ancient Greece, Homer, Hesiod, Cæsar
   and Lycurgus on money.......... 46
Carthage...................... 47-48
Rome......................... 49
The murder of Cæsar............... 52
Bank of Venice................... 54
Bank of Genoa................... 55
Bank Amsterdam.................. 55
Bank of Hamburg................. 56
The Tally system of England........ 57
The Bank of England.............. 60
The John Law money.............. 67
The French assignat............... 74
Bank of France................... 75
England's conspiracy against Napo-
   leon........................ 76
Colonial money................... 77
Continental money................ 84
Terrible conspiracy................ 86
Suppression of truth............... 86
No independent press.............. 89
Money of the Isle of Guernsey....... 91
Sketchley, the English statistition, on
   the Bank of England........... 92
National Banks................... 95
Crucify him...................... 97
Amendments of the Constitution.... 100
Alexander Hamilton steps towards
   the English system and the first
   United States Bank............ 102
Quotation from Burkey on the old
   United States Bank............ 105
The crash of 1819................ 106
Jackson's fight and the attempt to
   assassinate him............ 107-110
The wild cat banking system....... 111
Pennsylvania issues relief notes...... 113
Panic of 1857.................... 114
Panic of 1861.................... 118
The great conspiracy at work...... 119
The Hazard circular and its aiders
   by traitors in Congress....... 119-136
The banker's fraud and first demand
   notes........................ 137
Lincoln's letter.................. 139
The conspiracy in favor of an empire 145
Evidence that the bankers are in it... 146
The bank circular................. 147
What the New York Tribune and
   Times say.................... 148-9
The election conspiracy of 1868..... 149
Senator Sherman shows the cloven
   foot......................... 152

FINANCE IN PROPHECY.
INDEX.

	PAGE
The Bible dealings with governments..	265
Time space and matter	266
Space and matter	267
The hypnotic state	268
Four elements	269
The student and psychic phenomena	271
Man and the Bible	273
To develop a character	276
Man not what he seems	277
God	279
God, labor and rest	280
Man's descent from heaven	281
Re-incarnation taught in the Bible	284
God's week	287
Interest on money in the Bible	294
The church and usury	299
Sketch of Rothschilds	301
Daniel's Prophecy	303
Evidence of the last days	313
The United States in prophecy	313
End of Daniel's prophecy	314
The United States in God's plan	319
Christ's kingdom on earth	322
The Great Red Dragon	323
The English money power, the dragon	328
And reasons therefor from page...	329-34
The Mother of Harlots and beast, restored	335-38
The Roman Catholic church adopts pagan forms and ceremonies.	338-42
Morse's discovery of conspiracy	342
The seven headed beast	345
The future of the papacy	347
The woman sitting on the scarlet beast	348
The seven headed dragon	352-54
The image of the beast	354
The flag of England	355
The dragon, the beast and the image	355-60
The prophetic dates explained	360-64
And his number was 666	365-66

FINANCE IN PROPHECY.
INDEX.

Extent of money power..........253
Form of money...................254
What is money?..................259
The Bible dealings with governments 265
Time, space and matter..........266
Space and matter 267
The hypnotic state 268
Four elements 270
The student and psychic phenomena 271
Man and the Bible..............273
To develop a character..........276
Man not what he seems..........277
God 279
God, labor and rest.............280
Man's descent from heaven.......281
Reincarnation taught in the Bible.284
God's week 291
Interest on money in the Bible...294
The church and usury...........299
Sketch of Rothschilds...........301
Daniel's prophecy 303
Evidence of the last days........306
United States in prophecy.......313
End of Daniel's prophecy.........314
The United States in God's plan..319
Christ's kingdom on earth.......322
The Great Red Dragon..........323
The English money power, the dragon 325
And reasons therefor.......329 to 334
The mother of harlots and beast, restored ....334 to 338
The Roman Catholic church adopts pagan forms and ceremonies....338
Morse's discovery of conspiracy...342
The seven-headed beast..........345
The image of the beast..........354
The flag of England.............355
The dragon, the beast and the image 356
The prophetic dates explained....360
And his number was 666.........366
Repeated in lecture form...367 to 422
Our flag in the Bible......307 to 416
Political history of our country—Part 4 450
Treason—now we're to have a king 471

INDEX TO ILLUSTRATIONS.
Of Tables and Illustrations.
Frontispiece.
Table of dollars of nations....... 14
Table of fluctuations of gold...... 21
Table of interest................. 34
Money per capita................. 38

Illustrations.
The tally system.................. 58
Colonial money 82
Continental money 83
Money in circulation 172
Prosperity of Greenback days.....184
Prosperity of Bimetalism.........185
Gold backs 185
Egyptian coin 202
Celtic coin 202
Coin of Athens...................203
Different periods 203
Coins of Carthage 204
Coins of Rome....................
Wampum 205
The money power—the dragon...253
An ideal dollar..................254
Illustrated idea of the universe...279
The Zodiac 373
The scales 373
The Sun, Venus 374
Uranus 375
Nebuchadnezzar's vision 378
Stone cut without hands..........379
The winged lion 381
The bear 382
The four-headed beast............382
The beast with ten horns.........383
The three-crowned hat............384
Neptune 387
Three signs of the Zodiac........387
The ram 387
Paul Jones' flag 401
The first stars 402
The rattlesnake flag.............403
Betsy Ross making the flag.......404
The flag that Betsy made.........405
Old Glory 406
The woman who fled to the wilderness 410
The dragon and the man child....411
The seven-headed beast...........418
The image of the beast...........419
The ten-crowned beast 421
The harlot and the beast.........422
The financial cancer.............468
The body politic.................469
The traitor's king...............471
His coat-of-arms 472
His flag 474
The woman sitting on the beast..348
Mystery 350
10 usurers' countries or horns...353
Ring money 202
A safe, reliable plan............255

PREFACE.

In writing the preface of this book I will say that I had no idea of writing so extensive a work. Though for twenty years I have been gathering the matter for an extensive treatise on finance, I concluded that it would best reach the masses in an abridged or condensed form, so I compromised between the primer I set out to write and the extensive work contemplated for the future, and produced the forcible though condensed work in hand.

I will frankly admit I was led into the discussion of finance in prophecies by unseen forces, as stated elsewhere, and I will also frankly say that on the night of December 3rd, 1895, I was visited by a spirit and an angel in my own bedroom. I saw them as distinctly as I ever saw any earthly beings, and I was in the full possession of all my faculties. They came in answer to a prayer. I was thereby more fully assured of the righteousness of my course and encouraged to pursue my plans. To many this will seem the positive evidence of insanity or crankism. But to those who carefully read the work I can feel assured they will, at least, admit there is very much method in my madness, as no book was ever written containing more and better evidence of authority.

With the evidence the history of the world shows of opposition to reformers and advanced thinkers, especially when their reforms strike the rich, I may expect, first to be ignored; with fair success, ridiculed; with greater success, all manner of obstacles will be thrown in my path; and if the work is productive of great effect, my reputation, my liberty and my life will be put in jeopardy.

> "In parts superior what advantage lies?
> Tell (for you can) what is it to be wise?
> 'Tis but to know how little can be known;
> To see all other's faults, and feel your own;
> Condemned in business or in arts to drudge,
> Without a second, or without a judge:
> Truths would you teach, or save a sinking land?
> All fear, none aid you and few understand.
> Painful pre-eminence: yourself to view
> Above life's weakness, and its comforts too."
>
> — Pope.

That there might be some who would not care to read a work on theology, though it encomposed a part of the financial question, I recognized and so placed that part of the work by itself.

Upon revising this book I saw the necessity of deviding the book into four parts and of repeating that part of prophesy, tho in lecture form, and I invite all who wish to use the lecture, to do so, and to take orders for the book, and to send the orders to me, and I will devide the profits on your sales with you, when two or or more books are ord erd at one time. It is to do good that I seek. Price, manilla board 75 c'ts. Cloth $1.50 Nearly 500 pages, over 50 ilustrations with two large charts, for lecture purposes.
Lyman E. Stowe 131 Catherine st. Detroit. Mich.

PART ONE

FINANCIAL PHILOSOPHY

Having long seen the necessity of a work of reference or definitions used in the discussion of economic questions, and on July 3, 1894 being seized with an inspiration to write a series of questions and answers, that if read must enlighten the public on many points, I dropped all other matters and bent my energies to producing the following catechism, which I believe, will throw more light on the great questions of the day than anything heretofore given to the public:

Q. Why do we have hard times in a land of plenty, where undeveloped wealth is unlimited ready to pour out at the touch of man, and with plenty of idle men ready and willing to work?

A. Because men who deal in money reduce the volume of money so low that A waits for B and B for C and so on down the alphabet, and business is stagnated and Labor thrown out of employment and the prices of all property reduced until forced sales enables the privileged class to centralize wealth and enslave the people through the control of money.

Q. Are these men mean enough to do that?

A. Yes; for if men will corner railroads, wheat, pork, lard and all other commodities to make money out of, they will corner money for the same purpose.

Q. What is money?

A. John Stewart Mill, the economist, says, "Money is a

creation of law." Blackstone, the English Law Giver, also says, money is a creation of law and defines money thus: "Money is a measure of value by comparison whereby we ascertain the comparative value of all commodities. Therefore money is an ideal thing and stands in relation to the measurement of comparative values the same as the yardstick, the gallon and pound do to weights and measures of quantities."

Q. Have you any other evidence that money is a creation of law?

A. Yes; because you cannot pay a debt by force of law with any other commodity. A man may refuse to take wheat, corn, cattle, houses, gold, silver, or any other commodity, and sue and get a judgment, payable in money of the realm. But if money is tendered him he can never get a judgment payable in any other commodity in the world, unless the contract creating the debt so specified. This has been proven in many a Supreme Court decision, quoted in a pamphlet published by Richard F. Trevellick, Detroit, Mich.

Q. What is a pound?

A. A pound avoirdupois is a unit of measure by weight and is subject to divisable units. It must of necessity be fixed by law, otherwise there would be no stable measurement, and the pound vary according to the various estimates of more or less generous natures.

Q. What is a foot?

A. The foot is a unit of running measure, originally supposed to be the length of a man's foot. But men's feet vary in length and a more stable measurement was sought. The foot as finally adopted was composed of 12 inches, the inch based upon the measurement of three barley grains lying lengthwise. This was not satisfactory and the foot in America was established by law and is equal to 12.391,012 of the length of a second's pendulum in the City Hall of New York City. In other countries it differs somewhat from this.

Q. What is a bushel?

A. The bushel is the unit of value of dry measure. It and its subsidiary multiples are fixed by law. In New York the bushel measure must contain 80 lbs of distilled water at its maximum density at the mean pressure of the atmosphere at the level of the sea. This is the measure the law recognizes in settling all disputed measurements of dry measure, yet no one would be foolish enough to demand that every tool called a bushel measure should be tested with so much distilled water, or that the tool should be made of any specified metal, unless they desired to control the number of bushel measures, when they would demand that bushel measures should be made of some scarce commodity so the number of measures may be limited that they might better control them.

Q. What is a gallon?

A. The lawful gallon is the unit of liquid measure. In the United States it is the standard Winchester wine gallon of 2.31 cubic inches and contains 8.3388 avoirdupois lbs, or 58.372—1754 troy grains of distilled water at 39.83 Fahrenheit, the barometer being at 30 inches.

Q What is a dollar?

A. A dollar is a unit of measurement of comparative values. Like all other measures it is fixed by law, to prevent bickering and strife, and like all other measures it is an ideal thing. Its fractional proportions are mills, cents, dimes. No one ever saw a mill, coined yet it exists in the ideal and proves that the dollar and its fractional proportions like all other measures are ideal. But the tool which represents the idea is an entirely different thing.

Q. Should any of these tools be made of material possessing intrinsic value?

A. There is no substance but what contains intrinsic value. Some substances contain a higher intrinsic value than others, as for instance, iron possesses a greater intrinsic value than gold so if intrinsic value is required iron should be used for any or all of these tools rather than any other substance.

Q. What is intrinsic value?

A. Intrinsic value is that quality inherent in a substance making it useful for many purposes, and it exists just as much in the article if 10,000 feet under ground as when fulfilling its function in the hand of man.

Q. Can intrinsic value rest in anything but a natural product or the raw material?

A. No; for the moment the raw material is converted into a manufactured article it possesses a tool value and until the desire for the tool falls below the desire for the substance to fill some other purpose the intrinsic value is as much lost at though the metal or commodity were still 10,000 feet underground. When the jeweler or dentist melts up a gold coin it is because the intrinsic value of the metal is worth more to him than the tool value. But he, like the murderer has committed a crime, though of less degree, because he has taken what he cannot restore or give back. Because money belongs to the whole people, as it was created by law, and law belongs to the body politic. This is why Lycurgus of of old Spartia steeped his iron coin in acid destroying its malleability thereby destroying its intrinsic value that it might not be directed into other channels and its tool value lost.

Q. What constitutes tool or utility value?

A. Utility value rests alone in a manufactured article or a natural product appropriated for a special use and is separate from intrinsic or commercial value.

Q. Now you have given us a definition of intrinsic value and of utility value, please define commercial value?

A. Commercial value depends entirely upon the law of supply and demand and is applicable to any commodity, natural or manufactured that is desired by man—thus a thing may possess intrinsic or utility value and still command no commercial value.

Q. Please give us an illustra- wherein the three values may play a distinctive part?

A. Mr. Brown is one of a thousand men living upon an island. He manufactures plows, but few are required on the island but he has manufactured a large supply for sale on the main land; but the island is surrounded by an hostile fleet, and so his plows cannot be got to market, the island can make use of but few plows and as commercial value is a thing of conditions, the plows have been deprived of their commercial value as plows. But the utility value remains the same, so Mr. Brown chooses some one of his plows and makes use of it to cultivate a piece of ground to sustain life until he can go back to his former occupation. Meantime the people of the island have determined to defend themselves, but they need iron to make cannon, and shot, and timber to make carriages, and for other purposes. Someone suggests they use Mr. Brown's plows. Now the intrinsic value of the wood in the plow handles has been nearly spoiled altogether in consequence of cutting it up in so small pieces, as it cannot be replaced in its original mass. But the iron being fusible into one mass has not lost its intrinsic value for it can now be converted into any purpose required, and the demand for the iron has given commercial value to that substance far above the commercial value of Mr. Brown's plows. He hastens to dispose of his plows to reimburse himself for the loss sustained in the labor of manufacture, as the labor of manuture of plows is lost; which proves that labor does not always create wealth and that wealth is a thing purely conditional. Aristotle says; "And we call that thing wealth that fills the desire of man, lands, houses cattle, money." Thus money is wealth and depends upon conditions for its commercial value. But Mr. Brown wishes to obtain every dollar for his iron that he can, so sells his last plow. Now he must have a plow, he creates one from a piece of petrified wood, which answers the purpose. Others see him do this and do the same so the island is supplied with plows which possess a utility value. But as no one wishes to purchase plows, being able to supply their own, there is no commercial value worth speaking of attached to the plows, and the material contains but little intrinsic value, as it is not fusible and can be converted into few if any other purposes.

In California mining districts are dead cities, large stores, hotels and mansions entirely deserted, the mines have petered out. In consequence of the changed conditions the commercial value has been swept away—

the utility value has been somewhat impaired by the tooth of time so that it would require labor to restore the utility to it, the intrinsic value of the iron and stone remain the same though it is far removed from the use of man.

There may be thousands of other illustrations but this is sufficient to show that commercial value is a thing of conditions. It shows us that money being an ideal thing it is a stable measurement of comparative value. But the tool representing the measure depends for its exchange or commercial value, entirely on the law of supply and demand. This is as much the fact as that a yard stick measures three feet and that A may give a hundred dollars for a yard stick to be used in a great commercial transaction providing that yard stick is the only known correct yard stick available. Thus it is shown that it is an accurate representative of the ideal that is sought, and that the commercial and intrinsic value bear no relation to the ideal or utility value of the tool. Then it proves that when the government creates money it creates commercial value as it creates a tool that posseses a commercial value. But let the government create too many of the tools called a dollar and it reduces its commercial value, though the nominal or comparitive value remains the same. Ten mills make one cent, ten cents make one dime and ten dimes one dollar just the same. If the government issue too large a volume of money little damage is done. But if the government allow the volume of dollars to fall below the required necessities of legitimate business great damage is done, for the dollar representing all commodities is in greater demand than any other commodity, as it is a house, a horse, demand than any other commodity, as it is a house, a horse, clothing or any other commodity in a nut shell, and people will sacrifice all other commodities for that dollar, or sacrifice honor, virtue and all that is noble and good for money. Thus when money is scarce the tendencies of civilization are backward.

I heard some one say money is not wealth, you can't make a house of money, it is only a representative of wealth. No; money is wealth because men will sacrifice every other thing for money, thus the desire for it, under the law of supply and demand gives it value. It is true you cannot make a house of it, nor can you make a pair of boots out of a saddle, but that does not prove that the saddle is not an article of value, a unit of wealth. This is different, however, with the note of hand, the bank note or mortgage as all of these things are mere promises to pay money, and are not wealth but represent that the person who gave them, either has wealth or has made a misrepresentation. If however, there are too many of these promises on the market it is a very dangerous thing, for it shows there is too little money in circulation and debts are paid in promises so when these promises fall due, unless there has been an increase of money, the demand for the tool (dollar) is so great that its commercial value goes up and every other thing is sacrificed for money that debts may be paid and so save something out of the wreck caused by too small a volume of money.

Q. You have explained that the promisary note and the bank note are merely a promise to pay money and are not money--please explain what is currency?

A. Money may be currency but currency is not always money. A note of hand is neither money nor currency. A bank note is currency as it owes its existence to certain legislative enactements, though it is not money but a promise to pay money. Drafts and checks are also classed as currency, though they pass current but to a limited extent.

Q. Where did the term dollar originate?

A. Some writers claim the dollar was known or term used for money by some nations as far back as the year 1609, and coins so named of various value circulated in England at that date. The term dollar is taken from the Latin daleros, dale and the coin called dollar was first struck in the dale or valley of Joachim, in Bohemia. The dollar, the money unit of the United States was taken from the Spanish milled dollar so called because the edge was raised above or stamped. It was established under the confederation by resolution of congress July 6, 1786 fixing the silver dollar as the unit of American money and to contain 375-64-100 grains of pure silver and authorizing a mint. This remained a dead letter and was finally abrogated by the following enactments April, 1792.

SECTION 9. And be it further enacted, that there shall be from time to time, struck and coined at the said mint, coin, of gold, silver and copper, of the following denominations, values and descriptions, viz:

Eagles; each to be of the value of ten dollars, or units, and to contain two hundred and forty-seven grains and four-eights of a grain of pure or two hundred and seventy grains of standard gold.

Half Eagles; each to be of the value of five dollars, and to contain one hundred and twenty three grains and six-eights of a grain of pure or one hundred and thirty-four grains of standard gold.

Quarter Eagles; each to be of the

value of two and a half dollars and to contain sixty-one grains and seven-eighths of a grain of pure or sixty-seven grains and four-eighths of a grain of standard gold.

Dollars, or units; each to be of the value of a Spanish milled dollar as the same is now current, and to contain three hundred and seventy-one grains four-sixteenths parts of a grain of pure or four hundred and sixteen grains of standard silver.

Half dollars; each to be of half the value of the dollar or unit, and to contain one hundred and sixty-five grains and ten sixteenths parts of a grain of pure, or two hundred and eight grains of standard silver.

Quarter dollars; each to be of one-fourth the value of the dollar or unit, and to contain ninety-two grains and thirteen-sixteenths parts of a grain of pure, or one hundred and four grains of standard silver.

Dimes; each to be of the value of one-tenth of a dollar or unit, and to contain thirty-seven grains and two sixteenths parts of a grain of pure, or forty-one grains and three-fifths parts of a grain of standard silver.

Half dimes; each to be of the value of one twentieth of a dollar, and to contain eighteen grains and nine-sixteenths parts of a grain of pure, or twenty and four-fifths grains of standard silver.

Cents; each to be of the value of the one-hundredth part of a dollar, and to contain eleven penny weights of copper.

Half cents; each to be of the value of a half a cent, and to contain five and one-half penny weights of copper.

SECTION 20. And be it further enacted, that the money of account of the United States shall be expressed in dollars or units, dimes or tenths, cents or one-hundredths; and mills or one thousandths; a dime being the tenth part of a dollar, a mill the thousandth par of a dollar; and that all accounts the in public offices, and all proceedings inthe courts of the United States, shall be kept and had in conformity to this regulation.

These enactments alone should forever settle the question that money is the creation of law, and that it is an ideal thing, and that various substances may be used as a tool to represent the ideal.

Q. When was the first coin struck in this country?

A. The first coin was not struck until 1794. Thus showing that for at least nine years this country was without the tool called a dollar, or unit of measure of comparative values. As a substitute for the legal tool the people used foreign coins and other commodities. But foreign coins, while they were legal money in the realms that stamped them, were not money in this country; and that we might have a legal representative of our ideal unit of measurement of comparative values, certain foreign coins were made legal tender in this country by enactments that will be mentioned farther on. In 1793 all foreign coins, except the Spanish milled dollar, were demonetized or declared not a legal tender in this country.

March 2, 1799 there was an act passed regulating foreign coins, making them legal tender and acceptable for custums dues at certain fixed rates.

This proves again that money is a creation of law and that the money of one country is not money in another country, except it be made so by an enactment of law.

Again March 3, 1801, the law fixing the value of foreign coins was revised; and again April 10, 1806, and declaring them a legal tender.

Again March 30, 1823, the enactment was revised, so far as gold coins were concerned; again June 25, 1834 the silver coins, dollars of Mexico, Peru, Chili and Central America of not less weight than 415 grains each—and those restamped in Brazil of like weight.

Act January 18, 1837, coinage laws revised the standard for both gold and silver coin changed

Act of July 27, 1842, fixed the legal value of the English pound sterling at ($4.84.)

Act of March 3, 1843, again revised and fixed the value of foreign coins.

Act of March 3, 1849, authorized the issue of gold double eagles and gold dollars.

Act of March 3, 1855, silver three cent pieces were authorized.

Act of Feb. 21, 1853, silver coins, except the dollar, demonetized and the weight reduced. The half dollar or fifty cent piece was fixed at 192 grains, before 206 grains. All smaller coins reduced in proportion—made legal tender in sums not to exceed $5. Section 31 of this enactment provides for the issue of $3 gold pieces. There were few if any of this coin ever struck off.

Act of Feb. 21, 1857, all former acts making foreign coins a legal tender were repealed and section 34 made the Mexican dollar and a few other foreign silver coins a legal tender.

Act of April 22, 1864, the small penny or cent and two cent pieces were authorized, the cent made a legal tender to the amount of ten cents and the two cent piece legal tender to the extent of twenty cents.

Act of March 3, 1865, the three cent nickel piece was authorized and made a legal tender to the extent of sixty cents. One and two cent pieces were made a legal tender for only four cents and all other laws repealed.

Act of May 16, 1866, nickel five cent pieces were authorized and made legal tender to the extent of one dollar.

Up to Feb. 12, 1873, silver was considered the standard metal of this country, but by the enactment of this date the silver dollar was wiped out as the standard of our unit of measure and a gold unit substituted and the weight of the gold coins increased. Section 2 of this enactment provided for a trade dollar of 420 grains, leaving the subsidiary coins at the original weights and making all a legal tender in the sum of five dollars. This enactment was very clearly stolen through and was probably paid for with British gold. See article on conspiracy further on.

Act of March 3, 1875, silver twenty cent pieces authorized.

July 13, 1876, the trade dollar was demonetized.

Jan. 25, 1878, the following resolution passed both houses of Congress.

That all the bonds of the United States issued or authorized to be issued under the said acts of Congress hereinbefore recited are payable, principle and interest, at the option of the government of the United States, in silver dollars of the coinage of the United States, containing $412\frac{1}{2}$ grains each of standard silver; and that to restore to its coinage such coins as a legal tender in payment of said bonds, principal and interest, is not in violation of the public faith, nor in derogation of the rights of the public creditor. The Bland bill restoring the old silver dollar of $412\frac{1}{2}$ grains of silver, passed over the President's veto and became a law Feb. 28, 1878.

This did not restore silver to its former position of a free coinage with gold, but it gave us compulsory coinage of two million silver dollars per month, payable for both principal and interest of the public debt. Through trickery and influence the conspirators have prevented the government ever paying a dollar in silver for interest or principle of the bonded debt.

Undoubtedly the money changers had determined to get

rid of silver as soon as possible consequently the following trick was perpetrated:

The Sherman bill that became a law in 1890 stopped the issue of silver dollars and instead provided for the purchase of four million of ounces of silver per month, to be used as a security for silver certificates to be issued by the treasury department. The trick lay in the provision in the Sherman bill, for the repeal of the Bland bill and in 1893 the money changers shipped gold out of the country for the purpose of bringing on a panic that they might charge it to the Sherman bill and get up a popular cry for its repeal. Mr. Sherman voted to repeal his own bill and with its repeal the purchase and coinage of silver ceased, and we were left with the single standard of gold.

Q. How many governments are there that use the term dollar and do they all contain the same amount of silver?

A. The following table was published by the United States Treasury department:

Bremen, dollar valued at 73¾c
Prussian, " " " 69c
N. Germany, " " 69c
Saxony, " " " 69c
Denmark, " " " 105c
Norway, " " " 106c
Sweeden, " " " 106c
Mexico, " " " 99 8c
Liberia, " " " 100c
Ecuador, " " " 91c
Bolivia, " " " 95 5c
Central America, " " 91c
Peru, " " " 91-8c

Here are thirteen different nations using the term dollar as their unit of measure of comparative values, with dollars of light weight and valuations.

Now which is the dollar of the world? Is it the 78 cent dollar of Bremen, weighing 305 grains? The 100 cent dollar of Liberia weighing 450 grains or the 100 cent dollar of the United States, weighing 412½ grains? Does this not prove that there is no such thing as money of the world, as these dollars are not money except in the realm that issued them?

Q. If the government makes a dollar that costs but 5 cents and pays it to A for a day's work and A pays it to B and B to C, and so on through the alphabet to Y, and Y pays it back to the government for taxes, who has lost anything?

A. No body.

Q. Then who has gained?

A. The whole people.

Q. What are some of the arguments in favor of a cheap material over a costly one for our tool, the unit of comparative value?

A. I have before stated that a costly commodity cannot be used for two purposes at the same time, therefore when a substance is used for a specified purpose it is wise economy to use that substance that costs the least, in time and labor to produce, for when it is lost or worn out the loss is only to the individual, and will not cost the producer so much to replace.

In a speech delivered by John J. Ingalls, February 15, 1878, he says, "No enduring fabric of national prosperity can be builded on gold. Gold is the money of monarchs; kings court it. * * Its tendency is to acumulate in vast masses, * * in such volumes as to unsettle values and disturb the finances of the world. It is the instrument of gamblers and speculators, and the idol of the miser and thief. * * Whenever it is most needed it always disappears. * * *

No people in a great emergency ever found a faithful ally in gold. * * *

It makes no treaty it does not

break. It has no friends it does not sooner or later betray. Armies and navies are not maintained by gold. * * *

No nation ever fought a great war by the aid of gold; on the contrary, in the crises of great perils, it becomes an enemy more potent than the foe in the field; but when the battle is won and peace secured, gold reappears and claims the fruits of victory. In our own civil war it is doubtful if the gold of New York and London did not work us greater injury than the powder, lead and iron of the rebels. It was the most invincible enemy of the public credit. Gold paid no soldier nor sailor. It refused the national obligations. It was worth most when our fortunes were the lowest. * * *

It was in an open alliance with our enemies the world over. * but as usual, when danger has been averted, gold swaggers to the front."

I will add that it murdered two of our Presidents, (see conspiracies) and that it was cheap paper money that carried on our war and saved the nation.

Mr. Ingalls further says, "The gold value of the nickel five cent piece is exactly four sevenths of one cent; and the government has made a profit to this date of four million, six hundred and eighteen thousand dollars by this coinage." "I have heard these pieces called tokens." "They are tokens just as the silver dollar or the double eagle are tokens." They are convertible into any other lawful money. A nickel, worth four-sevenths of one cent will purchase five cents worth of any commodity just as certainly and cheaply as five cents worth of gold, because the nation has so decreed. The same is true of our subsidiary silver coinage, which has been alloyed to such an extent that the country is nearly six million dollars richer by the seigniorage."

Money which represents the comparative values of all commodities is a creation of law. Gold and silver require labor for their production. They have there uses in the arts and for ornaments, but as coin no person wants them, except to enable him to obtain other commodities. The holder of a paper dollar does not prize it because he can exchange it for gold, nor does the holder of the silver dollar value it because it contains a certain number of grains of metal.

The life of paper money averages but seven years. Had the government never issued a dollar of metal money, but all paper how many hundred millions of dollars better off would the government have been?

The cry that I want a dollar that is money if I go abroad is only the cry of knaves and fools for there never was a money of the world. The gold eagle is not money in London, it is not money in Paris or in Berlin. True it may be sold for English, French, or German money. So might wheat or any other commodity.

The man who travels abroad does not usually load himself down with gold, but deposits his money in bank and takes a letter of credit to a foreign bank and the foreigner does the same thing and the American uses the Englishman's money and the Englishman uses the American's money. And it is the same when the Englishman sells his silk for American gold or the American sells his wheat for English gold. the Englishman uses the American's money, and the American uses the Englishman's money, and even balances, are seldom settled in gold and never as money but the gold is weighed out as so much bullion or a commodity.

Q. Then if it makes no difference what material money is made of, will not at some times gold and silver as commodities rise or fall in value above or below the monetary value of the commodity in the coin, as the case might be? Can you state when such a thing ever took place?

A. Yes; gold and silver as well as any other commodities are subject to the law of supply and demand. But either end of the law may be effected by artificial means, and as Ingalls says, gold and silver is the tool of the gamblers. Men who deal in money will corner it the same as men who deal in wheat or other commodities.

During our late war, says Secretary Fessenden: "Experience cannot have failed to convince the most careless observer that, whatever may be the effect of a redundant circulation upon the price of coin, other causes have exercised a greater and more deleterious influence. In course of a few days the price of these articles rose from $1.50 to $2.85 in paper for $1.00 in coin and subsequently fell, in as short a period to $1.87 and then again rose as rapidly to $2.50; *and all without any assignable cause traceable to the increase or decrease in circulation of paper money.*"

The work of the gold gambler's of course, cornering it; and this is a nice thing for a basis for the people's money.

That gold and silver depend as much upon the law of supply and demand, for their commodity value as any other substance there is any amount of evidence to show. I will quote further in proof of this matter.

From the beginning of the Christian era to the fifteenth century, the precious metals were used almost exclusively for money. The mines failed and as the coins wore out and disappeared the contraction was so great that suffering was unparalleled. But rather let me give it in the words of the

U. S. SILVER COMMISSION OF 1876, VOL. I.

"At the Christian era the metalic money of the Roman Empire amounted to $1,800,000 000. By the end of the fifteenth century it had shrunk to less than $200,000,000.

During this period a most extraordinary and baleful change took place in the condition of the world. Population dwindled and commerce, arts, wealth and freedom all disappeared. The people were reduced by poverty and misery to the most degraded conditions of serfdom and slavery. This disintegration of society was almost complete. The conditions of life were so hard that individual selfishness was the only thing consistent with the instinct of self preservation. All public spirit, all generous emotions, all the noble aspirations of man shriveled and disappeared as the volume of money shrank and prices fell.

History records no such disastrous transition as that from the Roman Empire to the dark ages. Various explanations have been given of this entire breaking down of the frame work of society, but it was certainly coincident with a shrinkage in the volume of money, which was also without historical parallel.

The crumbling of institutions kept even step and pace with the shrinkage in the stock of money and the falling of prices. All other attending circumstances than these last have occured in other historical periods unaccompanied and followed by any such mighty disaster.

It is a suggestive coincidence that the first glimmer of light only came with the invention of bills of exchange and paper substitutes, through which the scanty stock of precious metals was increased in efficiency."

This is pretty good evidence that everything depends upon

the volume of money. But let us pursue this subject until we run it down to a certainty.

Prescott in his history of Peru tells us that gold was found so plentiful there by Pizarro that it fell in value to an enormous extent. The natives did not use it for money as their trading was all by barter, article for article. One of the Spanish soldiers traded a hatchet for his two handsful of gold and the native ran away for fear the man would want to trade back.

Says Prescott, "A quire of paper was sold for ten pesos-de-oro, eleven dollars and sixty seven cents of our money. Therefore the quire of paper exchanged for $116.70 in gold, reckoned in our money of to-day.

A bottle of wine sold for sixty pesos-de-oro, a sword for fifty, a cloak for a hundred and sometimes more, a pair of shoes for forty, a good horse for twenty five hundred."

Figuring in our money it would look so:

A bottle of wine,	$700.20
A sword,	$466.80
A cloak,	$167.00
A horse,	$29 175.00
A pair of shoes,	$350.10

All payable in gold and silver.

A thing that fluctuates like that is a nice thing for a basis for money, a'int it?

Burkey on money in his appendix, page 381, gives the following table of sliding scale of prices of gold in New York for 14 years and he quotes from the Tribune Almanac for 1876.

The left hand column of each year shows the lowest price and the right hand column the highest.

THE FLUCTUATION OF GOLD

DATE.	1862		1863		1864		1865		1866	
January,	PAR	105	134	160¾	151¼	160	197¼	234¼	136⅝	144⅝
February,	102⅛	104⅝	153	172½	157⅞	161	196⅝	216½	135⅛	140⅝
March,	101½	[illegible]	139	[illegible]	159	169⅞	148⅛	201	125	136¼
April,	101¼	102⅛	146	159	166¼	187	144	160	125	129⅛
May,	102⅞	104⅛	143½	155	168	190	128⅝	145¼	125⅛	141⅛
June,	103¾	109	140¼	148⅛	189	251	135⅝	147⅝	137⅛	167¼
July,	109	120¼	124¼	[illegible]	222	285	138	146⅛	[illegible]	156¾
August,	112¼	116¼	122⅛	129⅝	231¼	262	145⅝	148⅛	146¼	152¼
September,	116¼	[illegible]	127	143¼	185	255	142⅝	145	143¼	147⅛
October,	122	137	140⅝	156⅛	189	229	144	149	145¼	154⅝
November,	129	[illegible]	143	154	209	260	145¼	148¼	137¼	148⅛
December,	130	134	147	152¼	211	244	144¼	146⅝	131¼	141⅛

DATE.	1867		1868		1869		1870	
January,	132	137¼	133¼	142¼	134⅝	136⅝	119⅝	123¼
February,	137⅝	140¼	139⅝	144	130⅞	136⅛	115	121½
March,	133⅜	140⅞	137⅞	141⅝	130½	132¼	110¼	116⅝
April,	132⅝	141⅞	137½	140⅝	131⅝	134¾	111½	115⅛
May,	134⅞	138⅛	139⅛	140½	134⅛	144¾	113¾	115¼
June,	136⅜	138¼	139⅝	141¼	137	139⅝	110⅞	114⅛
July,	136⅛	140¼	140¼	145¼	134	137½	111⅛	122⅝
August,	139⅞	142⅝	143½	150	131¼	137⅝	114⅞	122
September,	141	140⅝	141⅛	145¼	130½	162¼	112¼	116¾
October,	140¼	145⅝	133⅜	140¼	128⅛	131¾	111⅛	[illegible]
November,	137⅛	141⅛	132⅛	137	121⅛	128⅝	110	114⅛
December,	133	137⅛	134¾	136⅝	119¼	124	110¼	111⅛

DATE.	1871		1872		1873		1874		1875	
January,	110¼	111½	108⅜	110¼	111⅝	114½	110¼	112¼	111⅝	113⅜
February,	110⅝	112¼	109¼	111	112⅞	115¼	111⅜	113	113¼	115⅝
March,	110⅛	111⅝	109⅝	110¼	114⅛	118¼	111¼	113⅝	114⅝	117
April,	110⅛	111⅝	109⅛	113¼	116⅝	119¼	111⅛	114⅝	114	115½
May,	111	112¼	112⅛	114⅜	116⅝	118⅛	111⅞	113¼	115	116⅞
June,	111⅛	113⅛	113	114⅜	115	118¾	110¼	112½	116½	117¼
July,	111⅛	113⅜	113½	115½	115	116⅝	109	110¼	111⅝	117⅝
August,	111⅝	111¼	112⅛	115⅜	114⅝	116¼	109¼	110¼	112⅛	114⅝
September,	112½	115⅝	112¾	115⅛	110⅛	116⅛	109⅝	110¼	113¼	117⅝
October,	111⅝	115	112¼	115⅛	107⅝	111½	109¾	110⅛	114⅛	117¼
November,	110⅝	112⅝	111⅜	114⅛	106⅛	110⅛	110	112⅛	114⅛	116⅛
December,	108⅝	110⅝	111⅜	113½	108⅛	112⅝	110¼	112¾	112⅝	115¼

John A Logan, in the appendix to the Congressional Record for 1874 says: "The price of gold is regulated just as the price of any other article of merchandise by the supply and demand." And then he gives us a table showing the difference in per cent in the rise and fall of gold from 1865 to 1874, which is substantially the same as the table here given.

Now our gold gambling friends will tell us that it was not gold that fluctuated in price from day to day or month to month, but it was the paper money that fluctuated. But this is easily proven false, as paper money bought the same amounts of the necessaries of life from day to day while gold would buy more or less as the case might be.

There was a policy of contraction of paper money adopted as early as April, 1865, and steadily pursued and the volume of paper money was growing less from day to day and all other values were shrinking in proportion, except gold, and that was fluctuating. What should make it go up 26 cents in June, 1866, fifteen months after the war, and the next September fall 24 cents? Why should it rise 17 cents in Agust, 1868, and then fall 17¾ cents the next November? Why should it rise 25 cents in September, 1869, four years after the war, and a steady contraction of paper money was going on, and then fall 31 cents the following month? There is no other possible answer than that the money changers were cornering it to gamble on. A nice thing for a basis for money, is it not?

William S. Jevons professor of political economy in the Owens University, England, says:

"There is plenty of evidence to prove that inconvertible paper money, if carefully limited in quantity, can retain its full value. * * But there is abundance of evidence to prove that the value of gold has undergone extensive changes. Between 1789 and 1809 it fell 46 per cent. * From 1809 to 1849 it rose in value 145 per cent."

Now this is not from a fanatical Greenbacker but from one of the great English professors and writers on the hard money side of the money question.

Adam Smith, another celebrated writer on political economy, says:

"The metals constantly varying in their own value they can never be made an accurate measure of value of other commodities."

And so I could pile up volumes of quotations from the most reliable men to show that the so-called precious metals are neither fit for money or a basis for money.

Colwell, in his "Ways and Means of Payment," speaks as follows:

"Another attribute, generally given to the precious metals, is that they are a standard of value.

This is inaccurate:

"Gold cannot in the mint be made the standard for silver, nor can silver be made standard for gold. Much less, taking the whole range of articles for human consumption, can they be made a standard of value to which all can be referred."

I have here given plenty of evidence that gold and silver fluctuate and are a poor thing to use for money and a worse thing as a basis for money, and they cannot even be held at a parity with one another. Are the bankers who insist on a gold basis blind to all of this; Then why do they cling to the old barbaric system and demand a gold basis? It is because by that means they can control the volume and thereby own the people, and control them as serfs and slaves. The proof of the fact lies in all historical records, and the evidence in what we behold before us. If mountains of gold and silver were found these selfish men would be demanding a diamond basis or some of the more expensive metals, of which there are a number of metals more valuable than gold or silver.

In 1894 when gold was discovered in California the bankers got so scared for fear money would become so plentiful that the people would become commercially free, that a short time after, the bankers of Germany, Austria, Belgium and Holand prevailed on those governments to demonetize gold, and adopt silver for a basis. But as it began to look as if silver would be the most plentiful metal, gold was remonetized and a systematic war waged against silver and one of the most damnable conspiracies the world ever knew has been organized to down all the government paper money, and silver as a basis, for a promissory bank notes, or as money above five dollars. When they were indeavoring to demonetize silver they worked upon the prejudice of the people, by declaring that there was but 58 cents worth of silver in the dollar and as poor men received most of their wages in silver it wronged labor, as the laborers dollar should be worth as much as the millionair's dollar. The redicn·ous and dishonest phase of this is the fact, that before the demonetization of silver the silver dollar with only 58 cents worth of silver would purchase as much of the necessaries of life as the gold dollar, but after they complete the demonetization of silver down to five dollars, silver will still be the money of the laboring man, with less purchasing power and gold will stand at a premium and be the millionair's money, a money that will measure his income and the tax imposed upon labor.

On the interesting testimony of Thomas Barring, we are assured that it was found impossible during the crisis of 1847 in London to raise any money whatever on a sum of £60,000 of silver.

This would be equal to $300,000, but silver was not a legal tender and money was scarce and silver was not even considered worthy as a security.

In 1855 Holland made silver the standard of value but coined gold without the legal tender quality and after about $18,000 worth of gold had been coined the demand entirely ceased

During a panic in India in 1864 silver was the basis, and in Calcutta you could not get a single rupee, 46 cents, on £20,000 of gold.

This proves beyond a doubt that people seek after legal tender money regardless of the material of which it is made.

Another of the dishonest arguments of the conspirators and their idiotic followers is that we want an elastic currency and that the gold basis promissory bank note system fills the want. But the fact is that the bankers contract the money, and expand the volume when it suits their interest. For example I will quote from Freeman O. Wiley, who quotes from the New York Tribune and other papers:

November 13, 1880 the Tribune editorially says:

"Money is unusually easy for the season. The loans are $324,970,900, the largest ever reported in the city"

This is certainly a glowing account but note what followed one month after. On December 15, quoting again from the same source:

"The bankers of this city have made a creditable effort to set themselves right. Loans were contracted $11,741,000 last week."

Here, did space allow, I would

like to quote the whole range of Mr. Wiley's argument and quotations, showing the disaster this contraction brought and the acknowledgment of the same by the press of the country.

The New York daily exchange says:

"Notwithstanding the stringency of the money market, the banks retired their circulation."

Oh, yes! They want an elastic currency that they may contract the volume of money at their sweet will; and that is really all there is to an elastic currency.

Mr. Wiley quotes from the N w York Mercantile Journal as follows:

"What about the future? This is a question we are beginning very often to hear. When for call loans men have paid one-eighth to one-fourth per cent per day, or say at the rate of 100 per cent per annum, for a little while, they are very anxious to know what is coming next."

So much for the banker's howl for an elastic currency; elastic for their benefit. If we have a volume of money large enough to meet the requirements of the people it will find its way to the proper channels at the proper time, and the bankers will not be able to corner it just when their interests can be best served at the expense of the people.

This brings us to the subject of volume. But we must first discuss

INTEREST ON MONEY

Q. What is interest on money?

A. Interest is any surplus advantage in returning what has been received.

Now mark the distinction. Any surplus advantage is interest.

You rent a house. You pay for the wear and tear and to keep up taxes, and other expenses.

That is not interest. But if the use of the money invested in that property is reckoned in, that is interest. Therefore, interest always means the reckoning of a return of a percentage for the use of money, borrowed or invested in an enterprise intended to return a profit.

There is no subject more delicate to handle than that of interest. One reason, because all profit is reckoned as interest. When in fact there is nothing in interest except a percentage on money loaned or promised for property received, or added to profits on account of money invested. That profit that comes naturally to the shrewd in trade or mechanics, as the result of industry, energy, perseverance and foresight, do not rightly belong to interest.

Q. Where does interest differ from usury?

A. In reality there is no difference. Usury means a percentage for the use of money, loaned or invested purely for interest.

"Take thou no usury of him or increase, but fear thy God that thy brother may live with thee." Leviticus XXV, verse 36.

Thus according to old Jewish teaching the charge of anything for the use of money was prohibited.

Thou shalt not give him thy money upon usury, nor lend him thy victuals for increase." Leviticus, XXV, 37.

If thou lend money to any of my people that is poor by thee, thou shalt not be to him as an usurer, neither shall they lay upon him usury." Exodus XXII, 25.

"Thou shalt not lend upon usury to thy brother, usury of money, usury of victuals, usury of anything that is lent upon usury." Deuteronomy XXIII, 19.

One would think this settled the question as what constitutes usury.

"I rebuked the nobles and the rulers

and said unto them. "You exact usury every one of his brother, and I set a great assembly against them." Nehemiah V, 7.

Here we cannot help asking of our ministers of the gospel, "Can you say that you 'rebuked the nobles and the rulers?'" They must answer, "Well hardly"

"I pray you let us leave of this usury." Nehemiah V, 10.

"In thee have they taken gifts to shed blood; thou hast taken usury and increase, and thou hast greedily gained of thy neighbor by extortion and hast forgotten me, saith the Lord God." Ezekiel XV, 5.

Here are but few of the quotations that may be taken from the Old Testament. But our church people try to excuse themselves for taking usury on the ground that those commands came under the old Jewish law and that there is not a word in the New Testament against usury, and then they quote the parable of the ten talents, Luke XIX.

Now if the reader will scan this chapter closely he will find Christ did not uphold the nobleman in taking usury. But he was illustrating to the people that they must not hide their light under a bushel, but go and spread it and obtain more light or they would fall into indolence and lose what light they did have.

As well accuse Christ of upholding murder because he gave us the parable of the good master of the vineyard who sent servants to the tenant and they were misused and sent back, then he sent his own son and he was murdered.

Now this is the way our good church people try to get out of a bad scrape.

Christ said he did not come to do away with the law but rather to fulfil it.

If we are under no obligation

to the old law on usury we are under no obligation to live under the ten commandments.

As for the New Testament containing nothing against usury, let me quote from Matthew XXIII, 24, 25.

"Ye blind guides, which strain at a gnat and swallow a camel"

"Wo unto you! Scribes and Pharisees, hypocrites! For you make clean the outside of the cup and of the platter, but within they are full of extortion and excesses."

How applicable this is to the many church people of today. No wonder they preach to small congregations and the church is losing its influence.

"And if ye lend to them of whom ye hope to receive, what thanks have ye? For sinners also lend to sinners to receive as much again." Luke V, 34.

So much for usury in the New Testament; and much more may be found by him who reads with care.

Murray on Usury, and he defends interest, says:

"There was no attempt at the defence of urury for fifteen hundred years after Christ."

I will here give several quotations from "Murray on Usury."

"Some writers have even gone so far as to place usury in the same category with the crime of murder. Cicero says that when Cato was questioned on the the subject, his only reply was: 'What is murder?'"

One Dr Wilson, in the reign of James I, in a discourse upon usury says:

"I well wish some penal law of death to be made against the usurers, as well as against thieves or murtherers, for that they deserve death much more than such men do; for these usurers destroy and devour up, not only whole families but whole countries and bring all folks to beggars that have to do with them."

St. Ambrose, in discussing it seems to think that it was confined to the Jews as an instrument of vengeance, to be used against their enemies, and says:

"Take usury from him whom you may lawfully kill."

Sir Edward Coke in speaking of this same text, describes it as a means confided to the Jews either to exterminate or pauperize their enemies, so that they should not be able to invade or injure God's people.

The English must look upon this matter in the same light, for they are the greatest usurers of the whole world.

The ancient Fathers of the church were very bitter against usury. St. Bazil portrayed the hypocricy of the professional money loaner in very strong language. He called them dogs, monsters, vipers and devils; and then proceeds to advise any sacrifice rather than borrow money upon usury.

Says he, "Sell thy cattle, thy plate, thy household stuff, thine apparel; sell anything rather than thy liberty; never fall under the slavery of that monster, usury."

It seems that in all history interest or usury has been the disturbing element of all nations at one time or another. The concentration of wealth in Attica 500 B. C. was due to the enormous rates of interest, 18 per cent, and it caused a clash between the oppressed and the oppressors: and Solon tried to abolish it but the people would not have it.

The Roman Empire was forever in trouble between the patricians or privileged classes and the plebeian or poorer class; and interest or usury was one of the bones of contention. Many attempts were made to prohibit interest by law and many times the rates of interest were changed.

Among the Romans twelve

per cent was the rate estalished by the Decemvirs, who compiled the laws of the Twelve Tables. In Rome interest was payable every month and was one per cent; hence it was called usura centisima, because in a hundred months it doubled the capital. So in reckoning the twelve months twelve per cent was paid. This law was afterwards abolished and interest laid under a total interdict. It was subsequently revived by the tribunes of the people in the 369th year of Rome. Ten years after interest was reduced to half the sum; but in the ear 411 of Rome all interest was prohibited by decree.

"Among the Romans usury was treated, during most periods of their history, as an aggravated species of theft and was punished with the utmost severity. The punishment of theft was only a forfeiture of double the value of the thing stolen; whereas in usury, the criminal was punished by condemnation, and forfeiture of four times the value of the usury taken. And the law in this respect seems to have been grounded on reasons of state; for, it is said, that usury was one of the most frequent causes of sedition and discord among men, and Cato, Seneca, and Plutarch inveighed against it, both at the bar and in the senate chambers. Cicero tells us in what abhorence it was held in Rome in his day."

For several ages the struggle against usury was carried on in England, until money loaning became an occupation so disreputable that it was left, alone, to the Jews to follow, until the 12th century

"At that period there was a company of Italians in London who called themselves merchant strangers" and who were the agents of the Pope in collecting his revenue in England. This company exacted four hundred and fifty per cent, per annum for the money they lent, and were guilty of the most cruel oppression. They evaded the law by charging nothing for the first three months, covenanted to receive fifty per cent for every month afterwards that it should remain unpaid and said they were no usurers, for they lent their money absolutely without interest, and what they were to receive afterwards was a contingency that might be defeated. They live in security, and were not kept in perpetual dread of being plundered, as the Jews were, being themselves Christians, and moreover, being employed by the head of the Christian church, their extortions were the more scandalous in the eyes of the people, and writers of the time complain that the Pope, by means of the Caursini, was as bad as the Jews.

At lenght so grossly oppressive were their extortions, that they drew down upon themselves the censures of the English clergy; and Roger, the then Bishop of London, having in vain admonished them to desist from their oppression, excommunicated them A. D. 1235. But through the Pope's protection, and their interest at Rome, they shortly afterwards caused the Bishop to be cited there to answer for his conduct, which induced the suspicion that the Pope was both their accomplice and partner in their spoils." (Murray.)

In 1730 Pope Benedict the XIVth addressed a brief to his subjects in which he, in affect, disclaimed the right of the church to interfere on the subject of usury and allowed the practice and settled the rate of interest and finally decided that unlawful interest alone was usury. Thus usury became a thing of geographical proportions, and what would be usury in one state would not be usury in another; and in some of our states there could be no such thing as usury as there are no usury laws in such states. Father O'Callaghan, who wrote upon the subject in 1840, tells how he was persecuted and driven from place to place and told by the bishops he must stop preaching on that subject or leave their diocese.

He refused and so was driven from pillar to post until finally summoned to Rome, but never received fair treatment.

Reader do you know the power of interest, do you know what it means?

"Interest means nothing more or less than conveying or stealing from the many to fill the purses of the few. The word itself is no other than a daring highwayman disguised in the garb of a legalized business. The harvests reaped by the swords of Attilla and Tamerlain were but as the gold dust swept from the floor of a western gambling saloon compared to the worlds of wealth wrung from the sweat of toil, by this relentless, ever-ready highwayman, called interest. This monster has not the decency of a common thief, a respect for his pal, but like the savage brute, the stronger live on the weaker, and the petty usurer of to-day is swallowed up by the giant usurer of to-morrow. This horrible system of legalized robbery is upheld and fostered for no other purpose than to satisfy the hell-begotten greed of man; and is tolerated only because each individual hopes to become a millionaire usurer. Vain hope."—Dynamite and the Torch.

To show the enormous concentrating power of interest note the table here given and figure for yourselves. When that class of people who are always howling, there is money enough, and condemn finance reformers, understand the difference between 3 and 12 per cent compounded annually, they too will get up and howl for more money.

The following are the sums that $1 will amount to in 100 years, loaned at the rates of interest mentioned and compounded annually

At 1 per cent,	2.75
" 2 "	19.25
" 6 "	340.00
" 10 "	13,809.00
" 12 "	84,675.00
" 15 "	1,174,405.00
" 18 "	15,145,207.00
" 24 "	251,799,494.00

And at 50 per cent it would eat up the world.

But many a debtor will look at these figures and say I do not pay compound interest. Oh no, you poor fool, nor do you live a hundred years. But that class of bankers that are trying to destroy the people's money, take compound interest, daily and on the people's money at that, and banking corporations do live hundreds of years and they are vampires without feeling or conscience.

Peter Cooper was always a careful business man. He was strongly opposed to the methods of many merchants who launched into extravagant enterprise on borrowed money, for which they paid exorbitant rates of interest.

Once, while talking of a project with an acquaintance, the latter said he would have to borrow the money for six months, paying interest at the rate of three per cent per month.

"Why do you borrow money on so short a time" Mr. Cooper asked? "Because the brokers will not negotiate bills for longer." "If you wish" said Mr. Cooper "I will discount your note for $10,000 for three years at that rate." "Will you do it? "Of course I will," said the merchant. "Very well" said Mr.

Cooper, "Just sign this note for $10,000 payable in three years, and give me your check for $800 and the tranfer will be complete." "But where is the money for me?" asked the astonished merchant. "You don't get any money," was the reply. "Your interest for thirty-six months at three per cent per month amounts to 108 per cent or $10,800; therefore your check for $800 makes us even."

Is it any wonder that through this engine of oppression the wealth of the world is becoming centralized in the hands of the few? Nor is this the worst of it. Through the money dealers controlling the volume they will expand it, and the business brightens, and under encouragement people will delve to get something ahead, and at three dollars per day and other things according, they can afford to borrow money at even ten per cent for a short time, they think, and they get in debt. But all at once the volume of money is drawn in. A waits for B and B for C, and sacrifices are made to meet obligations, and values shrink, wages fall, everything goes down in price except debts and interest. Labor brings but a dollar a day now, consequently debts treble, increased obligations are given and finally all their earnings, their hopes, their care for existence, is sacrificed to satisfy obligations, and even the poor innocent small banker, the product of the system, is in turn himself gobbled up by the great money kings who control the volume of money and says, "An elastic currency is necessary." Yes; neses-ary to his purpose to rob the masses.

Q. To abolish our present system of currency, would it not destroy commerce?"

A. No; for the moneyed men would be driven into the ranks of the producers. They would want an expanded volume of money, labor would be employed, business would boom and everybody would accumulate and be happy.

Q. But would we not have to have banks of exchange and deposit?

A. Yes; and the laborer is worthy of his hire, and the banker is a useful member of the business world. His pay should be a salary, fixed and paid by the government, as by nature of his business he handles the people's money, and money belongs to the body politic, consequently there is no branch of governmental function that so thoroughly belongs to the government to manage as the banking business.

Q. Would not interest have to be paid to the government, and would that not be usury as well?

A. No; for interest paid to the government would not mean interest but a system of taxation to defray expenses and the surplus, if there was any, would come back to the whole people.

Q. Would not such a system beget fraud?

A. No; no more than the United States mailing system begets fraud. But of course that fool argument is used by the money mongers and their hireling press to deceive the people.

Q. Why is not money loaning as righteous a business as commerce and trade?

A. Again I say because money belongs to the people, and the temptation to the banker to make money scarce is forever a menace to business and a block in the way of civilization.

Aristotle said, that "Money being naturally barren, to make it breed money is preposterous, and a perversion from the end of its institution, which was only to serve the purpose of exchange and not of increase."

Q. Can the rate of interest be governed by law?

A. Only in one way can the rate of interest be regulated by law and that is by the government issue of a volume of money sufficient for the demands of trade and by loaning direct to the people at a fixed rate, then no one would likely pay more than he would have to pay the government.

In the city of Detroit there is a very large workshop, costing many thousands of dollars, that is said to have been built with the interest on the wages of the men which had been kept back as a guarantee that the men would not leave without due notice.

Though volumes might be written in proof of the evils of usury or interest on money, yet I have said enough to set any reasonable man to thinking for himself, which if followed is better than all of the written books in Christendom. We will now proceed to discuss

VOLUME.

The Scriptures tell us "The love of money is the root of all evil." They might have added the want of money is produced by the love of money and is the visible expression of the evils.

As I have explained elsewhere money is a legal tender, an ideal, a thought, a substitute for legal demands, and hence its name, which means established by law, because it is in our power to change it and render it useless.

It has no productive force.

It can only pay debts.

It was invented by man to be the instrument of exchange, but not the object. But the lovers of the money have made it the object of life, they have made it scarce and brought want and ruin to millions of people.

Money has not the power to increase.

It does not grow, but is created by law—fiat.

It it the result of a legal custom and may consist of any substance.

When it is plenty people rejoice and prosper.

When it is scarce, people are distressed and want and ruin comes upon them.

The usury of money is a curse to the human family.

The want of money

Has debauched the world.

Has wrecked nations.

Has blighted industries.

Has been the chief source of crime.

Has filled alms houses and prisons.

Has driven women to prostitution.

Has driven both sexes to insanity.

Has filled thousands and thousands of suicide graves.

It is one of the great factors in all the differences among men.

In proportion to the volume of money is civilization rated.

A few years ago when everything of interest on the money question was being sought out, 1876 I think, the director of the mint in his reports gave the following amounts per capita of money in the United States and countries having a larger pro rata volume:

United States,	-	$22.29
Great Britain,	- -	23.76
Belgium,	- -	27 85
Netherlands,	- -	30.73
France,	- -	44.34

The amount of circulating medium in the degraded nations was as follows:

India,	$5.42
Mexico,	5.51
Peru,	4.85
Russia,	1.45
Turkey,	1.78
Columbia,	2.10
Sweeden.	5.73

These are the amounts that were in actual circulation. not including bank and treasury hoards.

Q. In what way can the volume of money be a test of civilization?

A. Because as money is plentyful the products of labor are rapidly exchanged and consumed. This keeps labor employed and the mind busy, for you know enforced idleness is the "devils workshop." Under favorable circumstances the tendency of man is upward, and the voluntary idle man has always something to attract his attention, and unless warped by an extreme greed for money, he finds an occupation that leads upward. Besides when money is plenty and labor employed, invention is stimulated, men's wants increase until the luxuries of our forefathers become our necessities, as our luxuries become the necessities of our posterity.

Our forefathers of a hundred years ago had no carpets on the floor, very few books and newspapers, very few if any pictures on the walls, a stove was not known, the photograph and the album that holds it, the piano, the house organ, the sewing machine, the beautiful chandalier, lamps, and the thousands of articles that we now think our necessities were unknown to our forefathers of that day, or enjoyed but by a very few, and not one in a hundred of the population could read. All of this too besides the vast amount of machinery necessary to create these things were unknown, and if it were not for our machinery we never could create such a vast variety of commodities and at no date was such progress made in invention, science and art as during our late war and the following decade. We then had nearly $80 per capita in circulation in the Northern States alone, and nearly everybody were getting homes of their own, and many of the laboring classes had homes furnished more luxuriently than the homes of the wealthy of our grandfather's days. But oh! what disaster was brought on by the money kings' policy of contraction of money, which will be referred to again farther on.

Through the instigation of this class the volume of money was contracted, people could not pay debts or exchange commodities, as money is necessary, a barter system is too slow, and thousands were thrown out of employment, factories went to decay; and suffering was unparalleled in this country, for the people once enjoying the comforts and luxuries of life suffer more when brought down to poverty than one who never knew those comforts. But the people were told there was an overproduction that had caused the hard times, and then again they were told that they had been too extravagant, that they must economise and live cheaper before they could hope for better times, and the foolish people believed this paradoxy; and they began to economise, and when their shoes and clothing were worn out they did not replenish, but suffered in rags or bought poorer, cheaper goods and thus economized the shoemaker out of employment. The shoemaker had but little to do and so helped him to economise clothing, and soon economised the tailor, the weaver and the farmer out of employment. And if this system is continued the sequence is that the carpets on the floor would go. Our forefathers had none. The music that cheers the heart of the little one must go, the pictures from the walls, and all those comforts that aid in refining man and softening his heart cease to be in demand and like in the dark ages, which I have shown were brought on by want of money, these things of beauty and enlightment will be classed among the lost arts.

Such enforced economy lessens the books and papers and closes the doors of the school house and church. The house tumbles down and for the want of means to rebuild; a hovel is erected, or the people are driven to the raw hides and poles and they are back with the barbarians of the plains. You say this is overdrawn? True, it is to suppose it to take place in a decade or two, but it would be the natural consequence of carrying such a false and pernicious system of contraction to its conclusion. But before the last stage would be reached the suffering by war, pestilence and famine could not be pictured; such is the direful results of continued contraction of the volume of money. While on the contrary a plentiful supply of the circulating medium will make a people independent, studious, patriotic and happy. *What man will not fight* for the wealth in his own pocket, even though it be paper, if it will pay his taxes? He knows it will pay his debts and exchange for what he wants, he cares nothing for gold and he is happy.

But the man who lives in a hovel and sees the wealth of the country represented in bonds, and they in the hands of a few, or of the foreign money kings has little or nothing to live for

He soon loses his love for his country and all is lost.

"Ill fares the land to hastening ills a prey,
Where wealth accumulates and men decay."

The Socialist reformers show their weakness and lack of understanding of finance by declaring we could get along without money, then they immediatly assert that we should use labor tickets, or printed slips representing a day's labor or its multiple. This is rediculous, as it would merely substitute an untried, clumsy system of currency for an old and well tried system. As both systems would require watchfulness and regulation it would be easier to regulate a system already understood than one that must be tried and learned.

Q. Would not prices finally settle to a small volume of money and so the country be as well off as with a large volume?

A. No; for when a people are accustomed to a large volume of money they can never safely go back to a small volume and I have shown that the nations using a small volume of money are the degraded nations. The volume of money should be so large that every man could have a fair supply in his pocket. During the war and for some years after, this was the case, and our people were the most independent and happy people on earth. Now there is not one man in ten with a cent in his pocket and the people are rapidly losing their independence and becoming abject slaves.

Q. Can you give us some historical facts to uphold this theory?

A. Yes. But before I proceed with the history of finance let me say that owing to the suppression of information by the privileged class, historical facts of ancient history, and even of modern history, are hard to obtain.

While still under the head of **VOLUME** we will discuss finance

IN HISTORY.

If we had ever so much history to draw from in a work of this nature it would be desirable only to give the salient points.

Of the financial history of China, India, Egypt, Assyria and Babylonia we have nothing worthy of note. Even Phœnicia, a strictly manufacturing and commercial people, there is nothing of their financial history to be obtained. But we know that all of those nations that exist today the volume of currency is small and they are degraded nations. Of the

HEBREWS OR ISRAELITES

We have nothing of finance until we reach Solomon's time. Solomon obtained much wealth from commerce, to which he gave much encouragement, and for several years kept his people at work on public works. Then he stopped and only looked after the pleasures of Solomon, aping the arrogant styles of foreigners, taking wives from among foreigners and aping their customs to please them. He demonetized silver, thus reducing the volume of money and brought distress and a rebellion headed by Jeroboam. It is said that this distress and disatisfaction was brought on by excessive taxation. But the people do not mind taxation when money is plenty, for then there is prosperity and they can afford to be taxed. But this trouble came with a contraction of the volume of money. The Bible says of this time, silver was of no account. Josephus says Solomon demonetised silver; that it was neither used to buy or sell. But we know that it had been used for money before that, for Abraham used silver to pay for the cave of Machpelah, which was used for a sepulchre for Sarah. Silver was used after that, because Judas Iscariot sold Christ for thirty pieces of silver. So it is evident that Solomon did what the money kings of today are doing, contracted the volume of money by demonetizing silver. And he ruined his country. Money became so scarce that usury became the curse of the land. This caused old Nehemiah to cry out, "I pray you let us leave off this usury." Neh. V. 10.

And he says, "I rebuked the nobles and the rulers and said unto them: 'You exact usury, every one of his brother, and I sat a great assembly against them." Neh. V. 10.

In Ezekial, chapter XXII, God tells why he drove the Jews out of the land he had given them. I recommend the reading of this whole chapter carefully especially verses 12 and 15 where God says:

"In thee have they taken gifts to shed blood. Thou hast taken usury and increase and thou hast greedily gained of thy neighbors by extortion and hast forgotten me, sayeth the Lord God. And I will scatter thee among the heathen and disperse thee in the countries and will consume thy filthiness out of thee.

Can any one now deny the evils of a contraction of the volume of money and the consequent curse of usury or interest on money?

The scattering of the Jews among the nations is the spawn that hatched the Red Dragon, the Jew money power, centered in Lombard and Threadneedle streets, London, England, and which the people of the world will arise and crush out, and the Jews with other people, will be made to see that the essence of selfishness, deception and dishonesty lies in usury or interest on money. We gather enough from

ANCIENT GREECE

To know the people were largely tinctured with Socialism, and undoubtedly, like our Socialists of today, thought that money must be based on something and that something must be labor or the product of labor, consequently oxen were largely used as money and a basis for currency a cheap metal. Undoubtedly the Augean stables, belonging to king Augeus of Elis, and said at one time to have contained 3,000 oxen, was his treasure house, 1194 B. C.

Homer and Hesiod never speak of gold or silver money. They express the value of things by saying they were worth so many oxen. Homer values the golden armor of Glaucus at one hundred oxen, and the brazen armor of Democles at nine oxen.

Cæser issued a cheap metal money, receivable for taxes and based upon cattle and bearing the devise of a horse, an ox, a hog, an ear of corn, as the case might be, to denote the different values of the pieces.

Some of the states or colonies of Ancient Grece adopted iron money as their medium of exchange.

Lycurgus the Law Giver of Sparta adopted a system of iron money, and that it might not be withdrawn from its legitimate purpose to be used in the arts, for iron was a scarce article in those days, he steeped it in vinegar to destroy its malleability.

Xenophon states that "most of the states of Greece have money which is not current except in their own territory."

Plato recommended a double currency in every nation: "A coin," he said "for the purpose of domestic exchange it must have value among the members of the state but no value to the rest of the world."

For visiting and using in other states he proposed a coin of intrinsic value, which would pass current in foreign states. But in this age that is not neccessary as foreigners will take our paper money if they can buy our goods with it.

But the money changers have always fought a cheap money, and when they are successful the people must suffer. In Attica 595 B. C. they had destroyed cheap money, and interest was high. There was a mortgage stone at the corner of nearly every piece of land, the money loaning class had their grasp on everthing, and they and their victims were about to clash and deluge the land with blood. But they finally agreed to arbitrate and consented to leave the matter to the philosopher Solon. He said he could do nothing for them except to draw up a code of laws, which if they accepted and obeyed, would save Attica from ruin. They consented. First he abolished all interest. The foolish people, hoping to some day become wealthy money loaners, refused to accept this as well as did the money loaners. He then ordered the mortgage stones taken up and the debt forgiven wherever the payments had returned a sum to the loaner equal to the principle first loaned, then to make it possible for the debtor class to meet their obligations he increased the volume of money by calling in all of the coins of the realm and recoining them and nearly doubling the volume by reducing the amount of metal in the coin.

This saved Attica from bloodshed and ruin.

Solon was asked by Crœsus, king of Lydia if the laws which he had made for the Athenians were the best that could be given them he said: "*Yes; the best they were capable of receiving.*"

All through the history of man there has been a continual war between the people and the privileged class. The privileged class, when defeated in one locality gathered their silver and their gold and hied themselves to some other country where they could gain privileges to rob the people.

After losing their power in Greece many of them retreated to Carthage. But people were more clanish in those days than at present and foreigners could not get a foothold with political influence in a day, so it took many years before their influence was greatly felt in Carthage, when they did get hold of Carthage their blighting influence soon destroyed the country as their devouring system of usury and selfishness will bring the most flourishing country to ruin, as surely as the army worm will wither and blast the most fertile and flourshing fruit tree when once it gets a fair hold upon it.

Carthage was the most prosperous nation on the globe at that time. Her white sails dotted the waters of the, then, known world, if indeed they did not reach to that of the new world. Her mines produced $10,000 per day of the precious metals, yet the metals were not used for money at home, but were kept especially for trade and commerce abroad. For home use Carthage had a leather money, and to prevent successful counterfeiting it contained a metal core, a compound of metals, the compound a secret of the government.

Carthage became very rich and powerful, but there was rising in the west a nation that was to eclipse her in all her glory. Rome was that rising power. Hannibal being a statesman as well as a general determined to conquer Rome, and almost singlehanded and alone. He hired his soldiers from foreign countries, equipped an army, marching through a hostile country, he crossed the Alps making friends of the Barbarians. He carried on along war, but finally was compelled to send home for assistance, for men and money. In pleading his cause he said, "It is now or never, for it is Carthage or Rome." But he had left an enemy in Carthage far worse than those he was fighting. The money power had destroyed the cheap money and come to a money of the precious metals. They had control of all government offices and established many useless institutions to make room for their people in office, thus taxing the people heavily to meet the expenses, and they considered only their immediate interests, so refused aid to Hannibal and recalled him. Hannibal withdrew from Roma, Scipio immediately followed him and was soon thundering at the gates of Carthage. A council of war was called and of course Hannibal was present, and in the discussion that followed Hannibal took no part but stood with folded arms and smiled at their tribulation. Senator Asdrubal Hoedus said, "Hannibal smiles and his country is in danger." "Yes," said Hannibal, "the smile of contempt for him who feels his country's loss, only, when his own interests are at stake, it is sorrow for Carthage."

With the destruction of the cheap money of Carthage came an era of corruption, even the judges became so corrupt that

Hannibal when made Preator was compelled to impeach the whole bench of judges, and he corrected other evils, and says Rollins the historian:

"They exclaimed vehemently against these regulations as if their own property had been forced out of their hands and not the sums they had plundered from the people."

Will the corruption already set in in this country cause a Hannibal or a Cromwell to arise and purify the nation? Surely none will deny that it is needed.

We will now note the difference in the financial changes between Carthage and

ROME.

Money is always scarce in new countries and prices high and interest runs up to almost an unlimited extent. There is always a vast amount of enterprise and push among those who venture everything to establish a home in a new country. Rome was the "Star of Empire" setting westward. She was rapidly increasing in population both by immigration and by extending her border by conquest. The volume of money was increasing but not in proportion to population, consequently there was always a strife between the privileged class and the producing class. And here is something I wish to forcibly impress on the minds of the people: the privileged class always tries to destroy the force and power of the people's leaders. Sometimes by circulating false reports, thereby turning the people against their own leaders, sometimes through bribery, sometimes by foisting their own friends into positions which they misuse and so betray the people, and sometimes by assassination.

The people seldom, if ever, assassinate a ruler or leader except they go in mobs, but where an individual does such work he generally does it at the instigation of a band of conspirators. I shall have occasion to call attention to some of these assassinations, while treating on this subject.

Now the bone of contention was money, land and political rights, or abused privileges, but interest on money was the leading evil. Marcus Manlius, a patrition, was one of the noble defenders of the people's cause. He was a soldier of great physical strength and when in 530 B. C. the Gauls attacked Rome the poorer classes withdrew and said they had nothing to fight for.

(This shows that oppression and poverty destroyed patriotism.) The soldiers retreated to the citadel on "Tarpin Rock," and one night when the Gauls attempted an assault, they scaled the rock, but before scaling the walls Marcus Manlius was awakened by the squak of the sacred geese. He sprang to the wall, and being a powerful man, he hurled the enemy down as fast as they came upon the wall, and made so much noise as to awake his comrades, who came to his assistance, and thus saved Rome. This gave him great honor and notoriety. The Gauls were soon compelled to withdraw when the people were coaxed back with the promise of amelioration of the existing political evils, land limitation of ownership, etc., etc. In this Marcus Manlius became one of the strongest defenders of the people's rights. The Patricians became enraged at this and determined to destroy him, and the foolish people consented to hurl him to death from the very rock where he gained his notoriety. This narative has no direct bearing upon the question of volume of money, nor have the two narratives following, but the reader should keep them in mind as they have a great bearing upon the historic facts that follow.

Notwithstanding the volume of money had been largely increased by reducing the metal in the coin, to carry on the war, population had increased, territory had increased, and much treasure was hidden and lost, consequently money was still scarce and prices of all commodities ranged high, as the producers were withdrawn from their occupations to serve in the army, so that the lower classes could hardly afford the humblest of food and clothing, while the privileged class lived in luxury. Paper, printing and engraving were not then known, so Rome could only increase the volume of money by reducing the metal in the coin. This debasing of the coin the money loaning classes would no longer stand.

The volume of money not being adequate to the wants of trade, and notwithstanding the many attempts to control rates of interest by law, usury was one of the greatest of the many abuses heaped upon the people by the privileged class.

We are now down to 133 B. C. Tiberius Gracchus, one of the tribunes, sought to enforce the the long neglected agrarian laws limiting the ownership of land to 500 acres also insisting on the wealth left to Rome by king Attalus of Pergamus by his will, to be distributed equally among the poor of Rome. This excited the animosity of the privileged classes who again set up the cry of ambition and collected enough fools from among the people to go down and murder Tiberius Gracchus and three hundred of his followers. Again I say, note the manner of exciting the prejudices of the people for the purpose of using them against their own interests.

Ten years after the death of

Tiberius Gracchus, his young and talented brother, Caius Gracchus being elected tribune, made a vigorous attempt to carry out the reform started by his elder brother. This included reforms in usury laws. He erected polling booths similar to those now used with the Australian system. At a new election he was counted out, (just as they do these things now a days.) the people indignant at this fraud and outrage arose in defense of Caius Gracchus, the patricians fearing him, hired an assassin to kill him, and then circulated the story that he called one of his followers to slay him. History gives us both sides of the story but students of history who understand human nature believe the patricians murdered him.

We are now down to 48 B. C. Julius Cæsar, a successful general, virtually ruled Rome sometime before his dictatorship. He sought to correct many existing evils, among which was the limitation of land ownership. He saw the abuses of the money matters. Up to his time the issuing or coining of money had been granted to a few wealthy families. Cæsar took this privilege from them and restored it to the government to whom it belonged. He also created a large volume of cheap metal money and started public works and paid it out to labor. This enraged the privileged classes. "The people loved Cæsar," Mark Antony said, and he said Cæsar put away the crown three times and we know history tells us Cæsar did not like to remain in the city among the corrupt politicians. He was a plain soldier and preferred the field, and notwithstanding this the privileged class determined to get rid of him, and for an excuse perpetrated their old trick, as in the case of

Manlins and Gracchus, they charged ambition, and knowing the manner of murdering these men was still fresh in the minds of the people, they dared not try it, so concluded it would be safer to murder him with their own hands, which they did March 15, 44 B. C. But Mark Antony said, *"They are all gentlemen"* We have just such gentlemen today who would not hesitate at any crime to further their ends.

History gives only the privileged class side of the story, and we must gather the facts in fragments, and they will no doubt deny them as they deny every fact that points at the wrong perpetrated by that class.

With the death of Cæsar soon came the death of cheap money, but Cæsar's successful wars had made Rome rich with the precious metals, they amounted to $1,800,000,000. But the mines now began to peter out and no new ones discovered and in consequence of many wars treasures were often hidden away and never found, so that the contraction of the volume of money was very great. This continued until civilization was nearly snuffed out, and the Dark Ages were the consequence, in which many of the arts were lost and the finer feelings of man smothered. (See Silver Commission's Report, page 19.)

With the destruction of commerce, which always comes if the shrinkage of the volume of money is great enough, came poverty, distress, and loss of patriotism, and the final downfall of Rome.

With the breaking up of the great Roman Empire, came a swarm of small republics. Each of these tried to excel the others in offering protection in opposition to individual privilege.

The Florenteens guarded their political rights with such jealous care that they held their elections every two months.

It was Venice, one of the independent cities that gave birth to the mother of our present credit system that turned the tide of commerce from a downward to an upward current, which gradually led to a higher state of civilization.

For many years the money center rested with two independent cities—Venice and Genoa.

Before I proceed farther I will give a brief description of the

BANK OF VENICE.

This bank was established in the year 1171, and fell with the fall of Venice in 1812, thus standing for nearly six and a half centuries.

The Bank of Venice was a government bank. The Venitian government was at war and needed funds and was compelled to resort to forced loans from its wealthy citizens, for which it gave credits in bank. These credits were transferable through a sort of tally system; in part or in whole, they were also receivable for taxes and dues to the government. The government entered into no obligation to repay the money. But Colwell, in his "Ways and Means," says: "Reimbursement of the loan ceased to be regarded as either necessary or desirable." Thus credits ran up and stood at a premium of 30 per cent above coin, but was finally fixed at 20 per cent above coin, and this because of their being accepted for all dues to the government. At first the government paid interest on deposits, but this was abolished in 1423, and all bills of exchange payable in Venice, whether domestic or foreign, were decreed payable through the Bank of Venice, unless otherwise specified in the contract. For the long existence of this bank Colwell says that they never suffered one panic. He further says:

"That the inhabitants of Venice were satisfied. We cannot doubt, as not an objection was ever made to the bank, at least none in extant, neither book, nor speech, nor pamphlet have been found in which merchant or dweller in Venice ever put forth any condemnation of its theory or its practice."

Now what have our gold bugs who scream fiat for the purpose of scaring investigators away from the grain of truth, to say of this bit of financial history?

Fiat, indeed! It was this fiat system that fanned the dying spark of civilization back to life.

THE BANK OF GENOA

Was a sister bank of the Bank of Venice, and was established early in the Thirteenth Century. Like the Bank of Venice it had its origin in the necessities of the State, though the loans upon which it was based were not forced but were the spontaneous offerings of the people. According to Caldwell the Bank of Genoa was the first to originate the bank note. The bank fell with the overthrow of the government at the same time of the fall of Venice.

For many years these three cities, Venice, Genoa and Florence, were the money centers of the world. But such a system of the people's money was not pleasant or desirable to the usurious class, consequently as the "Star of Empire" drifted westward the money loaning class sought pastures new, and for a time located in Amsterdam where favorable privileges were granted.

THE BANK OF AMSTERDAM

Was founded in 1609, on strictly commercial basis, and not to afford any assistance to the government. As before stated, Amsterdam was the commercial center of the world, and of course, offered the greatest inducement for a moneyed center.

The bank was established on the principle that coin once deposited, could never be withdrawn, but the people holding its notes knew that the specie was behind them, and it might just as well have been at the bottom of the sea, as it was not convertible. The bank's first capital consisted of silver coin, Spanish ducats, but foreign coins of all kinds soon flowed into the bank, and were received at nine per cent discount. These coins were melted up and the metal sold, which of course helped to enrich the banking company.

In 1672 when Louis XIV. penetrated to Utrecht, a great fear arose, and people who had accounts with the bank demanded coin, but this was met so promptly that confidence was restored. But 1790 the bank refused to return in coin a less amount than 250 florins.

Notwithstanding, it was supposed that the bank contained so much coin in its vaults, it became a heavy loaner to great corporations. It loaned the East India Trading Company more than 10,500,000 florins, which sum of course it was unable to make up to its depositors, and so it assigned its claims and expired. So much for the first failure of a specie basis promissory note banking institution.

THE BANK OF HAMBURG

Was established in 1619 on the model of the Bank of Amsterdam. It is still in existence, and is a flourishing institution.

For a number of years prior to the fall of Amsterdam the commercial center was gradually changing from Amsterdam to London, England.

Holland had become rich and prosperous, and no great contraction of the volume of money had ever taken place, and after the fall of the Bank of Amsterdam, Holland adopted a favorable currency system that has kept financial panics at bay.

England had for many years been a good stamping ground for the usurer—both Jew and Gentile.

The English nobility, or governing classes, were mainly the direct descendants of the old Vikings or Norsemen, a piratical class of adventurers from the far north, and of course were just the class to be bribed and influenced by the usurious money loaners, and as a nation she still pursues a piratical policy toward all weaker countries. But with all her faults she has always been a progressive country, and consequently always required a large volume of circulating medium. Like old Rome, for a great length of time she had no other means of increasing that volume than by reducing the amount of metal in the coin. Finally in the reign of Henry I., from 1100 to 1695, the tally system was adopted, a money fabricated out of wood. Says Jonathon Duncan, the historian:

"Its intrinsic value was no more than the value of the wood of which it was fabricated, but its representative (or commercial) value denoted large sums."

These were called "Exchequer values," and the system was similar to our greenback system, and it extended down to 1694, when the specie basis, Bank of England was established; then the tally system was abolished and it brought ruin. The result of this sudden contraction is given by Devant, as follows:

"The government appeared like a distressed debtor who was daily squeezed to death by the exorbitant greediness of the lender. The citizens began to decline trade, and to turn usurers. Foreign commerce had infinite discouragement.

"We are going headlong to destruction with carrying on a losing trade with our neighbors, and what has brought us to this low state?

"When paper money flourished (credits) and tallies performed all the offices of money, the great payments for land or rich goods, were therefore easily made, the king's duties paid, and all kinds of business easily transacted,"

Read this and stick it under the nose of the knave or fool who howls "Fiat!" the moment you speak of a government money made of a cheap material.

Q. Will you define the tally system and tell us why books of of reference do not give a better definition of it?

A. Yes. I, myself, have hunted through encyclopedias and books of reference with little satisfaction.

The reason so little is known of the system is on account of the prejudice against any system of finance, except a specie basis system, and when facts have come out in exposition of the matter, attempts have been made to suppress such matter as much as possible. I looked through many books of reference with little satisfaction until compelled to draw from many sources. I find that, in brief, the definition quoted here from the "Standard Dictionary" the most satisfactory:

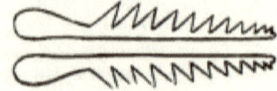

THE TALLY.

"Tallies from a piece of wood on which notches or scores are cut as marks of numbers. In all countries and in all ages tallies have been in use for keeping accounts. The falsification of an account is guarded against by splitting the tally in two through the notches, the debtor taking one-half and the creditor the other. In the English exchequer tallies were used from the Norman kings until 1685 (should be 1694) to record the debts of the state. The half of the tally given to the lender being called the "stock," and half retained in the exchequer the "counter stock," each bearing the date of the transaction and the name of the lender. Such stocks were negotiable, and when redeemed, were fastened to their counter-stock, and retained in the treasury. In 1835 the tallies accumulated in the exchequer were burned by order of the government, in the stoves of the House of Lords, a proceeding that caused the destruction of the House of Parliament by fire."

I will state that small amounts were designated by small notches and larger ones by larger notches. I will also state here that this was the system first in vogue with the Bank of Venice.

We must go back a little and refer once more to the debasement of British coins. Says Encyclopedia Brittanica: "At the close of the Thirteenth century the pound sterling contained what its name implied, a pound weight of silver, of 112 fineness, the penny, which was the commonest coin, containing a two hundred and fortieth part of a pound. Between this period and the first of the Sixteenth century her penny was reduced to one-third of its ancient weight.

The English pound now worth $4.84 of our money, if expressed in our dollars, would weigh less than five ounces, and the commercial value of the commodity worth about $2.80. The above valuation shows us that silver was the standard metal of England down to 1817.

From Henry, the VIII., there

was a continual debasement of the metal money down to 1551, and says the Encyclopedia Brittanica: "An attempt was made at the conclusion of this reign to issue a coinage of genuine quality, but as the base money continued in circulation, the attempt was futile." This shows us that the people preferred a money that cost but little for the material of which it was made, and that the desire for a high priced commodity came from another source, *i e.*, the money loaning class, who wished to make money out of it. To quote another:

"Queen Mary was anxious to restore the ancient standard, but found it impossible to do so. However, Elizabeth called in her father's and brother's base money at a low fixed rate, which gave her a considerable profit, and put into circulation money of the old character and quality. This was effected in 1560."

The contraction of the volume of money, through this change, was soon felt in the war of commercial distress, but the dire results of a dissatisfaction did not reach its hight until the autumn of 1642—82 years after when the civil war broke out under Cromwell. Dissatisfaction and rebellion do not follow immediately upon the heels of the cause, but take years to reach the point of explosion.

The metal in the coins was reduced again in Cromwell's time. But look at what a cost of suffering and blood that was necessary before the people got back to a cheaper and more plentiful money. For many years the goldsmiths of England were the bankers, but finally the

BANK OF ENGLAND

was founded by William Patterson, a Scotchman, in the year 1694. Its charter conferred upon it full power to borrow or receive money, and give security for the same under seal, buy or sell bullion, gold or silver. No special power was granted to issue bank notes, but the power to do so was assumed to belong to the general powers with which the bank was invested.

The whole amount of the capital stock originally subscribed was £1,200,000; it was handed over to the government as a special loan, the interest on which was secured by certain taxes designated for that purpose, and a sum of about £5,000 a year was allowed by the government for the management of the loan. The capital stock and accumulated profits were in 1878 about £88,000,000. The bank now has the privilege of issuing notes to about £70,000,000; no note shall be of less than £5 (or $25). Gold and silver are supposed to be held in bank for their redemption. This is false, as the government has come to the rescue of the bank on several occasions and allowed the bank to suspend specie payment and use the government fiat instead. This fiat is always the money to be relied upon when specie fails.

The most notable of these events occured from 1797 to 1825. The expensive wars with France forced the government to become a heavy borrower of the bank who to meet it it issued a large volume of paper promises, the specie in the bank became reduced and the government foreseeing the result came to the rescue by ordering the bank to suspend specie payments, this was sanctioned May 3, 1797; this continued until 1820 when an act was passed providing for the resumption of specie payments, which was not fully realized until May, 1823. I will here quote Burkey on the money question, who quotes from Colwell:

"The people of Great Britain were

obliged, therefore, to carry on their affairs for a period of twenty-five years with an irredeemable bank paper currency. During this period, notwithstanding the vast expenditures of war and the great burdens of taxation, Great Britain increased in wealth and prosperity more rapidly than at any other period in her history. The public revenues were increased from £23,126,000 in 1779 to £72,210,000 in 1815, at the close of the war with France, and stood at £54,282,000 in 1820.

"The amount raised by loan and and taxation during the time referred to, was never less in any one year than £47,362,000, during nine years it was over £70,000,000 a year, and for the years 1813 and 1814 it was respectively, £108,397,000 and £105,698,000. The loans negotiated by the bank for the government during the suspension of specie payment amounted to £350,000,000. During this period the Bank of England was a tower of strength to the government. But what after all enabled Great Britain to surmount all difficulties and come off victorious in one of the greatest contests of modern times was the wonderful development of her productive forces, occasioned by the abundance of money put in circulation by the war, irredeemable though it was. During this time 3,000,000 acres of unimproved land were brought under cultivation and the exportation of manufactured cotton goods increased in amount from £7,000,000 in 1801 to £27,000,000 in 1822. All classes of society participated in the general prosperity which prevailed, and during the entire period the nation never once suffered from a commercial crash or money panic.

"The guns of Waterloo, however, had hardly ceased to echo until the money power became clamorous for a return to specie payments. No one was so blind as not to be able to see that Great Britain was enabled by her paper money alone, to carry on the wars on the continent, and that by it alone were the people enabled to make such remarkable progress in commerce, agriculture and manufactures."

Doubleday in his "Financial

History of England," says, that with the contraction of the volume of money, to return to a specie basis:

"All things fell in value and real estate depreciated largely in value, and the real estate owners of the kingdom decreased in numbers from over 160,000 to less than 40,000. Business men, merchants and manufacturers were ruined by the thousands, wages were reduced and laborers thrown out of employment by the tens of thousands, and the public revenues fell off to such an extent that payments on the public debt ceased and have never, practically, been resumed."

Is it not strange that an intelligent people, like that of Great Britain will allow knaves and fools to take away from them the greatest blessing they ever knew and then never ask for its restoration? But no, it is not strange, for have not the masses always let the priest, the hireling press, and the political trickster do their thinking for them!

England suffered a financial panic in 1844 to 1847, and again the bank suspended specie payment (October 23, 1847), and afforded relief by issuing irredeemable paper money Ten years later, having by its attempted return to specie payment ruined the merchants and business of England, it was again obliged to suspend. The bank sought to retain its gold in bank by changing its rates of interest, which was done, during the panic of 1847 fifty-six times, ranging from three to ten per cent. In 1857 it changed its rates of interest eleven times, and then drew the gold out of the United States, and nearly ruined us. (See cause of panics farther on.) In 1866 the Bank of England suffered another suspension in consequence of the war on the continent of Europe, but this time it did not injure us because we had our greenbacks, although gold was shipped abroad to the amount of $45,000,000, and sold as a commodity at a high price.

I copy the following from "A Review of European Society," by J. Sketchley, an English statistician:

"In 1855 the Bank of England obtained the authority to increase its own issues to the extent of £470,000, being two-thirds of the lapsed note circulation of the provincial banks. This extra increase on behalf of the Bank of England was farther increased by £175,000 in 1865, so that the Bank of England can now issue £14,650,000 without having a grain of gold to meet the conversion of these notes. It may be asked what would the bank do if notes were presented for which it had not gold? Well such has been the case more than once, and on every such occasion, in steps the government and protects the bank against its own creditors. The note of the Bank of England is a legal tender everywhere, but at the bank itself. The Bank of England is not bound to honor its own notes.

"Now these notes are but 'rag money'; they are merely promises to pay bearer on demand the sum stated on the notes. Nor does the bullion of the Bank of England remain stationary. In 1845 it was down to £14,466,000. In September, 1879, it reached £35,225,000. In September,1881,it was down to £24,676,000,and at the close of 1882, it was only £29,751,000. Again when the bank has £30,000,000 of notes in circulation, and £20,000,000 of bullion in its coffers, it has n t that £20,000,000 to dispose of. If it pays out £10,000,000 of bullion it must call in £10,000,000 of its notes. Thus if the bank had £30,000,000 of its notes in circulation, and £20,000,000 of gold, only £5,000,000 and odd of the latter could be disposed of. Above that sum notes must be called in equal to the gold sent out.

"We now come to another part of the subject, namely, that of deposits. The general belief is that every one can withdraw his deposits, and in gold, whenever he thinks proper. But such is not the case. Deposits may be increased from tens to hundreds of millions, but gold does not so increase. In 1880 the total reserves in all the banks of the United Kingdom were only £33,000,000, while the deposits in the savings banks amounted to over £44,000,000, and those of the Post Office Savings banks to £40,000,000, and those of the Bank of England to £30,481,000. But even this forms a small portion of the deposits of the country. On January 18th, 1876, Mr. Robert Baxter read a paper before the Statistical Society of London on 'Principles which regulate the rates of interest, and the currency laws.' He stated that in 1814 the total amount of deposits in the United Kingdom was £70,000,000, while in 1874 it was £800,000,000. Only one gentleman present appeared to doubt the accuracy of that statement, namely Mr. Dunn of Parr's bank, Warington, who thought the total deposits did not exceed £600,000,000. Taking the latter figure to be true, and assuming that every bank in the kingdom gave its last ounce of gold, £570,000,000 of these deposits could not be paid, except in inconvertible paper; or as Cobbett would have said, 'in rag money'. But the probability is that if Mr. Baxter's estimate of £800,000,000 was above the mark, that Mr. Dunn's was below it, and that £700,000,000 would be near the truth. Nor could these deposits be paid other than in paper if all of the gold coin in the United Kingdom were placed in the coffers of the banks, being a total of only about £100,000,000. Here then is our position to-day Every bank note issued is a promise to pay bearer gold on demand: yet, of a note circulation of forty odd millions, nearly thirty-two millions are by law inconvertible. And while the total reserves of all the banks is only about £30,000,000, we have deposits amounting to about £700,000,000. What a glorious position for a nation to be in!"

Think of the United States in a worse predicament, and England ready to call our gold from us at any time. How are we to get the gold at any time, to meet our obligations except to buy it of them and pay their price, getting deeper and deeper in debt?

And that is why they have foistered this fraudulent system upon us.

Has the reader ever thought of our supposed gold basis and how he would get gold for his notes if there was a run on gold, and the banker refused to give it? If not let him inquire it will do him good.

After to the founding of the Bank of England they soon learned their power and how to pool their interests.

They also now had a government they could control and use for a battering ram, and the prosperity of that country was essential to their interests.

Though they did rob the people through the new systems of indirect taxation and by expanding and shrinking the volume of money at will, they deceived them and by pointing to increased possessions forced from small and unprotected countries, and to their own gilded palaces and exclaimed, "how rich we are getting."

The English people are truly a noble people, but the money loaning ruling class are a lot of vampires that are sucking the life blood from the world, through the financial and commercial arteries, and this class are mainly not Englishmen but infidel Jews. Napoleon recognized this fact when he said, "Give me the ear of the English people, I know I have been fighting a monied oligarchy."

It has long been the policy of England to push forward her commercial and financial interests into other countries and she beslimes them with her money and commerce, then when once in her folds, serpent like she crushes, then swallows them, by backing up her merchants and financiers with her army and navy. Thus a new system of warfare has been adopted and conquests are made more by commercial policies than by military force and tactics.

Now that we may fully understand the great financial questions of today we must consider England not as a people but as a nation in the hands of unprincipled men, or rather a monster corporation without a soul, without an attribute of humanity. But a monstrous unprincipled system that is using the nation as a battering ram to reduce all other nations to the will of the monster serpent (money power) that beslimes and crushes its victims before swallowing them. In the discussion of this question from this forward we will find the hand of the English Jew money loaner in it.

We will take up the subject of the

JOHN LAW MONEY.

Q. Who and what was John Law?

A. John Law was a Scotchman, the son of a goldsmith, and as I have before stated, in his time goldsmiths were the bankers. Therefore it is natural that John Law should have good ideas of finance. He was born in Edinburgh, Scotland, April, 1671. He studied mathematics and the theory of commerce and political economy with great interest. 1694 found him in London where in a quarrel over a love affair he fought a duel and killed his opponent. He was convicted of murder and sentenced to be hung, but escaped and fled to Holland, then the center of the commercial world. Here he observed with close attention the practical working of banking and financial business and conceived the first ideas of a banking system he afterwards tried to put in operation in France. In the year 1701 he published a book entitled "Money and Trade," in which he set forth views favorable to a system of money which should be used to employ labor, increase business and lower rates of interest. He offered his scheme both to England and Scotland, but of course it was rejected, as the money loaning power had full control of those countries, and Law's scheme was not considered favorable to their interests. He now offered his scheme to France, but on account of religious prejudices, as well as moneyed influences, Louis XIV. rejected the proposal, as he would not treat with a Huguenot. At this time religious prejudices ran high and the Pope and Cardinals were cheek and jowl with the great moneyed classes. D'Argenson, chief of police, expelled Law from France as a suspicious character. He had, however, become acquainted with the Duke of Orleans, and when in 1715 the king died and the Duke of Orleans became regent to Louis XV., not yet of age, Law again went to France and offered his scheme to the Duke of Orleans. In consequence of her long wars and the extravagance of her kings, France was in a state of bankruptcy. France was now friendly with England and thought it her duty to trade with her nearest friends. England had now adopted her new system of warfare. i. e., on commercial lines. Her manufactured goods were extensively used in France and of course she would dislike to see France, through any means, become a prosperous competitor. In consequence of the state of bankruptcy of France something had to be done and the Duke of Orleans accepted Law's proposition.

I must here state that the manner of collecting the revenues of France was through what was known as revenue farmers. That is the government would say to John Smith you collect the revenues of your bailiwick and retain such a percentage and return the balance to the government. Of course such a business would be very profitable to the agents; the agents were also the money loaners of France.

Law's scheme proposed that the government take the management of trade and currency, collect the taxes and free the country from debt. The revenue farmers objected and raised such a hubbub that Law's scheme was rejected. But Law was granted rights and privileges which enabled him to found a private bank, based upon a commercial trading company; this was styled *La Banque General*. The capital was six million livres, divided into 12,000 shares of 500 livres, payable in installments, one fifth in cash, three-fourths in *billets d'etat*. It was to perform the ordinary functions of a bank, and had power to issue notes payable at sight in the weight and value of the money mentioned at day of issue. Thus this became a specie basis bank, not what Law wanted, but we will pursue its course and see what it did. So great was the necessity for an increase in the volume of money that the bank was a great and immediate success.

The coin or unit of French money called the livre, is not now in use but has given place to the franc, which is about the same value, and five francs are about equal to one of our dollars.

The first issue of notes of this bank would not exceed $1,000,000 of our money, yet it started the wheels of business and created such prosperity that the demand for money was so great that even the revenue farmers clamored for a larger issue.

The bank was chartered May 2, 1716, and on April 10, 1717,

the government ordered the notes receivable for taxes. This gave the bank such a prestige that the notes were sought instead of gold, so the bank increased its circulation to 60,000,000 livres, equal to about $12,000,000. Prosperity was now so great that factories sprung up in every direction and people were rushing in from other countries to share in the good fortune of France.

France had never experienced such prosperity, her trade with other countries began to roll up to great proportions. In a year and a half her trading ships increased from 300 to 1,800. All of this excited the animosity of England and she determined to down France at any cost.

Henry Martin, the historian, tells us that England used every means to destroy this banking system. Dubois, a French cabinet officer, who had claimed to be a friend of Law's and had declared himself in favor of the bank, now accepted a bribe of 100,000 crowns per annum directly from the English secret service fund to intrigue against the bank. D'Argenson, former chief of police and several others were also in the pay of the secret service fund of England for the purpose of downing this bank system of money, restoring free trade and to weaken French patriotism by abolishing the large pension list.

The reader will here note the parallel of England's policy with this country, and point out the Dubois and D'Argensons of America. John Sherman and Grover Cleveland possibly might easily aid us to find them.

Though interest had been very high it now dropped to four per cent. As a means to destroy this bank a similar bank was started, and the shares and notes of Law's bank were bought up and a run on his bank instituted; but as Law's bank notes were acceptable for taxes they were preferable to gold, so gold flowed into the bank and the run had no effect. False friends now engaged the Regent to push Law's bank business farther. Our Lousiana, then a French colony, embracing a vast and unknown territory was given to Law by grant as a trading post. He established a trading company and merged the former East India and China company into the new company and styled it the West India Trading company.

The new company's capital stock consisted of 100,000,000 divided into 200,000 shares of 500 livres each. On the fourth of December, 1718, the bank became a government institution, and Law was made director and the name was changed to Bank Royal. Such a fever of gambling in stock was purposely excited that shares stood at a premium of fifty per cent. The note issue had now reached 110,000,000. Added to the power of the bank, was one to control the mints for nine years. And now unreasonable things were promised by the bank.

While Law held the confidence of the public, there were a number of deadly enemies to the bank who held its stock and would have gladly sacrificed it all to down the bank, as they would be reimbursed from the secret service fund of England. Again the rival bank, through conspiracy, made a run on the bank. But the government met this by a reduction of the metal in the coin, and withdrew privileges from the rival company which crushed it. England now resorted to counterfeiting and sent a shipload of counterfeit notes of the Bank Royal to France.

Now Law tried to benefit the state by taking its debts upon his shoulders to manage. The debt was over 1,500,000,000 livres notes were to be issued to that amount, and with these the state creditors were to be paid in a certain order. Shares were to be issued at intervals corresponding to the payments. The creditors were often not able to procure the shares as the shares were based upon the amount issued. Though the shares arose to almost a hundred per cent premium the bank did not benefit by this. Law had now more than regal power; the proudest aristocracy of Europe humbled themselves before him. He for a moment lost his head and changed his religion for the sake of policy. He became a Catholic, and at the same time was made controller-general of the finance in place of his great enemy D'Argenson, who was removed to make way for him. But like all great men whose success is phenominal, like Moses, Alexander the Great, Napoleon and others that may be mentioned, whose success produced a false pride, has proved their downfall.

The plans of the enemies of the bank had now matured, through gambling they had raised the price of shares forty times above their nominal value (i.e) a share of 500 nominal value now sold for 20,000 livres. The total value in shares had reached the enormous sum of 8,124,000,-000 livres which required 500,-000,000 of livres annually to pay five per cent on this sum. It was impossible to meet this, and now was the time for the enemy to flood the market with shares and take up coin and the price of shares, immediately declined, and as the notes were redeemable in coin they depreciated, or rather gold went up out of sight. The government came to the rescue and made the notes legal tender, but promised a dividend of forty per cent on shares, which of course it was unable to pay. On the fifth of March an edict appeared fixing the price of shares, for which the government had received but 5,000 livres each, at 9,000 livres, and ordering the bank to buy and sell them at that price.

There were now 1,689,000 livres of notes in circulation. Although they were a legal tender, the act converting them into coin had not been removed, this together with the gambling in shares was the weapon in the hands of scoundrels and emissaries of England to down the system. Law now lost his court influence and was obliged to submit to a decree reducing the shares and notes to half of their nominal value. This of course destroyed all confidence, and raised such a hubbub that it had to be repealed, but the mischief was done. Law was removed from office and the enemies of the bank proceeded to demolish the system. The bank was abolished but the notes still passed current nor could they be got rid of until the legal tender act was repealed some years later.

This great failure of a promissory note gold basis bank has always been held up as a great bug bear to scare people who advocate a government paper money, pure and simple, a full legal tender acceptable for all dues to the government. The Law scheme as carried out, was a mere speculative commercial business, assisted by the government, and turned into a gambling scheme by its enemies.

Thiers, the great French statesman, said that the edict of March 5, 1720, which made the shares convertible into notes, ruined the bank without saving the company.

Everything possible was done to make this thing odious, that no paper money system should again be tried.

Law was ostracized and lied about. But he left the institution a poor man, and became a wanderer. But, says Henry A. Martin, "Such great confidence had Peter the Great, then Emperor of Russia, in Law, that his agents followed Law for six months trying to prevail on him to accept the finance portfolio of Russia. But Law feared the Russian people and declined."

I have had great trouble to gather facts concerning this matter, and so completely has the matter been suppressed in the English language that nine out of ten students get the John Law money and the French assignat mixed up and suppose them to be one and the same thing. The contraction of the volume of currency, so suddenly, produced wide spread disaster. Of course the volume had been expanded beyond all reason for so small a country as France, and a country not accustomed to a large volume, and the sudden drop was the more disastrous. But the greatest evil did not effect that generation; but like the contraction in England under Mary, which was the indirect cause of the rebellion under Cromwell eighty years after, so this contraction was the indirect cause of the great French Revolution seventy years after.

There is no denying that the enemies of the Bank Royal were in open treason and as traitors should have been ferreted out and executed.

I will now take up the

FRENCH ASSIGNAT.

It was a product of the

French Revolution of 1790 to 1798. They were not money, but a species of bonds which were first based upon confiscated church property, afterward on other public lands. Though they were not money, they were used as currency. They were also at one time made redeemable in gold. They depreciated in value and the government was obliged to double the issue, and they depreciated still farther, and finally upon the overthrow of the revolutionary government and the formation of a responsible government under Napoleon, they became worthless.

To mix up the John Law money with the assignats, and compare them with an absolute government legal tender paper money, displays an ignorance of the subject. Even Napoleon used the assignats for a time, but in 1799 the

BANK OF FRANCE

was chartered. Like the bank of England, its notes were made legal tender by the government. Whenever it becomes necessary to expand the volume of currency there is danger of an inability to redeem in gold. Like the Bank of England it is a private bank, granting aid to the government, and receiving privileges and remunerations.

Although it is not, strictly speaking, a government institution, the government owns a large number of shares. It was through its legal tender notes that enabled France to spare so much gold and silver to pay the indemnity to Germany after the Franco-Prussian war, and still leave France in a prosperous condition.

As England's policy toward France from 1716 to the fall of Napoleon is an exact parallel with her policy toward the

United States from its earliest history to the present time, and as we are now about to discuss American finance, I must diverge a little to cite her policy toward Napoleon.

No matter what may be said of Napoleon's ambition he said he did not desire war and conquest, but peace, and his actions bore this out, for the moment he was at peace he sought to build up the industries of France. He abolished the schools that turned out lawyers, doctors and professional men, and established new schools that taught those things essential to the welfare of the masses and the industries of France, such as chemistry and its application to the sciences and arts. In fact, if his plans had been carried out, they would have made France the foremost nation in the world. He would have also perfected a national finance for those were his tendencies. But these things did not suit England and she sought to stir up other countries against him, through bribery and other means. She, herself, always taking a prominent part in the struggle.

As an evidence, in an old volume of "Doubleday's Financial History of England" I found that Pitt refused to accept the premiership of England until he was granted £60,000,000, or $300,000,000, for his secret service fund, which I find in a French history was used to bribe leading Frenchmen and leading men of other nations against France. This was not enough, so Russia was promised that if she would lure Napoleon into the rigorous climate of Russia in mid-winter and destroy everything before him even to the burning of Moscow if necessary, she should be reimbursed for her losses. This was done. The legitmate funds of the treasury were used, and when the people demanded to know what had become of those funds, Lord Castlereagh, secretary of the treasury, cut his own throat rather than divulge it. Such were the statesmen of England, England first, their own interests afterwards. This was commendable as statesmen, but horrible as a policy. Is it any wonder that Napoleon cried out, "Give me the ear of the English people; I know I have been fighting a moneyed oligarchy."

We have now reached American finance and will first discuss

COLONIAL MONEY.

As I have before stated, money is always scarce in new countries. So with the settling of our colonies it was no exception to the rule, and so for a long time much of the business of the colonies was done by barter or exchange of commodity for commodity. But disputes would often arise, and as an aid to peace and harmony many different things were made legal tender that debts might be settled lawfully and bickering cease.

The Indians found along the shores of Long Island Sound were more advanced in civilization than those further north. They used a circulating medium of exchange called "wampum," which consisted of beads of two kinds, one white, made out of the end of a periwinkle shell, and the other black, made of the dark part of a clam shell. They were highly polished and when strung together looked very pretty. The beads circulated among the Indians as money; the black being worth two white ones. The colonists came to use them, first in their trade with the Indians and then among themselves. In Massachussetts they became by custom the common currency of the colony, and were made legal tender for twelve pence.

Barter currency was established at an early day in the colonies; products of all kinds were made a tender in payments. Nails, lead, bullets, coon skins and tobacco, have all been legal tender in some section at some time in this country.

The first issue of paper money made in the colonies was by Massachusetts in 1690, four years before the Bank of England was established. The form of these notes or bills was as follows:

This indented bill of ten shillings, due from the Massachusetts Colony to the possessor, shall be in value equal to money, and shall be accordingly accepted by the treasurer and receivers subordinate to him, in all public payments, and for all stock [cattle] at any time in the treasury.

1690.   Signature of Committee.

They were not a legal tender, but receivable for taxes and property in the treasury. In 1692 it was ordered that these bills be received at 5 per cent premium over coin in the treasury, and the result was they circulated at a par with coin twenty years. In 1703 another issue of bills in the same form—₤15,000 —was authorized by act of Parliament, but they were not made a tender. But in 1712 an act was passed making them a tender for private debt. In 1716 another issue of £150,000 was authorized, not legal tender. These notes were distributed among the counties and put into the hands of trustees to be loaned to the people at 5 per cent. In 1720 another £50,000 was issued under similar conditions and purposes.

In 1720 bills were issued by Rhode Island. But these notes were made a tender for all debts, except otherwise specified by contract.

The colony of Connecticut issued similiar bills at various times between 1709 and 1731. New York began to issue bills in 1709; Pennsylvania, in 1723; Maryland, in 1733; Delaware, in 1739; Virginia, in 1755; South Carolina, 1730. The first bills issued by Virginia bore five per cent interest, and said Thomas Jefferson: "In a short time not one of them was to be found in circulation." This is another proof that money should be given no other attribute than that of a tool of trade Jefferson says. "Then we issued bills bottomed on a redeeming tax, but bearing no interest. These were received, and never depreciated a farthing."

In 1763 Parliament passed an act forbidding the issue of any more paper money. This of course was at the instigation of the money power.

In 1764 Dr. Franklin bore testimony, before the British board of trade, to the value of the paper money of Pennsylvania.

Here we must go back a bit and review the paper issue of Pennsylvania.

Benjamin Franklin, to this day honored and held to be one of the greatest philosophers the world ever knew, he who put the halter on electricity, the great power of the age; he whom friends and enemies of the country alike have reverenced and honored, nobly defended a fiat paper money. I here quote from Freeman O. Wiley.

"One of England's ablest orators and thinkers (Lord Erskine) said that,

'Those who met in convention to frame the constitution of the United States, constituted the wisest body of men that ever assembled on earth for a similar purpose."

And no mind was more active, no council more sought, and no voice more potent in that immortal convention, than that of Benjamin Franklin.'"

I will now quote a few passages from a lengthy article taken from Franklin's autobiography, and found in Freeman O. Wiley's "Whither are we Drifting as a Nation?":

"Want of money in a country discourages laboring, and handycraftmen (who are the chief strength and support of a people) * * And nothing makes more bad paymasters than a general scarcity of money."

Here is something I want the reader to particularly notice as it will be referred to again:

"Since men will always be powerfully influenced in their opinions and actions by what appears to be their particular interests therefore all those who are wanting courage to venture in trade now practice lending money on security at exorbitant interest, which in a scarcity of money will be done notwithstanding the law. I say all such will probably be against a large addition to our present stock of paper money, because a plentiful currency will lower interest and make it common to lend on less security,"
*   *   *.   Now it ought not to be wondered at if people from a knowledge of a man's interests do sometimes make a true guess at his designs, for interest, they say, will not lie."

I have before stated, on pages seven and eight, that money is a thing of conditions, it is wealth, as it is a house, a horse, in fact any thing a man wants in a nut shell. Evidently Franklin thought the same for in the article before mentioned he says:

"Men have invented money, properly

called a medium of exchange, because through or by its means labor is exchanged for labor or one commodity for another. And whatever particular thing men have agreed to make this medium of exchange, whether gold, silver, copper or tobacco, it is to those who possess it (if they want anything) that very thing which they want, because it will immediately procure it for them. It is cloth to him that wants cloth, and corn to him that wants corn, and so on of all other necessaries, it is whatsoever it will procure "

Of all the money systems that of Pennsylvania was the best. it was planted, nursed and cared for by Franklin. It was purely and simply a fiat money. It was loaned to the people in sums of £100 or under, but never over that sum; for it was the people's and not the speculator's money. The rate of interest was five per cent, which went to pay clerical and other expenses, and thus lessened taxes so the whole people received the benefit. This money was called proclamation money. It never was intended to be and never was redeemed in coin; and in 1759 there was outsanding £385,000 equivalent to $1,925,000; an enormous amount for so early a period and so small a population. As I have stated, money, like all other things depends upon conditions for commercial value. The conditions in this case were that the colony of Pennsylvania by authority vested in it by the king, issued the money and gave it commercial value; but when it ceased to be a colony and became a state, the conditions were lost, it ceased to be money and states refused to recognize either what they termed King George's money or the old Continental money. Expressly was this the case in New York, where the money changers had already got a foot hold.

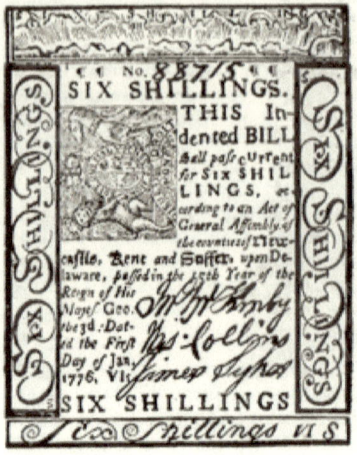

The above cut is an exact fac-simile of the Colonial money under the grant of King George. It was an absolute money as long as the law allowed. Once the law was repealed and then it ceased to be money. This is another proof that money is a creation of law. Below is the reverse side of the same bill.

The above cut is a fac-simile of the old Contenental promisory note. It never was money but was a promise to pay money, that is Spanish milled dollars which was money somewhere. The United States did not exist as a nation but as a belligerant power and had no authority to issue money. By comparing the above with the Colonial money the difference will be readily seen. One is money the other a promise to pay. Below is the reverse side or back of the same bill.

Even down to 1776 Delaware issued the King George or Colonial money, of which a fac-simile is here given, and as I here also give a fac-simile of the old Continental money you may see one was money and the other a promise to pay money. Even after the Revolutionary War North Carolina issued a large volume of legal tender money and it passed current for twenty years and stood at par with gold with no other conditions than that it was receivable for taxes, in which manner it was finally redeemed and destroyed.

One of the greatest bug-bears that have been used to frighten the American people from the discussion of the finance question is the old

CONTINENTAL MONEY

so-called, I say so-called, for these promissory, silver basis notes never were money. In the first place the conditions did not exist whereby they could be made money, as the colonies, like the Confederate States during our late war, were so many states in rebellion and had no recognized authority to emit bills of stable character, much less promissory notes promising something they did not have or could not get. Notice how these bills read, The first issue was in 1775 and read as follows:

> This bill entitles the bearer to to receive........Spanish milled dollars, or the value thereof in gold or silver, according to the resolution of Congress.
> ....

Other issues followed until the enormous amount of $350,000,000 had been put in circulation. The population was estimated in 1775 at only 2,448,-

000, and the entire property valued at less than $600,000,000. Is it any wonder that these promises to pay depreciated in value? Thomas Jefferson says that under the circumstances it was a wonder they ever passed current at all, yet they did stand at par with gold a year. But they were not money, never were money. The parties issuing them had no fixed power to issue money. They were metal basis promises to pay what the parties promising did not have and could not get. Thus the Continental money, so-called, is just the stuff the old Greenbackers and financial reformers object to; it is the kind of money the monied men howl for and they bring up their ghosts to scare people from investigating the question of financial reform.

It has been claimed that these promissory notes were made a legal tender but that is false. Congress passed a resolution of censure against all who refused to accept the notes and that was all they had power to do.

I have shown and will further show that the most stable money is a pure fiat money, made of a cheap commodity.

I have shown and will further show that gold and silver and their promissory note trash are the most unstable currency that the world has ever been cursed with, for as I have shown, gold and silver has deserted every country in its hour of peril. I have shown that the money power at that early day was exerting its influence and stood ready to devour the commercial prosperity of this country, and caused some of the states to refuse to accept or redeem either the Colonial money or the promissory Continental notes.

Before entering into a discussion of the money systems of the United States I want to state that I shall forcibly call attention to the the most

TERRIBLE CONSPIRACIES

the world ever knew. That their head center is in Lombard and Threadneedle streets, London, England, there is little doubt. That they have exerted a terrible influence upon all countries for the past hundred years is plain to be seen. That they will deny every truth that exposes them was to be expected, even financial reformers, some of them, show qualms of distress when these truths have been published, but there is not a thousandth part of the truth that has come to light. They have suppressed every evidence that lay in their power to suppress. The governments of the world from the little municipal government whose aldermen are bribed for a few dollars, up to the largest governments which are controlled by the great moneyed tricksters of the world, all, all are one mass of rottenness and corruption. And the pulpit and press are little better, though the influence these wield may be of a more covert kind, as, for instance, the

SUPPRESSION OF TRUTH

may sometimes be as flagrant a piece of dishonesty as downright theft. To be sure it is sometimes wrought by the change of public opinion or ignorance of the true state of affairs. The word "usury," that the Scriptures clearly define as increase, has been changed, first, through selfish motives, then it became public opinion. So Websters gives us the definition of public opinion; thus "usury" means only unlawful interest. Therefore the commands of Scripture are stretched in geographical proportions to cover all districts except those which have abolished all laws on usury. But many of our books of reference have been willfully tampered with.

A few years ago, I put the question to John M. Potter, then Editor of the Lansing Sentinel:

Q. "Do you think truths are suppressed in our books of reference?"

A. "Yes," said he, "the standard works of literature are suppressed and tampered with by the monocracy, college libraries invaded and works of art despoiled in the interest of monopoly. Some of the finest historical, scientific and economical works ever written have been suppressed and burned, because they taught principles of universal liberty. This has not only been done in the Dark Ages of the world but is done daily in every christian nation in the world. For over twelve years in my business as a newspaper publisher I have often found it impossible, in exciting campaigns, to get my paper delivered through the mails, and many exchanges are complaining of the same thing."

I wish to say right here that I published a pamphlet on the finance question in 1880 and had trouble to get it through the mails, but where the trouble was located I never could find out.

Mr. Potter went on: "Thomas Paine, the real author of the Declaration of Independence was forced from the country by religious intolerance, and his ablest works, the "Rights of Man," is never seen in academy, college or church, and it has been almost entirely eliminated from the libraries of the country. Wendell Phillip's greatest effor's are seldom seen, and attempts have been made to suppress those of Victor Hugo. Even the Encyclopedia Britanica has been interpolated and in some instances whole chapters have been left out which reflected upon the money power. In all editions published prior to 1860 there is a very strong article against banks, contraction and kindred evils. In fact the history of England's panic, of 1816 to 1825, is given and contraction is denounced as the most damnable and destructive measure any government can adopt to rob its people. In all editions published since 1860 all the best and most startling features of this article have been left out. The history of the Bank of Venice has been interpolated and changed to such an extent in the interest of banking schemes that almost all modern works on the subject are worthless. When Proudhon wrote his celebrated work, "Property is Robbery," he did it at the risk of his life and his personal liberty, both of which he nearly sacrificed. Not over eight years ago when General Weaver was a new as well as brilliant star on the political firmament, The North American Review gave him $500 to write an article on the "Financial Question," *which then as now was the most prominent question of the day.* The article was so truthful, plain and unanswerable that the monocracy trembled at the terrible exposition and influenced The North American Review not to publish it; and it has never seen the light of day, notwithstanding it cost said magazine $500. Even Webster's Dictionary has not escaped the despoiler. All the editions of this standard work published prior to 1860 give the definition of the word dollar to be a silver coin of $412\frac{1}{2}$ grains. All editions published since demonetization took effect, give the meaning of the word dollar, to be a gold dollar of twenty-five and eight-tenths grains of gold or a silver dollar of 412½ grains of silver."

I find the following items in a scrap book clippings from one of our papers, as near as I can make out, sometime in 1885.

NO INDEPENDENT PRESS.

At a dinner recently given the Press in New York, a journalist was called upon to reply to the toast, "An Independent Press." Knowing we had no independent press among the powerful papers of the nation, he for a long time refused to reply, but being insisted on to do so, said:

"There is no such thing in America, as an independent press, unless it is out in the country towns. You are all slaves. You know it and I know it. There is not one of you who dares to express an honest opinion. If you express it you know beforehand that it would never appear in print. I am paid $150 a week for keeping honest opinions out of the papers I am connected with. Others of you are paid similar salaries for doing similar things. If I should allow honest opinions to be printed in one issue of my paper, like Othello, my occupation would be gone. The man who would be so foolish as to write honest opinions would be out on the street looking for another job. The business of a leading journalists is to distort the truth, to lie outright, to pervert, to nulify, to fawn at the feet of mammon, and to sell his country and his race for daily bread, or for what is the same thing, his salary. You know this and I know it and what foolery to be toasting an "Independent Press." We are the tools and vassals of rich men behind the scenes. We are jumping jacks. They pull the string and we dance. Our time, our talent, our possibilities are all the property of other men. We are intellectual prostitutes."

None but the rich can run a great daily newspaper. They are money making enterprises; they make their money by selling their space and their influence. It is said a lie will travel ten miles while truth is getting on its boots. It is certainly so with newspaper lies.

Those who do not believe the press is influenced in behalf of moneyed men's schemes should read the bank circular further on, also what Mr. Windom, once Secretary of the Treasury, has to say in the matter.

In addition to the clipping above quoted I give the following from the same source, which goes further to show that large institutions are influenced in behalf of the great corrupt schemes of moneyed men:

"General Weaver some years ago having contemplated the issue of a work on the finance question, called upon the publishing house of G. P. Putnum's Sons, of New York City to negotiate for its publication. They replied that they would be frank with him, they could not publish this book, as they belonged to an association of publishing houses that agreed to publish nothing which was opposed to an exclusive gold basis currency. Mr. Weaver replied, 'Then I belong to an association that will not buy your books.'"

Even the great publishing houses of the world seem to be pooled with moneyed conspirators against the race and in favor of usury. And this deception and fraud and suppression of truth has always gone on since old Satan, the father of lies, through deception caused the human race to lose their inheritance and earn their bread by the sweat of their brows.

I find in a book entitled, "The Ancient Lowly," by B. C. Osborn Ward many evidences of the suppression of truth. He points out that recent archæological discoveries of stone tablets found in old Roman territory that one Eunus, of Sicily, marshalled at one time 200,000 workingmen, and with force of arms held the whole Roman empire at bay for ten years. History gives us no account of it. He shows that nearly 1,000,000 of men were crucified at different times for taking part in labor strikes, that 6,000 were crucified at one time on the Apian Way. He also shows that the unsuccessful strikes of all ages have been made unsuccessful by the bribery of their leaders.

A few years ago when the Supreme Court gave its decision in the Julard vs. Greenman case on the currency question in favor of the greenback legal tender, not a paper in Detroit dared publish it, or at least did not publish it and we had to depend on the pamphlets for our information regarding it.

I will now give some of my own experience in this same line.

I have had great trouble to find in books of reference evidence of truths I was in search of, truths I know had been published in earlier editions. I could not find the tally in Encyclopedia Britannica or in the great American Encyclopedia. Surely so great a matter as the tally system described on page 57 should be easily found and fully explained.

What I find concerning the John Law money, in Encyclopedias, is very meagre and unsatisfactory. Concerning the French assignat, the information is still more unsatisfactory.

Professor Jevons, in his work on Money, gives a very interesting article concerning the issue of paper money, by Daniel De Lisle Brock, on the

ISLAND OF GUERNSEY.

The people of the island wanted a covered market, but they could not raise the funds necessary for its erection. A deputation of the principal persons called upon the governor to ask his advice and assistance in the matter. The governor asked in what way he could assist them. Times were very hard in the island, and money very scarce, they thought if they had a market building at least an exchange of commodities might be made.

They told him their difficulty was a financial one. He replied that if that was their only difficulty he thought he could surmount it. He inquired if there was plenty of material on the island to build it, and above all had they the skilled artisans and laborers required. Certainly they had these. The governor then explained that as governor he would sign, stamp and declare legal tender, four thousand pound notes. With these you can pay for your material and labor; go on and build your hall. The hall was built. It contained eighty stands, which rented for about five pounds each per annum. At the end of a year the rents paid amounted to £400. These notes were cancelled and so on for ten years when the whole of the notes were paid in and destroyed. There was no money borrowed, no great profits paid; but strange to say, prosperity reigned while these notes were in circulation, and stagnation came when they were destroyed and the people wondered at the hard times.

J. Sketchley, in a work entitled, "Review of European Society" gives the same story; several other prominent writers have done the same, but for some unexplained reason they have omitted the dates. Desiring to fix the date I naturally refered to my books of reference for the desired information.

But not one word on the subject could I find, not even the governor's name. Though I did find in Encyclopedia Britannica that in St. Peter's in Guerncey there was a grand new market hall built in 1873-4, but not a word of the financial part. Surely so unusual and important a matter as this was not omitted through carelessness?

Some years ago the first volume of Henry A. Martin's history of France, translated by Mary L. Booth, published by Walker, Wise & Co., Boston, Mass., was placed in my hands. the book came from the Detroit Public Library. I found the book went into every detail of government; in fact the most perfect history I ever saw. I sought for the remaining three volumes, but an entirely different work was brought me, To be sure it was by the same author and by the same translator but not the same publishing house; and it was in comparison like a candle to daylight. The balance of the volumes to the edition I required, to the astonishment of the Assistant Librarian, could not be found. I wrote to Walker, Wise & Co., but my letter was returned as such a publishing house was not in existence. As the book was published in 1865 and this was at least twenty-five years after, I could get no clue to members of the house. I wrote to the other publishing houses, but of course got no satisfaction. Then at great expense to myself, I wrote to many second-hand book dealers and offered $100 for the four volumes, and when I went to another city I made diligent inquiry but was never able to procure the coveted volumes. Undoubtedly the book, in the English language, has been suppressed.

'Albert J. Chapman, one of

Detroit's brightest and ablest lawyers, and one of the best posted men on the money question in the world, once told me that desiring to get the report of the Secretary of the Treasury for 1867, as it contained important evidence of the great silver conspiracy, he found on diligent inquiry that almost any other year might be had but not of the year desired. He finally wrote to Representative——— who after a long time sent him a copy with the statement that it was very hard to get but after some fibbing he was enabled to obtain it.

Is all of this an evidence of conspiracy?

Answer me this, why is it the brightest men of the country like my friend Chapman, honest and unassuming, should be ignored and left out in the cold, while disreputable men are pushed to the front? It is easily answered. The money power have no use for such men, and the fool people will not pick them up, as they prefer to follow their big mock sheperds, though they are given dirt instead of salt. If there is no undue influence used, why is it such men as Oliver P. Morton, John Sherman and the hero statesman, John A. Logan who all defended the greenback cause nobly, and then suddenly became silent on the subject or outspoken opponents to the cause they so nobly defended? Certainly we cannot help but look back to the Dubois and D'Argensons of France and wonder!

Let those who like deny there is a conspiracy and a powerful band of conspirators. In the light of history, how can we believe them!

Since the above was written I find the following evidence of conspiracy, which I quote from the National Watchman, one of our brightest reform papers:

The article below quoted gives strength to the utterence of one of our great New York dailies some years ago and quoted elsewhere. "That they (the banks) are so thoroughly organized that no act of Congress can overcome or resist their decisions."

NATIONAL BANKS.

"The baneful influence of national banks upon the legislation of the country has become apparent to all. The methods by which their influence is maintained are sometimes problematical but occasionally brought out with minute distinctness. An example of this kind came to light as far back as 1876 in the course of the speech of Hon. J. M. Bright in Congress. Mr. Bright gave out the following letter as sustaining his declaration that the banks had accumulated a fund for corrupt legislative purposes:"

WASHINGTON, D. C., JUNE 1, 1876.
214 D Street, N. W.

Dear Sir:—I was told some months since by Dr. Egbert, member of Congress from the 27th district of Pennsylvania, that when he was president of a national bank, I think in Mercer, Pennsylvania, that they were assessed one dollar upon each thousand dollars of their circulation as a fund to secure legislation in their interests; and, he said, he supposed this was general throughout the country. This would give an annual fund of about $350,000 and you yourself can compute its corrupting influence as well as any one. Dr. Egbert was six years at the head of a national bank.

Yours, very truly,
EGBERT HASARD.

HON. J. M. BRIGHT.
Washington, D. C.

When Dr. Egbert returns I will introduce him to you and he will repeat it.

"That letter was submitted to Mr. Egbert, who sits near me here, and was approved by him, and he is ready, so far as he is concerned, to testify, and there is other testimony on the subject."

"If these corporations are permitted

to come here to influence legislation of the country, I think it is time that a check and rebuke should be given to them. I proclaim here that they are the enemies to human liberty and the constitutional rights of the people, the invaders of the legislation of the country. Their relation is a pecuniary one; it is one for the purpose of trafic; it is one for the purpose of making the people bleed money. There is nothing in harmony between them and the industries of the country except as they can make profit out of them."

I do not wish it understood that I think all bankers are cognizant of these wrongs, for of course they are not. We all know of bankers we feel would spurn the very idea of supporting the atrocities perpetrated by this band of conspirators, yet they unconsciously aid the guilty by being blinded by their interests. And after all there is not so much difference in human nature. There is none so bad that there is no redeeming quality and none so good that evil does not exist somewhere in their nature, if circumstances only brings it out. It was the great pirate, Captain Kid, whose business it was making widows and orphans, when his men got into a quarrel and were butchering each other, shouted, in trepidation, "Men, for God's sake, desist. Can ye not see ye are making widows and orphans?"

It was a noted hard character, and a notorious prostitute, that interfered and saved the lives of the Band of the 6th Massachusetts when they were assailed by plug uglys, while passing through Baltimore at the opening of the late war, and this at a great risk of their own lives.

Bulwer Lytton tells in a foot note in his strange story, of an eminent Spanish philanthropist and philosopher who murdered a dear friend for a few pieces of ancient coin t' his collection might be complete. There is no doubt that many a banker's hand has flown to his pocket when his sympathies have been suddenly aroused by some sudden misfortune, even to a stranger, if forcibly brought to his attention, and then he might coolly walk to his office and order some poor widow out of his house because she could not pay the rent.

But that is business, and business knows no friends or mercy. In business he will cast his vote with the unprincipled of his order, favoring a contraction of currency, when if he would stop to think, he should see that it fills alms houses and prisons, and makes prostitutes, paupers and suicides. Blinded by his interests he will condemn the reformer, while he could not be made to believe that in his society, there are as gentlemanly criminals as ever "scuttled a ship or cut a throat."

Of course they would not suppress or deny truths or persecute, or murder a reform agitator who stood in their way, they are ready to

CRUCIFY HIM.

SAYS, WILLIAM SHAKSPEARE,

"When it was found that Jesus was accomplishing too much good in the world; when it was found he was assailing sin and wrong in high places; that he championed the right and condemned the wrong, he drove out the "money changers," he rebuked hypocrisy, he sat at meat with "publicans and sinners, and was in speech and word, of the people, who felt the sorrows of the people, and meant by his sword of truth to slay the enemies of God and love," then they cast about for something to condemn him. His words and sayings were tortured and misapprehended to mean anything and everything but the good and highest well being of society, until the cry set up by the High Priests "Crucify Him" was taken up and repeated by those he sought to aid. And strangest of all, even those he had worked with, even Peter, when the trial hour came, denied he ever knew him; and when at the last solemn moment and he was left alone—"alone in the Garden of Gethsemane"— when the supreme moment of loneliness and fear o'erswept his being, none stayed to hear the cry: "My God! My God! why hast thou forsaken me?" And this is the pathway all reformers must tread. And the poor, petty, cowardly souls will whimper when the great truths thundered by their comrades are denied by the guilty parties, just as any thief will deny the evidence of his guilt. And these poor souls who fear truth will deny their comrades and help the scoundrels to deny the evidence of their guilt.

The reader will please excuse this digression. But as I shall point out some ugly evidence of terrible conspiracies I wish to lay a solid foundation.

So thoroughly was the usurious money loaning system organized that it stood ready to devour this country the moment it stepped into the world a full fledged nation, and that power began its intrigues at once. Notwithstanding the States had surrendered all power or control over the question of money to the Federal Government— the object being to secure to the people a uniform and stable medium of exchange. Hence it was that clause was inserted in the Constitution expressly prohibiting States from coining money, emitting bills of credit, etc. But this wise provision was soon totally subverted by the money power through the instrumentality of the banks of issue, modeled on the British system of bank currency, and the currency of the country has been subject to the control of that power ever since. At the close of the revolution four banks of issue were established in the United States: one in each of the states of New York, Massachusetts, Maryland and Pennsylvania.

This immediately brought up the question of constitutional rights.

From the very start to the present time there has always been, among the moneyed classes a strong tendency toward a centralized government; and so jealously did the framers of the Constitution guard the rights of the people from the wiles of the aristocratic, oppressive class, that it will be well here to quote a few paragraphs from the Constitution. I will first quote from the Declaration of Independence :

"We hold these truths to be self-evident: that all men are created equal; that they are endowed by their Creator with certain inalienable rights; that among these are life, liberty, and the pursuit of happiness. That to secure these rights, governments are instituted among men, deriving their just powers from the consent of the governed.''

And this is carefully provided for by safeguards all through the Constitution reiterated in the first paragraph of the Fourteenth Amendment.

That the rights of the people shall be carefully guarded against usurpers of power, may be seen in articles first and second of the first amendments of the Constitution.

"Congress shall make no law respecting an establishment of religion, or prohibiting the free exercise thereof;

or abridging the freedom of speech or of the press; or the right of the people peaceably to assemble and to petition the government for a redress of grievances."

That no false charges might be brought against the people so assembled, that might be forcibly used against them, in Article III. section three, paragraph one, reads thus:

"Treason against the United States shall consist only in levying war against them, or in adhering to their enemies, giving them aid and comfort; no person shall be convicted of treason; unless on the testimony of two witnesses to the same overt act, or on confession in open court."

How wisely did our fathers guard the rights of the people. Look at the following:

ARTICLE II.
AMENDMENTS OF THE CONSTITUTION.

"A well-regulated militia being necessary to the security of a free state, the right of the people to keep and bear arms shall not be infringed."

Now that the people might not, in the heat of passion, get into bickerings with foreign powers, Article I. section seven, paragraph eleven, it is reserved to Congress alone "to declare war, grant letters of marque and reprisal, and make rules concerning captures on land and sea."

Now mark with what fear they dreaded the encroachments of the aristocratic classes. In paragraph two, Article I. they retain the right, "to coin money (i. e. create) regulate the value thereof; and of foreign coin, and fix the standard of weights and measures." Now it is very clear they feared the wiles of the moneyed class for mark here Article I., section nine, paragraph seven:

"No title of nobility shall be granted by the United States; and no person holding any office of profit or trust under them shall, without the consent of Congress, accept of any present, emolument, office or title of any kind whatever, from any king, prince or foreign state."

Now notice the government reserves to itself the right to create money and regulate the value thereof and in the following positively prohibits the states exercising those rights or of declaring war, placing them in equal importance:

Article I. section ten, paragraphs one and three: "No state shall enter into treaty, alliance or confederation; grant letters of marque and reprisal; coin money; emit bills of credit; or make anything but government money a legal tender for debt, pass any bill of attainder, expost facto law, or impairing the obligation of contracts; or grant any title of nobility. * * No state shall, without the consent and control of Congress, lay any duty on tonnage, keep troops or ships of war in time of peace, enter into any agreement or compact with another state or with a foreign power, or engage in war, unless actually invaded, or in such imminent danger as will not admit of delay."

Now it should be plain by the above quotations that the intention of the framers of the Constitution was to throw all the safeguards, possible, around the people and to curtail the powers of the moneyed class, and that the government reserved to itself alone the right to coin money and emit bills of credit, and that any granting of powers of issuing money or emiting bills of credit to individuals, corporations or even states, is unconstitutional. But we now see where the moneyed classes have usurped those powers, and to what terrible extent of crime they have gone to, in furthering their hellish schemes of robbery.

At the close of the Revolution the aristocratic money power

was headed by Alexander Hamilton who was the Secretary of the Treasury. In a speech delivered June 18th, 1787 he said.

"I believe the British goverment forms the best model of government the world ever produced. * * All communities divide themselves into the few and the many. The first are the rich and well born, the other the mass of people. * * Nothing but a permanent body (a House of Lords) can check the independence of democracy."

And this is the man, the first Secretary of the Treasury, who urged the establishment of a National Bank, modeled upon the British system, a system that has proven a tyrant and a curse to the world. The Bank of England, not a government institution, is granted by that government—that but a short time since granted privileges of piracy—the right of issuing 14,650,000 of bank promises to pay gold, without a grain of gold behind it, and the government makes these notes a legal tender except to the bank itself. The Bank of England is not bound to honor its own notes.

In 1852 the Bank held £20,751,000 specie in its vaults, with an issue of £30,000,000 in notes and a deposit of the people's money of £750,000,000. Where would this little handful of gold be if the people demanded their money in gold? And this is the gold basis system that Alexander Hamilton desired to fasten on this country and the money class have ever since been working for. In 1863 in the House of Representatives in a speech delivered in support of the National Bank Bill, Hon. E. G. Spaulding, a banker of New York, boldly asserted that

"It is now most apparent that the policy advocated by Alexander Hamilton, of a strong central government, was the true policy."

Here we get the spirit of the money power.

The first bank of the United States, with a capital of $10,000,000, was chartered by Congress, February 25, 1791 for a period of twenty years; Jefferson who was then secretary of state gave a written opinion denying the power of Congress to incorporate a bank of issue. Madison, who was in Congress, opposed it in a powerful speech, as a violation of the Constitution.

In 1811 the bank applied to Congress for a renewal of its charter, but it was not granted. Clay and other leading statesmen opposed its recharter on the ground that it was "unconstitutional, and anti-American, and strictly a British institution."

Now disregarding the Constitution, prohibiting the rights of states, to grant privileges to emit bill of credit, governors of states did grant such privileges, and in 1815 we had, says Jefferson, probably a hundred banks of issue. In 1814 a bill was passed over the governor's veto in Pennsylvania, chartering forty banks alone, with a capital of $17,000,000. Thirty-seven of them went into operation at once, and suspended six months after. Such a sudden fluctuation of prices proved a great disaster, but mind you these were specie basis promissory note concerns with no fiat behind them.

The people needed money and the government here made a great mistake in not furnishing a plentiful supply of legal tender notes and paying out to labor thus getting the money into circulation.

Specie basis banks are always required by law to redeem their notes in specie, but as they are always authorized to issue notes to three times the amount of specie held, and as they often exceed their authority, any one may readily see the utter impossibility of the redemption of the notes, if there chances to be a sudden demand for gold.

Kellogg tells us that in 1849 the specie held in the banks of Connecticut for twelve years was $478,719, while the average amount of their loans to the public, during the same time was $11,669,457—more than twenty-four and one-third times as much money as the banks had in specie.

"The annual interest on $11,669,457 was $700,167 if they could have loaned only their specie, the interest would have amounted to but $28,723. The banks gained from the public annually $671,444 above the interest of their specie, and in twelve years, $8,057,328. They collected this interest in advance and made their dividends half yearly to their stockholders; therefore it is proper to compound this interest half yearly, which would swell their gains nearly $12,000,000, or $1,000,000 annually."

The specie basis concerns have been compelled to suspend specie payments as follows in 1800, 1814, 1819, 1825, 1834, 1837, 1839, 1841, 1857, 1861. And all of this is brought up as argument against a government issue of money and in favor of the rotten gold basis system.

Says Burkey: "In March, 1809, a legislative committee of the state of Rhode Island made an examination into the affairs of the Farmer's Exchange Bank of Glouscester, and it was found that they had $58,000 of its notes in circulation, and only $18.16 in its vaults for their redemption. Before the end of the year a general suspension of the banks of New England took place, and it was discovered they were nearly all in the same predicament. * * In 1814 all of the banks outside of New England * * were compelled to suspend, which brought great disaster."

Again the government made

the mistake in not furnishing a stable substitute for this rotten system. And in 1817 the second great Bank of the United States was established. This of course was a private institution though the government held one-fifth of the shares, four-fifths were supposed to be held by foreigners though it was ascertained that forty members of Congress in 1818 held stock of the concern. Probably most of it given them to secure their support.

I will again quote from Burkey.

"The second Bank of the United States began business on the twentieth day of February, specie payments were nominally resumed. But the extent and character of the resumption that took place may be gathered from the following case, cited by Sumner in his 'History of American Currency:, 'In 1817 a case at Richmond—after specie payments were resumed—gave an insight into the state of things. A man having presented ten one hundred dollar notes for redemption was refused. He could not get a lawyer to take his case against the bank, for a long time. Finally, having obtained judgment, the sheriff was sent to collect. The president of the bank was taken before the court, but refused to pay. The bank was closed by the sheriff, but soon after opened and went on.' The gold basis system had now been in operation long enough to produce its legitimate fruits, accordingly we find that here and there the people were becoming alarmed at its encroachments upon the public. The following is an extract from a report of a legislative committee of the state of New York in 1818:

"'Of all aristocracies none more completely enslaves a people than that of money, and in the opinion of your committee no system was ever better devised so perfectly to enslave a community as that of the present mode of conducting banking establishments. Like the siren of the fable they entice to destroy. They hold the purse-strings of society and by monop-

olizing the whole circulating medium of the country, they form a precarious standard, by which all property in the country—homes, lands, debts, and credits, personal and real estate of all descriptions—are valued, thus rendering the whole community dependant upon them, proscribing every man who dares to expose their unlawful practices. If he happens to be out of their reach so as to require no favors from them, his friends are made the victims, so no one dares complain.
* * Their influence already begins to assume a species of dictation altogether alarming, and, unless some judicious remedy is provided by legislative wisdom, we shall soon witness attempts to control all selections to offices in our counties—nay the election to the very legislature. Senators and members of the assembly will be endebted to the banks for their seat in this capitol, and thus the wise end of civil institutions will be prostrated by corporations of their own raising."

How much this reminds one of the utterances of the National Bankers of a few years ago. "Soon they, the banks, will be so thoroughly organized that no act of Congress can overcome or resist their decision."

Again I quote from Burkey:

THE CRASH OF 1819.

"In 1818 the bank of the United States had discounted to the amount of $43,000,000, and had $2,000,000 in specie. It had established eighteen branches and its notes could not be signed fast enough for the public. To increase its reserve of specie it had bought $7,000,000 of bullion abroad, at a cost of $800.000 for expenses, but it was exported as fast as it was imported. The Bank of England, which had been in suspension since 1709, was preparing to resume specie payments, was drawing specie from every source that was available. In April, 1818, less than fifteen months after the bank of the United States started, it was believed to be insolvent. A committee, appointed by Congress to investigate its affairs, reported a resolution requiring the bank to show cause why its charter should not be forfeited, the resolution was lost, as forty members of Congress were stockholders in the bank. The bank now resorted to vigorous measures to save itself from bankruptcy, and in a little over two months was once more solvent. It had however ruined the country. The amount of bank notes in circulation in 1814 was $45,000,000; in 1818, $100,000,000.

"In 1819 the volume was reduced to $45,000,000. In August 1819, 20,000 people were out of work in Philadelphia and a similar state of things existed all over the country; wheat was twenty cents a bushel in Kentucky, at Pittsburg flour was $1 per barrel, lumber $2 per thousand. One who presented a bill to the bank for redemption had to make oath that the bill was his own and that he was not an agent for any one; this had to be done before a cashier and five directors and he had to pay $1.37½ expenses on each bill."

This of course was done that they might retain the specie in the bank. Volumes might be written in description of the suffering of the people at this period. It was not the increased volume of money that did the mischief but the sudden collapse in consequence of contraction. Had this been government fiat money of course it would never have happened. The disaster was caused by the rotten gold basis system they now so much howl for. This panic lasted several years, but in 1823-4 banks were started everywhere, New York alone chartered about fifty banks. The bank of the United States issued $3,000,000. But as before the gold basis bubble soon burst. England, as always will be the case, whenever we try the gold basis system, needed gold, drew it out of the country, the banks again tumbled and brought down ruin with them.

Says Sumner's History of American currency:

"The banks, although based on 'hard money' and professing to pay coin were in a state of chronic suspension. The press of the country was completely subsidized; Congress as well as state legislatures, bowed in abject submission to the mandates of the money power; and even the Supreme Court of the United States did not escape its contaminating influence."

President Jackson was elected in 1828, and immediately let it be understood that he should oppose the bank as it had failed of its purpose. As its charter would expire in 1836 he determined not to precipitate matters, but let it run until that time. But the bank had now determined to fight to the bitter end. The re-election of Pres. Jackson would take place in 1832. The bank had determined on his defeat, and, says Hon. W. D. Kelley, in a speech delivered at Indianapolis, August, 1875.

"Through its branches and its control over state banks, its power extended into every part of this country. Millions of dollars (belonging, as subsequently appeared to depositers and stock holders) were squandered for the purpose of corrupting the people."

The government funds had been deposited with the banks but they had already been withdrawn or they would have gone the same way.

"Statesmen, Congressmen, brawling politicians, editors, all succumbed to its influence. * * After a careful survey of the field, and a thorough canvass of Congress, it was determined by the bank that a renewal of its charter should be applied for during the session of Congress immediately preceeding the next general election in 1832. The bill passed Congress by a majority of eight in the senate and twenty-two in the house. As was expected it was returned with the President's veto on the 10th of July, 1832. The contest was then transferred to a wider field and carried on with excessive virulence. The money power every where went to work to defeat Jackson. In Philadelphia for example, the bank would order business men to hold public meetings in its behalf, in order that it might ascertain who were its friends, and who were courageous enough to stand by the government in its efforts to redeem the people, and then in turn it would appoint places for the assembling of the different trades in order that the employers might see who of their workmen had opinions which they dared mention."

It was during that debate in the house that John Randolph said:

"Charter a bank with $35,000,000, and let it learn its power, then bell that cat if you can. It will overawe Congress and laugh at your laws."

The charter of the bank expired in 1836, but it had two years to wind up its affairs, but, says Thomas Benton, in his "Thirty Years in Congress."

"Instead of preparing to close its business, it resorted to new and desperate measures to prolong its power. In January, 1836, a bill was 'sneaked' through the state legislature of Pennsylvania by bribery and corruption, entitled, 'An act to repeal the state tax, and to continue the improvements of the state by railroads and canals and for other purposes.'"

"Under the vague generality of 'other purposes,' was found a charter for the United States Bank, adopting it as a State Bank. The people of Pennsylvania were astounded and met in masses; the act was repealed, and an investigation ordered, but as usual in such cases it amounted to nothing."

The bank still did business until October 9th, 1839, when it closed its doors in rottenness, only to come up again in the nation's distress in a new form, called the National Bank System. The rottenness of this system could not be half told in one volume. Pitt, the English statesman, forsaw the rottenness of this system, for when Alexander Hamilton first brought forward his banking scheme in 1791, Pitt said:

"Let the Americans adopt their funding system and go into their banking institutions, and their boasted independence will be a mere phantom."

My father-in-law, Benjamin F. Chase, who well remembered incidents of the great fight of the United States Bank, often told me that there was no doubt that the attempted assassination of President Jackson was instigated by the bank power, for it had even been threatened in some papers; and a statement made that they had a gun that was a sure thing as it would explode under water. This was the first heard of the percussion cap. President Jackson well knew who had tried to take his life for he reprieved the poor tool, and stated that it was the men behind him that he desired to get hold of. They tried to intimidate the President long before this for when the bill to renew the charter was on its passage, large numbers called on him and at first said to him:

"President Jackson, if you veto this bill it will ruin the business interests of the country." Said the President: "I have given the matter my close attention and I will answer for that."

They then adopted harsher means and said:

"President Jackson, if you veto this bill we will ruin the business interests of the country." "What," said the President, "you threaten to ruin the business interests of the country?" "I will give you men twenty-four hours to get out of the city of Washington, if found here after that time your corpses will grace the walls of the capitol building.'

It will be well to notice here that in 1880 their kind made the same threat: "To ruin the business interests of the country." But as this will be referred to farther on I will now take up the

WILD CAT BANKING SYSTEM.

The English moneyed men had never desired or intended to let a rival system get a hold in this country, hence whenever the gold basis system seemed to get in a fair way to make a good showing, the Bank of England was in real or pretended distress, and as the capitalist always managed to get hold of a great amount of our securities, during the distressing times of a panic, they would rush these securities on the market, offer them for bank notes at a sacrifice, which of course they could do having bought them for a song. They would now send the bank notes to their respective banks and demand the coin. This bursted the banks and left our own people with the worthless notes. So English capitalists were waxing rich while our people were suffering the consequence. As soon as things became settled and very low prices prevailed, the gold was loaned back to our people who again would issue a large number of notes, when the same thing was enacted over again. The crash of 1837, 1839, 1841 and 1857 were all of the same nature. In 1837 upon examination into the standing of New England banks it was found that the best of them had but $1 in gold to redeem $11 of their paper. In the West it was far worse. From 1837 to 1841, many banks were started up in out-of-the-way places. A log building was put up and called, say, the city of Podunck, another one might be called Wild Cat, etc. etc. Now a fine lot of bank notes would be printed. The devices were very imposing and pretty. Some representing the various branches of industry and some scenes of the wilderness: such as a wildcat in the act of springing upon its prey or the body of the note printed in black and a dog printed in red on one end. [I have some of these notes still in my possession.] The notes were given to an agent who would exchange them for the notes of a similar bank in a far distant state. These notes were loaned on all kinds of security or exchanged for any kind of property. So common was it for a man to have a carpet sack full of these notes that it originated the term "carpet baggers," a term so often given to politicians, in the south after the war.

These notes were supposed to be redeemable in gold. But as the banks could not be found, the whole thing being a fraud, the bubble soon burst and brought great distress upon the people. And this rotten gold basis fraud, belonging to the enemies of a true government money, is often brought up to scare people who would attempt to look into the matter, and fools take up and repeat the cry, "Oh! you want a wild cat money;" which is the very thing their masters want and we do not want. After this bubble burst the distress of the people was terrible; and now let us see where the people got relief. I here quote from Burkey, page 44.

"In 1745 Virginia was badly in need of money or a medium of exchange. A paper money bottomed on a specific tax was issued, which afforded abundant relief, and as we learn from Jefferson, never depreciated a farthing in value. But a more marked instance of the value of money as an element of production is furnished by the experience of Pennsylvania during the present century. In 1841 the people of Pennsylvania were on the verge of bankruptcy. The state was unable to pay the wages of laborers for work done on the public works. There was no money, consequently trade and production were completely paralyzed. The state of Pennsylvania in this crisis issued $3,100,000 of what were called relief notes, bearing simply a promise that they would be received by the treasury of the State in payment of all taxes and other obligations due the state."

"These notes were taken greedily." But the banks would like to have squelched them.

"Banks inserted in the front of their books an agreement that the depositers should receive on check the same kind of money he deposited, and then took these notes. They discounted paper with them. The wheels of industry were set in motion by these notes, which promised nothing but that they would be received in payments of state taxes. The state paid her domestic creditors, and these hastened to pay theirs or to supply their wants by purchases. Crops, for which there had been no market, moved; the loom and the spindle were again heard; labor, lifted from dispair, found work and wages, and with the great resources of Pennsylvania, under full and free development, she was soon exporting more than she imported. Gold and silver flowed in upon us. 'We then were wise enough to know,' says William D. Kelly, of Pennsylvania, from whom this was first quoted, 'that it is labor not gold and silver that maintains the public credit.'"

So after all we see that a tax receivable paper—though the state could not make it a legal tender—was what saved the country again when the rotten specie basis system had nearly ruined it. During the panic of 1893 the Governor of Mississippi did a similar thing and the banks set up a howl that it was unconstitutional, and he was summoned before the United States authorities to answer to the charge of overriding the Constitution. Of course it was unconstitutional, but no more so than the granting of bank charters by the state or United States authority. "But it makes a difference whose ox is gored."

However if the United States will not furnish us with a plentiful supply of money our states should have the privilege of doing so, and we should not be dependant upon a rotten and dishonest banking system.

After the fall of the wild cat banks more restrictions were thrown around the banks and government inspectors called upon the banks periodically to inspect the amount of specie and see if the required amount of specie, one-third of the issue of paper, was in the vaults.

All manner of schemes were worked to trick the inspectors. In cities it would be ascertained what banks the inspector would visit first, when after inspection of the coin in the first he would be taken into the president's office and wined and entertained until the gold could be put in a wheel barrow and taken to the next bank, and he would be let go where he would inspect the same gold over again and again. In country places where this could not be done kegs of nails, or refuse scrap iron, was put up and labeled as so much gold, and as Samuel Cary once said in a speech delivered in the Detroit Opera House: "When the bank failed it was not for the want of gold enough but for the want of enough nails that the banks failed."

BEFORE THE PANIC OF 1857.

We seemed to be getting along quite fairly. But England had passed through the

Crimean War in 1853, to 1856, and in consequence she had another crisis, she must have gold to bolster up her system, and as before our securities were gathered up, rushed over here and exchanged for bank notes, the bank notes taken to their respective banks and the coin demanded. And as if to make assurance doubly sure to bring on a crisis here, a seeming preconcerted run was made on the strongest bank in the country, as if it went down it must carry the majority of other banks with it. This bank was the Ohio Life and Trust Company. It closed its doors August 24, 1857. Nearly all other banks soon followed or partly suspended and their notes were at a discount of from five per cent to ninety-five per cent, and every business man had to carry a little book called the bank note detector to know what money was good or what money was bad, and even then the notes were fluctuating so rapidly that it was impossible to tell just what a bank bill was worth. A workingman might receive his pay in notes considered good at night and in the morning they were worthless. *And this was a gold basis system.* Times were terribly bad, everything cheap, but there was no money to buy with and everybody was destitute. In 1858, my mother's taxes on 2½ acres of ground in the city of Flint was forty cents. I accidently found twenty cents in silver on an old circus ground and the news spread all over Genesee county, that the widow Stowe's son had found half enough money to pay her taxes.

Gold was discovered in California in 1849, and in Australia in the early fifties, but in those slow days it took several years for us to feel the effects of it.

But we were slowly recovering from the dire results of the panic of 1857, when the war broke out in 1861. At this time the government recognized no other money than gold and silver; silver the 412½ grain dollar was the standard money of the nation. Before going farther I must state that during the panics of 1837 to 1839 the government lost $2,000,000, with the banks so that in 1840, the Independent Treasury Act was passed. But a new Congress coming in the next year repealed it. However in 1846 it was re-enacted and remained in force until it was suspended in 1861 to allow the Secretary of the Treasury to deposit with the banks, in aid of loans that he was to receive. However the secretary deemed it prudent to immediately withdraw the deposits, and he refused to deposit with them farther except as bonds afterward were deposited with the banks for disposal. The banks, however, expected the government to deposit with them and check out, and allow them to issue an unlimited volume of notes which the government would have to back. Thus they would get the benefit of the whole issue, and the government have to borrow back its own notes. Under an act of July, 1861 the Secretary was authorized to negotiate a loan of $250,000,000, for which he was authorized to issue coupon bonds, or registered bonds or treasury notes, in such portions as he might deem advisable. The banks agreed to take up this loan, and did furnish the government $80,000,000, of gold, and I defy any man to show where the government ever received another dollar of gold by loan during the war. When the bankers found their scheme would not carry their patriotism, we hear so much about, vanished and they had no more gold for the government. When it was ascertained that the bankers had no more gold to loan the government, it raised a general indignation among our leading men in Washington. Statesmen remembered that we had issued, in a time of need, treasury notes that were as good money as gold and silver. These issues were made in 1812, 1813, 1814, 1815, and from 1837 to 1848, $100,000,000, with and without interest, and in 1857 20,000,000, full legal tender notes that were preferred to gold. Hence they argued that we could resort to that measure again. I was in Washington at that time and well remember the many expressions of contempt for the bankers by the most of our statesmen. I read in one of the morning papers of a hot debate on the subject the night before. When Thaddeus Stevens, chairman of the Finance Committee said: "Very well, let the bankers go, we will issue treasury notes that will pay all dues public and private." "Yes," said Zack Chandler, "and damn, it we'll demonetize gold and silver." But Oh! what a change came over Mr. Chandler. But Governor Begole says it was after Mr. Chandler *got hold* of $50,000.000 bonds that he wanted paid in gold. Many more of our statesmen also changed their minds suddenly, and in the light of history we may easily judge what caused the change. At this time there was about 1,600 state banks in the United States with a circulation of $20,000,000, of this circulation about three-fourths belonged to the Northern States. The northern banks held in specie for the purpose of redemption, about $60,000,000. Of the $250,000,000, loan act of

July 7th, 1861, $50,000,000 might be issued non-interest bearing demand notes, the balance in bonds running twenty years at not over seven per cent.

The government paid out the demand notes to the extent of $50,000,000, altogether. This with the $60,000,000 gold received from the banks, which the government immediately paid out, started the wheels of business, and says Spaulding's "Financial History of the War:"

"The disbursments of the government for the war were so rapid, and consequent internal trade movement was so intense, that the coin paid out upon each installment of the loan came back to the banks, from the community in about a week."

If the government issue of a few millions of non-interest bearing notes, and paid out for war and destruction, should so quicken exchange and start the wheels of business, why, when a financial panic is upon the people causing untold distress, unsettling of homes filling alms houses, prisons and suicides' graves, should not the government come to the relief of the people and issue paper money and pay it out for labor to beautify the land and thus relief distress? This could not be considered a debt as the life of paper is but seven years, there is no interest on it and as it disappeared the government (who are the people) would be so much ahead and no one would be the loser. But the money kings won't have it so, as they could make nothing out of it.

THE CRASH OF 1861.

England now began to demand our gold, and according to "Spaulding's Financial History of the War," December 7th, 1861, the banks had $42,800,000, in specie, but by the twenty-eighth day of the same month it had dwindled to $29,300,000, and the banks suspended specie payments. But why did we not have a panic, and consequent loss to business and the the people? I answer, because we had a substitute for the specie that was shipped to England in the demand notes and greenbacks issued shortly after; so the crash of '61 injured nobody.

NOW COMMENCED.

The most damnable conspiracy the world ever knew.

The infidel Jew money-kings in Threadneedle and Lombard streets London, England, who now through their money control the world, assisted by their cohorts and bribed statesmen on this side, sought to cripple and enslave the people of America, and while we were knocking the shackles off from four millions of colored chattel slaves they were forging the golden fetters to bind over sixty millions of people in commercial slavery, far worse than chattel slavery. I will here point to evidence that has sometimes been denied, but I will point to circumstances substantiating its truthfulness. About this time there was a circular published in England and mailed to their alies in this country called

THE HAZARD CIRCULAR
WHICH READS-

"Slavery is liable to be abolished by the war power and chattel slavery destroyed.

"This I and my European friends are in favor of, for slavery is but the owning of labor and carries with it the care of the laborer, while the European plan, led on by England, is capital control of labor, by controlling wages.

"This can be done by controlling the money. The great debt that capitalists will see to is made out of the war, must be used as a measure to control the volume of money.

'To accomplish this the bonds must be used as a banking basis.

"We are now waiting to get the Secretary of the Treasury to make this recommendation to Congress.

"It will not do to allow the greenback, as it is called, to circulate as money any length of time for we can not control that."

This circular was issued in 1862 and "confidentially" circulated among the bankers. The evidence of its truth may be found in other utterances from the same source as well as the policy shaped here.

Henry C. Baird, in an article published in the *Philadelphia Enquirer,* and reproduced in the Irish World under date of April 5th, 1879, quotes from a speech by Lord Huskinson in Parliament, as follows:

"To give capital a fair remuneration, labor must be kept down."

Again from the London Times:

"An inexhaustible supply of cheap labor has so long been a condition of our social system, whether in town or country, whether for work or pleasure, that it remains to be seen whether a great enhancement of labor would not disturb our industrial, and even our political arrangements to a serious extent. Two men have been after one master so long, that we are not prepared for the day when two masters will be after one man; for it is certain, either, that the masters can not carry on their own business as well, or that the men will comport themselves properly under the new regime. Commercial enterprise, and social development require an actually increasing population, and also the increase shall be in the most serviceable—that is the most laborious—part of the population, for otherwise it would be at the command of capital and skill."

Comment upon the above is not necessary, as the manner of carrying out their schemes is prima facie evidence of their plots.

The Hazard circular tells us:

"We are now waiting to get the secretary of the treasury to reccomend the National bank system, to Congress." Which he did in his first annual report to Congress, December 10, 1861. that Chase was honest but deceived and unduly induced to make this reccomendation is proved by Mr. Chase's utterance afterward, when he said:

"My agency in procuring the passage of the National Bank Act was the greatest mistake of my life. It has built up a monopoly that effects every interests in the land, It should be repealed, but before this can be accomplished, the people will be arrayed on one side and the banks on the other, in such a contest as we have never seen in this country."

After the people, headed by President Jackson, defeated the old United States bank, Thomas Benton said:

"Jackson has beaten the bank; yet the bank power is not conquered, but like a royal tiger driven to the jungle, will return again, with all her whelps."

We find the bank element did return and we will now note what took place. You will notice the National bank system was reccomended to Congress as early as December 10th, 1861 and a bill prepared, but it was not pressed until 1863 nearly two years after, and at a time when it was of no use to the government and as the Hazard Circular said they would be; the bonds are used as a basis for the National bank circulation. If this does not imply a cut and dried conspiracy, what does?

By an act of Congress, approved February 12th, 1861, the Secretary of the Treasury was authorized to issue $10,000,000, demand notes not bearing interest, but payable in specie on demand at the Treasury or Sub-Treasury. This in addition to the $50,000,000, authorized July

17, making $60,000,000 in all, so enraged and frightened the money changers that they strengthened their organization and prepared for a war on the government. Now as there was no gold in the Treasury to redeem these notes with they rapidly ran down in value, because they were not a legal tender, but mere promises to pay what the government did not have, therefore they were mere promises, based on a lie, which proves again that money is a creation of law and without fiat, or law, no currency is stable.

The government now seeing that to issue promises to pay something it did not have or could not get, would destroy its credit and the value of its notes altogether, sought new measures to meet its demands. Thaddeus Stevens, chairman of the finance committee, now prepared a bill that would give the government plenty of money; a full legal tender, good for all dues public and private.

Now the money power saw that if this bill passed the people would find out what money really was and so they sought to destroy the force of the bill No sooner was the bill made public than the bankers went to Washington in droves, as many as five thousand being there at one time, says one authority. They organized in a formal manner by electing S. A. Mercer of Philadelphia, chairman, and invited the finance committee of the senate and the ways and means commit ee of the house, to meet them at the office of the Secretary of the Treasury, January 11, 1862. The invitation was accepted. At the meeting which followed the bankers spoke in opposition to the bill, but submitted the following plan for raising money:

"1. A tax bill to raise $125,000,000,

over and above duties on imports, by taxation.

"2. Not to issue any demand notes except those authorized at the extra session of Congress in July last.

"3. Issue $100,000,000 at two years, in sums of five dollars and upwards, to be receivable for public dues to the government, except duties on imports.

"4. A suspension of the Sub-Treasury Act, so as to allow the banks to become depositors of the government of all loans, and to check on the banks from time to time as the government wanted money.

"5. Issue six per cent twenty-year bonds, be to negotiated by the Secretary of the Treasury, and AND WITHOUT ANY LIMITATION AS TO THE PRICE HE MAY OBTAIN FOR THEM IN THE MARKET.

"6. That the Secretary of the Treasury be empowered to make temporary loans to the extent of any portion of the funded stock authorized by Congress, with power to hypothicate such stock, and if such loans are not paid at maturity, TO SELL THE STOCK HYPOTHICATED FOR THE BEST market price that can be obtained."

Some of these measures were favored but most of them were opposed.

The house committee, through Mr. Spaulding, bitterly opposed the measures, as it placed every opportunity in the hands of the bankers to gamble in government stocks, and in many ways to swindle the government.

I quote the following from "Burkey on the Money Question."

"Thus while the masses were exerting every energy to sustain the government, the money power was plotting to get control of its finance, in order that it might be enabled to prey upon the people in the hour of their extremity. How well it succeeded will duly appear."

And this is the nobility of the moneyed class, that we hear so much about, who sprung to the country's aid in its hour of danger.

I will here, before we go farther—that we may fully understand definitions and terms—explain the names and kinds of obligations issued during and for some years after the war.

The acts providing for government issues will be found farther on, but here I wish merely to define different kinds of paper issues. From a table copied from "Burkey on Money."

The following are the names and amount of bonds and debt statement October 31st, 1865.

Bonds, 10-40's so called because they could be paid in ten years or might run forty years at the government option bearing five per cent interest:

Due in 1904,	$172,770,100
5-20s, six per cent, due 1882-84-85,	659,259,600

Bonds, 6 per cent, due			1881	$265,347,400
"	5	"	"	1874,	20,000,000
"	5	"	"	1880,	18,415,000
"	6	"	"	1867,	9,415,250
"	6	"	"	1868,	8,908,341
"	5	"	"	1871,	7,022,000
"	Pacific R.R.	"	1895,	1,258,000
"	Texas indemnity (funded)			760,000
Bonds, treasury notes, etc., past due				613,930

Total Bonds	$1,163,769,611

The following are the amounts and kinds of legal tenders and currency in circulation at the same date as above.

Compound interest notes due in 1867-68 so called because the interest was compounded:

Amount,	$ 173,012,131
Seven-thirty treasury notes, so-called because they bore 7-30 interest, due in 1867 and 1868, amount,	$ 830,000,000
Temporary loan notes	99,107,745
Certificates of indebtness due in 1886,	55,905,000
5 per cent treasury notes due Dec. 1, 1865	32,536,901
United States notes	428,160,509
Fractional currency	26,057,469
Total	$1,244,779,825

Most of the above were legal tender, and all receivable for government dues.

National bank notes	$185,000,000
State bank " etc.,	65,000,000
Treasury notes, greenbacks etc.	1,644,779,825
Total currency in circulation in the Northern States alone	1,894,779,825
Total bonds and currency called debt, Oct. 31, 1865.	$2,808,549,437

Registered bonds are those registered at the Treasury Department to the name of the person who owns them, and cannot be paid to any others unless regularly transferred and it is a good safeguard against theft. Other bonds are made payable to bearer.

A standard coin dollar means prior to Feb. 12th, 1873, the silver dollar of 1792, containing 371 and 4-16 grains of standard silver. This was dropped out by the act of 1873 and the 25 8 grain gold coin substituted. But the coinage of the gold dollar as a coin was prohibited by act of Congress, September 26th, 1890. These coins are sometimes referred to as standard coins or primary money as they are used as a basis for promissory note currency. But primary money is a misnomer as there is no such thing as primary money, as promissory notes are mere currency and not money at all as I have stated.

The difference between treasury notes not bearing interest and those bearing interest is merely this. A treasury note bearing interest and not a legal tender is simply an evidence of security of indebtness, it does not bear the attribute of money but a person might take it hoping to dispose of it, as he would a promissory note of a friend, rather than wait for the money.

Treasury notes are made receivable for dues to the government, while bonds are not consequently treasury notes pass as currency, and if they bear interest it is a detriment to them as currency, as they are withdrawn from circulation and hoarded for gain which proves a detriment to business.

Now we will notice the bankers always fought the issue of non-interest bearing treasury notes, of any kind, and have always used their influence to have them converted into interest bearing bonds to get them out of the way and saddle the country with a great debt, just as the Hazard Circular claimed they would.

As I before stated, Thaddeus Stevens drew up a bill to create a full legal tender paper money that should pay all dues, public and private, that would be as good for the bond-holder as for the musket-holder, or the plow-holder, or merchant. But the bankers were there to prevent it. And that what I say is true I must give a little testimony. Mr. Fessenden, once Secretary of the Treasury, when speaking of this subject said:

"It is quite apparent the solution of the problem may be found in the unpatriotic and criminal efforts of speculators, and probably of SECRET ENEMIES, to raise the price of coin, regardless of the injury inflicted upon the country."

I will now give the testimony of so good an authority as Mr. Lincoln in his message to Congress as early as 1861, and I want the reader to bear this in mind as I shall show that it was for this sentiment that Mr. Lincoln was assassinated by the money-power conspirators.

"Monarchy is sometimes hinted at as a possible refuge from the power of the people. In my present position I would be scarcely justified were I to omit exercising a warning voice against returning despotism. THERE IS ONE POINT TO WHICH I ASK ATTENTION. IT IS THE EFFORT TO PLACE CAPITAL ON AN EQUAL FOOTING WITH, IF NOT ABOVE LABOR, IN THE STRUCTURE OF THE GOVERNMENT. I bid the laboring people beware of surrendering a power which they already possess, and which, when surrendered, will surely be used to close the door of advancement to such as they, and fix new disabilities and burdens upon them till all of liberty shall be lost."

Now we will give the testimony of Oliver P. Morton, Indiana's great war governor:

"There is gathered around the Capitol of this nation a gang of miserable stock jobbers, with no more conscience than pirates, inspired solely by a greed for gain, and they thundered successfully at these doors until they drove this government into the most pestiferous acts of bad faith and legalized robbery that ever oppressed a free nation since the dawn of history."

Now this should be enough evidence as to what kind of *gentlemen* these moneyed men were who "came to the government's rescue in its hour of peril."

When this bill of Mr. Stevens was on its passage the bankers went into the Senate, then a small body of men with very low calibre of brain, with few exceptions. There they could best exert their influence. Although their influence was not lacking in the House. No stone was unturned to destroy this bill and foist one of their own upon the public.

Quoting from Wiley's "Whither are we Drifting as a Nation" he quotes from an open letter from Peter Cooper to John Sherman, and in turn quotes from Secretary Chase as follows:

"When I was Secretary of the Treasury, the question arose how should the soldiers in the field and the sailors on the ships be fed? I found that the banks of the country had suspended specie payments. What was I to do? The bankers wanted me to borrow their credit or pay interest on their credit. They did not pay gold, or propose to pay any themselves, but wanted me to buy their notes. I said, no gentlemen; I will take the credit of the people, and cut it up into little bits of paper."

In April, 1878, the Chicago Inter-Ocean was asked:

"How much gold and silver did Congress borrow to carry on the war from 1861 to 1865?" The reply was: "None; the receipts from customs were sufficient."

This of course meant for the specie demands of the government. As I before stated, I defy any one to show where the government ever received, by loans, more than $80,000,000 of specie during the war. But the bankers determinately fought the legal tender act and insisted on the exception clause on the back of the greenback, forcing the government to refuse to take its own money, and refusing to take the same kind of money for the interest on their bonds that they insisted that the soldier, the business man and the farmer should take. To use the words of Mr. Stevens in the great argument at that time he says:

"But while these men have agonized bowels over the rich men's cause, they have no pity for the poor widow, the suffering soldier, the wounded martyr to his country's good, who must give half of it to the shylock to get the necessaries of life. I wish no injury to any, nor with our bill could any happen; but if any must lose, let it not be the soldier, the mechanic, the laborer, and the farmer."

Such were the noble appeals made by our statesmen, like Stevens, Mason, Spaulding and others, against the sophistries of Roscoe Conkling of New York, and of Vallandingham of

Ohio and other defenders of the shylocks.

Mr. Stevens, further, says in speaking against the amended bill:

"I maintain that the highest sum you could sell your bonds at would be seventy-five per cent, payable IN CURRENCY ITSELF. That would produce a loss which no nation or individual doing a large business could stand a year.

"I contend that I have shown that such issue, without being made money, must immediately depreciate, and would go on from bad to worse. I flatter myself that I have demonstrated, both from reason and undoubted authority, that such notes, made a legal tender, and not issued in excess of the demand, will remain at par and pass in all transactions great and small, at the full value of their face; that we shall have one currency for all sections of the country and for every class of people, the poor as well as the rich."

Mr. Steven's defence of his bill was forcible and lengthy and finally closed the debate Feb. 6th, 1862, and was adopted by a vote of 93 to 59, it now went to the Senate where it was mutilated, so, to use the words of Mr. Stevens, "the father of it did not know it." It bore these amendments:

1. That the legal tender notes should be receivable for all claims and demands against the United States of every kind whatever, "*except for interest on bonds or notes, which shall be paid in coin.*"

2. That the Secretary might dispose of United States bonds "*at the market value thereof, for coin or treasury notes.*" The bill was also otherwise amended and a strong attempt to strike out the legal tender act altogether, but the latter was lost even in the Senate. It then went back to the House. Here Mr. Stevens called the attention of his, col-

leagues to the amendments, saying:

"*They are very important and in my judgment, very pernicious, but I hope the House* will examine them."

On the 19th Mr. Spaulding opened the debate in the House when he said:—

'I am opposed to all of these amendments of the Senate which make unjust descriminations between creditors of the government. A soldier or sailor who performs service in the army or navy is a creditor of the government. The man who sells food, clothing, and the material of war, for the use of the army and navy, is a creditor of the government. The capitalist who holds your seven and three-tenths treasury notes, or your six per cent coupon bonds, is a creditor of the government. All are creditors of the government on an equal footing, and all are equally entitled to their pay in gold and silver.
* * Who then are they that ask to have the preference given to them over other creditors of the government? Sir, it is a very respectable class of GENTLEMEN, but a class of men who are very sharp in all money transactions. They are not generally among the producing classes—not among those who, by their labor and skill, make the wealth of the country; but a class of men who have accumulated wealth, men who are willing to lend money to the government, if you will make the security beyond all question, give them a high rate of interest, and make it payable in coin. Yes, sir; the men who are asking these extravagant terms, who want to be preferred creditors, are perfectly willing to lend money to the government in her present embarrassments if you will only make them perfectly secure, give them extra interest, and put your bonds on the market at the market price (a price that they will fix) to purchase gold and silver to pay them interest every six months. Yes, sir; entirely willing to loan money on these terms. Safe, no hazard, secure, and the interest payable in COIN."

It will here be noticed that only the interest is expected in coin, the principal in the greenback paper money with which they bought the bonds. But we will soon see them claiming both interest and principal in coin (and posing as the saviors of the country) not only coin, but in one, and a scarce kind of coin at that. On the 20th Mr. Stevens again on the floor in the House said;

"Mr. Speaker, I have a very few words to say. I approach this subject with more depression of spirits than I ever before approached any question. No personal motive or feeling influences me. I hope not, at least. I have a melancholy forboding that we are about to consummate a cunningly devised scheme which will carry great injury and loss to all classes of the people throughout this Union, except one. With my colleague, I believe that no act of legislation of the government was ever hailed with as much delight throughout the whole length and breadth of this Union, by every class of people, without exception, as the bill we passed and sent to the Senate. * * It is true there was a doleful sound came up from the caverns of bullion brokers, and from the saloons of the associated banks.

"Their, cashiers and agents were soon on the ground and persuaded the Senate, with but little deliberation, to mangle and destroy what it had cost the House months to digest, consider and pass They fell upon the bill in hot haste, and disfigured and deformed it, that its very father would not know it. Instead of its being a beneficent and invigorating measure, it is now positively mischievous. * * It makes two classes of money —one for the bankers and brokers and another for the people. * * Why give them the additional advantage. * * The banks took $50,000,000 of six per cent bonds, and shaved the government $5,500,000 on them, and now ask to shave the government fifteen or twenty per cent, half yearly, to pay themselves interest on these very bonds. They paid the fifty million in demand notes, not specie, and now demand the specie for them."

Finally a conference committee was called. In which Mr. Stevens fought nobly for a full legal tender money; and says Judge Kelly in a speech of Jan. 12, 1876:

"I remember the grand 'Old Commoner.' (Thaddeus Stevens) with his hat in his hand and his cane under his arm, when he returned to the House after the final conference, and shedding bitter tears over the result. 'Yes,' said he, 'WE HAVE HAD TO YIELD; THE SENATE WAS STUBBORN. WE DID NOT YIELD UNTIL WE FOUND THAT THE COUNTRY MUST BE LOST OR THE BANKS BE GRATIFIED AND WE HAVE SOUGHT TO SAVE THE COUNTRY IN SPITE OF THE CUPIDITY OF ITS WEALTHY CITIZENS.'"

And so the bill passed in its crippled state and the first (greenbacks) legal tender notes were issued under the act of Congress of February 25, 1862, bearing this pernicious amendment:

"THIS IS A LEGAL TENDER FOR ALL DEBTS, PUBLIC AND PRIVATE, EXCEPT DUTIES ON IMPORTS AND INTEREST ON THE PUBLIC DEBT, AND IS EXCHANGABLE FOR UNITED STATES SIX PER CENT BONDS, REDEEMABLE AT THE PLEASURE OF THE UNITED STATES AFTER FIVE YEARS."

Is it any wonder that gold brought a premium when there was a special demand created for it, and when the government dishonored its own notes. If the people could have paid all dues with the government paper money would they have sought for gold, or gold gone up? Certainly not; yet there are fools and scoundrels to-day who will claim, in the face of this evidence to the contrary, that the government had to buy gold of these bankers to deal with countries abroad, whereas she bought nothing abroad. And with this scoundrelly conduct of the bankers they tried to deceive the people and make them believe this wicked amendment came from the

Committee of Ways and Means. Says Mr. Stevens:

"This was partly the fault of letter writers, and partly the fault of stock-jobbing money editors I perceive the money article of the Philadelphia press of Monday of this week, represents the bill was reported by the Committee of Ways and Means, notwithstanding the papers of last week stated its true origin. I suppose these money article editors are some dishonest brokers who make gain by their misrepresentations."

Now the money power had the foundation of their plans fully matured. They had forced the government to issue a large volume of bonds that they were allowed to depreciate until able to buy them at a very low price and pay for them in paper, not gold, as I have shown. Now their aim is to depreciate both bonds and greenbacks, and force the government to buy gold. This scheme was carried out until the government was robbed of millions and millions. Their National Bank institution was established. They were permitted to deposit bonds (that they had bought at a great discount) with the government, where they were kept safe from burglars, fire and loss. The government returned them interests, from 5 per cent and upwards, semi-annually in gold, then gave them 90 per cent in National bank notes, all free from taxation, to start their banks with. Oliver P. Morton once said on the floor of Congress, they did not pay to exceed 60 cents on the dollar for the bonds. Then at that rate for $60,000 a man could start a bank, draw interest on one hundred thousand, at 6 per cent, paid in gold semi-annually, then receive ninety thousand dollars to loan to the people at from 7 to 10 per cent. The banker was supposed to retain

20 per cent in his vaults, but in those flush days when the banks were full of deposited money it was easy to add $10,000 to the $90,000, buy another $100,000 bond, start another bank and thus draw interest in gold on two hundred thousand dollars and have one hundred and eighty thousand dollars in bank notes for a reserve and to loan to the people. And much larger frauds were perpetrated than that: As for instance the government deposited its money in a certain New York bank and the government's own money was used to purchase bonds with and the surplus shave saved to the banker. And the government was defrauded out of millions of dollars in this manner. As will be noticed farther on, by reference to the acts published, the heft of the bonds were not issued until after the war, and that to take up non-interest bearing legal tender paper money there was no necessity of ever issuing a dollars worth of bonds.

The heft of the bonds were issued to gratify the shave shops and to pay the exorbitant rates of interest. Here is a table showing the amount of interest paid on the public debt from June 30, 1861 to June 30, 1877.

June 30, 1861	$6,112,296.18
" " 1862	13,190,324.45
" " 1863	24,729,846.61
" " 1864	53,685,421.69
" " 1865	132,987,350.25
" " 1866	133,067,741.69
" " 1867	135,684,011.04
" " 1868	140,424,045.00
" " 1869	130,694,242.80
" " 1870	129,235,498.00
" " 1871	125,576,565.93
" " 1872	117,357,839.72
" " 1873	140,947,588.27
" " 1874	107,119,815.21
" " 1875	103,093,544.57
" " 1876	100,243,271.00
" " 1877	97,000,000.00
Total	$1,596,854,901.10

I have given the statement showing the bonded debt in 1865 was but $1,163,769,611.89.

Thus it will be seen that we paid in those seventeen years, in interest alone, $433,085,289.21 more than the original bonded debt, and one-half of that bonded debt was fraud or shave. Now if we add the bonded debt created in the issue of bonds after the war to take up legal tender notes that ought to have been left in circulation which was $1,644,779,825.66.

Now in the total government issue of bonds and all kinds of obligations including notes or greenbacks the whole amount or total issue to 1865, was $2,808,549,437.55. If we have paid as much interest in the past eighteen years as we did in the seventeen years from 1861 to 1877 we have paid $385,160,364.65 more than the whole government paper interest and non interest bearing frauds and all. But we have not paid quite as much interest in the past eighteen years as in the former seventeen, as the government paid off some of the indebtedness and converted some of it into smaller interest bearing obligations.

But inasmuch as we have counted the many millions of non-interest bearing paper which was in no way the bankers' money and have made no account of what has been paid on the principal we have much more than paid our just debt twice over, and according to the basis of justice established by Solon, spoken of on pages 45 we should now repudiate the balance of the whole debt. But it would be claimed that it would injure the innocent holders of bonds. Well; we grant that is true. But no great reform can be carried out without injury to some one's interests. If we now pay the balance of the whole bonded debt in legal tender paper money, the prosperity and happiness that it would bring to all would more than compensate all for any trifling loss of the depreciation in the purchasing power of the money they receive. But if they grumble at that how much more should the people grumble at the greater value they have been compelled to pay by the increased purchasing power of the money, brought about by the contraction of the volume of currency.

When the bonds were issued wages averaged $3.00 per day, but when much of the interest was paid wages would not average one dollar per day, consequently we have more than paid the public debt many times over.

Since the foregoing estimates of public debt crookedness was written, my attention was called to the following statement made by Senator Jones of Nevada, in a speech January 22, 1894:

From 1862 to 1858 United States interest bearing bonds were sold to the amount of -	$2,049.975.700
Discount on coin consi'red	1,371,424,238
Profit to purchasers	678,551,462
There has been paid as interest	2,538,000,000
Premium for bonds not due	58,000,000
Paid on principal of bonds	1,756,000,000
Total paid	4,352,000,000
Add profit to purchases	678,551,462
And it amounts to	5,035,551,462

Thus it will be seen we have paid nearly three billions more than the original debt. The people would be justified in refusing to pay another dollar of the fraud, as a fraudulent debt cannot be collected by law, but if we did we would have to fight the combined powers of Europe.

But I must go on exposing

THE FRAUD.

It will be remembered that the act of July 17th, 1861, and of February 12, 1862, creating, the former $50,000,000 old demand notes of not less denomination than ten dollars and the latter $10,000,000, in bills of not less denomination than five dollars, making altogether $60,000,000 demand notes not bearing interest but payable on demand at St. Louis and Cincinnati, and that the government had no gold to redeem them and there was a general suspension of specie payments the banks refused to accept them, except on special deposit, and of course they ran down in value. But the bankers wished to get rid of them as otherwise it would be a glaring evidence that even the crippled greenback would soon be sought more than the gold demand notes. So the act of February 12th, 1862 made them a full legal tender, acceptable for all dues public and private and twelve hours after they were made a full legal tender they rose to a par with gold and remained there until every dollar disappeared.

It must be remembered that the majority of the great money loaners of this country are and always have been largely the agents of the Europeon money kings, though many of our own bankers reaped harvests from the great fraud perpetrated on the government in its hour of peril.

The bankers, through the exception clause, depreciated the greenbacks, that they might buy them cheap and gamble in gold, getting the gold every six months on the interest on the bonds, they forced the government to purchase it back at their own price, they also forced the merchants to pay them their own price for the gold, as the merchant had to have gold to pay custom dues with. If the government had been allowed, by these gentry to take its own notes for all dues, no one would have ever wanted gold, and gold would never have gone above the paper dollar, as no one would have wanted it.

I know there are knaves and fools that will claim, the government had to have gold to use abroad. But I and all other well informed men have steadily denied that the government ever bought anything of consequence abroad to carry on the war. But the reader need not take the say so of such a fanatic as I but here are the words quoted from Secretary McCulloch's report for December 4, 1865.

"The fact that means have been raised without foreign loans, to meet expenses of a protracting and very costly war, is evidence not only of great resources of the country, but of the wisdom of Congress in passing the necessary laws, and of the distinguished ability of the immediate predecessors of the present secretary in administering them."

The above should forever settle, in the mind of the reader, the question that our government in no way depended on, or received assistance from other countries. I will state however, that there may be no chance for controversy that at the beginning of the war the government purchased 60,000 stand of old Belgian rifles that were soon cast aside as useless, one reason for casting them aside was the calibre was much larger than our own, which in consequence created trouble. We also had to pay for the Russian fleet in our waters, as a check to England, at the time of the Mason-Slidell affair. Though this did not come in directly but ostensibly as the payment for the Alaskan acquisition. Therefore it will be seen that our bonds did not go abroad until all was safe, after the war. Though the foreign money power was aiding in carrying out their hellish plot all of the time. The bonds were depreciated and bought at a low figure with a depreciated currency, and finally when the war was nearly to a close their plans were ripe to raise the value of money and bonds that they might get a dollar for what, Oliver P. Morton said, cost them not to exceed sixty cents. The scheme to contract the currency was ripe, and ready to carry out the moment the war closed. All knew after the battle of Gettysburg, and fall of Vicksburg that the war was drawing to a close. But with President Lincoln in the chair, their contraction schemes would never carry. It was plain to be seen by his message to Congress in 1861, quoted on page 126 as well as by the following letter that as soon as the war was over he would turn his attention to other and more dangerous enemies of the country.

LINCOLN'S LETTER

"Yes, we may all congratulate ourselves that this cruel war is nearing to a close. It has cost a vast amount of treasure and blood. The best blood of the flower of American youth has been freely offered upon our country's altar, that the nation might live. It has been indeed a trying hour for the republic; but I see in the near future, a crisis approaching that unnerves me and causes me to tremble for the safety of my country. As a result of the war, corporations have been enthroned and an era of corruption in high, places will follow, and the money power of the country will endeavor to prolong its reign by working upon the prejudice of the people until all wealth is aggregated in a few hands and the republic is destroyed. I feel at this moment more anxiety for the safety of my country than ever before, even in midst of the war. God grant, that my suspicion may prove groundless."

The above letter was written by Mr. Lincoln just prior to his assassination. That letter and his recommendation to Congress in 1861, which has been, before quoted, shows that Mr. Lincoln thoroughly understood the situation, and would, as soon as his hands were free, correct the evil.

The money power saw this. Mr. Lincoln must be removed, or all of their plotting and planning was for naught. It was easy to play upon the vanity of such a man as Booth—he would live in history any way and he might escape and pose as a hero abroad. What persuasive influence was used it matters not. No body else than the money power had any interest in Mr. Lincoln's death. The south could gain nothing by it, the leaders saw this and neither rank or file rejoiced at the death of the great man, but indignantly denied all possible participation or knowledge of the affair. As all thinking men have long since dropped the idea that southern sympathy had any direct bearing upon the matter. But the great criminals, like all thieves, when in danger of discovery, try to divert attention by crying stop thief and point to someone else. They trumped up the story and put it in the mouths of fanatics to repeat, and so the obsurd story that it was the Jesuits that plotted his destruction was put in circulation. But I ask, what could the Catholic church, or this educational order, gain by the death of such a noble man? I answer, nothing but a petty revenge, which, likely, did not exist. No body could possibly gain anything, but the money power.

What? You profess to believe they would not do such a thing? But you foolish things who think that, do you not know that the pages of history run red with the stories of conspiracies against great men? Do you not know that kings, princes, prelates and popes, who stood in the way of ambitious and greedy men have been put out of the way to gratify their desires? Do you not know that in all ages there have been a plenty of Judas Iscariots who would sell their Saviors for thirty pieces of silver? Have I not shown how Hannibal was driven from Carthage by this class because he made them give up their hold upon the people—how they worked upon the prejudice of the people and caused them to destroy Marcus Manlius and Tiberius Gracchus, how they hired an assassin to murder Caius Gracchus—how they assassinated Cæsar with their own hands—how they treacherously put Napoleon on the Island of St. Helena—how they attempted the assassination of President Jackson?

What, they have no motive! Is not the enslavement and rule of the world, through their infernal system a motive great enough?

Would these men, who would not hesitate to prolong the war, by crippling the government, when they knew it meant the limbs and lives of thousands, hesitate at plotting at the life of one man who stood in their way though he be a Jackson—a Lincoln—or a Garfield? No one else had such a motive for the destruction of Lincoln as did these men. Nor am I charging that one banker in a thousand knows anything about the plotting of ruin that is going on. There are thousands that would fight these terrible wrongs today if they were not misled by their supposed interests. But as I have before pointed out that Benjamin Franklin said, that we could judge them by their interests, and the great capitalist who intend to rule the world through their pernicious systems, through falsehood controling the small bankers like so many puppets.

The war closed. Their machine was all ready to put in motion, to enhance the value of the bonds and currency they had purposely run down, that they might get control of it. They had control of the banks and wished no other kind of money to compete with them. They had caused the government to put a ten per cent tax on all state banks of issue and so got rid of that system. They now made war on the government money, by declaring we must return to a gold basis. The people did not ask this, it was only the bankers who demanded it. And they claimed, to get o a gold basis, we must contract the currency. They did not say that the government must get rid of its bonded debt as soon as possible, but they made war on the non-interest bearing paper and the legal tender bonds as these were competitive paper with their own. Secretary McCulloch, who was at first a friend of the people, as Henry Cary Beard the statistition said. Secretary McCulloch said to him: "I do not care if the greenback goes to $2.75 in gold, the people have money to do business with any way." But Mr. McCulloch now became the friend of the money kings for in his report for 1865 he recommended to Congress, that the compound interest notes shall cease to be a legal tender at once. What harm was there in their remaining a legal tender as long as they were out? None but that they were a competitive money with National bank currency. In the same report he tells the inexperienced national bankers must learn that their notes are not money but promises to pay. What use was there of getting rid of real money and keeping promissory notes in the field? None but to further their schemes.

Now Secretary McCulloch in his report, as early as December 5, 1865, using the following sophistries, recommends the contraction of currency, and from this war is made on all government legal tender paper money. I will criticise as we proceed. That in large type of course is my own. Says the Secretary:

"On a basis of paper money, for which there is no outlet, all articles needed for immediate use, of which it became a measure of value, (comparative value he meant, of course) felt and responded to the daily increase of the currency."

(Mark this, prices are good.)

"So that rents and the price of most articles for which there has been a demand have been, with slight fluctuations, constantly advancing, and are higher now with gold at forty-seven per cent premium than they were when it was at one hundred and eighty-five. Even those which were affected by the fall of gold upon the surrender of the confederate armies, or by the increased supply, or diminished demand, are advancing again to former, if not higher rates."

What? the product of labor going up and the producer getting the benefit, and the rise and fall of gold nothing to do with it, but the large volume of money the cause? Thank you, Mr. Secretary; thank you for the information

"The expansion had now reached such a point as to be absolutely oppressive to a large portion of the people, while at the same time it is diminishing labor and is becoming subversant of good morals."

"Oppressive" to whom, Mr. Secretary? To the moneyed class only. "It is diminishing labor;" why? Because labor is becoming independent and need not be enslaved. "Subversant of good morals." Labor will not bend the knee and bow the head to the moneyed kings.

"There are no indications of real and permanent prosperity in our commercial marts, in splendid fortunes reported to have been made by skilful manipulations at the gold room or the stock board."

Ah how his heart beats for the poor souls who have made fortunes in the gold gambler's den, they are not fixed as they will be when his contraction scheme is carried out.

"No evidence of increasing wealth in the facts that railroads and steam boats are crowded with passengers, and hotels with guests; that cities are full to overflowing, rents and prices of the necessaries of life, as well as luxuries, are daily advancing."

What, no evidence of prosperity when the people are happy and enjoying themselves with plenty, can travel and do not have to slave to keep the wolf from the door?

"All these things prove, rather that a foreign debt is being created, that the number of non-producers are increasing and that productive industry is being diminished."

The people must be kept down or they will not be slaves. Just what the Hazard circular said. But, that manufacturing was diminishing is a lie, for not until the contraction of the volume of money went into operation did factories diminish and labor become dependent, demoralized and the land filled with tramps.

That Mr. Lincoln's fears, expressed both in his first message, and in the letter just quoted, were well grounded, and that the sentiments, favoring a monarchy, expressed by Alexander Hamilton and his followers, has never died out but is still pushed forward, is evident from the fact that as early as 1868 they started the publication of a paper called "The Imperialist," which was intended to start the ball in motion to prepare the people for the overthrow and destruction of our free institutions. Many remember this paper and there are still copies of it in existence. Mr. Gordon Clark, author of "Shylock" speaks of it and quotes from a little book "Imperialism in America" by Mrs. Sarah E. V. Emery, of Lansing, Michigan.

"The paper was published at No. 37 Mercer street, New York. Its figurehead was an imperial crown, its motto, "The Empire is Peace—Let us have Peace." It was published by the "Imperial Publishing Co.," but was an anonymous sheet, no name of editor, proprietor or correspondent appearing on its pages; among its advertisements was one of the banking firm of Morton, Bliss & Co. If rumor makes no mistake, Levi P. Morton was the member of the firm that gave its patronage to this traitorous sheet."

Its introductory was as follows:

"Though UNANOUNCED this Journal is not unexpected. The platform of The Imperialist is revolutionary: ITS OBJECT IS TO PREPARE THE AMERICAN PEOPLE FOR A REVOLUTION THAT IS AS DESIRABLE AS IT IS INEVITABLE.

"WE BELIEVE DEMOCRACY TO BE A FAILURE."

"We believe, in short that Democracy means lawlessness, corruption, insecurity to person and property, robbery of the public creditors, and civil war, that the empire means security, public faith, and peace."

"We believe that the national faith, if left in the keeping of the populace, will be sullied by the sure repudiation of the national debt, and that AN IMPERIAL GOVERNMENT CAN ALONE SECURE AND PROTECT THE RIGHTS OF NATIONAL CREDITORS.

"We believe that A SMALL PER CENTAGE OF THE AMERICAN PEOPLE CAN BE CONSIDERED FIT, BY CHARACTER OR EDUCATION, FOR THE UNRESTRICTED EXERCISE OF SELF-GOVERNMENT."

This paper did not live long and why? Because at that time they found it treading on dangerous ground to openly advocate imperialism, in the face of so much patriotism just expressed in the great war.

The people must be brought to it by slow degrees of suffering and servitude. *Ye Gods!* how prophetic were Mr. Lincoln's words:

"The prejudices of the people will be worked upon."

The money power could use the machinery then in operation and make both parties subservant to their will; and now note ten years later what the New York Tribune has to say on the matter, January 10th, 1878:

"The capital of the country is organized at last, and we shall see whether Congress will dare to fly in its face."

The next day it says:

"The time is near when they (the banks) will feel themselves compelled to act strongly. Meanwhile a very good thing has been done. The machinery is now furnished by which, in any emergency, the financial corporations of the east can act together at a single day's notice, with such power that no act of Congress can overcome or resist their decisions."

Again read the above and tell us if Macauley, the great English historian, was not right when he said the money power would hesitate at nothing to farther their ends, that if the Copernican system of astronomy had interfered with the moneyed class it would have been utterly denied and defeated.

McCulloch's report for 1865 was in line with their action but he was yet halting between two positions, hence the revelations of facts coupled with the sophistries he offers.

"There is no fact more manifest than that the plethora of paper money is not only undermining the morals of the people by encouraging waste and extravagance, but is striking at the root of our national prosperity by diminishing labor."

Keep down Labor or you can not control it, seems to be the burden of the article.

"The evil is not at present beyond the control of legislation, but it is daily increasing, and if not speedily checked, will at no distant day, culminate in wide spread disaster. The remedy, and the only remedy within the control of Congress, is in the opinion of the Secretary, to be found in reduction of the currency."

Whatever else is denied surely the Secretary's report urging a contraction of currency should not be denied, though they have denied that there ever was a contraction or that any of the interest bearing debt was a legal tender. In fact they have denied every truth that has exposed their hellish plots. Now here is other evidence of their plot in

THE BANK CIRCULAR,

which was issued to American bankers during and since the war:

"Dear Sir: It is advisable to do all in your power to sustain such daily and prominent weekly newspapers, especially the agricultural and religious press, as will oppose the issuing of greenback paper money and that you also withhold patronage or favors from all applicants who are not willing to oppose the government issue of money. Let the government issue the coin and the banks issue the paper money of the country, for then we can better protect each other. To repeal the law creating national bank notes or to restore to circulation the government is-ue of money will be to provide the people with money, and will therefore seriously affect your individual profits as bankers and lenders. See your member of Congress at once and engage him to support our interest, that we may control legi-lation.

"Signed by the Secretary
"JAMES BUELL."

Is it any wonder the people have been deceived, and as Mr. Lincoln said, "their prejudice worked upon," when the press and the pulpit and our representatives have been influenced against us?

Sure, as Thomas Benton said they would, "the bank institution has returned from the jungle with her whelps," and as John Randolph said they would "they overawe Congress and laugh at our laws."

They knew what the contraction of the volume of money would do and started in to educate the people to the idea of submissive slavery. About the same time that the above appeared the following appeared in the New York World:

"The American laborer must make up his mind henceforth not to be so much better off than the European laborer. Men must be content to work for less wages. In this way the working man will be nearer to that station in life to which it has pleased God to call him."

They should have said, to which it has pleased the money power to call him.

So from the independence that Mr. McCulloch admitted the people to possess in 1865, they have fallen to dependent seris, slaves and tramps in 1876 to '78 and since.

The New York Times sees the consequence:

"Those farmers who are land poor must sell and become tenants, in place of owners, of the soil. The hoarded, idle capital must be invested in these lands, and turned over to the poor farmers, who will at once be set upon their feet, not to go and loaf about towns and villages, spending their money while it may last, but to buy with this money stock, fertilizers, implements and machines, and go to work to cultivate the soil profitably."

Here should be added—profitable to the money kings. So we here see everything fits into this great conspiracy, and proves how well grounded Mr. Lincoln's fears were for the welfare of his country.

The contraction policy went on. The non-interest bearing paper as well as legal tender obligations were converted into long time bonds.

In 1867 the bank of England had one of her colicky qualms, or financial panics; she must have gold. This called the gold out of our country but we still had enough government paper money in circulation to carry us through, so we hardly noticed the flurry.

The money kings had everything pretty nearly their own way now. They had bought the bonds for sixty cents on the dollar or less and now wished to realize one hundred cents, to do this, they knowing the interest only was payable in coin, the principal in lawful currency or greenbacks, to make it payable in gold it was necessary to have an act passed by Congress and approved by the President. Therefore, the cry went up that the government credit must be strengthened, though why the government credit needed strengthening three years after the war was over and the bonds all sacrificed at a low figure no one attempted to explain. But, the Rothschilds owning several hundred millions of 5 20 bonds, they had determined to make a great profit upon them so they ordered their special agent here, August Belmont, to see that a plank called government credit strengthening act be got into the Democratic Platform, as the presidental campaign of 1868 was near at hand.

August Belmont, special agent of the Rothschilds, himself a large bondholder and chairman of the Democratic National Committee, evidently thought this would be an easy job for him to do, it was not to be supposed that it could be got into the Republican platform. Says Burkey on money, page 227:

"Mr. Belmont was instructed, by Baron James Rothschild as early as March 13th, 1868, that unless the Democratic party went in for paying the 5-20 bonds in gold, it must be defeated. The first step necessary was to educate the people. Consequently the hireling press, the great papers in large cities took up the song of government credit strengthening act, and the country papers, of course, fell into line. Through shrewd manipulation the convention was to be held in New York July 4th, 1868.

"Mr. Belmont and his satellites were unable to control the convention, as leading men said if the party wished to get back into power it must come before the people with an honorable purpose. The government credit strengthening act plank was rejected, and the following plank substituted:

"'Resolved, Third: when the obligations of the government do not expressly state upon the face, or the law under which they were issued does not provide that they shall be paid in coin, they ought in right to be paid in the lawful money of the United States.'

"When this plank was presented the cry went up 'read it again, read it again.' It was read and re-read. But, this plank doomed the party to defeat. The session was a stormy one and nearly broke up in confusion. It has been claimed and never successfully denied that August Belmont then owned a $60,000 interest in the New York World, the leading Democratic newspaper, and that he turned that interest over to Manton Marble, editor and part proprietor of that paper. On the fifteenth day of October, a few weeks before the general election, the World, to the consternation of the democracy throughout the country, came out in a leading editorial denouncing Horatio Seymour for the presidency, as unfit and unavailable, and advising his withdrawal. Such an act of treachery had never been equaled in the annals of politics."

But this was not enough. Benjamin F. Butler charged, and he seldom made a mistake in such matters, that at a dinner, where Belmont, and Schenk, chairman of the Republican National Committee, were present, the matter was fixed up and the government credit strengthening act plank went into the Republican platform. The people went on and held the election, or thought they did, but it was all fixed at that dinner. Now apparently the people acquiesced in this robbery. But the hireling press went on upholding the fraud by declaring that the 5-20 bonds should be paid in gold. But if so what was the use of all this trouble, and even now an act must be passed and approved, to make it legal. The bill was presented March 12th, only eight days after Grant took his seat. It was carried after a hot debate in which Senator John Sherman in a speech in the Senate, February 27th, 1868, uttered the following sentiments:

"I say that equity and justice, are amply satisfied if we redeem those bonds at the end of five years in the kinds of money, of the same intrinsic value it bore at the time they were issued. Gentlemen may reason about the matter over and over again, and cannot come to any other conclusion; at least that has been my conclusion after the most careful deliberation.

"Senators are some times in the habit, in order to defeat the argument of an antagonist, to say that this is repudiation. Why, sir; every citizen of the United States has conformed his business to the legal tender clause. * * Every state in the union without exception, has made its contracts, since the legal tender clause, in currency and paid them in currency."

"Art thou fallen from heaven, Oh! Lucifer! son of the morning?"

Mr. Sherman has apparently ever since been a staunch defender of the interests of the moneyed kings. It is due him that he might have honestly changed his mind. But Benjaman Franklin said that by their interests we might judge them; and in a parallel case, Henry A. Martin, the French historian, tells us that cabinet officer Dubois, in 1716, received a hundred thousand crowns per annum, direct from the secret service fund of England, for changing his mind.

It is a well known fact that Henry Clay and Daniel Webster, during the fight with the old United States Bank, uttered just as brave words as did Mr. Sherman and then were hushed into silence, and the otherwise brilliant record they left has been clouded by that silence.

Senator Morton declared that:

"We should do foul injustice to the government and the people of the United States, after we have sold these bonds on an average for not more than sixty cents on the dollar, now to propose to make a new contract for the benefit of the bondholder."

It was farther shown, conclusively, that the 5-20 six per cent bonds of the United States were not regarded either at home or abroad as payable in coin. Mr. Lawrence, of Ohio, called attention to the fact, that on the thirtieth day of November, 1867, (over two years after the war was over) our 5-20 six per cent bonds sold in London at 70⅜ cents while New Brunswick and Cape of Good Hope six per cents, sold at 105.

As a farther evidence the Honorable Thaddeus Stevens subsequently declared, that "when the bill was on its final passage, the question was expressly asked of the chairman of the Committee of Ways and Means, and expressly answered by him *that only the interest* was payable in coin.

"If I knew," he added, "that any party in this country would go for paying in coin that which is payable in other money, thus enhancing it one-half; if I knew there was such a platform, and such determination on the part of any party, I would vote on the other side, I would vote for no such speculation in favor of the large bondholders—the millionaires—who took advantage of our folly in granting them coin payments of interest."

I will quote from Burkey on money:

"Congress and the President had done everything in their power to make the 5-20's payable in gold, but the Rothschilds and the money power generally were apprehensive as to the future, inasmuch as the act of Congress of March 18th, 1869, was in violation of the terms of the contract under which the bonds have been issued, and might be repealed. No time was lost, therefore, in inducing the Secretary of the Treasury to pay off these bonds in gold. By means best known by themselves, Mr. McCulloch had been induced to redeem about $150,000,000 of these bonds, during his administration of the Treasury, and the process was continued under Boutwell and his successor, until the 5-20 bonds issued under the original act of February 25, 1862, were all redeemed in gold or its equivalent.

This single act of robbery, for it is only one of the many acts of robbery, which have been perpetrated by the money power during the past few years under guise of law, will foot up about as follows:

"Amount of 5-20 six per cent bonds $500,000,000.00.

"Interest in gold at six per cent compounded semi-annually, for ten years, $403,096,132.71.

"Total cost of the $500,000,000 bonds at sixty cents on the dollar $300,000,000.

"Net profit in ten years in gold $603,096 132.71."

To make assurance doubly sure that the bonds should all be paid in coin and that it should aid in contracting the volume of money, "An act to authorize the funding of the national debt," was passed and approved July 14, 1870. This act provided:

"That the Secretary of the Treasury is hereby authorized to issue in a sum or sums not exceeding in the aggregate $200,000.000 coupon or registered bonds of the United States, in forms as he may prescribe, and of denominations of fifty dollars, of present standard value, at the pleasure of the United States, after ten years from the date of their issue, and bearing interest, payable semi-annually in such coin, at the rate of five per cent, per annum."

Three hundred million dollars of like bonds, bearing four and one-half per cent interest, redeemable after fifteen years, and also a sum of bonds bearing four per cent interest, redeemable after thirty years—in all not to exceed $1,000,000,000. By the act of January 20, 1871 this act was amended so that the amount of five per cent bonds was increased to $500,000,000.

Thus $1,800,000,000 of the government paper was funded in these bonds. The government non-interest bearing paper and all legal tenders rapidly disappeared.

General Butler said in his speech before the Chamber of Commerce, of New York City, in January 1875, and he challenged any man in that city to contradict him:

"After the 5-20 bonds were issued—I say from that hour during the whole war, and until the strength, power, credit, and stability of the United States were assured by Lee's surrender at Appomatox Court House, not a single dollar of gold or silver was subscribed or paid by any banker or capitalist in America or Europe for a bond of the United States."

Henry C. Carry, the best authority on political economy in America and the peer of John Stewart Mill, says that five months after Lee's surrender there had not been a bond of the United States sold in Europe and only $200,000,000 of our state, railroad and corporation bonds were held there.

Secretary McCulloch, in his report for 1868, says:

"The opinion that the country was benefited by the sale of securities abroad is founded upon the supposition that we HAVE RECEIVED REAL CAPITAL IN EXCHANGE FOR THEM. This supposition is to a large extent unfounded. Our bonds have gone abroad to PAY FOR GOODS without which they might not have been purchased. Our imports have been increased by nearly the amount of the bonds which have been exported."

Thus it is shown that the bonds were actually used as a circulating medium at home and abroad.

Of course the above does not refer to the bonds bought by the European syndicates through their agents and held here for dishonorable purposes.

It will be noticed that the last act quoted showed the bonds were to be redeemed in coin No specified coin was stated. Now the money power had gained everything they desired so far.

They would now try to get themselves paid in a specified coin, one of the most scarce commodities if possible. Consequently in 1873, they, through a trick, got silver demonetized and though silver was re-monetized they still persist. It was always intended that the bonds and interests should, only, be paid in the one scarce commodity, gold. But as this subject will be discussed under the head of Bi-Metalism we will proceed with the story of funding and contraction.

I here again quote from "Burkey on Money:"

"In January, 1875, the bullionists found themselves strong enough in Congress to pass a law decreeing specie resumption January 1, 1879. The composition of the House of Representatives, at this time is worthy of note, and should open the eyes of the people to the necessity of sending a different class of men to represent them in that body. The Honorable Moses W. Field, of Michigan, in a recent speech, gives a detailed statement of the professions and callings of the members of the Forty-Third House, of which he was a member, as follows:

" 'The Forty-Third Congress, to which I belonged, was composed o three hundred seventy-nine members. In this number there were six lumbermen, thirteen manufacturers, seven doctors, fourteen merchants, thirteen farmers, three millers, one land surveyor, one priest, one professor of latin one doctor of laws, one barber, one mechanic, ninety-nine lawyers and one hundred and eighty nine bankers, which includes stockholders in National Banks.'

"Thus it will be seen that almost a majori y of members were bankers or interested in National banks."

Is it to be wondered at that we have had such vicious financial legislation when the people—instead of sending men to legislate for them whose interests are identical with their own, they send men whose interest are diametrically opposed to their own.

Of course the great panic of 1873 was the direct result of the vicious contraction policy.

The resumption of specie payments for 1879 gave an excuse for a more rapid contraction, and as a farther evidence of the thorough understanding of the plot and the effects of contraction. I quote here an extract from a letter written December 4, 1866, by E. G. Spaulding, a Buffalo, New York banker, sent to Secretary McCulloch:

"You no doubt now, to a certain extent, HAVE CONTROL OF THE CURRENCY OF THE COUNTRY and I think you will, of a necessity, contract moderately,' so as to preserve a tolerable easy money market. There may be OCCASIONAL SPASMS OR TIGHTNESS for money, but generally, I shall look for plenty of money, FOR AT LEAST ONE YEAR TO COME."

So this banker at least knew that a contraction of the volume was going to make money scarce and seemed to fear the result to some extent. But among the contraction schemes was one to get rid of the

FRACTIONAL CURRENCY.

In 1863 about twenty millions of fractional currency was issued. This issue was forced upon the authorities by the inexorable logic of events. Gold and silver having disappeared, as they always do in every emergency, the people were forced to invent for themselves such substitutes as they could, and postage stamps, despite all of the inconvenience of using them gummed, was the change used until in 1862. On July 17, the President approved "An act authorizing payment in stamps and prohibiting circulation of notes of less denomination than one dollar." The act authorized the Secretary of the Treasury to issue the fractional currency, but it was not until 1863 that the full amount of the $20,000,000 was issued.

But this amount was increased about $5,000,000 a year until it reached about $46,000,000.

The act of 1875, approved January 4th, authorized the issue of silver coin to take the place of this currency.

About $40,000,000 five per cent bonds were issued to purchase silver to take up the handiest fractional currency any people ever knew. Now the life of paper fractional currency averages no more than five years. Thus in thirty years the government would have saved $20,000,000 which would have lessened taxation to that amount, less cost of production. Now in thirty years the government will have paid in interest, compounded, the amount of the bonds twice over, $80,000,000.

This with the original $40,000,000 amounts to $120,000,000. The life of silver is but thirty years, when at the end of that time the government will be out $120,000,000 and have none of the silver left. The government has lost and the individual has lost and the community has been deprived of a handy nimble currency to gratify the hell-be-gotten greed of the money kings.

THE REFUNDING OF 1881; OR THE BANKER'S REBELLION.

About $200,000,000 six per cent bonds fell due this year.

The Congress, in session just prior to Mr. Garfield's election was flooded with petitions from the people asking that these bonds be paid with legal tender paper money, and if they found this impracticable to pay them with silver dollars, of which the Treasury was so full that there was talk of having to build additional room to accommodate it. The law clearly granted the Secretary the privilege of redeeming with this silver. The bankers demanded long time, high interest bonds. The people continued to urge Congress to pay these bonds in legal tender paper, or silver, or at least to convert them into small interest bearing bonds payable at the government option. The bankers were incensed at this and threatened if either one of these things was done, they would ruin the business of the country. This appeared in many of the papers throughout the country and has gone down in history as the banker's rebellion of 1880. The reader will remember that this is just what the bankers threatened President Jackson with, and then attempted his assassination. Apparently, to give force to their threat and intimidate Congress, they began contracting their loans, which proves they can use the contraction of currency to destroy business if it suits their ends. They were warned, by some of the New York papers, that they had better stop as the people would find out how they did it and they might loose their power. Many of the congressmen were looking for re-election, consequently they were afraid of the bankers on the one hand and of the people on the other. That they had reason to fear the bankers is borne out by what Mr. Greeley said when he ran for President in 1872, which is as follows:

"There is gathered around the capitol of this nation a gang of miserable stock jobbers, with no more conscience than pirates, inspired solely by a greed for gain and they have thundered successfully at the doors until they drove this government into the most preposterous acts of bad faith and legalized robbery that ever oppressed a free nation since the dawn of history."

With all of this in view no wonder a timid Congress was afraid of the bankers on the one hand and the people on the other. They adjourned without taking action on the bond question.

The bankers had reason to believe they would have, in President Garfield's administration, favorable consideration. Why? Because Mr. Garfield had, with great power, defended some of their measures, and he was branded by greenbackers a tool of the money power. Besides on the eve of the Chicago Convention that nominated him for President, Mr. Garfield at a banquet in New York among the moguls of Wall street eulogized Alexander Hamilton and his financial policy. He that had advocated monarchy and established the diabolical English system of finance, in this country.

Mr Garfield was a patriot, a man of good parts, ambitious and shrewd and he did this for a purpose. That he was ambitious is shown by his remarks to his mother on the occasion of his inaugural ceremony:

"Mother this seems to good to be true." Again on his death bed, almost the last words he uttered: *"Shall I live in history?"*

Mr. Garfield well knew that it would be a long time before the people would understand the cause of their trouble and that if he would help them, he must obtain the presidency, which he could not obtain without currying favor with the money kings. Politicians will never forget his shrewd manipulations of the Chicago convention which gave him the nomination, which was at that time equivalent to election. Mr. Garfield took his seat on the fourth day of March, 1881. Now he had the highest office within the gift of the people. The natural desire of an ambitious man would be to go down to his grave as one of the fathers of his country, with Washington, Jackson and Lincoln. To do this he must do some great act that would endear him to the hearts of the people and thus he could be elected by the will of the people. History told him the people loved a leader when they were prosperous and happy. He might bring all of this about by paying the public debt and creating prosperity among the masses. That he had come to this conclusion is shown by the following utterances:

"The people will remember the the bankers and capitalist of Wall street as the Germans remember robbers of the river Rhine, who never came out from their strong-holds but to plunder and rob them."

Again he said:

"Whoever controls the volume of money in any country is absolute master of all industry and commerce."

Almost the first thing Mr. Garfield did after taking his seat was to instruct his Secretary of the Treasury, Mr. Windom, that he did not need an act of Congress to convert the bonds into small interest bearing bonds, payable at the government option. Mr. Windom proceeded at once to carry out these instructions.

It was plain to the money power that if Mr. Garfield lived he would find means to pay off the public debt, wipe out the bonded system and abolish the National banking institution, which would be a necessity if the bonds were paid. Under these considerations, Mr. Garfield was a dangerous man to the interests of the money power. Greater reasons would exist for their taking his life than the taking of the life of Lincoln. Why? Because they had more at stake now, having gone so far with their scheme they could not think of turning back, if it cost the lives of thousands, besides it might appear to them that Mr. Garfield was a traitor to their cause, instead of the great detective and public benefactor that he was. At any rate Mr. Garfield was shot on the second day of July, 1881. Immediately it was flashed over the wires, apparently without thought or consideration, that it was the work of a crazy office seeker. But Guitean proved to be the sharpest man in the house at the trial, and when he thought he did not get the defense that he believed he ought to have he threatened to expose some one. Suddenly there was a report that a bungling attempt was made to take his life and he was closely confined and guarded and no one except the authorities allowed to see him. It would be an easy thing to quiet him now by telling him, "The feeling runs high against you; you will be killed if you are seen." "Keep still you fool and you will be reprieved on the gallows, at the last moment." Then dead men tell no tales. When it was discovered that Guitean was not insane but likely the tool of some band of conspirators it was charged to the stalwarts, a faction of disgruntled Republicans. Of course this was a rediculous story unless there was something back of it, for what sense would there be in killing a man that in so short a time they could defeat and thus gain a greater satisfaction. But even if it was the stalwarts; who were the leading men of that faction?

Some of them, we know, were persistent defenders of measures favorable to the moneyed kings.

Have we now exhausted all of the circumstantial evidence pointing to a conspiracy of the money kings? Not by any means. The following was clipped from a Detroit paper in 1886, if I remember right. I have unfortunately, for the strength of this article, mislaid my memorandum of dates, but I am pretty sure the article was copied from the New York Herald of that year. It appears under the following caption:

"GUITEAU'S CONSPIRACY."

EVIDENCE WHICH WAS SUPPRESSED BY COLONEL CORKHILL.

THE REPORT OF A PRIVATE CONVERSATION IN WHICH THE PUBLIC PROSECUTOR OF GUITEAU MADE SOME STARTLING STATEMENTS ABOUT A CONSPIRACY.

"New York, July 8.—The Herald publishes a special from Long Branch in which the correspondent, commenting upon the death Colonel Corkhill, says that he knew Corkhill intimately and knew that he possessed certain secret information about Guiteau which has never been made public. The writer states that on one occasion Corkhill complained to him that some of his actions during Guiteau's trial had even been interpreted as showing an imperfect sense of duty. Corkhill told the writer he was obliged to act as he did and suppress certain items of interest which would have ruined well-known public men and shocked the nation.

He went on to say that he was waited upon after the trial by a lady who proved to be Guiteau's first wife, who used his aid to procure a pension. She made certain statements to him which revealed a long standing and carefully worked out plot in which well known public men were interested and Guiteau was to be the tool. Names, dates, the steamer on which Guiteau was to be spirited away, reports of conversation at the meeting place of the conspiracy, in a well known restaurant were all plainly exhibited.

The writer farther states that Corkhill showed him a piece of paper containing the names of two of the conspirators. It fitted exactly in the mutilated letter produced in the evidence by Corkhill in the trial of Guiteau and which had been the cause of the abuse being heaped upon him. Corkhill bitterly complained that one of the men whose name was on the piece of paper had been specially active in injuring him. He said he had damaged his professional reputation in his effort to prevent a great scandal from leaking out, but he would finally defend himself from unjust imputations."

Some time prior to the publication of the above quoted article and before Mr. Corkhill's death, it had been hinted that Mr. Corkhill, at the proper time, would divulge some suppressed evidence concerning the Guiteau trial that would be startling, but be it remembered Mr. Corkhill dropped dead and I have watched closely ever since, but have never seen the cause of his death published.

Is this all? No; for what became of Mr. Windom?

Encyclopedia Brittanica tells us that Mr. Windom took the responsibility of the refunding business of 1881 upon his own shoulder, beside he made a number of bitter utterances against the money power. Mr. Windom said, in a letter written to the Anti Monopoly League in New York:

"The capitalists have bought and are buying largely the Associated Press, and are controlling all the avenues of intelligence."

Is it any wonder you hear

nothing from the press, in defence of the people? Mr. Windom was a dangerous man to the interests of the money power. Though often favoring them through policy. He was called back to the secretaryship under Mr. Harrison, the cleanest administration since Lincoln's. He had not long been in his seat, when at a banquet at New York, he had just delivered a brilliant little speech, he, too, suddenly drops dead. Now it is possible these men died from natural causes. But in this enlightened age when chemistry produces such wonders, it is possible, through chemical action, to produce the apparent effects of almost any disease.

There is a Mexican weed, that one drop will produce insanity, two drops acts entirely different and will produce paralysis and eventually death. Now we of occult powers often see evidence of wrong doings of men, though we may not always be able to weave so strong a web of circumstantial evidence as here presented.

We see men who have fought nobly for the cause of financial reform, just as they had reached a position of influence or produced a work of power whereby they could influence the leading classes, they would quietly drop out of sight, become violently insane and have to be taken to a retreat, never to recover, or perhaps show symptoms of insanity which would cause them to commit an act foreign to their natures which would disgrace them and soon bring them to death, or perhaps they are stricken with paralysis of which they soon expire. So many of these cases have come under my observation that I no longer doubt that some of it is the work of a band of conspirators.

That some of the greater agitators have not yet been reached by this power while weaker ones have gone, is no evidence against this theory, as their agents may be more active in one locality than another or may experience greater opportunities in one locality than another. Take for instance our own city of Detroit.

The Honorable Moses W. Field, who did more for the early organization of money reformers than any other man in America, was ostracised, and slandered traduced, finally, afflicted doing things entirely foreign to his nature—showing symptoms of that same strange insanity that had overtaken others. I know Mr. Field was a man of fine parts, an honorable gentleman, a fine robust physical nature and I believe he died a martyr to the cause of financial reform.

John H. Eakin was a personal friend of mine and for many months an office companion. I never saw anything that would lead me to think insanity was lurking in his make-up, but he was a fearless advocate of financial reform, carrying his ideas to influential people, to professional men, and even into the church. In this way he was doing effective work which it would be for their interest to stop. He went violently and incurably insane.

Richard F. Trevellick, a famous advocate of the cause, for years, had just completed his phamphlet giving Supreme Court decisions on the question. With this he could approach a class of leading citizens who hitherto had given the subject but little attention and he was approaching professional men besides carrying the war into

Africa, so to speak. Just when he got where he could do the best execution he is seized with paralysis and in a few months dies. This struck his friends with astonishment, as no one would have believed the seeds of paralysis were lurking in his robust form.

Lyman A. Brant, a well known labor agitator, a newspaper man and ex-member of the state legislator, better known than Lyman E. Stowe, who is a fierce writer of articles on financial reform. Lyman A. Brant was often taken for Lyman E. Stowe and as he died a few days ago in an insane asylum, it is possible, Lyman A. Brant died for Lyman E. Stowe, or it is possible all of this was the result of natural causes, but the casual reader cannot but admit that it is a strange coincidence that so many of this class are afflicted in such a peculiar manner.

Benton's prophecy seems a true one: Jackson did not kill the old money reptile, but like the Bengal tiger, she has returned from the bush with all her whelps.

Through natural occult powers we see, we are taking our lives, our liberties, our reputations in our hands and while we see this, we know that we have power to ward off some of the evil, but if we have to submit to the inevitable destiny, like Sampson, we may by our death accomplish more than in life.

Connected with the story of Mr. Garfield's death I will relate a little story, though foreign to the subject in hand and not offered as an argument, it will no doubt interest the reader as a strange coincidence:

The day of Mr Garfield's death I left my office early in the afternoon badly fatigued and much indisposed. I hastened home and sought a darkened room and lay down and slept a troubled, dreamy sleep. I slept all of the afternoon and until next morning when I awoke bright and feeling well except somewhat perplexed over a vivid dream that still haunted me. In this dream, vision, or whatever it was, I saw Mr. Garfield, in fact was at his bedside just before his death and alone with him. He related the cause of his death, said he had been misunderstood by friends and wronged by foes and he wept at his country's misfortune. The scene was so sad and impressive that when I awoke my face was bathed in tears, several times this dream was partly repeated, but at what time I first dreamed it, I do not know. But so forcibly was it impressed on my mind that when on my way to my office the next morning, on meeting a letter carrier I said to him "If I hear of Garfield's death, I shall believe I visited his deathbed last night in a dream." "Why," said he, "did you not know that Mr Garfield died last night at four o'clock." I certainly did not. But strange to say some weeks after on seeing the illustrated papers the room that I saw with all of the faces and positions, of people in attendance and surrounding appearances were pictured just as I had seen them in my dream and still stranger the papers stated that for a few moments before his death Mr. Garfield was alone just as I had seen him while in that conversation.

It may be claimed that my mind was effected by the great national sorrow. But it is fair to state here that I did not like Mr. Garfield and believed him an enemy to the country who bad better be out of the way than not, though of course I could not sympathize with the assassin, nor sanction such a measure of disposing of him. But from that night he has found in my heart a place as a loved and martyred President.

SUMMING UP ON THE EVILS OF CONTRACTION.

Says David Hume in his essay on money:

"It is certain that since the discovery of the mines in America, industry has increased in all nations of Europe * * we find that in every kingdom into which money begins to flow in greater abundance than formerly, everything takes a new face; labor and industry gain life; the merchant becomes more enterprising, the manufacturer more diligent and skilful and even the farmer follows his plow with more alacrity and attention. * * It is of no manner of consequence with regard to the domestic happiness of a state whether money be in a greater or less quantity. The good policy of the magistrate consists only in keeping it, if possible, still increasing; because by that means he keeps alive a spirit of industry in the nation and increases the stock of labor, in which consists all real power and riches. A nation whose money decreases is actually at the time weaker and more miserable than another nation which possesses no more money but is on the increasing hand."

Says Mr. Dunning on "Philosophy of Price":

"Money is the life-blood of a nation business prospers and workingmen are employed at good wages. Make it scarce, all business languishes; merchants become bankrupt and laborers are starving; who don't know this."

In 1868 John Sherman, when speaking of contraction, said:

"The appreciation of the currency is far more distressing than senators suppose. Our own and other nations have gone through that process before. * * It is not possible to take the voyage without the sorest distress to every person except a capitalist, out of debt, or a salaried officer, or an annuitant, it is a period of loss, danger, lassitude of trade, fall of wages, suspension of enterprize, bankruptcy and disaster."

John A. Logan in his speech reported in the appendix to the Congressional Record, 1874 says:

"There are many who firmly believe a return immediately to a specie basis, though oppressive for a time would ultimately prove most beneficial. But I, for one, can see benefit only to the money holders and those who receive interest and have fixed incomes. I can see as a result our business operations crippled and labor reduced to a mere pittance. I can see the beautiful prairies of my own state, which were beginning to bloom as gardens, with the cheerful homes rising like white towers along the pathway of improvement, again sinking back to idleness. I can see the hopes of the industrious farmer blasted as he burns his corn for fuel, because the price will not pay the cost of transportation. I can see our people, of the west, groaning and burdened under taxation, to pay the debts of the states, counties and cities, incurred when money was abundant and bright hopes of the future were held out to lead them on. I can see the people of our western states, who are producers, reduced almost to the condition of serfs to pay the interest on our state, county and other private debts to the money lenders of the East."

I think I have offered enough evidence to prove the baleful effects of a contraction. But I will give one more testimony quoted from Wiley's, "Whither Are We Drifting":

"That of the Monetary Commission appointed by joint resolution, August 5th, 1876, and consisting of three United States senators and three members of the House and three secretaries, whose duty it was to inquire into the change which had taken place in the relative value of gold and silver; the cause of the change and whether permanent or not and what effect upon trade and commerce."

The following gentleman composed that commission:

John P. Jones, Lewis V. Bogy, of the Senate.

Randall L. Gibson, George Willard, of the House.

Richard P. Bland, William S. Grosbeck, of Ohio, Professor Francis Bowen, of Massachusetts, George M. Watson, of Maine, were appointed Secretaries.

The findings were as follows:

"The true and only cause of the stagnation in industry and commerce, now everywhere felt, is the fact everywhere existing of falling prices, caused by a shrinkage in the volume of money."

Now this contraction of the volume of money has been going right along, or if it has at any time seemed to stop and increase, it has not increased in proportion to increase of population and business which is equivalent to a contraction.

But right in the face of all evidence for years, the hireling press lied and deceived the people and told them there had been no contraction.

I have quoted the recommendation to Congress by Secretary McCulloch, December, 1865, I have quoted the law itself, I now quote such testimony as John A. Logan, who in a speech in Congress, reported on p. 139, of appendix in Congressional Record, for the year 1874, he says:

"The circulating medium has been contracted $1,018,167,784."

If this is not enough evidence of a contraction here is an extract from President Grant's message for 1873:

"In view of the great actual contraction that has taken place in the currency, and the comparative contraction continuously going on due to the increase of population, increase of manufactures and all the industries, I do not believe there is too much of it now, for the dullest season of the year.

"During the last four years the currency has been contracted directly by the withdrawal of three per cent certificates, compound interest notes and seven-thirty bonds outstanding on the fourth day of March, 1869, to the amount of sixty-four millions of dollars. During the same period there has been a much larger comparative contraction, due to increase of population, manufactures, etc."

Counting certain bonds that were a legal tender, and that in 1865, the South was not yet using our money to any great extent, the per capita in the northern states would reach $80 and such prosperity as ours, no country in the world ever experienced. But I do not wish to give the agitator's figures but will give the statement of the shrinkage of volume, by the Chicago Inter-Ocean, a good reliable Republican paper. The following is a table copied from Freeman O. Wiley's "Whither Are We Drifting As a Nation," as he copied it from the Chicago Inter-Ocean, in answer to a letter dated from Schonburg, Iowa, July 1st, 1878.

The question was asked what has been the amount of money in circulation, each year, since 1865. Here is the answer by this good Republican authority:

"We have heretofore republished this table and those who wish it for reference should preserve it:

Year	Currency	Population	Amt. Per Capita
1865	$1,651,283,378	34,819,581	$47.42
1866	1,803,702,726	35,537,143	56.76
1867	1,330,414,677	36,269,502	36.68
1868	417,199,773	37,016,989	22.08
1869	750,025,089	87,779,860	19.19
1870	740,039,179	38,558,371	19.10

1871	734,244,774	39,750,073	18.47
1872	736,348,912	40,978,697	17.97
1873	738,291,479	42,245,110	17.48
1874	779,031,589	43,550,756	17.89
1875	778,176,750	44,896,705	17.33
1876	735,358,832	46,285,344	15.89
1877	696,443,394	47,714,829	14.60
1878	540,540,187	58,935,306	11.23
1879	534,425,558	50,155,783	10.65
1880	528,554,297	52,660,456	10.23
1881	610,682,483	53,210,269	11.48
1882	657,504,084	54,806,557	11.97
1883	648,105,895	56,550,814	11.47
1884	561,475,988	58,144,235	10.18
1885	533,405,001	59,888,562	8.90
1886	470,574,361	61,776,218	7.64
1887	423,452,211	63,335,774	6.67

Here says another Republican authority, the Chicago Express:

"The red torch of the vandal lighted up the whole country from Pittsburg to Chicago."

This called a brief halt in contraction. But let me here give the words of the Chicago Express, except that I will at each date quote the shrinkage of volume, as given by the Inter-Ocean. But if allowance were made for all bonds that passed current as money, the shrinkage would be nearly double that given here.

Says the Chicago Express:

"On the twelfth day of April, 1866, Congress passed a law authorizing the Secretary of the Treasury to sell 5-20 bonds and with the proceeds retire United States currency, including greenbacks."

On December 4th, 1866, E. G. Spaulding, a Buffalo, New York banker, a member of Congress, wrote to Secretary McCulloch as follows:

"You no doubt now, to a certain extent, have control of the currency of the country and I think that you will, of necessity, contract moderately, so as to preserve a tolerably easy money market. There may be occasional spasms or tightness for money, but generally I shall look for plenty of money for at least one year to come."

When this letter was written

the country was in possession of $1,906,687,770 currency.

Following remarks in italics are mine. The cause of variation in estimates of volume of currency is due to the fact that certain bonds were considered money by one party and were not by others, but my table, before given on page—shows exactly what bonds were legal tender though many others passed current.

DURING THE YEAR 1866

with $56.76 per capita we had but 520 business failures in the whole country involving a loss of but $17,625,000.

Labor was well paid and fully employed.

1867

This year the work of contraction was vigorously pushed,—the volume contracted to $36 68 per capita and there were 2,386 failures, with a total loss of $56,218,000.

1868

During this year $473,000,000 of money was destroyed, the volume brought down to $22.08 per capita, 2,608 failures, with a loss to creditors of $63,774,000. Money began to tighten and financial "spasms" were frequent.

1869

During this year over $500,000,000 of money passed into the cremation furnace *bringing the volume to $19.19 per capita* and producing 2,799 business failures and a loss of $75,054,000. Money growing tighter and wages lower.

1870

This year $67,000,000 of money was destroyed, per capita $19.10 and 3,551 failures took place involving a loss of $88,242,000. Money very scarce and wages of labor were reduced all over the country.

1871

Thirty-five millions of money this year is retired, per capita, $18.47, with 2,915 failures and a loss of $5,220,000. Wages cut still lower.

1872

Only about $12,000,000 was destroyed this year, per capita, $17.97, but such had been the strain upon the business of the country for the past five years that this proved the last straw to 4,069 business firms, involving a loss of $121,058,000. More cutting of wages and strikes talked of.

1873

This year the per capita stands at $17.48. The storm reached its climax. Business had hoped that with every returning season, prospects would brighten and money would become plenty. Instead of this, however, notwithstanding but $1,609,000 were destroyed, the people became panic stricken and 5,183 business firms were precipitated over the bankruptcy precipice, with a loss of $228,499,000. Five hundred thousand men were thrown out of employment, wages cut down all over the country and strikes are of frequent occurrence.

1874

Notwithstanding the terrible results of last year, the wine press of contraction still creaks on its hinges of death, as around and around it sweeps out of circulation $75,484, certificates indebtness, which had been e legal tender money, 60 treasury notes, $6,886,-

045 legal tenders, $3,000,000; fractional currency and $1,000,000 bank notes, producing 5,830 failures at a loss of $152,239,000 to creditors; per capita $17.89. A million idle men begin to tramp for work, wages still decline and strikes more numerous.

1875

"Volume $17.33 per capita. The volume was contracted, $42,817,413 and the failures reached 7,740 with loss to creditors of $201,160,000. Two millions of laborers out of work, famine and hunger stare them in the face and tramping becomes a profession.

1876

"*Volume down to $15.89 per capita.* According to the most reliable estimates, the contraction of the currency this year, in the destruction of greenbacks and the withdrawal of bank currency, amounted to about $85,000,000, with 9,092 failures and $191,111,000 loss. This does not include losses to stockholders, by foreclosure and sales of railroads.

"What a record for ten years who wonders times were hard and men idle? Still with all this array of wreck and ruin, with the finger-board of contraction, at the close of each year, pointing to the cause, the people were asleep, or on their knees praying for some interposition of Providence in their behalf, while John Sherman went marching on, with the torch of death, to burn the remaining $300,000,000, of the people's money. Three million men are out of employment. Bankruptcies multiply with great rapidity. The tramp nuisance culminates, wages are cut down to starvation prices. Strikes, riots and general consternation seize the people and the circulation is cut down to $696,000,000.

1877

Volume $14.60 per capita.

"The torch of the vandal lighted up the country from Pittsburg to Chicago. These are the foot-prints of that red-mouthed despot, the money power, which is still forging chains for the limbs of Americans."

I must now take up this where the Chicago Express left off.

1878

The volume of currency shrank to $11.23 per capita and this year the number of failures reached 10,478; amount of liabilities, $234,383,132. But this year gave us remonetization of silver in the Bland Bill, two to four millions a month of silver dollars to put in circulation which began to flow out at the close of the year, and

1879

was the year of specie resumption; per capita, $12.65. The increased silver brought us the boom of 1879, failures dropped down to 6,658; liabilities $98,000,000.

1880

The boom was walking on. Increase of currency through silver is doing its work, the failures have shrunk to 4,735; liabilities only $65,000,000. But the latter part of this year there was an attempt to frighten Congress by the bankers, known as the bankers' rebellion of 1880 and they contracted their loans very heavily and when money is scarce the contraction of credits is equivalent to a contraction of volume of currency and the consequence was that the volume ran down to $10.23 per capita.

1881

Failures increased to 5,583 liabilities at $81,000,000. But confidence was in full blast and business was booming on confidence, emigration was increasing and consequently the volume of currency was shrinking but credits were more than taking its place.

1882

The volume had increased a little, per capita to $11.97; but the strain for money was great and failures increased to 6,738; liabilities $101,000,000.

1883

The volume per capita was 11.48. Credit is so largely in excess of cash that the strain is increasing, failures were 9,184; liabilities, $173,000,000.

1884

The volume of money per capita this year is given as $10.17. Failures, 10,910; liabilities, $226,000,000 and the country is piling up credit preparatory to a tremendous smash.

1885

Volume of money per capita $8.90. Failures 11,212, liabilities $267,340,264. The papers are declaring there is lots of money, but business is mainly done on expanded credit.

1886

Volume of money per capita $7.64. Failures 12,292; liabilities, $229,288,238. Business is lagging, credits are not being pushed and failures are falling off a little.

1887

Volume per capita $6.67. Failures, 12,042; liabilities, $835,121,888. Credits still growing.

1888

Little change in the volume of money. credits that have taken place of money are being urged. Failures, 13,348; liabilities, $247,659,156.

1889

No change in volume: tendency to push credits. Failures, 13,277; liabilities, $312,496,742. A tendency to still push credits.

1890

The last year looked dangerous, credits are enormous but the time is not yet ripe to pluck the goose, but something must be done.

John Sherman comes forward with the fourth act of his silver demonetizing scheme, known as the "Sherman Bill." This repealed the "Bland Bill" and gave to the country a forced purchase of four and a half million ounces of silver per month and the putting in circulation of silver certificates to that amount. That increased the currency two and a half million dollars per month over, the best the secretary would do with the "Bland Bill." This increase of currency stimulated trade, strengthened credits and business boomed, more on credit than on cash by many times, yet the increase of cash had a good effect and brought failures down to 10,672; liabilities, $175,032,826.

1891

The volume of credit is expanding beyond the limit of reason and cash is in great demand. As a business man I find I can discount bills and buy goods at almost my own figures for cash. But I found myself warning everybody to stand from under, the bubble is about to burst. Increased business, from the stimulant of a little more money and failures increased to 12,394; liabilities, $193,178,000.

1892

There is as yet no material change except that everything looks shaky, like a great balloon inflated and ready to soar or collapse. Many business houses are shaky. There are signs that the business people are trying to hedge, preparing for the storm, failures, 10,270; liabilities, $108,595,248.

But the blow is yet to come.

1893

The fifth act of the silver drama is on now. The conspirators are now ready to prick the bubble. Says Gordon Clark, author of "Shylock," a work on finance:

"It is pretty well known that, as early as the 12th of March, eight days after the inauguration of their President, the Banker's Association issued to its members what has become known as

"'THE PANIC BULLETIN.'"

"'Dear Sir:—The interests of national bankers require immediate financial legislation by Congress. Silver, silver certificates and treasury notes must be retired and the National bank notes, upon a gold basis, made the only money. This will require authorization of from $500,000,000 to $1,000,000,000 of new bonds as a basis of circulation. You will at once retire one-third of your circulation and call in one-half of your loans. Be careful to make a money stringency felt among your patrons, especially among influential business men. Advocate an extra session of Congress for the repeal of the purchase clause of the Sherman Law and act with the other banks of your city in securing a petition to Congress for its unconditional repeal, per accompanying form. Use personal influence with Congressmen particularly, let your wishes be known to your Senators. The future life of national banks as a fixed and safe investment depends upon immediate action, as there is an increasing sentiment in favor of government legal tender notes and silver coinage.'"

If this is not sufficient evidence of a bankers' conspiracy, I here quote farther from the same authority:

"As long ago as December 24th, 1877, The New York Tribune said:

"'Last week a long list of firms at Chicago was carefully filed away for future use, by strong banks here. "Why?" it was asked. 'Because this is a list of firms who support "Bland's Bill,'" so spoke an old banker of note."

Again the Inter Ocean of August 20th, 1893, said:

"Early in the winter a bank president, conversing with a Chicago man of business, said to him: 'Mr. Jones, we are going to make the West pay up this summer.'

"'But why should you press your crditors?' asked Mr. Jones. The reply was: 'Well, we think it would make you a little more thoughtful about currency matters and drive you from your foolish ideas about silver.'

"Reporting a conference between New York bankers and the United States Secretary of the Treasury, the Sun of April 27, 1893, said:

"'There is a determination also to show the miners of silver the evils of the Sherman Law. * * This work has been started by a number of bankers in the solid communities of the East. They are daily refusing credits to the South, South West and West.'"

"On the 20th of April the Sun added:

"The statement of Mr. Carlisle to the New York bankers makes it clear that while Mr. Cleveland works in Congress the bankers will be expected to work, not in New York only, but throughout the country, doing their utmost to pinch business, in the expectation of causing a money crisis that will affect Congress powerfully from every quarter."

"The financial report of the Philadelphia Press, under date of September 22nd, contained this frank confession:"

There are ominous rumors on the street that New York will put the screws on the Senate. * * There is no question but that the banks of New York are still withholding money from merchants while possessing millions of idle cash, because of tacit arrangement not to unloosen it until the senate votes for repeal."

What does every organization say becomes of all traitors?

"The penalty of treason is death." "Conspiracy against the country is treason."

The cost in life and human suffering, this conspiracy has entailed cannot be estimated. But it again must be redeemed in blood, though thousands of innocent ones must suffer that the guilty may be punished. Such is the inevitable reward of corruption. "He that lives by the sword must perish by the sword."

In compliance with demands of the conspirators', credits were contracted and a vast quantity of gold shipped out of the country to create a panic. Many of the smaller bankers, innocent of crime, were compelled to close their doors. The great credit inflated business boom collapsed.

Even such business men as Andrew Carnegie, in an article in the North American Review, admitted that the business had been done with eight per cent cash against ninety two per cent credit, and others claimed the difference much greater than this in favor of confidence paper. The crash was terrible. Failures, 15,508; liabilities, $382,153,676.

Thousands and thousands of firms went out of business that were never reported as failures.

The suffering and loss caused by our great Civil War, was no comparison to that produced by this terrible panic, which was wilfully brought on by selfish men. Had the government issued a few hundred millions of dollars, of full legal tender paper money and started public works and paid it out for labor, the wheels of business would have moved on, and much of this suffering and loss have been avoided.

Nor would this paper money have been in the form of a debt, there would have been no interest to pay. The life of paper is but seven years, it would soon have worn out and disappeared, and the country been that much richer for the work accomplished. The people would have been saved the suffering and the whole community benefited.

The pretence was here for the repeal of the "Sherman Act," and the stoppage of the coinage of silver. Money is extremely scarce, failures and suffering on the increase and Congress dallies and does nothing. The moneyed men are all powerful, running the country deeper and deeper into bonded debt. The money power are determined to accomplish their hellish work and destroy all non-interest bearing paper money and come alone to a gold standard, regardless of what it costs the people in suffering and wealth. But the people are awaking and they will soon look upon a certain class of moneyed men as so many vipers or mad dogs that must be got out of the way at any cost. Let these men beware for they are building their own funeral pyres, though they may be destroyed by the wrath of a Sampson that perishes with them.

1894

There were many promises and great hopes of a revival of business. But a duller year for business, this country never saw. Number of failures, 13,895; liabilities, $172,993,856. Though there is a slight falling off in the number of failures and amount of liabilities, the bottom is being knocked out of everything except one's debts, as it takes more of the products of labor to get a dollar 'than ever known in this country before, debts are really doubling up. But the value of property is shrinking out of sight.

1895

The great money loaning conspirators, are preparing for the struggle of the metals, and are putting money in their various great enterprises to employ labor. so to start the wheels of business and start the credit system, thus creating a fictitious business boom to aid them in carrying out their hellish plot of a

GOLD STANDARD.

This scheme is not because they want gold for money, or for a standard, nor the gold itself, but that they may use it as an engine of oppression.

They know well there is not gold enough in the world—or even gold and silver together to do the business of America alone and to issue more promises to pay, a thing you have not got or cannot get, is a fraud, a delusion and a snare and that is all that it is intended for. But this brings us to the subject of

BI-METALISM.

OR THE SILVER CONTROVERSY.

TAKE YOUR CHOICE
OUR OWN HOME AND CARRIAGE.
The greenback days of 1860 to 1870, Bi-Metalism or Monometalism.

BIMETALISM, 1873.

This is a mere matter of dog eat dog, with silver the under dog in the fight.

The big gold gambling dog wants the "lion's share" of the plunder, while the silver mine owners are fighting for a better price for their product. The people have by far the greater interest with the silver or under dog, as the demonetizing of silver lessens, the volume of

MONOMETALISM, 1894.

money and increases the value of the debts, requiring more labor or the products of labor to pay those debts. But it would be a blessing if the people would demand the demonetizing of both metals and insist on a scientific paper money, such for instance as described herein. Or if as the golden calf worshipers say; God made gold money and law has nothing to do with it. It can make no difference if the government coin both gold and silver, free, but take the legal tender quality from them both and put it on to an exclusive paper money, this will test the whole thing. But we all know that it is not because they want gold for money, for the sake of gold, but, because they can, by that means, control the volume of money, thereby enslaving the people of the world. And to carry their ends they resort to bribery and influence the governing classes, the bench, the professor, the pulpit and the press until the whole mass is one nest of rottenness and corruption. Here are some of the

FALLACIES THEY FEED FOOLS ON.

They speak of gold and silver as the precious metals, when in fact there are a number of metals more useful, that are much cheaper and a number less useful that are much dearer. For instance, take gold and silver out of the world and the masses of the people would hardly miss it. But, on the other hand take iron out of the world and every railroad must cease to exit, every steamboat, every mill, every mechanical tool, would be lost, every building fall to pieces and every household be disrupted, every individual affected and civilization drop back to a barbaric state. Thus it will be seen that the intrinsic value of iron is many thousand times greater than gold.

The commercial value of the smelted iron ore is but a few cents per pound at the outside, a little more than the cost of labor in production. But they claim for gold that its value is given to it because it costs a dollar's worth of labor to produce it. This is a deception. If all of the cost, in worry, sweat and toil, suffering and death, to say nothing of wasted fortunes, were counted against gold, it would be so expensive, that many dollars would not buy one grain of it. But the commercial value is given it by the law of supply and demand. And if the nations of the earth would demonetize it, there would not be another dollars worth mined in a hundred year, on account of the falling of in demand.

Q. Will you please give us the value and qualities of some of the metals.

A. Yes. But it is a fact that if asked to name the most valuable metal, there is not one in a hundred but what would mention gold first and silver afterward. But let us see how near the truth they would come.

Gallium is worth $3,250 per ounce troy, or $39,000 per pound. The Vanderbilts are said to be worth $200,000,000, if so, they could purchase 312 tons of gold and have something left over, but they could not buy three tons of gallium.

There is not one person in a thousand that ever heard of this metal, as it was not discovered until August 27th, 1875. Its utility value is comparatively nothing, the world has got along very well without it. Its commercial value rests alone in its scarcity. Like gold and all other metals, it depends upon the law of supply and demand for its commercial value and the supply end being extremely small gives it great commercial value, though the demand end is extremely limited.

Many of the metals in the following table have very little, or no utility value, while iron the cheapest metal, has the greatest intrinsic or utility value. Lead comes next, copper next, then tin, zinc and so on.

TABLE OF NAMES AND VALUES OF METALS.

Metal	Dollars	Cents
Gallium	$9,000	
Vanadium	3,840	
Glucinum	3,264	
Zirconium	3,000	
Lithium	1,960	
Didymum	1,920	
Cerium	1,920	
Indium	1,896	
Zittrium	1,728	
Tantalum	1,720	
Erbium	1,680	
Strontium	1,536	
Niobium	1,526	
Barium	975	
Iridium	650	
Asmium	640	
Palladum	400	
Gold	240	
Chromium	200	
Lanthanium	175	
Platinum	130	
Rhodium	112	
Telurium	108	
Potassium	30	
Silver	12	
Aluminum	9	
Cobold	5	
Nickle		60
Block-tin		50
Zinc		18
Copper		12
Lead		6
Iron		3

Of course many of these

metals are compounds, others elementary substances.

Here are the metals that have been used for money: Iron, lead, copper, tin, nickle, silver, platinum, gold. Russia used platinum for money until, discontinued in 1845, and when she demonetized it, it fell in value quite materially, notwithstanding its scarcity and the fact that there is a large demand for it, for electrical and other purposes.

I have shown that many of the high priced metals have little or no intrinsic or utility value.

Senator Stewart in a recent speech said:

"There is no such thing as intrinsic value, in a commercial sense. The light of day, the heat of the sun and the air we breathe have intrinsic qualities and are essential to animal life, but they have no commercial value because their quantity is unlimited. Commercial value, results from the desire to possess, and limitations of quantity. If the stamp of all the governments of the world were removed from both gold and silver coin and neither of these metals could be used as money, their principal value would be destroyed. The desire to possess them for any other purpose would be trifling. They wou'd not be costly enough for ornaments and the supply on hand would be sufficient for an indefinite period for use in the arts.

"In this is found the true theory of money."

Here is a list of some articles, that possess a high commodity value, that are now used for money. Gold, silver, copper, nickle, by the great nations. Oxen, among the Zulus and Kaffirs of Africa. Tin forms the standard of value of the great fair of Nishni Novgorod. In the retired districts of New Guinea female slaves are the standard of value. The

Solomon Islands use strings of shell beads about the size of shirt buttons, well made and strung in fathom lengths of two kinds, red and white. This is the basis of currency. Dogs' teeth however are the gold of the coinage, but only two teeth from a dog's jaw are a legal tender. A hole is drilled in each and when a native has accumulated a sufficient number he strings them together and wears them as a collar. Such a collar may be worth as much as $100. Porpoises' teeth are one-fifth the value of dogs' teeth and rings of a marblelike stone, are also current coin. Cocoanuts, pigs, wives and slaves and tobacco are all money.

Ten cocoanuts equal one string of white beads.

Ten strings of white beads equals one string of red beads, or one dog's tooth.

Ten strings of red beads are equal to fifty porpoise teeth.

Ten porpoise teeth equals one good quality wife.

One marble ring one human head.

One human head, one good pig.

One good pig, one medium young man.

Among some of the native Australians green stone and red ochre are used as money. Iron spikes are still used by some of the tribes of Africa for money, chocolate, cocoanuts and eggs are used in some parts of South America for money. Norway even now uses corn for currency and in India, cakes of tea pass as currency and in China pieces of silk, and in Corea sheets of paper still pass as currency.

In 1709 when Peter the great of Russia overran Sweden and carried away all metals of great value, copper became so valuable that small pieces of the size of our old fashioned coppers were coined into pieces of the value of nearly a dollar of our money.

Afterward as it became more plentiful huge plates of copper were coined and became the currency of the realm.

Gold and silver as money antidates history itself.

Two thousand years before Christ, Abraham, the Chaldean sheperd, returned to Egypt, "very rich in cattle, in silver and gold." Mark at this period silver is mentioned before gold. Afterward, says the Bible record, he bought the cave of Machpelah where his bones were to rest, beside those of Sarah, his wife, for which he paid "four hundred shekels of silver current money with the merchant." A shekel was worth about fifty cents of our money, consequently he paid about $200 dollars for the cave.

Before proceeding farther I will give the values, in our money, of some of the ancient and modern coins in the following coin tables.

	DOLLARS	CENTS
A Mite		1-5
A Farthing		2-3
A Gerah		11¼
A Piece of Silver		13
A Penny		15
A Bekah		27¼
A Drachma		30
A Shekel		55¼
A Stater		60
A Talent of Silver	1,656	
A Talent of Gold	26,496	

This table is from Potter's Bible Encyclopedia.

A table such as the above is of but little use to us except we know the purchasing power of the coin. But as that was continually changing as the ages rolled on, we have but little data whereby to place our judgment.

In Ancient Greece in the days

of Pericles, B. C. 469 to 429, in which time, Encyclopedias say, times were good, the laboring classes received as follows: Common labor three obolo—equal to three and one-half cents, consequently his pay was about ten and one half cents per day. A gardener got about fourteen cents, a wood sawyer (lumberman), nineteen cents, a carpenter seventeen and one-half cents, a scribe or secretary of a public office, fifteen cents, and very long hours.

At this time beef was worth about three to four obolo or more than the common laborer got per day. The poorer classes could eat no meat except now and then a little wild game. They lived mainly on a sort of pea or bean, with leeks, and herbs, and corn, or what we call wheat. Their clothing was of the poorest sort.

We may judge by this, how the laborer fared who received the penny a day (fifteen cents worth of silver) spoken of in Matthew II, 9, 13. But we are assured by one authority at least that this word penny was a mistranslation, the original Roman word was "denarius" and its purchasing power, at that time, of food and necessaries of life, was $3.20. But here we are in the dark as much as ever, for what quantity and quality were the goods, in comparison to our productions of today?

And think of the price that Judas Iscariot got for our Savior, thirty pieces or $3.90. Either it was not for the money that this act was done or Judas Iscariot had as small a soul as some of our capitalists of today.

Those asses who prate about the money of the world are requested to observe the following table and try and ascertain the purchasing power of the different pieces in their respective countries and they will see the folly in the idea of universal money.

The two dollar gold-piece of Newfoundland value	$2.02.70
The Shanghai, Tael of China	1.03.10
Ruble of Russia	.54.40
Rupee of India	.34.22
Florin of Austria	.34.50
Mahbub of Tripoli	.62.90
Bolivia of Venezuela	.14.00
Peso of Mexico	.75.80
Silver Yen of Japan	.75.20
Silver dollar of the Central American States	.09.80

But the strangest coin of them all is the

REIS OF BRAZIL.

The basis of currency is an imaginary unit, the reis, 1,000 of which make a milries, worth, apart from exchange, about 50 cents. The lowest nickle coin is 100 reis, worth 5 cents, below these are copper coins; 20 reis being equivalent to one cent.

Thus one pays 7,500 reis for a meal for himself and wife at a restaurant; 2,000 reis to a boatman to take you ashore from the steamer; 1,000 reis for a bottle of beer; 500 reis to a guide for pilotage through a public building; 200 reis for a ride on a street car; 100 reis for having his boots blackened.

As an offset to this, it is said that in the southern part of Russia the peasants use a coin of such small value that it would take 250,000 of them to buy an American dollar, and these coins are so scarce that a man who has a hundred is looked upon as rich and one who has a thousand is considered very wealthy. Think of this, comfortable, well off, with one-fifth of a cent, wealthy with two-fifths of a cent, rich with two cents and a nabob with five cents.

Ye who are wise will see by this the folly of talking about

wanting money that is money if you go abroad. But the silly, vaporing fool that is only fit to be the slave of a usurious, hypocritical, falsifying master will whine. "I want the money of the world, money that is money if I go abroad."

It is said that a cubic inch of gold is worth $210; a cubic foot, $362,370; a cubic yard, $9,797,762. This is valuing it at $18 an ounce. It is estimated that we have $6,000,000,000 of gold in the world, and if so, according to the above estimate it would not occupy a cubic space of twenty six feet. But it is very doubtful if there is any such amount of gold in existence, for we should deduct at least one-third of the production for wear and loss. If we do this, we can figure, by the following estimate and table, the amount of gold still in existence pretty accurately.

I have given the United States Silver Commission's Report for the amount of the precious metals at the beginning of the Christian Era to be two billion eight hundred million dollars. But by the close of the fifteenth century it had dwindled to less than two hundred million dollars.

We will now note the following annual production of the precious metals of the world, from the discovery of America to 1872 inclusive.

From the Director of the United States mint as quoted by the "Columbian Advocate:"

PERIODS	GOLD	SILVER
1493-1520	$ 3,855,000	$ 1,954,000
1521-1544	4,759,000	3,740,000
1545-1560	5,657,000	12,959,000
1561-1580	4,546,000	12,447,000
1581-1600	4,965,000	17,400,000
1601-1620	5,662,000	17,538,000
1621-1640	5,516,000	16,358,000
1641-1660	5,829,000	15,224,000

1661-1680	6,154,000	14,006,000
1681-1700	7,154,000	14,200,000
1701-1720	8,520,000	14,779,000
1721-1740	12,681,000	17,921,000
1741-1760	16,356,000	22,158,000
1761-1780	13,761,000	27,128,000
1781-1800	11,823,000	36,534,000
1801-1810	11,815,000	37,161,000
Total	$125,993,000	$271,523,000

The world's production of gold and silver for the calender years of 1811 to 1889 inclusive.

YEARS	GOLD	SILVER
1811-1820	$ 7,606,000	$ 22,474,000
1821-1830	9,448,000	19,141,000
1831-1840	13,484,000	24,788,000
1841-1850	36,393,000	32,434,000
1851-1855	131,248,000	86,827,000
1856-1860	136,946,000	37,611,000
1861-1865	131,728,000	45,764,000
1866-1870	127,537,000	55,652,000
1871-1872	113,431,000	81,849,000
1873	97,200,000	82,120,000
1874	90,750,000	70,673,000
1875	97,500,000	77,578,000
1876	103,700,000	78,322,000
1877	114,000,000	75,240,000
1878	119,000,000	84,644,000
1879	109,000,000	83,383,000
1880	106,500,000	85,636,000
1881	103,000,000	89,777,000
1882	102,000,000	96,230,000
1883	95,400,000	98,986,000
1884	101,700,000	90,817,000
1885	108,400,000	97,564,000
1886	106,000,000	92,772,000
1887	105,000,000	94,265,000
1888	109,900,000	103,316,000
1889	118,800,000	117,951,000
Total	$2,494,691,000	$1,877,514,000

Gold and silver produced in the United States from 1890 to 1893 inclusive.

PERIOD	GOLD	SILVER
1890	$32,845,000	$ 0.485,000
1891	33,175,009	75,416,000
1892	33,014,981	82,101,010
1893	35,955,000	77,575,75

Taken from the "Report of Director of Mint."

By a careful study of these tables it will be observed that

the lowest production of these metals was in 1493, the highest was in 1889; that up to these dates there was a continual fluctuation in the annual product from $5,805,000 to $236,451,000. As these commodities are subject to the law of supply and demand like all other things. It will be seen that they are an unfit thing to use as a basis for promissory notes. And one can not help ask the question. Why should two commodities of such fluctuating value be used for a basis for promissory notes when the whole range of products would make a greater and safer security? But as absolute money is better than promissory notes, why use them at all? except you wish to grant a power to corporate bodies of selfish men on purpose to rob the people.

It will be noticed that there has been much more gold produced than silver—that is in value. Though the ratio of the production of silver has been steadily on the increase.

In 1493 there was $38 of gold produced to $19 silver. In 1892 there is $118 of gold to $162 of silver.

It will also be remembered that the obligations of the United States could be paid in silver as well as gold and the production of silver in the United States has caught up to and gone past that of gold. Consequently the conspiracy against silver effects the United States more than any other country.

As I have before stated this whole silver question is brought forward first to rob the people by forcing them to pay twice the amount in value that the bond holders had first, fixed upon that they could rob the country off and secondly at this time to attract the attention of the people from the more vital question of a scientific paper currency that would upset the robbery system of controling the world by controling the volume of money. As a means to this end they must have something for an argument so there is much blatherskite talk about the ratio in the value of gold and silver in past times. Wherever there has been any great change in the comparative values of gold and silver, from one to sixteen—that is in valuation of one pound of gold to sixteen of silver, since 1600 B. C., it has been because of local conditions.

If the nations of the earth were to coin both gold and silver at a ratio of sixteen to one there is no doubt that the price would range at that rate or if they were coined at any other ratio they would remain at that ratio. But it is the interest of some large creditor nations, like England, to demonetize silver that they may force the debtors to pay a larger amount, thereby enslaving the world. Such a thing as free coinage of silver by those nations, cannot be looked for. Whether the United States could force the nations to recognize a standard of 16 to 1 by resorting to that measure is a question to be solved. But it makes no difference one way or the other. The United States has a just right to return to a free coinage of silver at a ratio of 16 to 1 and to pay her obligations in silver. For the benefit of those who would like to know the comparative values of gold and silver, I will here give the range from 1600 B. C. to the present time.

Before Christ 1600—1 to 3.33. Authorities; Inscription Karnak, tribute list of Thothmes. (Brandis.)

Before Christ 500—1 to 13, Persia (Boeckh.) Page 144.

Before Christ 470—1 to 10. Asia Minor. (Boeckh.) Page 12.

Before Christ 300—1 to 10. Greece. Depression of gold caused by the influx of gold, by the successful wars of Alexander

Before Christ 49—1 to 8.93. Rome. Caused by the influx of gold by Cæsar spoiling the Gauls.

Cæsar's headquarters were at Aquilia, at the head of the Adriatic, where there was also a gold mine, which at this period became very prolific.

From the beginning of the Christian Era to 161 A. D. the ratio was from 1 to 10.97 to to 1 11.99 or counting the debasement of the Roman coin, about 1 to 11.

A. D. 438 Byzantium and Rome 1 to 14.40. Theodosian code. Arbitrary.

A. D. 1351. From this date to the discovery of the new world, the ratio varied from 1 to 12.30 and 1 to 12.80.

A. D. 1494—1 to 10.50. Fixed arbitrarily by mint regulations—England and Germany. MacLeod's Political Economy.

1640—1 to 13.51
1665—1 to 15.10   } France, Mint regulations.
1679—1 to 15.00
1680—1 to 15.40

I will now give a statement of the fluctuation in the ratios of gold and silver from 1687 to the demonetization of silver by Germany and the United States, and the stoppage of free coinage. As quoted by the Columbia Advocate, from Dr. A. Soetbeer; for 1687 to 1832 from 1833 to 1878. Pixley's and Abell's tables from 1879 to 1889 daily cablegrams from London to the Bureau of the Mint.

The following shows the fluctuations of gold and silver and shows the highand lowest points reached during the periods.

1687—1 to 14.94   1793—1 to 15.00
1697—1 to 15.20   1808—1 to 16.08

1702—1 to 15.52	1809—1 to 15.98
1728—1 to 15.11	1813—1 to 16.25
1729—1 to 14.92	1814—1 to 15.04
1737—1 to 15.02	1843—1 to 15.93
1738—1 to 14.91	1859—1 to 15.19
1746—1 to 15.13	1861—1 to 15.50
1760—1 to 14.14	1865—1 to 15.44
1790—1 to 15.04	1869—1 to 15.60
1872—1 to 15.63	

After the repeal of the Sherman Act and the complete closing of the American mint to silver that metal dropped until it would take over thirty-two pounds of silver to buy one pound of gold. But at the same time everything else shrank in value. I will here quote from a speech of The Hon. John P. Jones, of Nevada, who states in a table, he says, was prepared for him by the Bureau of Statistics of the Treasury Department, Washington D. C., that in 1873 a bushel of wheat would bring $1.14 gold or silver and today would bring $1.12 in silver; but would bring but 87 cents in gold. In 1873 a pound of cotton would bring 16 cents in gold or silver but today would bring thirteen cents in silver bullion, but would bring only ten cents in gold.

A pound of cheese, that in 1873 cost the purchaser eleven and three-fourths cents, gold or silver, now brings twelve cents worth of silver bullion and but nine cents in gold.

He quotes the range of prices of many other articles which showed about the same rise in the price of gold and shrinkage in price of commodities; which proves to us that the extra demand given to a metal by using it for money increases its commercial value, and that if gold or silver were entirely demonetized their commercial value would shrink to insignificance.

The fallacy in the cry for an

HONEST DOLLAR.

When the banker tells you he wants a gold dollar because he wants to be honest and pay gold you tell him he is a liar. For he never pays gold if he can help it, but pays his rag promissory notes.

There is comparatively no gold in circulation as money.

The great majority of the people seldom see or get a piece of gold.

The fallacy of a gold basis, of being able to get gold if you want it, is exploded by the fact that if there is a demand of any consequence for gold it slinks out of sight and you can not get it at all.

Q. Is the price of gold fixed by law?

A. Yes. By the provisions of its charter, the bank of England is obliged to purchase every ounce of gold bullion offered, that is nine hundred and two-thirds fine and pay for it £3, 17s, 9d—$18.92 per ounce but other bullion and coins she can shave and speculate in. This alone would establish a fixed price for gold.

This act was passed July 19, 1844, and has never been repealed. It fixes the price of gold as much as an act, by any reliable demand, could fix the price of any other commodity. If the same authority were to fix the price of silver at $20 per ounce, in the same manner, every ounce of silver would bring $20, less the freight or exchange.

COINAGE

Q. Was gold and silver always used as money?

A. Its use antidates history.

Q. Was it likely the first thing used for money?

A. No. Of course it is natural to suppose barter or

trade, commodity for commodity, constituted the first commerce.

As many commodities, such as game, fish, berries, etc., etc., were perishable and would decay before they could be used or traded, some indestructible commodity would be selected as a standard measure of comparative values. As there were no statute laws, of course this was adopted by common consent.

As the diversity of commodities increased, it became necessary that the standard should be devisable into fractions Consequently, beads made of polished seeds, shells and animals' teeth, highly polished and strung together as a thing of ornamentation, was probably the most universally known as money by primitive men. As the metals were discovered they came next.

Q. Were the metals first used in coin or by weight?

A. Certainly as coin.

The first coins were, probably mere nuggets of metal, pierced and strung together like other things used for ornamentation. As man progressed these ornaments assumed more artistic shapes, and so the primitive jeweler was the first coiner of money.

After beads came rings, and archæology gives us some samples of this early coinage.

Most writers state that the metals were first used by weight. But weights and measures were evolved by progressive man long after money became necessary. These writers also give the earliest coinage as dating with the Lydians, 700 B. C. Herodotus credits the Lydians with the invention of the art of coinage. This, however, is a mistake as there is good evidence that both gold and silver were coined in India long before the coinage credited to the Lydians.

Homer speaks of brass coins in Greece, 1184 B. C. But the Egyptians used ring money long before this, as Egyptian monuments show us that rings were used for money at a date long prior to this, and nearly 2000 B. C. Abraham brought back with him pieces of gold and silver.

ANCIENT RING MONEY.

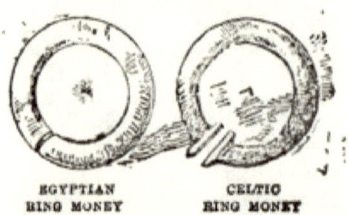

EGYPTIAN RING MONEY   CELTIC RING MONEY

Of course as man progressed in commerce tricks of trade came into use and fixed weights and measures grew out of this. The smallest unit of an indivisable substance would naturally be chosen as the unit of measure of weight. Therefore the little Arabian bean carot was undoubtedly the first thing fixed upon as a standard of weights. Afterward the barley corn was undoubtedly used as a standard of both weights and measures. As the demand for the metals increased the value increased; tricksters, naturally, varied the size of the rings and debased the metals and measures were adopted to overcome the fraud.

But as men of more or less generous natures would meet in business and bickering take place, fixed, statutory laws became necessary, and the science of money, weights and measures are still developing (see weights and measures pages 2 to 4)

Perhaps making money—as a government function—a legal

tender unit of measure might properly be credited to the Lydians. Though the date would have to go back seven or eight hundred years or more before Christ, as Lycurgus made iron money in Sparta, 900 B. C , and as he steeped it in vinegar to destroy its annealability it would seem to prove that making money was a government function and intrinsic value considered a detriment. This is borne out by the fact that 500 B. C., Solon, of Athens, recoined the money of the realm, reducing the metal in the coin nearly one-half.

COINS OF ATHENS, 500 B. C.

Volumes of very interesting matter might be written on coinage alone. The London Museum contains 165,000 specimens of coins, most of them that have been money but are not today. Their intrinsic value would not compare with that of their weight in steel, and the commercial value of the commodity would fall many thousand times below their commercial value as curiosities. But their greatest value is to the student of history.

As no coin was dated prior to 400 A. D it is very hard to fix the date of ancient coin.

AES

The earliest Roman coin, 500 B. C.

These 165,000 specimens of coins, once money but now money no where, are one hundred and sixty-five thousand points of evidence to prove that money is a creation of law.

Coins of Alexander the great, 578 B. C., probably the strangest and least known coin is that represented in the cut below.

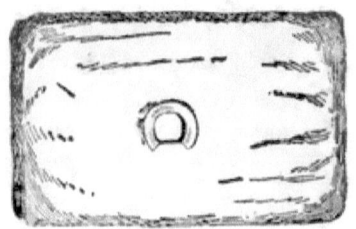

Carthagenian leather money, 200 B. C., as described by Rollins. A piece of leather with a metal core.

ROMAN SEXTIUS- 250 B. C

COIN OF CLEOPATRA AND MARC ANTONY
500 B. C.

JULIUS CÆSAR,
About 50 B. C.

WAMPUM OF THE NORTH
AMERICAN INDIANS.

The standard of our own silver dollar was taken from the Spanish mill dollar which was almost, a universal standard of money when our first dollar was authorized, 1792.

Many make the mistake in supposing the corrugated edges on the piece is the milling but it is not. The milling is the plain, raised edge of the piece and is for the protection of the coin. The corrugation is called the reading.

The two metals have always fluctuated as to the standard of coin value.

Senator Jones says that kings David and Solomon used silver as the standard. He has made a slight mistake as King David did and Solomon did until he fell away from the ways of God and demonetized silver and brought on the rebellion under Jeroboam (see pages—)

Mr. Talmage in a sermon, gives the wealth of Solomon as £680,000,000 in gold and £1,028,000,377, silver. But he does not give his authority.

The ratio at which gold and silver were first coined was the ratio at which they had gone into use by weight.

In Lydia and Greece it was

thirteen and one third of silver to one of gold.

In the time of Philip of Macedonia, gold was the most plentiful of the two, in Macedonia and Asia Minor.

Far back in India, the metals were used five of silver to one of gold.

Boeckh, in his economy of Athens, says:

"The value of gold is more variable than that of silver, which, therefore, may be considered as the standard of price for gold as for other commodities."

Silver was the standard money of England until 1816 when the gold standard was adopted, and the value of gold coins as compared with silver, was, from 1257 to 1664, regulated by proclamation.

The Napoleonic war with France, ran England deeply in debt. The money power behind the bank of England bought up the consols with a plentiful cheap money, and desired their interest in a scarce, high priced money. Consequently paper was contracted and silver demonetized and through that the English people were robbed.

As before stated the money power of England was now enthroned with a vast leverage behind them. They were soon enabled to lend money to the nations of the world, and through the process of funding and refunding and the mighty gains of compound interest, were able to dictate terms to any nation they did business with.

There were, however, other great capitalist, in other nations who were trying to shape national affairs to suit their interests; so when gold was discovered in California and and Australia, it was thought money would be so plentiful that the people would be independent; so they sought to demonetize gold, which was done by Germany, Austria, Holland and Belgium. But as long as the bank of England was buying every ounce of gold at $18.92, gold could not shrink in value to any great extent. England would not demonetize gold because several of her colonies produced gold but no silver of consequence. Though Holland coined $18,000,000 it was not a legal tender and there was no demand for it, and they stopped its coinage.

It was soon found, however, that gold was not so plentiful as was supposed and these nations remonetized gold.

The power of the money loaners, that rule England with a rod of iron, have their branch house in Frankfort and a special agent in every county. Through usury compounded their power is rolling up. Almost every nation is in debt to them and they have not lost sight of their method of destroying the power of France in 1716 and are using the system of bribery to corrupt the world.

They have steadily worked to the end that there shall be but one metal used for a standard of value that they may be able, through controling the volume of money, to control the world.

STANDARD METAL

Standard gold or silver means the standard, government rule for mixing alloys with the metals. The standard of both metals is that of a thousand parts by weight, nine hundred shall be of pure metal, and one hundred of alloy. The alloy of gold is silver and copper, and the alloy of silver is copper, and the standard metal is after the alloy is added.

The standard dollar is the one that measures all other dollars, which are promises to be paid in the standard mill dollar.

The Spanish mill dollar had been almost a universal standard of money the world over and until 1792 was the unit of measures of comparative values in the United States of all commodities including gold.

In 1792 our silver dollar of $371\frac{1}{4}$ grains of pure silver or 416 of standard silver was authorized. The dollar containing $3\frac{1}{2}$ grains more of alloy than the present silver, but the same amount of pure silver.

The gold eagle (for there was no gold dollar,) contained $247\frac{1}{2}$ grains of pure gold which would make the dollar—had there been one—contain $24\frac{3}{4}$ grains of pure gold.

The act of June 28, 1834. reduced the amount of gold in the coin and made the eagle or ten dollar piece, contain 232 grains of pure gold or 23.20 of pure gold to the dollar.

The act of January 18th, 1836, reduced the alloy in the coins to one-tenth of the weight. The standard dollar by that act contained $371\frac{1}{4}$ grains of pure silver or $412\frac{1}{2}$ grains of standard silver, the same as our dollar now contains.

This shows us that silver was the recognized standard and gold was changed to conform to the silver dollar.

We now had no more changes in the coinage laws until 1853.

France had made a bid for silver by changing her ratio to $15\frac{1}{4}$ to 1. This demand was rapidly calling our silver away and our government now reduced the metal in the fractional coins. See coinage laws, pages

---

There had never been but few silver dollars coined. Now there was none as the bullion in the dollar would sell for more than the face value of the dollar.

Although we had an authorized dollar from 1792, Spanish mill dollars of seventeen penny weights and seven grains was a legal tender with us until February, 1857.

The reader will remember the Hazard and bank circulars and how the plot states that this country would be saddled with a great debt, through the expenses of the war, and old citizens and soldiers will remember how that war was needlessly prolonged until the debt piled up, almost to fabulous proportions you will also remember that after the debt was swelled as great as they dared to let it go, that through the plans already laid they made a vigorous war on all paper money, that they, the conspirators, could not control. We will also remember the manly position Mr. Sherman took on the occasion, of the passage of the pernicious, so called, government credit strengthening act. But in the light of what we will now find we must ask ourselves if Mr. Sherman was not taking that position to throw dirt in the eyes of the American people as to his real nature and purpose.

The reader will also remember how one Dubois, a French cabinet officer, sold himself for a hundred thousand crowns per annum of British gold, paid direct from the English secret service fund, to intrigue against French finance.

Well in 1865, several of the European nations, led by France, saw through the designs of England and sought to avert it, so formed what is known as the "Latin union." This union consists of France, Belgium, Italy, Switzerland and Greece.

Their object was to form a union of nations and fix upon a common standard.

This was done among those nations called the Latin union, and acquiesced in by Prussia.

It must be stated here, however, that all of the nations of the Latin union were first in favor of a gold standard until overruled by the influence of France. But a secret war had been waged against silver as soon after 1849 as it was discovered that gold was not going to be so plentiful as had been supposed.

In 1867 however, the Emperor of France extended an invitation to the United States and all European nations to hold

A CONFERENCE IN PARIS

for the purpose of extending the principles of 15 to 1 throughout the commercial world.

The invitation was accepted and one, Samuel B. Ruggles, was appointed commissioner for the United States.

It is easy to be seen why England should desire that the United States should not join the union but should demonetize silver. She being on a gold basis and her moneyed men, who control her, owned a large amount of our bonds. They had increased their value by the large destruction of our paper money, that is, by reducing the volume of money, they reduced the price of labor and the products of labor so that if one bushel of wheat would pay three dollars of debt before the reduction of the volume of money, one bushel of wheat now would not pay one-third as much of the debt as before or only one dollar instead of three dollars of the debt. England being a large buyer of the products of our soil and having large manufacturing interests. She wished to destroy our manufacturing and commercial interests and drive us to agriculture for her benefit, besides by reducing the volume of our money she would reduce the price of our products; and the interest on the great public debt would purchase more of those products. Consequently she could afford great amounts of money for bribing influence to demonetize silver.

Whether Mr. Sherman was honest in his convictions or not, we know history tells us England did bribe Dubois of France and Senator Stewart says just before that conference in 1865. Mr. Sherman did go to England and he did write a powerful letter to Mr. Ruggles, advocating the single standard.

The letter referred to was dated May 18th, 1867, and was originally written in English, was represented in the French translation a few days afterward.

Mr. Sherman was chairman of the Senate Finance Committee and of course his letter bore great weight, and the United States did not join the union. But every energy was bent to shape the scheme for a successful demonetization of silver.

If we find our milk skimmed, and there is cream on the cat's whiskers we may wrongfully suspect the cat, but circumstantial evidence point to the cat as the thief.

Now the cream seems to be sticking to Mr. Sherman's whiskers and men have been hung for treason with less evidence to convict.

The Government Credit Strengthening Act virtually repealed the act of paying the bonds in lawful currency and substituted an act paying them in coin, and at that time they dare not specify the kind of coin. Mr. Sherman seemed to be in favor of the people's cause here. But we will watch his work for the future.

Now if we could pay our debts in coin, it meant the silver as well as gold, for silver was our standard at that time.

Our mines in the West were producing prodigious amounts of silver which would enable us to pay our debts in silver as well as gold and we could do it almost as cheaply as before in paper. But it would not enable the British money kings to carry out their hellish plot against this country, so silver was demonetized.

It may be laid down as an axiom that evidences of debts never depreciate when there is enough wealth behind them to pay what they call for on their face. But the burden of paying may easily be increased by controling the power of production and thereby reducing the value of the product that must be disposed of to meet that obligation.

This country was rich in silver and could easily pay its debts in that kind of money which it had a perfect right to do, or the moneyed conspirators' scheme would have been so stated at the time of the passage of the "Government Credit Strengthening Act."

The science of finance is one which, unfortunately, very few people devote much attention to, and it is unfortunate for this country that it is so. Tolstoi tells us it is "The root of all evil." And a false system is certainly the root of much evil. While those who have studied the question closely, declare that a system based upon scientific principles is one of the most valuable factors in a community for the equitable distribution of the products of labor, and an instrument of economy, the value of which is almost beyond computation.

While the people slept in fancied security, even allowing themselves to be robbed by the "infamous Government Credit Strengthening Act" and other kindred dishonest legislation, they still paid no attention to the more damnable scheme of demonetization of silver, of which Sherman's letter to Ruggles seemed to be the first visable blow struck against silver.

On the sixth day of January, 1868, Mr. Sherman introduced a bill in the Senate, apparently to assist in the unification of the coins of nations. But in effect making gold the single standard, and section three of the bill limited the legal tender of silver to $10. This bill was defeated mainly through the power of the minority report of Senator E. D. Morgan, of New York. Thus Ruggles and Sherman were shelved for the time being.

Says Senator Stewart:

"From the establishment of the mint, in 1792 to 1873, there was no year in which there were not more or less legal tender silver coins struck, at the mints. There were many years in which there were no dollars coined, but there was no year, month or day, Sundays and holidays excepted, when the owner of silver could not take it to the mint and have it coined into dollars or some other denomination of silver coins.

"The total amount of silver coinage previous to 1873 was $105,437,025.60. Only about $8,000,000 of this amount was legal tender silver dollars, but all the balance was full legal tender silver money, excepting the subsidiary coin, coined after 1853.

"Between 1860, the date of the opening of the Comstock mine, and 1873, the demonetization of silver, there were 4,887,610 standard silve dollars coined; in the year of 1871, $1,115,706; in 1872, $1,100,106; and between January 1st and February 12th, 1873, the date of the passage of the mint act, there were $.93,600 coined."

These figures are taken from the report of the Director of the Mint for 1890, page 247.

I call particular attention to the fact that there were coined during the years 1871 and 1872, 2,232,210 standard silver dollars and then there were coined between the first day of January, 1873 when the mint act took effect, 293,600 standard silver dollars. If the coinage had continued at the same rate during the entire year there would have been coined in 1873, $2,492,185.

The statement which eminated from the senator from Ohio that the silver dollar was obsolete at the time of the passage of the mint act, and which statement has been constantly repeated by the gold press and gold orators ever since, is absolutely untrue.

The above shows us that free coinage meant that any one who had gold or silver bullion could take it to the mint and have it coined at the ratio of 16 to 1. But now we will find the sly thrust to assassinate free silver coinage.

On April 28th, 1870 a bill was introduced by Mr. Sherman and referred to the committee on finance, *entitled a bill revising the laws relative to the mint, assay offices, and coinage of the United States.*

This bill did not eminate in the usual way, but originated in the treasury department and was sent to Senator Sherman, chairman of the finance committee, accompanied by a letter of recommendation from George S. Boutwell, Secretary of the Treasury. Mr. John Jay Knox was Deputy Comptroller of the currency.

Says Senator Stewart in speaking of this subject:

"Mr. Knox was soon after promoted from that office to the presidency of a leading National bank, one of the great financial institions of New York. Such promotions of treasury officials who have been faithful to the banking interests have been too frequent to escape observation."

The bill contained seventy-one sections and was evidently to cover up deception, for it was not what the bill contained but rather what it did not contain wherein the deception lay. The bill was so constructed as to seem to be a mere codification of the mint laws of 1853. But by leaving out certain wordings silver became demonetized as soon as this bill would go into operation.

On December 19th, 1870, the bill was reported to the senate with amendments. On the ninth day of January, 1871 the bill came up in the Senate and was discussed in committee of the whole.

Says Senator Stewart:

No allusion whatever was made during the discussion to sections 15 and 18; in fact there was nothing objectionable. It was not what the bill contained but what it did not contain that worked the wrong and demonetized silver."

Portions of this bill were discussed at great length and finally Mr. Sherman called for a vote by yeas and nays on the passage of the bill and he voted against the bill, evidently because the amendments to the bill destroyed the true purpose of the bill:

"On January 13, 1871, on motion of Hon. Wm. D. Kelly, the senate bill was ordered printed. On February 25, 1871, Mr. Kelly, the chairman of the committee on coinage, reported the bill back with an amendment in the nature of a substitute, when it was again printed and recommitted."

The bill was never heard of

again at the session and was never debated in the house.

In an article, by Senator Stewart, entitled "True History of the Demonetization of Silver" and published in the National Watchman in the spring and summer of 1895, Mr. Stewart points to many apparent subtile tricks of Senator Sherman, and clearly and forcibly comments upon his acts in the matter.

March 8th, 1871, Mr. W. D. Kelly, chairman of the Committee on Coinage, introduced another bill supposed to be for mint regulations, but which if enacted would have demonetized silver as completely as the one previously offered. The trickery in this bill was also discovered and opposed in such a manner as to bring on a lengthy and heated discussion in the House. The discovery of the deep laid and far reaching trickery in the bill was made by Hon. Clarkson Potter, of New York, who was himself in favor of a gold standard, but who could not sanction the trickery and evils of this bill.

In consequence of the hot discussion on this bill it became so odious that it was abandoned by its friends and a substitute offered.

In pushing this bill through there was a great deal of trickery, and juggling resorted to, and finally an unusual thing: the barefaced crime of pushing the bill through without a reading; for the substitute was fraught with as much evil as the original bill.

The bill was finally amended and passed February 12th, 1873.

Here is the amendment that demonetized silver:

"The silver coins of the United States shall be a trade dollar, a half dollar or fifty cent piece; a quarter dollar, or twenty-five cent piece; a dime, or a ten cent piece; and the weight of the trade dollar shall be four hundred twenty-two grains troy, the weight of the half dollar shall be, respectively, one-half and one-fifth of of the weight of said half dollar; and said coins shall be a legal tender at their nominal value for any amount not exceeding $5.00 in any one payment.

It will be seen by the foregoing that by a trick the silver dollar of our daddies was left out, and so the silver dollar was demonetized.

While this act stopped a legal tender coinage of a dollar for the future it did not demonetize the coin of the past that was in circulation. But the revisers of the General Statutes, incorporated in the revision a clause, without authority of law, demonetizing all silver coin, including the dollar.

Q. Have you any evidence of trickery or cause of evil influence in this matter?

A. Yes. First I have shown that England, that is her Jew money loaners, are the creditors of the world, and the gold basis is for their interests. They buy nearly everything abroad. Their money has gone into nearly every enterprise in our country and in fact everywhere else.

They have destroyed American money to make room for theirs. They own more land in America than would make two such islands as England. They want tenant farmers, and they desire to make the rest of the world produce cheap for their benefit, as the volume of money grows scarce, people will sacrifice the products of labor for a little money. But the debts owed to them do not decrease, while the interest they receive and the dividends on their investments in railroads, mining interests, brewing and all other business; has a greater purchasing power.

Of course England wants a gold basis and I have pointed out, her unprincipled methods of the usage of France from 1716 to the fall of Napoleon. Will she hesitate to use the same dishonorable means to down this or any other country? Of course not. These Jew descendants of an ancient usurious people who were driven from their own land and have fastened upon England with their tentacles, as the devil fish fastens upon its prey, will not hesitate to reduce the world to pauperism for their benefit, though it brings war, pestilence, and famine. It was their influence that prolonged our late war. It was their money, their armies, boats built in their docks, we were fighting and it was their money that bribed the legislatures, and our politicians, our newspapers, and our pulpits, and our judges, for what? I have proven by the Hazard circular, and the bank circular and by other testimony that they have done it—to get this country deeply in debt; to buy our bonds cheap; to destroy American money to make room for theirs; to get their bonds payable in coin; to demonetize silver, that their bonds might be paid in gold, a scarce metal; to bankrupt merchants and manufacturers; to despoil the producer; to defraud labor; to drive the small business men and laborers to agriculture, that they might have tenant farmers to till the land they stole; subvert the liberties of the people; to destroy the Republic, and enslave the Americans. To hell with England and her Jew money loaning scoundrels. Our own capitalist are blinded by gold or they would see that shortly they will be devoured by the monster giant usurer.

Q. You have made an assertion, where is your evidence?

A. First. "Gold is a wonderful clearer of the understanding; it dissipates every doubt, and scruple in an instant, accommodates itself to the meanest capacities, silences the loud and clamorous and brings over the most obstinate and inflexible. Philip of Macedon refuted by it all the wisdom of Athens, confounded their statesmen, struck their orator's dumb, and at length argued them out of their liberties."—Addison.

Says Gladstone the English Premier:

"There is now the greatest aggregation of wealth in the hands of the few since the days of Julius Cæsar, and therefore, on the other hand, the greatest poverty and want known to the civilized world for nearly two thousand years. Just in proportion as the wealth aggregates in the hands of the few, the common people become poor and dependant."

Yet this same Gladstone says England is the creditor nation and should oppose the double standard of gold and silver.

Before the British Royal Commission of 1868, on international coinage, Mr. Jacob Behren, a noted British merchant and member of the Associated Chambers of Commerce, after answering special and technical questions, was asked, in conclusion, "if there was anything else he wished to state?" He replied:

"I would only state that, in my opinion, the general introduction of gold all over the world has been one of the greatest possible blessings to England. I believe that England would be now the very poorest country in the world if the silver standard abroad had been kept up, and gold had not been generally introduced. Gold would otherwise have been very much reduced in value, and we should have had all the gold poured into England. All the debts owing to us would have been paid in the depreciated currency; and, therefore, I believe that England ought to be very thankful that it has been introduced, and ought to give every facility to its circulation."

Early in 1872, Ernest Seyd, an English banker, came here with $500,000 to influence legislation in the interest of the single standard (gold). This was announced in both English and American journals. But since then it has been denied by the money power. But we will have to bring proof of it.

Says Mr. Hooper, Chairman of the Committee on Coinage, in the Congressional Record of April 9th, 1872, page 2,032:

"Earnest Seyd, of London, a distinguised writer and bullionist, who is now here, has given great attention to the subject of mint and coinage. After having examined the first draft of this bill (for demonetization of silver) he made various sensible suggestions, which the committee adopted and embodied in the bill."

Is this evidence enough? If not why did they wait so many years before denying it.

Judge Kelly said he saw the original bill and it was in Ernest Seyd's own hand writing.

Why did they not deny it before the death of Judge Kelly?

Is this evidence enough?

Well if not, here is an affidavit made by Frederick Lockenbach, a prominent citizen of Denver, who says he was once a member of the New York Produce Exchange. He says that in a conversation he had in London, in 1874, that he brought up the subject of rumored corruption in Parliament. Seyd replied that the corruption in our Congress was far worse than in Parliament. This was at the dinner table. After dinner in a private conversation Seyd resumed the subject, and after pledging Mr. Lockenbach to privacy, he spoke, according to the affidavit, as follows:

"'I went to America in the winter of 1872-3, authorized to secure, if I could, the passage of a bill demonetizing silver. It was to the interest of those I represented—the governors of the Bank of England—to have it done. I took with me £100,000 sterling, with instructions if that was not sufficient to accomplish the object, to draw another £100,000 or as much more as was necessary.' He told me German bankers were also interested in having it accomplished. He said he was the financial advisor of the bank. He said, 'I saw the committee of the House and Senate and paid the money and stayed in America until I knew the measure was safe.' I asked if he would give me the names of the members to whom he paid the money—but this he declined to do. He said 'Your people will not now comprehend the far reaching extent of that measure—but they will in after years. Whatever you may think of corruption in the English Parliament, I assure you I would not have dared to make such an attempt here as I did in your country.'"

The Silver League sent a copy of the above affidavit to every paper; in the country. But of course the press that would not publish the Supreme Court decision on the great greenback question—(Greensman vs. Jewlard) would not publish such an article as this.

Is this evidence enough? Well if not the Scriptures say, "that through their own mouths ye condemn them," so the following is quoted from the Banker's Magazine for August, 1873:

"In 1873, silver being demonetized in France, England and Holland, a capital of one hundred thousand pounds ($500,000) was raised and Ernest Seyd, of London, was sent to this country with this fund as the agent of the foreign bondholders and capitalist to effect the same object which was accomplished."

It is now claimed this can not be found in that journal of that date—and may be it never appeared in what is now known as the Banker's Magazine. But we have pointed out how matters have been interpolated, or ripped out of other works where it was thought necessary to conceal the truth. We can not say that was the case here, but some of us remember of seeing it published in a paper of that or a similar title.

Now as farther evidence in this matter we will go on and point out the results of this great influence.

The Rotschilds have a branch power in Germany, and when at the close of the Franco-Prussion war, and France was compelled to pay Germany the large indemnity of one thousand millions of dollars. It was thought, now is the time for Germany to change her standard, so in December, 1871, Germany decreed the gold standard and commenced the coinage of gold and stopped the coinage of silver. Before this Germany had but very little gold, but she had about $400,000,000 of silver, but these silver coins were not demonetized until July, 1873, when the exclusive gold standard was established and the mark adopted as the unit. Silver was made subsidiary and limited to ten marks for each inhabitant with a legal tender limit of twenty marks. Therefore Germany did not really demonetize silver until after the United States did.

It was well understood that France and the Latin Union must soon follow. But here is something most writers have lost sight of.

A few years after the Franco-Prussian war our newspapers were commenting upon the strange fact that Germany with her one thousand millions of indemnity was depressed and business bad, while France who had that enormous amount to pay seemed prosperous and happy. They never seemed to understand why it was so, but the kernel in the cocoanut was this: That France, to enable her to spare the coin to pay Germany, created a large amount of small bonds and bank notes which passed as money and lubricated the wheels of business. Trade and commerce were quickened, invention ran high, the French people could consume, exports increased, gold flowed back into France, and what at first seemed to be a misfortune proved a blessing and remained so until France contracted her paper and demonetized silver, then discontent came back and presidents were murdered.

On the other hand Germany, whose fortune it was to receive that great amount of money, was nearly ruined, because of the demonetization. Business became stagnated, a veritable hegira of its people took place. From 1873 to 1879 the emigration from Germany numbered 1,546,000 souls, and now Emporer William is cudgeling his brain to find how he can keep his people quiet and keep socialism down.

In the United States it was different. The people here had to be educated or deceived, and the conspirators sought the latter as the safer and quicker way, and, as I have shown the trickery in the House and Senate, I will now show General Grant's position on the question and ask what influence turned his head. Listen to the words of Mr. Grant, to his friend, Mr. Cowdry, a New York banker, written Oct. 6, 1873. Mr. Grant had before expressed himself in favor of a large volume of money, as you will remember. Now he says:

"Our mines are now producing almost unlimited amounts of silver, and it is becoming a question, what shall we do with it? I suggest here a solution that will answer for some years, and suggest to you, bankers, whether you may not imitate it—to coin our silver and put it in circulation. Now keep it there until it is fixed, and then we will find other markets. The South and Central American countries have asked us to coin their silver for them. There never has been authority of law to do so. I trust it will now be given * * we will become the manufacturers of this currency with a profit, and shall probably secure a portion of our pay in the more precious metals."

Now note that President Grant wanted all the silver coined, and kept in circulation, he also wanted our government to coin the silver of other countries and this was in October, 1873, after he had signed the bill to demonetize silver. But it will be remembered that the bill demonetizing silver was stolen through by a trick and here is the evidence that, Mr. Blaine, speaker of the House, knew nothing of it and most of the Senate knew nothing of it and the President did not know it until five days after he signed it. Notwithstanding the old party press and speakers are adding evidence of their conspiracy and falsehood by denying these facts. Even Mr. Horr, in his discussion at Chicago, last July, denied that this bill was surreptitiously stolen through.

The following is quoted from an article by Senator Stewart on the "History of Demonetization of Silver" published in the National Watchman, July, 1895:

"DEMONETIZATION UNKNOWN AT THE TIME.

"The Senator from Ohio (Sherman) says, 'Sir, I would rather stand this day before you defending a law which has been denounced and vilified, as this has been, boldly announcing that I did read the law, and that I knew its contents, than to plead the baby act and say I did not know what was pending here before us for two or three years as an act of legislation."— Congressional Record, August 31, 1893, p. 925.'"

Says Mr. Stewart;

"Such a charge under ordinary circumstances might be regarded as a reproach. If I stood alone I would not feel complimented by the charge. But I was in illustrious company, and I will now introduce some of these associates to whom the charge of 'pleading the baby act' equally applies."

Senator Thurman, on the 15th of February, 1878, in a debate said:

"I can not say what took place in the House but know when the bill was pending in the Senate we thought it was simply a bill to reform the mint, regulate coinage, and fix up one thing and another and there is not a single man in the senate, I think, unless a member of the committee from which the bill came, who had the slightest idea that it was even a squint toward demonetization.'—Congressional Record, Volume VII, Part 2, Forty-fifth Congress, second session, p. 1064.

Senator Conkling, in the Senate, on March 30, 1876, during the remarks of Senator Bogy on the bill (S. 263) to amend the laws relating to legal tender of silver coin, in surprise, inquired:

"Will the senator allow me to ask him or some other senator a question? Is it true that there is now by law no American dollar? And, if so, is it true that the effect of this bill is to make half-dollars and quarter-dollars the only silver coin which can be used as a legal tender?"—Congressional Record, Vol. IV, Part 3, Forty-fourth Congress, first session, p. 2082.

Senator Allison, on February 15, 1878, when the bill (H. R. 1093) to authorize the free coinage of the standard silver dollar and to restore its legal tender character, was under consideration; observed:

"But when the secret history of this bill of 1873 comes to be told, it will disclose the fact that the House of Representatives intended to coin both gold and silver, and intended to place both metals upon the French relation instead of on our own which was the true scientific position with reference to this subject in 1873, but that the bill afterwards was doctored, if I may use that term, and I use it in no offensive sense of course."—

Mr. Sargent interrupted him and asked him what he meant by the word "doctored." Mr. Allison said:

"I said I used the word in no offensive sense. It was changed after the discussion and the dollar of 420 grains was substituted for it."—Congressional Record, Vol VII, Part 2, Forty-fifth Congress, second session, p. 1058.

The reader will notice this admission that the bill was doctored and foreign matter substituted after the discussion was over. If this is not an evidence of conspiracy and fraud, what is? (Author)

"On February 15, 1878, during the consideration of the bill above referred to, the following colloquy between Senator Blaine and Senator Voorhees took place:

Mr. Voorhees, "'I want to ask my friend from Maine, whom I am glad to designate in that way, whether I may call him as one more witness to the fact that it was not generally known whether silver was demonetized. Did he know, as speaker of the House, presiding at that time, that the silver dollar was demonetized in the bill to which he alludes?

Mr. Blaine. "'I did not know anything that was in the bill at all. As I have before said, little was known or cared on the subject. [Laughter.] And now I should like to exchange questions with the senator from Indiana, who was then on the floor and whose business it was far more than mine to know, because by the designation of the House I was to put questions; the senator from Indiana, then on the floor of the House, with his power as a debator, was to unfold them to the House, did he know?

Mr Voorhees. " 'I very frankly say that I did not.' " (Ibid., P. 1063)

Senator Beck, in a speech made in the Senate, January 1878. said:

"It (the bill demonetizing silver) never was understood by either House of Congress. I say that with full knowledge of the facts. No newspaper reporter—and they are the most vigilant men I ever saw in obtaining information—discovered that it had been done."—Congressional Record, Vol. VII, Part 1, Forty-fifth, second session, p. 260.

Senator Hereford in the Senate, on February 13, 1878, in discussing the demonetization of silver, said:

"So that I say that beyond the possibility of a doubt (and there is no desputing it) that the bill which demonetized silver, as it passed, never was read, never was discussed, and that the chairman of the committee who reported it, who offered the substitute, said to Mr. Holman, when inquired of, that it did not effect the coinage in any way whatever."—Ibid·, p. 982.

Senator Howe, in a speech delivered in the Senate on February 5, 1878, said:

"Mr. President. I do not regard the demonetization of silver as an attempt to wrench from the people more than they agree to pay. That is not the crime of 1873. I charge it with guilt compared with which the robber of two hundred millions is venial."—Congressional Record. Vol. VII, Part 1, Forty-fifth Congress, second session, p. 764.

In the face of the evidence given elsewhere that Ernest Seyd, an English banker, brought $500,000 here for corruption purposes and that the national banks raised $350,000 per annum to procure legislation for their interests.

I say if here is not evidence enough, of deception, fraud, and crookedness, what more do you want?

With such an array of evidence of conspiracy, as I have brought here, is it not enough to fill one with fear that the ballot must be a failure and nothing but a bloody revolution, the gallows and the guillotine will ever purify the social atmosphere.

The fetid atmosphere of a hot summer's day is only purified through electrical discharges that often takes some lives, and I fear the social atmosphere will only be purified in a similar way.

Gen. Garfield, in a speech made at Springfield, Ohio, during the fall of 1871, said:

"Perhaps I ought to be ashamed to say so, but it is the truth to say that, I at the time, being chairman of the Committee on Appropriations, and having my hands overfull during all that time with work, I never read the bill. I took it upon the faith of a prominent Democrat and a prominent Republican. I do not know that I voted at all. There was no call of the nays and the yeas, and nobody opposed the bill that I know of. It was put through as dozens of bills are, as my friend and I know, in Congress on the faith of the report of the chairman, of the committee; therefore I tell you, because it is the truth, that I have no knowledge about it."

Judge Wm. D. Kelly, the man who first introduced the bill claimed to have put it in the hands of Mr. Hooper and that at that time he knew nothing of the clause in the bill demonetizing silver. Mr. Hooper was a banker and had been a staunch friend of the people as well as, had Mr. Kelly.

Now some of these many, who claimed to know nothing of the fact, that it demonetized silver, were honest in their assertions of no knowledge of the matter, while others may have been influenced by Mr. Seyd's five hundred thousand dollars and were afterward ashamed of their action.

President Grant declared he knew nothing of it until four days after he signed it, and the above letter to his friend, Cowdry, which was not published until it appeared in the Chicago Tribune, March 30, 1878, would indicate that had Mr. Grant known of this fraud at that time he would have vetoed the bill instead of signing it. But mark what a change, after he had taken a a trip around the world with the nabobs.

When the people had become aroused and demanded the remonetization of silver and the Bland Allison act was passed over the head of President Hays, Mr. Grant in a letter to Judge Strong, said:

"If I were where I was one year ago, and the seven years previous (meaning in the presidential chair), I would put my unqualified veto upon the bill."

What influence so changed Mr. Grant's views?

Now let us see where this influence has still continued.

I will here give the text of the Bland act, which passed over the President's veto by the necessary two-thirds vote of the House and Senate:

"*Be it enacted by the Senate and House of Representatives of the the United States of America, in Congress assembled:*

"That there shall be coined at the several mints of the United States, silver dollars of the weight of $412\frac{1}{2}$ grains troy, standard silver, as provided in the act of January 18, 1873, on which are the devices and superscription provided by said act, which coins together with all silver dollars heretofore coined by the United States of like weight and fineness, shall be a legal tender at their nominal value for all debts and dues, public and private, except for all debts and dues where otherwise expressed and stipulated in the contract; and the Secretary of the Treasury is authorized and directed to purchase, from time to time, silver bullion at the market price thereof, not less than $2,000,000 worth per month, nor more than $4,000,000 worth per month, and cause the same to be coined monthly, as fast as so purchased, into such dollars; and a sum sufficient to carry out the forgoing provisions of this act is hereby appropriated out of any money in the treasury not otherwise appropiated. And any gain or seigniorage arising from the coinage shall be accounted for and paid into the treasury as provided under existing laws relative to the subsidiary coinage; provided, that the amount of money at any one time invested in such silver bullion, exclusive of such resulting coin, shall not exceed $5,000,000; and provided, further, that nothing in this act shall be construed to authorize the payment in silver of certificates of deposit, issued under the provisions of Sec. 254, of the Revised Statutes.

"Sec. 2. All acts and parts of acts inconsistant with the provisions of this act are hereby repealed.

"Sec. 3. That immediately after the passage of this act the President shall invite the governments of the countries composing the Latin Union, so called, and of such other European nations as he may deem advisable, to join the United States in conference to adopt a common ratio between gold and silver, for the purpose of establishing internationally the use of bimetalic money and securing a fixity of the relative value between those metals; such conference to be held at such place in Europe, or in the United States, at such time within six months as may be mutually agreed upon by the executives of the governments so invited, or any three of them, shall have signified their willingness to unite in the same. The President shall, by and with the advice and consent of the Senate appoint three commissioners, who shall attend such conference on behalf of the United States, and shall report the doings thereof to the President who shall transmit the same to Congress, said commissioners shall each receive the sum of $2,500 and their reasonable expenses, to be approved by the Secretary of State, and the amount necessary to pay such compensation and expenses is hereby appropriated out of any money in the treasury not otherwise appropiated.

"Sec. 4. That any holder of the coin authorized by this act may deposit the same with the Treasurer or any Assistant Treasurer of the United States in sums of not less than $10 each, corresponding with the denominations of United States notes. The coin deposited for or representing the certificates shall be retained in the treasury for the payment of the same on demand, said certificates shall be receivable for customs, taxes and all public dues, and when so received may be reissued."

It will now be noticed that this act does not restore free

coinage of silver but that the secretary is to buy not less than two millions nor more than four milllions of dollars worth per month and coin the same and that it can be used to pay all u s and debts. It will also be remembered that no Secretary of the Treasury has ever bought and coined more silver than he was obliged to, that is, two millions per month and that it has been hoarded as much as possible or paid out for current expenses but never on the public debt to any extent, but there has been a steady war made on silver ever since and in 1890 our *honest?* John Sherman introduced his bill, called the

SHERMAN ACT.

It passed July 14, 1890.

It directs the Secretary of the Treasury to purchase silver bullion to the amount of 4,500,000 ounces per month at the market price, not exceeding one dollar for 371 grains of pure silver, and to issue in payment for such purchase of silver bullion, treasury notes of the United States, redeemable in coin, and when redeemed may be reissued. Such treasury notes shall be a legal tender in payment of all debts, public and private, except where otherwise expressly stipulated in the contract, and shall be receivable for customs, taxes and all public dues. and when so received may be reissued:

"That the secretary shall each month coin two million ounces of the silver bullion purchased under this act into standard dollars until July 1st, 189 , and after that time he shall coin of the silver bullion purchased under this act, as much as may be necessary to provide for the redemption of the treasury notes herein provided for. That upon the demand of the holder of any of the treasury notes herein provided for the secretary shall redeem such notes in gold or silver coin, at his discretion."

It will not take a sharp observer to see the trick in this act. You will notice, first, it is intended to please and blind the public by seeing the Bland bill and going it $2,500,000 better, to use a gamblers phrase. This would show the public that the volume of money was to be increased. But the silver was not to be coined but paper put out, to be redeemed in gold or silver and here lies the trick. In 1893 the conspirators brought on a panic by first shipping the gold from the country, then taking these notes to the treas- and demanding coin. Of course the treasurer, who always favors the moneyed element, did not use his privilege and redeem these notes in silver but redeemed them in gold.

The panic that was purposely brought on had to be charged to some cause, and as was before intended it was charged to the Sherman Act and a demand made that it must be repealed. They even went so far as to call a special session, to repeal that act, which was done to the extent of repealing the purchasing clause, which virtually demonetized silver or at least stopped further coinage, and Mr. Sherman, the father of the bill, who before voted against his own bills when they were deprived of their venom now voted to repeal the only redeeming quality of his own bill, called the Sherman Act. But the repeal of this act brought no relief, consequently it cannot be the cause of the panic, but the direct cause was the small contraction of currency by the shipment of gold, this shattered and curtailed credits which were used for money, and so lessened the tool of trade that business had to stop, and values are shrinking to meet the small volume of money. It now remains to be seen whether the people of the world will submit to slavery, degradation and go back in civilization or whether we shall have a world-wide revolution which will erect a guillotine in every large city where the heads of the guilty and the innocent together shall roll into the basket as they did in Paris during the great French Revolution. Every indication points to the latter.

I must now go back to the panic of 1873. Professors, preachers and the press were bribed or influenced to deride the greenbacks and declare it was a war measure and the cause of all of our trouble. Unthinking people and fools took up the cry, and it was dubbed "Rag Baby." But now arose a class of philosophers, thinking men and students who defended the greenback from rostrum, press and stump. But they found the moneyed men of the world, the press, the pulpit, and the college, arrayed against them, with nothing but the naked truth for a defense. At first the only arguments of the conspirators was that of derision for the rags, rags, and the nurses of the rag baby. But the greenbackers simply met this with logic: What if they were

RAGS?

What is the star spangled banner itself but a rag; our bibles and our books are rags; the world's history is written and printed on rags. The moral tablets of literature are only graven on rags. The monumental tombs of classics lore, that shed their beacon light from the world's dawn are rags from base to capital. The papyrus rolls of Ancient Egypt, and the ponderous folios of Confucious, that antidate history itself are rags. The deeds of our property; the bonds, and the bank notes are rags and what of all this? It is not the material but what they represent that gives them value and all the gleanings of the ravished mines of Galconda, the gold of Ophir, and the famous wealth of the Ormus and the Ind, with, that gathered from the mines of California and Australia to boot would not weigh a pennyweight against the value of these rags.

No more did they call them rags. But the metals alone were money, fitted by nature for money. This was shown to be false as each metal must receive alloy before it was fit for money and it was proved that money was a creation of law.

Then it was, "can you make money by simply calling it money? If so let us call a milk ticket milk, and you can feed the babies with it." And fools laughed at this, would be wit. But we asked them . "If you call a gold piece wheat can you feed the people with it?" Then with one breath we were told "there is money enough in the country if you have got anything to buy it with." We pointed to the fact that western people were burning wheat and corn for fuel because they could not sell it and coal miners were starving for that grain because they could not sell their coal, and we were told there would soon be a European war which would create a demand for our grain and the sale would bring us more money and better times. The fools did not think they were acknowledging that we needed money and this would bring it and that they were actually wishing for war and destruction to bring us what we could easily provide ourselves, if allowed.

Then it was a declaration that the panic was brought on by our speculation, too many factories, too many railroads built to no where, that money was wound up in these things, this caused the hard times. It was pointed out that the money would not be destroyed but would still be in existence and awaiting investment, but it was shown that you could hardly borrow money without exorbitant interest and the demand of unreasonable security. Then it was overproduction, there was too much of everything produced. The granaries groaned with their burdens and the people tramped and starved. The factories produced so much that they were glutted, and the people were barefooted and in rags. They then declared for the Malthusian theory, population had increased faster than nature could provide and so people suffered. This horrible theory was advanced in England during the panic of 1823, by a minister of the gospel, and brought forward to do duty here and was hailed with delight by church hypocrites who should have remembered that God said, multiply and replenish the earth; and they should have remembered that the earth was but sparsely settled and there was an abundance of wealth ready to pour out at the touch of man but we needed a tool of exchange of which we had been robbed. So we had produced too many people on the one hand to consume too much products on the other, so all must suffer. Such foolish arguments were met with logic and fact, and then they resorted to calling names. The advocates of justice were cranks; blatherskites, hoodlums, socialists anarchists, and everything but gentlemen.

But the greenbackers went on sewing the seed of truth. Some fell on rocky places and for the lack of nourishment sprouted and withered, some fell on the wayside and was trampled under foot, and some were chocked by the tares, but some fell in good ground and increased a thousand fold. The conspirators continually sowed tare among the wheat by aiding the prohibitionist, and the A. P. A., and the socialist, and every other so called reform organization which contained just enough simple reform to dazzle and attract the attention of the people from the vital issue. They brought up the mutual banking systems of Scotland and of Canada. But the greenbackers pointed to the fact that mutual banking merely meant the substituting of promissory notes for money and no promissory note system, drafts or checks can take the place of legal tender money. And so the great truth went on spreading, for

"Truth crushed to earth will rise again
The eternal years of God are hers
While error wounded writhes in pain
And dies amidst her worshippers."

A mighty party has been formed that is soon to sweep the whole country declaring for a truly scientific paper money that will forever sweep away the power of the usurer, the rich oppressor and poverty. It will start the wheels of business. It will set the idle to work. It will give the poor a chance to earn homes. It will make the waste places blossom like the rose, and labor will be independent. Two masters will seek one laborer, not as now a hundred laborers seeking one master.

The moneyed men know this and so they wish to stem the tide and divide the issue and they have retreated to their last fortification but one. They have allowed the great silver question to engross the minds of the people, rather than lose all, and their last ditch will be war. They are now putting off the great struggle with lies, lies, and the press and the pulpit are aiding them. Even the government officials seem to be in league with the conspirators.

We know that the Republican party, which was the father of the greenback, deserted its child, deserted the principles of Lincoln, Chase, Thadeous Stephens and that class of true republicans, to follow the standard of the money power. The first time that Cleveland was president he was supported by the bankers though they had all been republicans but at a meeting of the Bankers Association at St. Louis June, 1888, 300 bankers voted for Cleveland to 52 against him, and so succesfully did he accomplish their work that he has been their candidate ever since, and when elected a second time on a free silver platform he *stultified himself and his party, by always* working in the interest of the foreign money loaners. The party can never be trusted again, for "you can not believe a liar when he speaks the truth."

Even the treasury department is charged with being an auxiliary of the National Banking Association. Listen to the words of Hon. Haldor E. Boen, of Minnesota, in a speech in the House, June 5, 1894:

"Never since Hugh McCulloch came into the treasury has there been any honesty in that department in dealing with the volume of currency, but a perpetual subservience to the money power is manifest in all reports of that department ever since. In fact, it has been manipulated by the different secretaries of the treasury for the interests of Wall street to such an extent that today the treasury of the United States is looked upon as an annex to the National Banking Association.

"It is a well known fact that the treasury department stands in closer relation to the National banks of the country than it does to the people or their representatives in Congress.

"The volume of currency is purposely made to appear large in order to deceive the people into believing that the amount of currency in circulation does not and will not control the prices of labor and its products."

Mr. Boen then quotes extensively from carefully prepared tables by Mr. N. A. Dunning which shows up deception, among which are the following:

"They say we have a greater volume of currency in circulation then ever before."

Then they go on with these stereotyped

LIES

"The total amount of gold in the country is estimated at $519,156,102 of which the treasury reserve is $96,519,833. In banks (controller's report) reserve $103,417,876, leaving among the people $317,218,393."

And nothing is allowed for waste, and it is a well known fact that jewelers and dentists are continually drawing on this stock for the arts, about one-third of the coinage is used annually in this way. Who ever gets a dollar of gold?

Dr. Kimble, Director of the Mint for 1889, pages 42 and 43, says:

"There must be some error in the estimates as $275,000,000 of the estimated gold can not be accounted for."

This would leave but $42,218,393 with the people:

"It is estimated that there is of silver in the country $496,747,573, held in U. S. Treasury (Treasurer's Report), $25,636,299; in banks, $15,315,656; among the people $455,795,018."

Gold bullion and silver bullion and the certificates that represent them are both counted as money in circulation which can not be, as when the certificates are out bullion must be in.

Out of $46,961,000 fractional currency ever issued there is proof that $15,000,000 of it has never been accounted for yet it is put in to swell the volume of currency supposed to be in circulation. There is supposed to be in circulation of greenbacks $346,681,016. The banks are reported to hold of this $160,346,021. Where is the rest of it? The average life of paper money is but seven years. This money has been out twenty-eight years with portions of it occasionally renewed. Let any business man look over his receipts of paper money from day to day and he will find he seldom sees a greenback. It is all silver certificates or national bank notes. The great bulk of this money has been destroyed, yet it is counted as money in circulation. The destruction of all kinds of paper money is great, yet the whole volume issued is counted as in circulation.

The contraction of currency has increased the value of money so that money loaning is the only profitable business left, so banking institutions, loan offices and trust companies are more numerous than factories, and the law requires these institutions to hold a reserve fund, and they must obey the law or lose their charters, and these institutions hold up in reserve $909,-

581,127, yet all of this is counted as money in circulation.

When we had our large volume of money in circulation at the close of the war, there were but few banking, loan and trust institutions in the country. The money was new, and but little of it was lost by wear and tear. As before stated, our volume of money was great—at least $70 to $80 per capita—and business was good; while now we cannot have over $25 per capita, and we have no business to speak of, and debts are increasing, and the money loaners gobble all.

So much for their lies.

We clip the following from *The National Watchman* of Washington, D. C.:

SENATOR VEST ON PER CAPITA CIRCULATION.

Senator Vest, in a recent speech at Fayette, Mo., declared there was only only $3.84 per capita in circulation. This statement is very gratifying to us, since we have long been designated as the "per capita crank" of the reform movement. We were the first to take up the question in detail and designate, item by item, the deduction to be be made, and show by figures the real volume per capita in circulation. In a newswaper discussion with the late Secretary Windom, we took the Treasury statement in detail and so thoroughly disclosed and proved their unreliability that Mr. Windom declared to us personally in his office at the Treasury Department that large deductions ought to be made from the amount declared to be in circulation. We have contended for fifteen years that the reserves held in banks, either for prudential reasons as or by statute law, can not and ought not to be counted in circulation among the people. To this proposition Secretary Windom also consented. Gradually, but surely, the idea has gained a standing that the Treasury figures are grossly erroneous upon that point, and an increasing number of Senators and Congressmen last year challenged their correctness. Now comes Senator Vest, one of the most intelligent and fearless of that body, and boldly declares that there is only $3.84 per capita in circulation, instead of the $25 as claimed by the Treasury Department. Senator Vest says:

"We are told now by these distinguished apostles of the single gold standard, that this country has too much money; and that there is today in circulation among the people of the United States $25.07 for every man, woman and child in the country. Oh, how happy we are without knowing it! Twenty-five dollars and seven cents, and they furnished us with Treasury report showing us this delightful condition of affairs. I have here a compilation which I have made from the official reports of the Treasury Department, issued in 1893 by the Secretary of the Treasury, showing how this estimate is arrived at. Read it, Col. Radcliffe, you are younger than I am. My friends don't leave because we are going to read a few figures. These statistics constitute the essence of the whole controversy."

COL. RADCLIFFE READS FOR MR. VEST.

Col. Radcliffe, a venerable man with a gray beard, read as follows:

"On July 1, 1893, the Secretary of the Treasury in his report, gave the amount of money in circulation as $2,323,547,077. On examination it was found that in this statement an error had occurred by reason of counting both the gold and silver in the Treasury and the outstanding certificates which represented them. Another statement was then made showing he amount of money in circulation to be $1,738,954,057, or $584,593,923 less than the amount first reported. Of this sum there were $597,687,683 in gold, $615,861,484 in silver and $525,594,883 in note. In this aggregate of money in circulation among the people, the Secretary includes $78,541,683 of gold bullion and $119,113,911 of silver bullion not coined, and which could not be in circulation. If this sum be deducted we have left $1,541,298,593.

of this amount $96,519,888 in gold coin, $25,636,899 in silver coin and $19,956,496 in notes were locked up in the Treasury vaults, and, therefore, not in circulation. If these sums be deducted we have left $1,399,191,385. But this is not all. The report shows that in 1893 there were 3,781 national banks having reserves, by law of $573,000.000, after deducting which there remains $885,291,385. In addition to this, there were in 1893, 5,685 state savings and private banks, having reserves amounting to $307,046,268. which leaves in circulation $581,255 067. But how does the Secretary know that in 1893 there were $597,697.685 in gold bullion and coin in circulation? He took the amount of gold in the Treasury and in the national banks on June 30, 1892, $115,000,000, and added to it the estimated total of gold in circulation, $20,000,000, thus making $135,000,000. To this he added all that had been coined at the mints since 1872, with the gain or loss of gold exported or imported as registered at the Custom Houses, deducting $1,500,000 each year for the industrial arts, which is far too little."

"The Secretary assumes that every dollar coined since 1872 is still in existence, and that none have been lost or destroyed by fire, shipwreck or otherwise. I do not believe that there is any such amount of gold in circulation as $597,000,000. I do not believe there is a gold coin today in this audience, and the same statement can be made anywhere in this country. If the treasury report is correct, it is a sad commentary upon the patriotism of those among us, who see the government paying an enormous bonus to the Rothschild syndicate to obtain gold in order to maintain its reserve.

"It would be correct, in my opinion, to deduct at least $250,000,000 from the estimate of the Treasury for the amount of gold in circulation, and this would leave the total amount of money in circulation $331,255,067.

"Besides this the Secretary in his estimate counted $119,332,550 of silver and $77,415,223 of gold coin, or $196,747,673, without deducting any amount by reason of losses by fire and shipwreck or otherwise, and if we fix the sum at $49,674,-767, as the total loss from February 28, 1878, to November 1, 1893, it will leave as the whole amount in circulation $281,580,300. From this amount there should be deducted at least 10 per cent on the amount of national bank notes now outstanding, to cover losses by fire, flood and otherwise, which would make another deduction of $17,871,387 —leaving in actual circulation $263,-708,913 The total population of the United States by the census of 1890 was 62,622,850. If we add 10 per cent increase for the five years which have elapsed since 1890, our population is now at least 68,884,475, making the per capita circulation $3.84 instead of $25, as claimed by the single gold standard advocates.

"The result, and I think I have not overstated it, is that instead of $25.07 in circulation for every man, woman and child in the United States, there is in reality $3.84. And if, in order to cover all errors, we make this $5, or even $10, per capita, what is the comparison with the circulation we have had in the past? What is the comparison with the condition of this country immediately after the war, when we had unrivaled prosperity and all men were busy and happy? We had then a circulation of $67.26 per capita, and I ask the men of my age, and even younger men than myself, here today, to go back in memory to the condition of the United States at that time. I assert here now—and nobody knows it better than myself, for I came back legged from participation in that strife I assert that there never was such prosperity in this country as in the five years immediately following the war. I declare here now that until this miserable system of contraction of the currency was put upon the people by the Republican party the hum of business and the hymn of prosperity and content ascended from every home in the land.

"But it was said that we must go to specie payment, and Hugh McCulloch, Secretary of the Treasury, bought in seventy-seven odd millions of greenbacks to bring the circulation down. Mr. Sherman, as Secretary of the

Treasury, continued this unholy work. What was the result? Seven long years of misery and distress, while the financial life-blood spurted out from the fingers of the American nation and gloom settled thick upon the land.

"Take the official report of Hugh McCulloch, made to Congress in 1865, in which he said that notwithstanding the ravages of war and the loss in labor this country had made unparalleled strides in prosperity. He declared, and it was the truth, that the people were out of debt; that they were prosperous and happy; that new enterprises were being originated; that manufactories were being started, railroads were being built, and that the farmers were putting new improvements upon their lands. The bankers and money lenders saw that their prey were escaping; that money was plenty; that there were no votaries in the temple of the red demon of gold which was the place where they obtained their gain. What did they do? They established this system of contraction to grind their victims down once more, and immediately the clouds gathered, the sunshine disappeared, and famine and despair once more strode upon the earth; and here we stand today, at the end of the road, confronting the legitimate outcome of these years of contraction. Shall we go now permanently to the single gold standard forever, or shall we have gold and silver, the money of the constitution, which our fathers left us?

"I have been called a great many names, and I know I will be called a fiatist and an inflationist next, but if inflation will bring back prosperity to our country and energy to our people, then in God's name give us a little inflation. If we can again bring back to darkened homes the sunshine and joy of other days, let us inflate."

They told us it was the tariff question that caused hard times. We must have high tariff and we must have free trade, but we pointed to the panic of 1857 with free trade, and to the panic of 1873 with a high tariff; to good and bad times with free trade, and to good and bad times with high tariff. We pointed to bread riots in free trade England, and to labor disturbances in protected Germany. They have had to give up the tariff question and accept the financial question in part. They are in their last line of works. They will now resort to fraud; your vote will be counted out. The next President will be a Republican, counted in by an overwhelming majority. But the next the people will elect and seat, but they will never seat him without shedding rivers of blood. The money power will see, that with the seating of the people's President their power is gone for ever, and their bonds will be paid in the people's money and interest scarce. They will declare that the people have gone mad, and they will raise armies of hirelings, but the people will not be put down. They will then call in the aid of England. Will she respond? Will a power that has reduced her own people to slavery, and the work people of one of her colonies to *one and a one half pence per day where salt is one and one-half pence per pound* —a day's work for a pound of salt, in a land where in 1878 seven millions of people died of starvation and the tax on salt alone *was thirty-five million dollars;* will this power hesitate to help enslave America? *No!* but she will not dare to try it alone— her own people are of our blood and of our language, and they will rebel against it. But the money power will form an alliance between Germany, Austria, Italy, Belgium and England. Even the churches will be united —a new pope enthroned, who will declare God-like powers, and arbitrate their differences, and the combined powers will be brought against us, and the bloodest war the world ever knew will be waged against us, and the Scriptures shall be fulfilled, men will go down in war "and seven women shall take hold of one man to be called of his name." The money powers will assume that they are right, and point to the precedence of collecting a fraudulent account as of Nicaragua at the cannon's mouth, which was not done for the sake of the few thousand dollars, but as a precedent to show the United States what they might expect. But Russia will not be with them: she will find it a good time to get an opening to the sea and the head of her church at Jerusalem; and France will not be with them, she will find it a good time to get back Alsace-Lorraine; and the reformers of the world will find it a good time to carry out their cherished hopes, and so the world will be involved in war, "and the stars of the heavens (the kings, princes and the nobles) will fall to the earth like a tree casting her untimely fruit before a mighty wind," and England "the hammar that has broken the nations to pieces, shall in turn be broken to pieces," she will lose her rich colonies, and Michael, the manchild, born of the woman that fled to the wilderness (the United States—the woman the church, Puritans, Huguenots, Quakers, and all who came for religious liberty) shall wax strong and rule the world with a rod of iron.

Some such a system of finance as here given will be adopted, and the power of usury gone forever.

"BUT"

OH! FOR A STATESMAN who is also a warrior and who loves his country before himself, who can see that all things are built up by accretion and die away by erosion, that our country must expand until it reaches the borders of this hemisphere.

Oh! for a statesman who can see that by employing the people, creating wealth, is better than supporting armies, police, judges, lawyers, and paupers and criminals, and that this can be done through the financial system here offered.

Oh! for a statesman who can see that a war of carnage and blood is productive of less suffering and wrong than the war that the money power of England is waging against us. She has destroyed American money to make room for her's that has gone into our railroads, our mines, our breweries, our mills, our factories, and in fact every great enterprise, and she is binding our people in slavery through golden fetters of debt fraudulently obtained.

AROUSE!

Oh, Americans! ye lovers of freedom! listen no longer to the lies of the hireling press, the pulpit, paid priesthood, who care not for God or right, or the college professor, whose golden path is paved with financial falsehoods to deceive the tender mind, "for in the last days deceivers shall wax stronger and stronger, lying and and loving a lie, and making a lie," but they shall be swept away by the sword of truth.

Oh, Americans! put away your differences, and your many organizations, and form one mighty organization. Arm yourselves and drill for you have a mighty foe to meet. When the usurpers have got your seat of government and your flag, treat them as rebels and usurpers; do not let them brand you as such. Stick to your country and your flag—*your flag*; let no dirty red rag, or any other device, take the place of our God-given banner, whose blue field and starry array typify God's pure heavens that covers all mankind, and the land that justly belongs to the lovers of equality before the law; whose broad stripes typify the stripes that liberty must endure to sustain their rights; whose blood-red color, typifies the blood that flows in all men's veins alike, be he prince or pauper, wise or fool, whose brilliant white represents the purity of the government our forefathers intended, and that we should defend to the last drop of blood.

The south was wrong, but unfortunately through the mistakes of our forefathers. She had the constitution with her. Had their leaders been wise enough to have quickly seized our capitol and stuck to our flag we never would have whipped them. So stick to your capitol and your flag. Arm and defend the justice of our government and put down the usurpers who will count you out and defend their lies by force. We can never be safe until we drive England from this continent, for she is our worst enemy.

It was England's intrique, English guns, English bullets, English boats, and English money that was our worst enemy during our late war, not the English people, for they were our friends, but the English piratical nobility, urged on by the *triced* Jew money loaners, the descendant of those God drove from Jerusalem for taking usury and greedily gaining one of another, and to whom he said "I have smitten my hand against you * * * and ye shall be scattered among the heathen, and among the countries until thy filthyness shall be consumed out of thee." This

—250—

whole subject is so mixed, with scriptural prophecy, and finance and prophecy are dry reading to the unitiated, that I will give you "finance in prophecy" in the form of a running story.

I have piled up evidence enough already to prove that money is a creation of law, and that legal tender money is the only safe thing to do business with. Austria has been doing business for years with a paper currency, but in 1893 attempted specie payments, which she has never been able to maintain, before nor since.

Russia, during the reign of Queen Catherine, was at war with Turkey and had to resort to treasury notes, which carried her through the war; again with the aid of treasury notes she fought her battles with Napoleon, and again in 1770 she issued notes which carried her through two wars, but for years she has been unable to sustain a specie basis currency, and now she is about to attempt to sustain her specie basis system, but with the rest she will be plunged in war to keep her dissatisfied people quiet.

CONSTITUTIONAL MONEY.

Here are the state cases in which the constitutionality of the legal tender money are passed upon, and where the same may be found, and what the judges said in some of the cases:

Carpenter vs. Northfield Bank (39 Vt. 46).

Shollenberger vs. Brinton (52 Pa., St. 9).

Verges vs. Gibony (38 Mo., 458).

Brown vs. Welch (26 Ind., 116).

Latham vs. United States (1 Ct. of Cl., 149).

Lick vs. Falkner (25 Cal., 404).

Curiac vs. Abadie (Id., 502).

Kierskie vs. Hedges (23 Ind., 141).

Britenback vs. Turner (18 Wis., 140).

Jones vs. Harker (37 Ga., 503).
Reynolds vs. Bank of the State (18 Ind., 467).
Wilson vs. Trebilcock (23 Ia., 331).
Met. Bank vs. Van Dyck (27 N. Y., 400).
Hague vs. Powers (39 Borb. N. Y., 427).
Roosvelt vs. Bull's Head Bank (45 Ind., 579).
Murry vs. Gale (52 Id., 427).
George vs. Concord (45 N. H., 434).
Van Husan vs. Kanouse (13 Mich., 303).
Hintrager vs. Bates (18 Ia., 174).
Maynard vs. Newman (1 Nev., 271).
Milliken vs. Sloat (Id., 573).
Borie vs. Trott, (5 Phil., Pa., 366).
Johnson vs. Juey (4 Coldw. Tenn., 608).

The above are copied from the reports of court decisions which were not merely questions of the constitutional power of Congress to issue legal tenders in time of war or peace, but the whole matter of the necessity of all acts for whatever purposes not prohibited by the Constitution.

Chief Justice Chase, in Hepburn vs. Griswold, stated that:

"The constitutionality had never been called in question, except as to its retrospective effect, and then by the submission of the people to this and contemporaneous construction of other courts, bring to its relief a general principle of law, which has all the force of law itself. The mere fact that there is a concurrence is an argument in favor of the proposition, which is concurred in by the different courts."

Attorney-General Akerman, in arguing in favor of the constitutionality, said:

"Congress has never hesitated to enact what should be legal tender in payment of debts. The right to thus enact has been assumed in twenty-four statutes, passed in presidences of Washington, Jefferson, Madison, Monroe, Jackson, Tyler, Polk, Fillmore, Pierce, Lincoln and Johnson. * * * The Constitution nowhere declares that nothing shall be money unless made of metal."

It would be interesting reading to give the whole range of these reports had I space to do so, but I have piled up argument enough to show that anything that a government sees fit to make money of can be declared legal tender, and that our intelligent people have found a full legal tender paper money, in sufficient volume, is the best thing that a government can declare legal tender.

Juillard vs. Greenman (U. S. Reports. Vol. 110, p. 421).

SUPREME COURT DECISION.

"Congress has the constitutional power to make the Treasury notes of the United States a legal tender in payment of private debts, in time of peace, as well as in time of war.

"Under the act of May 31st, 1878 (ch. 146), which inacts that when any United States legal tender notes may be redeemed or received into the Treasury, and shall belong to the United States, they shall be reissued and paid out again, and kept in circulation. Notes so reissued are a legal tender.

"Submitted to Supreme Court, 1884, decided March, 1884, the opinion of the court being delivered by Mr. Justice Gray:

" Upon full consideration of the case the court is unanimously of the opinion that it cannot be distinguished in principle from the cases heretofore determined, repeated under the names of the Legal Tender cases (12 Wallace), Dooley vs. Smith, (13 Wallace) R. R. Co. vs. Johnson (15 Wallace), and Maryland vs. R. R. Co (22 Wallace.)

This should forever set at rest the question of the rights of government to issue paper money, pure and simple.

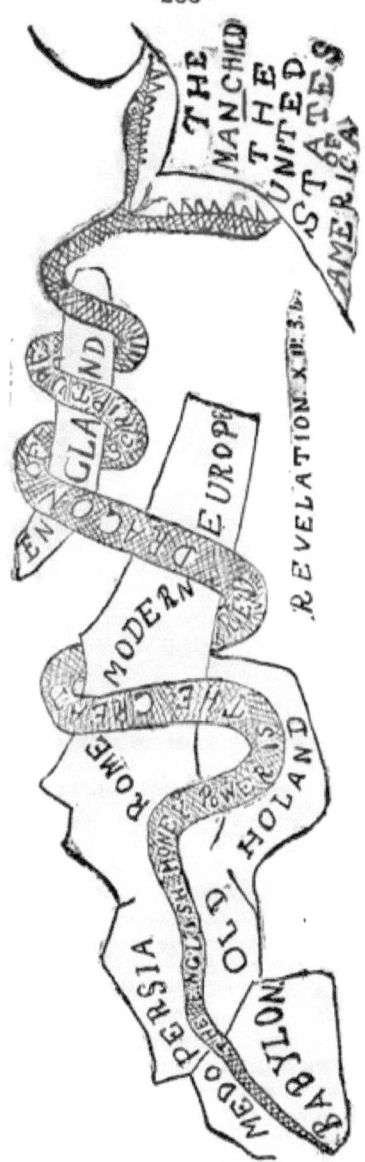

This cut fairly represents the money power as we can gather from history. It has devoured and ruined every country that it got a thorough hold of. There is no doubt it is the "Great Red Dragon" spoken of in Revelations.

A money like this, with a full legal tender act, acceptable for all dues, public and private, is absolute money.

The government has a perfect right to establish such a system as described in the book, "WHAT IS COMING," and called the *Sea Level Stable Value Money System*, without a change of the Constitution. Else what does the Constitution mean when it says that the government, "shall coin money and regulate the value thereof and foreign coin"? With such a system we could never have hard times. If you want good times, post yourself and help to make them.

Read "WHAT IS COMING!" the most complete work on finance ever written. Mailed free on receipt of cents, by the author
  LYMAN E. STOWE,
131 Catherine St.

A Safe and Reliable Plan
FOR THE ISSUE AND REGULATION
OF A GOVERNMENT PAPER MONEY.

Section 1. The Secretary of the Treasury shall be authorized to issue $200,000,000, of full legal tender paper money, good for all dues public and private. This issue shall be in denominations of one, two, five and ten dollars bills. Further issues shall follow as required until the conditions imbodied in section five are brought about, then shall the issue cease until again ordered to go on by further conditions there in mentioned.

Section 2. Our navy shall be increased, at once, second to non now known.

That patriotism may be fostered and a stimulant to early enlistment in case of war and that he who spring to his country's call may rest assured he will be dealt as liberally with as the tardy one who reluctantly takes up arms, and that only when great inducements are offered. Equalization of all soldiers bounties shall be settled at once, and the amount paid to the living soldiers or to his heirs if he is dead, and a bill formerly before the house, known as the per dime pension bill, shall be passed and become law and enforced at once; and further be it enacted that all public works shall be pushed forward at the greatest possible speed and as many new works benefical to the public good ordered as seem necessary to set idle labor at work and this money shall be paid out for all expenditures on such beneficiaries, and it is further enacted that all current expenses and all other expenses shall be paid in the same kind of money, of bills of the same and of larger denomination as becomes necessary for conviuience, except where contracts made prior to July 1st, 1895, strictly specify on the face thereof that they shall be paid in other kinds of money or commodities.

Section 3. Whenever a state or county desires to borrow money, to push public work, the government shall loan to such states or counties at one per cent. The state or county to give bonds for security.

That this money may be put in circulation as quickly as possible and that the machinery of the present banking system may be utilized the Secretary of the Treasury be instructed to loan the banks money at one per cent, at the rate of seventy-five per cent of the paid up capitol of the bank borrowing money. The government to hold a first lien on the capital stock and assets of the bank.

Section 4. It being known that all productive enterprise returnes on an average but three per cent, all interest abo e three per cent shall be denominated usury and any bank demanding a greater interest than three per cent, or refusing to loan on ample real estate security, at three per cent and still attempts to loan at a higher rate shall forfeit its charter.

A person should be able to borrow at the rate of fifty per cent of the assessed value of the property offered as security.

Section 5 The Secretary shall appoint a competent agent in each state to investigate and each agent shall report to the secretary when there is no longer an involuntary idle man in his state and the agent shall also ascertain and report the average price of five hundred staple commodities The list of commodities shall be furnished by the secretary of the treasury and when the avrage price of such commodities for the hole United States has been ascertained the secretary shall record the same and at this point the issue of money shall cease until the average price of that five hundred articles shall fall below that fixed sea level when the issue of money shall be resumed and paid out as before until the average price of those five hundred commodities has again risen to that fixed sea level. Always at this point the government shall cease to employ extraordinary labor until such time as it may be deemed necessary to employ idle labor as a balance wheel to prevent disaster. In case of influx of money from abroad or the giving up of hoarded money, which would cause the average price of the five hundred commodities to rise above that fixed sea level an increased revenue may be provided for to create a surplus in the treasury and thus reduce the out standing volume of money and bering down the price of the five hundred commodities to that fixed sea level. In this way a stable measure of comparative values may always be maintained.

Section 6. The government shall grant free coinage of gold and silver at the ratio of sixteen to one and otherwise regulated by the coinage laws of 1837, except that such coins shall be a legal tender only for the payment of bills created prior to July 1st 1895, and so specified on the face thereof that they shall be paid in such coin.

Section 7. The government shall obligate itself to pay no bills in other than this legal tender paper money after July 1st, 1895, unless unforseen conditions demand it and then by special act of congress only.

Section 8. That the government may obtain gold and silver to meet demands of former bills at the lowest possible price the secretary shall appoint special agents and they shall be continually on the watch quietly purchasing those metals for the government. Such agents shall be secretly appointed and the fact of their business kept a secret and if any one of them divulge his business to any other person, he shall be discharged from the government employ and he shall be subjected to a fine of five thousand dollars, or imprisonment for five years or both as the aggravation of the case may seem to warrant. Be it further enacted that if any number of people form a conspiracy or combination to raise the price of those metals, that they may be benefited at the government expense, they shall be considered guilty of conspiracy and treason and if convicted shall be punished by death.

Some of the matter in this article may seem foreign to the financial question and as measures belonging to other departments of government, but they are essential corrolaries of a stable system of a measure of comparative value, as they are a means of distribution as well as a balance wheel to the system Besides the navy other necessaries of war would be needed if we once obtain commercial liberty as the money loaners of the world would form a conspiracy to turn the crowned heads against us and we would be compelled to fight or submit to commercial slavery again.

The government purchases comparatively nothing abroad, consequently needs no gold and silver except to pay certain outstanding obligations. This system would not destroy those metals but on the contrary, they like all other commodities being subjected to the law of supply and demand, the demand end would be effected by the demonetization and the price would fall. As our money is not money in any other country the metals in the form of bullion would answer the commercial man just as well as coin and cost less labor to procure them. Our prosperity would force other countries to follow our example and the Lord only knows how far the price of those metals might fall; but the bankers will never willingly except this system as they could not control the country and two hundred per cent is not enough for them.

There has been a hellish attempt to deceive the people and make them believe that private corporation gold basis promissory note currency is better than a full legal tender, tax receivable paper money, by comparing the John Law gold basis gambling scheme currency of 1716, the French confiscated church property basis, assignat of 1789, the continental gold basis currency of 1876 and the wild cat state bank notes of a later period.

With such a scientific government paper money as herein described. And it is supposed by many that we have no authority worth speaking of in favor of a pure governmental paper money as against the private corporation paper promises to pay a metal money, which is an institution of a barbarous age, and one that present civilization has outgrown.

But they never mention the legal tender notes of the first United States Bank from 1710 to 1811: or the treasury notes without interest from 1812 to 1815. All legal tender, and which Galatin and Campbell, Secretaries of the Treasury say were equal to coin though bankers opposed them as they do greenbacks now. The notes of the Bank of the United States from 1816 to 1836 were full legal tender. They were for twenty years, at home and abroad, preferred to coin.

From 1837 to 1848 $100,000,000 in treasury notes without interest were preferred to coin. In 1857 Congress authorized the issue of $20,000,000 treasury notes, full legal tender for all debts due the government. And they were preferred to coin.

The demand notes of 1861 were gold basis promisary notes to be redeemed in gold, and they ran down in value. But Congress put on the fiat and by law made them legal tender, acceptable at the custom houses and in twelve hours they increased in value 20 per cent and stood at par with gold until they all disappeared. Now where is your fool that howls "fiat?"

There will be a great effort to saddle this country with a tremendous gold bearing bonded debt. It should be opposed by every honest man and if carried should be repudiated or paid in paper money.

WHAT IS MONEY?

FOR THE BENEFIT OF THOSE WHO SCOFF AT paper money and government control of the issue of money, let us quote some authorities on the subject:

WHAT IS MONEY?

"Money is a creation of law."—John Stuart Mills, Economist.

"Money is a creation of law. It is a measure of value, by comparison, whereby we ascertain the comparative values of all merchandise, or it is a sign which represents the respective values of all commodities."—Blackstone, the English Law Giver.

Attorney General Ackerman, in speaking of the legal tender act, said: "We repeat, money is not a substance, but an impression of legal decree."

"The theory of the intrinsic value of money has been abandoned by the best writers and speakers."—Encyclopedia Brittanica.

"Metalic money, while acting as coin, is identical with paper money in respect to being destitute of intrinsic value."—North British Review.

"An article is determined to be money by reason of the performance by it of certain functions, without regard to its former substance."—Appleton's American Encyclopedia.

"Money is an ideal thing; the coin or government legal tender paper bill is the tool or visible expression of that ideal thing. The tool that represents that idea depends as much upon the law of supply and demand for its value as does the **wheat** or any other commodity.

Congress alone has the right to issue money and regulate the value thereof."—Our Constitution.

"If Congress has the right, under the Constitution, to issue paper money, it was given them to be used by themselves; and not delegated to corporations or individuals."—Andrew Jackson.

"The general government ceases to be independent, it ceases to be safe, when the national currency is at the will of a company"—Thos. H. Benton.

Read the following extract from a speech of John C. Calhoun of South Carolina, delivered in the United States senate during the panic of '37-38; "We are told there is no instance of a government paper that did not depreciate. In reply I affirm there is none, assuming the form that I propose, that ever did depreciate. Whenever a paper receivable in the dues of a government had anything like a fair trial it has succeeded."

"When all our paper money is made payable in specie on demand, it will prove the most certain means that can be used to fertilize the rich man's field by the sweat of the poor man's brow." —Daniel Webster.

"Whatever a government agrees to receive in payment of the public dues, as a medium of circulation is money, no matter what its form may be, trading notes, drafts, etc. Such bills or paper issued under the authority of the United States is money."—Henry Clay, in the Senate, 1837.

"Gold and silver are not intrinsically of the same value with iron No method has hitherto been found to establish a medium of trade equal in all its advantages, to bills of credit, made a legal tender."—Benjamin Franklin.

"I sincerely believe that banking institutions are more dangerous to liberty than standing armies."—Thomas Jefferson's Work's Vol. VI page 608.

"Bank paper must be suppressed and the circulating medium must be restored to the nation, to whom it belongs. It is the only fund on which they can rely for loans; it is the only resource which can never fail them, and it is an abundant one for every necessary purpose. Treasury bills, bottomed on taxes, bearing interest or not bearing interest, as may be found necessary, thrown into circulation, will take the place of so much gold and silver." Thos. Jefferson's Works Vol VI. page 199, letter of Sept. 11th, 1813.

"I have ever opposed money of bankers; not of those discounting for cash, but of those fostering their own paper in circulation and thus banishing our cash. My zeal against these institutions was so warm and open at the establishment of the bank of the the United States that I was derided as a maniac by the tribe of bank mongers who were seeking to filch from the public."—Thomas Jefferson in a letter to President Adams, Jan. 24, 1814.

"Charter a bank with $35,000,000, let it establish and learn its power, and then find, if you can, means to b il that cat: it will be beyond your power, it will overawe Congress and laugh at your laws."—John Randolph.

"As a result of the war, corporations have been enthroned, and an era of corruption in high places will follow, and the money power of the country will endeavor to prolong its reign by working upon the prejudices of the people until all wealth is aggregated in a few hands, and the republic is destroyed. I feel at this moment more anxiety for the safety of my country than ever before, even in the midst of the war. God grant that my suspicions may prove groundless."—Abraham Lincoln.

We believe that circumstantial evidence shows that Mr. Lincoln's position backed by such utterances, cost him his life.

"Whoever controls the volume of money in any country is absolute master of all industry and commerce." —James A. Garfield.

Now let us handle gold and silver for a few minutes. King Soloman demonetized silver, the lessor metal, and brought destruction and ruin to his country.

Five hundred B. C., the precious metals were found inadequate to the needs of Greece. Solon reduced the metal in the coin, thereby expanding the currency, and thus saved Attica from a deluge of blood.

Five hundred years later Julius Cæsar found the precious metals insufficient to supply the circulating medium of Rome, and he took the privilege of coining money from the wealthy families, to whom it had been granted, and restored it to the government, to whom it belonged, and he created a cheap metal money, and established public works and paid it out to labor; thus creating good times and the peaple loved Cæsar, but the wealthy senators murdered him with their own hands.

The Romans, on several occasions, were compelled to reduce the metal in the coins to increase the volume of money to carry on their wars.

"At the Christian era the metalic money of the Roman Empire amounted to $1,800,000,000, by the end of the Fifteenth century it had shrunk to less than $200,000,000. * * * History records no other such disastrous transition as that from the Roman Empire to the Dark Ages. * * * It is a suggestive coincidence that the first glimmer of light only came with the invention of bills of exchange, and paper substitutes, through which the scanty stock of the precious metals was increased in efficiency."—Report of the United States Silver Commission of 1876.

England was compelled to reduce the metal in her coin several times and the money changers tried to force her back, but failed. She was finally compelled to adopt paper and suspend specie payment.

Gold deserted the United States on several occasions and always brought disaster until we resorted to paper money, when the absence of gold did not trouble us until we attempted to get back to a gold standard, when it brought ruin and dispair.

Henry A. Martin, the French historian, tells us that France tried to adopt a system of paper money, but the money changers crippled it as did our bankers cripple our paper money during the war, yet such prosperity did that money give France that England determined to destroy its power and paid from her secret service fund one Dembies, a cabinet officer, a hundred thousand crowns per annum t intrigue against this money and as much more to M. D'Argenson for the same purpose.

It would not be hard to point out the Dembies and D'Argensons, judging by their work.

The bankers told Andrew Jackson if he vetoed the old United States bank bill they would ruin the business of the country.

He vetoed it and some one tried to assassinate him; he well knew what for.

In 1881 Congress was flooded with petitions to pay the bonds with paper or silver, or to convert them into small interest bearing bonds, payable at the goverment's option. The bankers said if you do either we will ruin the business interests. This is known as the bankers rebellion of 1881. Freeman O. Wiley! whither are we drifting as a nation. Congress failed to do either, but Garfield did convert them into small interest bearing bonds and circumstances point to that, and his utterences upon the finance question at that time as the cause of his assassination.

The bankers hate the people's money and are determined to convert it into interest bearing bonds; there is $496,000,000, of it that cost the people comparatively nothing but if converted into bonds it would cost us eleven millions of dollars per annum to pay the interest.

On page 239 of this book, which was first published in 1895, says there will be an attempt to saddle this country with debt. We have now an estimated and inflated value of 140 billion of wealth, with 85 billions of debt from National to corporate, to say nothing of private debt and open account, and the cost of living higher than ever known, and millions of people out of employment.

Lord Macaulay, the English historian, said the moneyed classes would hesitate at nothing.

Indeed they are more dangerous to humanity, justice and honor than a band of pirates, or wild beasts. What we must have is a powerful secret society to meet them on their own ground.

Upon revising "What Is Coming," I found page 264 left blank, so thought I would use it to sing the praises of the author, who finds published praises are paid for anyway, and the reformer has so many enemies, there are more who stand ready to dig his grave than sing his praises.

Though I am the author of 23 books, large and small, and have many letters of thanks and congratulations, so far from the press giving me a kind word, some of the papers and magazines squirm when I offer a book for review, or politely decline to advertise Astrology, and return my money, or give me rates so high they are prohibitive, otherwise advertising in papers and magazines is a waste of money for "What Is Coming" never had $10 worth of advertising done for it, yet it sold itself 2,000 copies. Bible Astrology is now on its third thousand, and I will soon publish the letters of firms who have declined to review the book, or accept my money for advertising.

Whether I am a prophet or not, is plainly seen by the illustration above, which is taken from my "Poetical Drifts of Thought," published in 1884. The original drawing was made in 1866, and a gasoline engine predicted at that time.

:38 Catherine St., Detroit, Mich.

PART TWO.

FINANCE IN PROPHECY.

It will seem strange to many that a *theological* subject should be discussed at the same time, and between the same covers, inclosing one on *political economy*, but, from the fact that the signs of the times and many scriptural passages would go to show that they belong together. From Genesis to Revelation the Bible deals with governments, far more than with the individual. Comparatively few, but rigid instructions, are given to the individual, while all the aim and purpose seems to be to establish or restore a perfect government.

The Ten Commandments and the added one by Christ, "Love one another," together with the instruction that "pure and undefiled religion before God is to visit the widow and the fatherless in their afflictions, and keep yourself unspotted from the world," is sufficient, if followed out, to insure a participation in the government of Christ's kingdom, and a final rest in heaven.

Christ says: "For where two or three are gathered together in my name, there am I in the midst of them." There is no dogma or creed preached here, and one man has as much right to set up a creed as another, so long as he adheres to this and teaches in the name of Christ, for "Jesus said unto him, Forbid him not, for he that is not against us is for us."—St. Luke IX., 50. Therefore, I shall give my own understanding of Scriptures, adhering to Christ's teachings in its sweetness and simplicity.

If I seemingly go outside of the Scriptures for truths, it is not to set up false doctrines, but because that book is not large enough to hold instructions in all the branches of science, and for aught we know the twenty-three books of the Bible that are lost, when found may contain the very things that I am inspired to write here. I use the term *inspired* in the sense that all authors must admit to —that all productions of deep thought are partly the result of unseen forces.

If God is omnipotent and omnipresent, he is the author of all things, and is in everything. Consequently there can be no place without Him, not even the most minute atom or smallest space can exist but what He is in it; therefore we must be as much a part of God, as a finger is a part of one's self.

Our individuality is but to ourselves, each a part of the eternal whole, necessary to that eternal whole. Each in acting one ramification of a gigantic plan, and the better we act our parts, the greater harmony, and the pleasanter our periods of peaceful rest must be, and as Christ said, "The kingdom of God is within you."—Luke 17. 21.

It shows to us that there is a condition of mind, so all other things must be a condition of mind, and all things must be for a testimony to the purpose of his plan. But why a plan, and what the purpose of the plan? In this work we have not room for a lengthy philosophical discussion of the subject, but will take the matter up at as near first principles as the finite mind can grasp.

TIME, SPACE AND MATTER

are, and always have been, matters of great concern to the

philosophical thinker, but in my estimation there are three things that do not exist in the economy of God.

Time is eternity—an everlasting now—to the conception of man divided by events. This is proven by lengthy dreams, which are known to flash through a man's mind in an instant, and by the life time that in an instant runs, panoramic like, before a drowning man.

SPACE AND MATTER

must now be treated from another standpoint, nor do I expect to prove to the satisfaction of any person that these things do not exist. I only wish to get as good a foundation for a starting point for my main question, as possible.

In discussing space I must admit that the finite mind cannot conceive of its own existence or that of the Almighty, of which man is an infinitesimally small part, can exist without a space in which to dwell, but to the senses of man himself, he can never be positive that that space is real. It may be a condition of mind, but it will be found easier to decide that matter only exists in the condition of mind, or at least, that man can never be certain that it exists in real indestructable substance.

In a dream you see new places, new faces, you walk, you ride, and though confined in your little 8x10 bedroom, as dark as Egyptian midnight, the daylight you see is as real and as beautiful as any daylight. The space you look into or traverse is just as real as any, the substance is real substance to your mind. You would not believe you were dreaming at the time, but, you say, I awoke to real life. Pshaw! cannot you see you may be dreaming now, and may awake to a life much more real than this life, which is so full of contradictions and absurdities? Can you positively swear that you are not dreaming this moment, and will awake and say, What a strange book I was reading. Then, if that be true, man can never be fully satisfied but what he is in a condition of mind subject to some more powerful mind, and sees what that mind desires him to see; or he may be subject to some condition of which natural cause has brought his own mind, and nothing is really what it seems. Thus,

THE HYPNOTIC STATE

gives us to understand how it was possible for God to create the World or universe from nothing.

Let us take twelve people, all good hypnotic subjects, to six of them I will say: "Behold what a beautiful rural scene, the rolling ground, the green grass, the shrubs and flowers, the bees and the birds, how grand the music, and sweet the perfumed air. The orange trees are laden with fruit. Sit you down and feast. Here is a place for a picnic. But, my! how warm. You perspire at every pore. Lay by your coats and capes." They do my bidding. These six are in a world entirely their own. They do not see me or the other six of their companions.

I can become a god to them for the time being, if I will. I can leave them partly subject to their own minds, or hold them entirely subject to mine.

They could not make themselves sweat, but I cause them to perspire freely.

I now take the other six and picture to them a winter scene: "The beautiful lake of glary ice, with its band of merry skaters; the snow-clad hill with its happy coasters: the sleighing parties; the shouts of joy and jingling bells." They see and hear it all, but it is entirely blank to the six pic-nicers in the summer scenes.

I have them shiver with cold, appropriating the garments that the others left off, while the others sweat without them. Each party is unconscious of the presence of the other, though in touching distance of one another.

Each party has a world of their own that others do not see.

Then if I can do this, and make a world for my fellow man, how much more can the great God of the universe do? He can grant us, who are parts of himself, an ego to exist forever, or destroy that individuality at will, taking us back into the undivided whole, to be re-established into an identity where it may please him. He can will as many worlds or systems as he pleases, and clothe them with all the intricicies of creation that pleases his fancy, and which becomes a science for us to study and finally to trace back to mind itself, as we seem to do in chemistry.

In my recollection it was taught that there were four elements—earth, water, air and fire. Now we know they are not elements, but are compounds, and we find there are seventy-one elements, and each atom acting upon the same law or principle that we act—of like and dislike, love and hate, attraction and repulsion. This is not all. We see it is possible each element is dissoluable into ether, a substance which penetrates all other substances, and possibly back to mind itself.

Cook, in his "New Chemistry," says: "Every atom of matter seems to possess its proportion of mind." But if God is everywhere, there is no matter, but all is mind, though possibly subject to a central government as man is controlled by the nervous force centered in the brain.

As it is impossible for us to conceive of a center without a circumference, it is impossible for the finite to comprehend the infinite. But the action of chemistry teaches us that mind is active in the smallest atom of matter, and we see apparent reason displayed in the plant that seems to exercise intelligence in seeking water or light, and that intelligence increases as the higher organic matter becomes more perfect. Man, standing at the head of organic matter, sees the possibility that he is the result of organic matter, and that when the organization ceases he ceases to exist as an intelligent entity, forever. On the other hand, it is no stranger that we should live again than that we now live, nor is it any stranger that we have lived before than that we now live.

For reasons that will be given farther on this matter can never be settled to the satisfaction of all men, but there are three classes that have solved the question satisfactorily to themselves.

The materalist, with a great deal of reason, for he believes that there is no mind outside of organized matter, and the more perfect the organization, the more perfect the mind.

The theologian rests his belief upon faith, and the most intelligent ground their faith in the Bible, of which twenty-three books are lost, which the Bible speaks of, and how many more we don't know, or what they would reveal to us if we had them, besides there are many interpolations. So we can expect to get but little satisfaction from him, even if he be right.

Now, as theologians are divided and quarreling among themselves, each creed and sect declaring all others are wrong and sure to be lost, we must turn to the very fundamental principles of their doctrine to get the nearest to the truth, or safest grounds on which they can stand, and we will find Christ says:

"Except ye be converted and become as little children, ye shall not enter the kingdom of heaven."—Matt. 18:3.

Now a man with a dogma to crowd upon others *willy-nilly*, is hardly like a little child to be lead. Again Christ says: "For where two or three are gathered together in my name, there am I in the midst of them." He did not say two or three of this church or that church, but two or three in his name. Therefore an abiding faith in God and in Christ the Son of God is the safest ground for them to tread, and let every one decide for himself his peculiar dogma and manner of worship.

THE STUDENT OF PSYCHIC PHENOMENA

basis his beliefs on much broader ground. He accepts all the truth that science may teach, acknowledging evolution with all of its daily evidence to be a fact. He watches the expression of thought in the most minute atom, and traces it to the broadest intelligence of man. He pries into every phenomena of nature. He understands there are more wonders in the invisible world than ever dreamed of in our wildest imagination. He goes into the intricicies of hypnotism, and sees that it is possible to create, to the human mind for the time at least, a tangible something from thought, or mind alone. To what is real to some and superstitution to others, he delves in to get the real kernal of truth.

He calls upon the Astrologer, the Phrenologist, the Palmist, the Clairvoyant and the Spiritualist, and the Physiognomist. Here he is surprised to find they all, more or less accurately, give a description of his former life and manly attributes, and some of them go so far into the future as to prove to him, beyond a doubt that man has a destiny laid out before him. If these people are truthful and adepts in their profession, he finds they all agree in the main. He is satisfied now that his destiny is laid out, and that the professionals of six different branches of science are able to traverse the path of his past life, and a large portion of his future life. He sees how it was possible for Christ to tell the woman at the well of her past life and of her future. John 4:17.

Many who have been deceived by fakirs, or have not developed far enough into a spiritual mind to receive a satisfactory reading, will deny that there are any truthful professionals in these sciences, or that anything of our future life can be foretold. But I know whereof I speak and "the proof of the pudding is after eating."

Now, if man has a destiny that can be read, it is proof to the student of psychic phenomena that there must have been a destiner, for this is beyond the control of the most intelligent man. He is now in a shape to believe in and receive communications from the unseen world. Though his efforts here are blocked, and communications unsatisfactory and meager. He does not give up, for he knows that every science has had to stem the tide of popular prejudice and pave its way, step by step, with the sweat and toil and labored energies of the faithful student seeking truth. Hypatia, the Grecian scholar, was torn limb from limb, burned to ashes, and the ashes scattered to the winds; Galileo was imprisoned; Bruno burned at the stake; Columbus put in chains; Fulton called a crank, to say nothing of the thousands of christian martyrs that have suffered because they tried to evolve something better than the stagnated principles and exploded theories of threadbare and degraded ages. The student of psychic phenomena will not stop here. After proving that man has a destiny, and that there is a destiner, and that he can communicate with unseen beings. He is determined to determined to develop his theories and find out all that may be found out. He is now ready to accept almost anything as truth until proved false, thinking it better for mankind to believe a hundred lies, until they fall to pieces of their own rottenness, than to dispute one great truth, and thereby stand a stumbling block in the way of human progress. He has found that faith is an absolute necessity to the gathering of truth. He finds that the man who attends the spiritual seance without charity and faith, will get little satisfaction. What does this lead him to? It leads him back to Bible teaching. He finds faith is an absolute necessity. Though "faith without works is dead." No progress could be made without faith. Even the seed would not be planted without faith, or the harvested food taken into the stomach without faith or the stomach assimilate without faith. Though you have all of the faith in the world and have not charity for others weakness, what availeth it. Here let me quote from I. Corinthians XIII.:

"Though I speak with the tongues of men and of angels, and have not charity, I am become as sounding brass, or a tinkling cymbal.

"And though I have the gift of prophecy, and understand all mysteries, and all knowledge; and though I have all faith, so that I could remove mountains, and have not charity, I am nothing.

"And though I bestow all my goods to feed the poor, and though I give my body to be burned, and have not charity, it profiteth me nothing.

"Charity suffereth long, and is kind; charity envieth not; charity vaunteth not itself, is not puffed up.

"Doth not behave itself unseemly, seeketh not her own, is not easily provoked, thinketh no evil.

"Rejoiceth not in iniquity, but rejoiceth in the truth;

"BEARETH ALL THINGS, BELEIVETH ALL THINGS, HOPETH ALL THINGS, ENDURETH ALL THINGS."

I have put the above in caps to draw especial attention to the necessity of faith.

"Charity never faileth: but whether there be prophecies, they shall fail; whether there be tongues, they shall cease; whether there be knowledge, it shall vanish away.

"For we know in part, and we prophesy in part.

"But when that which is perfect is come, then than that which is in part shall be done away."

After reading the above you can see why you have not received better satisfaction in your investigations. You had no *charity* for those who were trying to aid you, you had no faith in your work, and you could not see through the vail. You went seeking lies and you got lies.

Go up the broad Mississippi and you will find its muddy waters swelled by many filthy currents, at length you reach the broad Missouri, whose waters seem more muddy than all the rest, though it be fed by many a clear mountain stream, while the Mississippi itself, above the Missouri, is tolerably clear. But trace up all of these streams, and if they do not, sooner or later become dry beds, you will find they are fed from the living waters of some mountain stream or spring. But the great currents become muddy as they flow through the low lands. The great Christian Church is likened to the mighty Missouri. It started with pure waters at the fountain head, but it has become filthy, carrying its filth to the masses, adding mud to the aggregate of streams that flow to the sea—the people—because it has lost its tolerance, charity. If the above be true we must not expect to gain the whole truth and perfect satisfaction until that which is perfect has come—then that which is imperfect shall be done away.

"When I was a child, I spake as a child. I thought as a child; when I became a man I put away childish things.

"For now we see through a glass darkly, but then face to face: now I know in part; but then shall I know even as also I am known.

"And now abideth FAITH, HOPE, CHARITY, these three: but the greatest of these is CHARITY."

Become as a little child, in the name of Christ, seeking truth with *faith, hope and charity*, making the study of religion a science, and we will unbar the gates of heaven, for "the kingdom of God is within you."

The student of psychic phenomena, now driven back to the Bible, wonders why it is veiled in mystery? Why God did not see to it that the books were kept together and properly translated, so that bickerings and quarreling over it would not be necessary. He then reasons that no substance can be brightened without friction, the human mind is no exception. Then he wonders if the divine mind would ever recognize joy if it had never thought of sorrow, know sweet from bitter or sour from sweet, if he had never thought of the opposite.

Then he recognizes the fact that it is quite possible that it was necessary for man, in a great measure, to work out his destiny. If so, the Bible is purposely veiled that he should unroll the puzzle and so develop a character.

This is not all he sees that all nature is against him. A continual struggle for an existence is his lot, with weeds and thorns to block his way. And pain, and sickness and death, his lot, and the worst thing of all to contend against, is his own selfish nature. He quotes one of our great poets:

"Man's inhumanity to man,
Makes countless thousands mourn."

He wonders why a just and alwise God should make this so? He is told it is because of Adam's sin. But he knows that no just man, much less a just God, would punish the children for what the parents did thousands of generations ago. Then he reasons that it must be metiforical and the Garden of Eden is something more than a patch of earthly ground of vegetation, and he seeks the truth. But where? From the fountain head of wisdom. "Ask and ye shall receive; knock and it shall be opened unto you." He knocks, and it is opened, he asks and does receive all that his finite mind can hold. He reasons, and with the aid of God, reaches this conclusion. There is no such thing as matter; God is a mighty principle that takes in all things. That there is nothing without him. This being the case, there can be no matter.

Taking the liberty to coin a

phrase that will convey to the mind the existence of an imponderable something in the form of a pandrible substance, I will say we are mere specks of concentrated principle revolving upon an axis, and that unconscious motion is the the only motion that we have. Our bodies and all our seeming motions are but thought—not mere imagination of our own, but the thought of the great controling principle, sent out on currents of his will, which reaches us, and becoming reality to us, we all see as near alike as our different standpoints will allow.

Thus our specks of concentrated principle or mind floating in a sea of mind, and reached by currents of will power. I just had this last assertion most beautifully illustrated to me. Professors Wallace and Howard, clairvoyants, advertised here in our city, and I called upon them. According to instructions, I wrote ten questions, differing from each other in purpose as much as possible. No one was present when I wrote them. I folded up the little pieces of paper and mixed them up and threw them on the table. There was no possible way for them to know what questions I had asked, if any, or to know one from the other. Yet the young man made no mistake in picking out the paper containing the question, handing it to me without looking at it, and answering it correctly.

Now this could not be mind reading, as I could not have picked out the questions, and some of them I had forgotten I had asked them. Then how did he get it? I answer that he got it in this way. When I wrote the question or even thought of it, it was stamped in the sea of mind surrounding me, and he having the sixth sense, that is being evolved in man, very highly developed, read it in this sea of mind. And this also accounts for the fact that two people often think of the same thing at, seemingly, one and the same time, while, in fact, one of them thought of it, and it immediately flashed on a current of mind and impressed the other person, and, speech being so much slower, both spoke seemingly at once. This also accounts for the approach of one person being sent ahead to one or more people who exclaim: "Speak of the devil and he will appear."

Again I say, the finite mind cannot comprehend the infinite being of which each of us is a part.

The cut below will convey the writer's idea much better than can be done in cold print. The central figure or the eye represents the source from which all power flows. Though, as we cannot conceive of a center in a boundless space, the center is everywhere, or, in other words, the great principle of love of knowledge, truth, kindness, and all that will bring universal happiness. The direct rays emanating from the center, represents the will power of this principle. The large circle represents the will power bringing order out of chaos. The next larger circle represents governments, some on the direct lines of his will, and ready to aid others farther away from those lines. The third line of circles represents communities in more or less direct communication with the perfected plan of God.

The very small dots are the individual beings, smaller or or greater as the case may be. Each individual or community are surrounded with an atmosphere or influence, which results for their immediate good or bad, as the case may be. But all for ultimate good, as there is nothing really bad. Bad only as it affects our condition of mind at the time being.

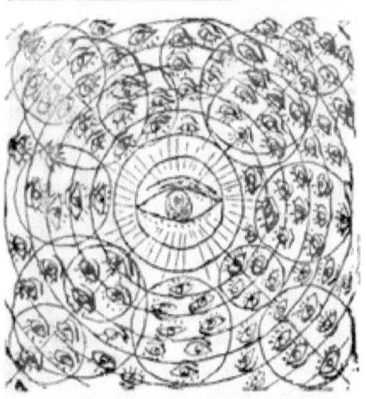

It will be seen by this cut, and the former description, that it is the author's design to picture a great sea of mind, divided into concentrated parts floating in a sea of thought. Each individual is subject to his surroundings. He can aid his personal circle by getting as near to the direct rays or purpose of God as his understanding will allow. By his personal efforts he will aid the community. The community may aid the nation, and when once the current of truth is drawn upon, the stream increases, as the typifing of any great body of water represents, that pressure rapidly widens the stream. Thus prayer is the first step toward inviting that pure current.

GOD

Now having established the thought of a universal sea of mind, and no matter. The understanding of the purpose of this controlling principle becomes our next work. As there is nothing but God, what must be the occupation of such a being? How does he exist, and for what purpose?

Such a being must occupy his powers, and knowledge must be his aim.

What, he then does not know all things? you say.

I ask, could he know joy if he had never thought of sorrow? Could he know bitter from sweet had he never thought of the opposite, or if he knew them could we know them without experience—and we a part of him?

Very well then, he directly or indirectly, is laboring for knowledge, either for the central principle or to convey it to the ultimate portions of himself.

Therefore, he is everlastingly laying plans for us to solve, either for his direct knowledge or for us, an indirect knowledge.

"Wisdom," says the Scriptures, is the principal thing; therefore "get wisdom; and, with all of thy getting get understanding. Exalt her, and she shall promote thee: she shall bring thee to honor, when thou dost embrace her. She shall give to thy head an ornament of grace; a crown of glory shall she deliver to thee."

From this we must judge that the allegorical story of the tree of knowledge placed in the Garden of Eden was for a good purpose, and even the tempter placed there for a good purpose. It is new our duty to find out that purpose.

GOD HAD HIS PERIODS OF LABOR AND HIS PERIODS OF REST. GEN. 2:2.

This is typtfied in our Sunday or seventh day, in the millinium or seventh thousand year, and finally in the great period of rest called Heaven.

That this might be well and thoroughly forced upon the attention of man for his future study, the Mosaic law was very severe, even to the stoning to death the man who was caught gathering sticks on that day.

In this period of rest, called Heaven, all of man's desires are gratified, so long as he observes the law. First he must think of God, the creator of all things. Thus he displays his faith. I have before shown how necessary faith is. I will now illustrate again by the twelve hypnotic subjects. We will say ten of them are perfect subjects, the eleventh one says, "Yes; I am willing to be hypnotized *if you can do it.*" Here he displays his lack of faith in a positive denial of my powers, and the whole matter rests with himself. He has no faith that I can hypnotize him, consequently cannot enjoy the pleasure of the rural scene, fruit, flowers, music, and other temporary gifts within my power to bestow. The twelfth man, in a melancholly manner, says, "I would like to enjoy what I know you can give to these people, and I sincerely hope you will be able to bestow those gifts upon me in the same manner." Now he has expressed his lack of faith as much as the former. His desire may be all right, but his lack of faith is eminent.

This lack of faith can only be overcome by a constant sacrifice of personal desires and determination to believe the truth, when the clear mountain stream, of the water of life, or source of all purity, is tapped and allowed to flow in and push out the roilly waters of the low lands, or individual selfishness. I say individual selfishness, because the second law, or rather the third law, as the first law of heaven, is order. But to obtain one's desires in Heaven, as before stated, we must first think of the great Creator with faith that he can give us those desires. The next thing we must harbor no individual selfishness, which is the third law, but must think of the masses and forbear to wish for something that would make some one else unhappy, for in that case we would turn Heaven into a hell. We can see that by the fearful strife for an existence here on earth, through the selfishness of man, nature has given us an abundance of everything in undeveloped wealth, but the few selfish have monopolized the land, and all gifts of nature, and prevent their fellow man from earning an honest living.

But, Heaven itself would become monotonous, after a while, for this reason, mind cannot understand what it has not experienced, and this is why the boy can never learn through the experience of the father, though told a thousand times he must turn the machine himself, before he understands how the wheels go round, or the labor required to set it in motion.

Confine a number of people in a room, give them music, books, games, and all that their conceptions require, and for a time it will be heaven for them. But after a time all of these things become old and stale, and the going over and over again becomes monotonous. They look across the street and see people, seemingly enjoying something different, their desires are awakened, they wish to get over there, and though out in the street it is slush and mud, and storm, but what of that, they will brave hell itself before they will longer remain in that place; that that was once their heaven, but now their hell. Thus the inhabitants of Heaven willingly eat of the forbidden fruit of the tree of knowledge and are driven from the Garden of Eden, and go down, down into chaos, only to come up through one of God's plans, under the law of evolution. First in the gaseous matter, then in the fire, then in rock, then in the soft earth, then in the vegetation, then in the reptilian life, then in the lower animals, then to man. (*See Stowe's Poetical Drifts of Thought.*) Nor does he stop here, but he lives and dies, and is born again for many times. Each time drawing nearer and nearer to that heaven which he left, finally reaching there, on a higher plane than when he started, enjoying more because he knows more, and where he will remain until it becomes monotonous, when he will again, willingly eat of the forbidden fruit, forbidden only providing he wished to remain, but if he wishes greater joy he willingly eats of the tree of knowledge, and goes down into God's workshop or school room forever aiding the great Creator, of which he is a part, enacting one ramification of God's mighty plans. And of which we are given here in shadows enough to feed our desires for knowledge, and enable us to understand and enjoy the experience after our return to Heaven.

"Hence there is more joy over one sinner who repents, than the ninety and nine who never went astray."

The old soldier had a high aim and purpose when he enlisted for the war, though he knew he would suffer, and even today he suffers for his good work done over thirty years ago, yet where is there one who would trade that experience today for any earthly blessing. He learned a bitter lesson, that has become a morsel sweet to remember.

At each death man goes into the spirit life, where he reviews his past life, and rests until willingly returning to this life, chosing here the part he shall play in some combination with others. Possibly as a victim of a murder, or the murderer himself. Thus experiencing all phases of life.

If the murderer overcomes his desire, he has strengthened his will power, which will always stay by him and push him higher in his work that he may graduate that much quicker. He that would have been the victim, dies of accident, or disease, as his part has been fulfilled.

The question is asked, Why do we not remember some of our former lives?

Who wants to be told of a novel before he reads it? Who would solve a puzzle, or remember it afterwards that had already been explained to him? We came here for experience and did not wish to bring anything of former lives into this one, except it is a part of a former life that we have in some way neglected to fulfil. When on rare occasions it is brought back to this one, hence we have the musical prodigy. The natural thief, mathematician, or any other born wonder. It is this way that man's destiny is placed before him, and which may in part be read by clairvoyants. But how much the individual may overcome, only God knows, hence we get no perfect clairvoyant readings.

I am asked here: "What other authority have you for advancing this Buddistic doctrine of reincarnation?"

I answer, first that it is not a Buddistic docrine, but is a biblical doctrine.

"What? A biblical doctrine! We never heard of such a thing. Where can you find it in the Bible?"

Well, hear what Christ says about it, Matt. 11:10-11:

"Verily, I say unto you, among them that are born of woman there hath not risen a greater than John the Baptist; and if ye will receive it, this is Elias, which was for to come."

This is plain enough. But, few would receive it at that day.

Elijah, in the Greek, is rendered Elias; rendered in English translation both Elijah and Elias.

Now let it be remembered that the II. Kings 2:11 tells us this:

"And it came to pass, when the Lord would take up Elijah into heaven by a whirlwind, that Elijah went with Elisha from Gilgal. And it came to pass, as they still went on and talked, that there appeared a chariot of fire and horses of fire and parted them both assunder; and Elijah went by a whirlwind into heaven."

This was 880 years before Christ

Now let us see what was promised about this matter. Malachi 4:5 says:

"Behold, I will send you, Elijah, the prophet before the coming of the great day of the Lord."

Now if you will turn to Luke 1 you will see with what care God provided for and watched over his messenger upon his reincarnation, with Zacharias for an earthly father and Elizabeth for an earthly mother.

Matt. 17: 10-14: "And his disciples asked him, saying, why then say the scribes that Elias must first come? And Jesus answered and said unto them, Elias truly shall first come; but I say unto you that Elias is come ALREADY, and they knew him not. Then the disciples understood that he spake unto them of John the Baptist."

Again in Mrk 9:11:13:

"And they asked him, saying, Why say the scribes that Elias must first come? And he answered and told them, Elias, verily cometh first; but I say unto you that Elias is indeed come, and they have done unto him whatsoever they listed."

Remember they beheaded John. Is not this evidence of reincarnation? It is not positive that they understood it that way, at that time? See what Heb. 13:2 says of it:

"Be not forgetful to entertain strangers: for thereby some have entertained angels unawares."

Now that the dead shall come up and live and reign with Christ in his kingdom a thousand years, is shown us in many places, and especially in Revelations, chapter 20:

"Blessed and holy is he that hath part in the first resurrection; on such the second death hath no power; but they shall be priests of God and of Christ, and shall reign with him a thousand years; but the rest of the dead liveth not again until the thousand years were finished."

This has reference to the millennium, of which is Sunday, and no work is to be done on that day, but more of this as we proceed.

Man declares the beast has no soul, but perishes with death. But the beast possesses every attribute of man, only in a lesser degree. He suffers and dies. He loves and he hates. He remembers and he forgets. He sorrows and he joys.

Chemistry and all nature provides a recompense. But man claims a recompense for himself, but denies a recompense for the suffering brute creation. But reincarnation, under the evolution theory, gives a recompense for all, and makes our many lives so many school days. With our periods of rest. The spirit state is shadowed in our night, the reincarnated condition as our day. The millennium thousand years as our Sunday, and this brings us to God's plan on this earth.

We are told that he made the world in six days, and finished or rested on the seventh.

Man has never told us of what he made the world. But as scientist cant conceive of something being made from nothing, he concludes that matter always existed. But as God is everywhere, he would have to be in every part of matter, and there can be no room for God and matter, consequently the world of matter is but an idea, or thought of God, which rests in a condition of our mind, the same as the worlds I built for my hypnotic subjects, as that rests in the condition of their minds. But as they are already under a greater control than mine; my control is subject to that greater control. And so hypnotism stands a testimony for a good purpose.

Some one says, then it is all imagination.

No; for imagination belongs to the individual, while the hypnotic state sees a picture drawn from another powerful mind, and in our life, which is a more powerful condition of life, what we sense becomes a greater reality.

Then God made the world in six days. Yes, but he had no reference to our twenty-four hour day, when he was talking.

"How do you make that out?"

First, Because he did not make the sun until the fourth day, which was left on purpose until that day, as a point of evidence to aid us in our study.

Secondly, When he placed Adam and Eve in the Garden and told them they must not partake of the forbidden fruit, that he really intended they should eat of, and placed a tempter there that they might be tempted to eat and so obtain knowledge. He said: "But of the tree of knowledge of good and evil, thou shalt not eat of it: for in the day that thou eatest thereof, thou shalt surely die."—Gen. 2:17.

But the serpent said: "Ye shall not surely die."

Now Adam lived nine hundred years, and Bob Ingersol says the serpent told the truth and God lied. And the theologians, try to get out of it by twisting it around and saying God did not mean what he said, but he meant a spiritual death. But we have better evidence than that for God was not talking about Adam's twenty-four hour day, but about his thousand year day.

"But, beloved, be not ignorant of this one thing, that one day is with the Lord as a thousand years, and a thousand years as one day."—II. Peter 3:8.

Now no man ever lived a thousand years, not even Mathuslah.

Is this all the evidence that we have of this thousand year day?

No for we have the evidence that God does his work in weeks, and that seven, and three, are prophetic numbers. Therefore, every seventh thousand year God allows man a millennium or rest of a thousand of our years.

This is typified in our Sunday, as well as in the old Jewish law. God commanded that every seventh year the land should be allowed to rest.

"And six years thou shalt sow thy land, and shalt gather in the fruits thereof:

"But the seventh year though shalt let it rest and lie still; that the poor of thy people may eat: and what they leave the beasts of the field shall eat. In like manner thou shalt deal with thy vineyard, and with thy oliveyard."—Exodus 23:10-11.

Three is a prophetic number. The week is divided in three parts. It was two thousand years from Adam to the flood, and then a change of dispensation. It was two thousand years from the flood to Christ, and then a change of dispensation.

It is now nearly two thousand and we are about to have another change of dispensation, and the millennium year or Sunday of a thousand years will be ushered in.

Now before I proceed with this I must show that the world was inhabited before Adam's time. But God commenced this week's work with Adam's time for a starting point.

We have both in geology and archæology evidence that the world has existed many more than six thousand years. And the fact that Cane went to the land of Nod and took himself a wife i. e. is biblical evidence. And this has always been a stumbling block for Bible students, but it is a proof that the world was inhabited before Adam's time. But our week started with Adam, and will close with the eve of the millennium Sunday, when another week of labor will commence.

"And Satan will be loosed for a season to deceive the nations."

And those who are not fit to take a higher sphere must go on through six thousand years of strife, living and dying, and being born again.

"And I saw thrones and they sat upon them and judgment was given unto them: and I saw those of them that were beheaded for the witness of Jesus, and for the word of God, and which had not worshipped the beast, neither his image, neither had received his mark upon their foreheads, or in their hands; and they lived and reigned with Christ a thousand years.

"But the rest of the dead lived not again until the thousand years were finished. This is the first resurrection.

"Blessed and holy is he that hath part in the first resurrection, on such the second death hath no part, but they shall be priests (to others) of God and of Christ, and shall reign with him a thousand years.

"And when the thousand years are expired, Satan shall be loosed out of his prison.

"And shall go out to deceive the nations, which are in the four quarters of the earth, Gog and Magog to gather them together for battle: the number of whom are as the sand of the sea."—Rev. 20:4-8.

This is not to take place until the end of the millennium.

Now this shows us that people do live again and die again, and that knowledge is the end and aim of the whole matter, and God does use lying spirits or angels to act as lying spirits for the purpose of leading man on to his studies or experiences.

See I. Kings 22:20 23:

"And the Lord said, Who shall persuade Ahab, that he may go up and fall at Ramothgilead? And one said on this manner, and another said on that manner.

"And there came forth a spirit, and stood before the Lord, and said, I will persuade him.

"And the Lord said unto him, Wherewith? And he said, I will go forth, and I will be a lying spirit in the mouth of all his prophets. And he said, Thou shalt persuade him, and prevail also: go forth and do so.

"Now therefore, behold, the Lord hath put a lying spirit in the mouth of all these thy prophets, and the Lord hath spoken evil concerning thee."

Now this shows us that if God's plan requires deception to lead his people in the way of knowledge, he uses it, and we are enabled to understand every phase in the great drama of life, and Shakespeare was inspired when he said:

"All the world's a stage,
And all the men and women merely players.
They have their exits and their entances;

And one man in his time plays many parts.

His acts belong to seven ages."

– As You Like It. Act 1., Scene 7.

I have here stated that at the end of the thousand year millennium, Sunday, that those who are fit to go to a higher sphere, will go, but the rest of mankind, both in the fleshy condition of mind and the spirit state, will go on waring in strife, brightening the mind as it only can be brightened, by the friction of "the survival of the fittest."

The idea of flying away to Heaven immediately after death is both unreasonable and unbiblical. There are none fit for Heaven as they are, and to change them suddenly at death, would be to make other persons of them, and life would be for no purpose.

What would be the use of a child attending school with its hardships, if at the end of the quarter, though he was in the primary grades, he should be boosted into college without finishing his study of the lower grades?

The Jews were undoubtedly the direct descendants of those who were not able to graduate on the close of a former week of God's work—hence they were called "the children of the devil," or "the lost sheep."

Those of mankind who had not yet had a chance to graduate could not be classed with the Jews.

The first two thousand years from Adam was used to populate the world with mankind from the spirits of the lower animals, these were the primary classes. With few exceptions, the spirits of the former inhabitants who were unfit for a higher sphere, remained in the spirit state of rest. But at the end of the two thousand years the flood swept the earth, and a change of dispensation took place. The same as at the end of a week. As undoubtedly the sinking of the continent of Atlantis was at the close of the last week of God's work, as at the close of this millennium thousand years, Satan will be loosed to deceive the nations and bring them to a terrible war, and then the destruction of the whole by fire before the starting of a new week of work.

With the beginning of the second third of the week, or the new dispensation, came a higher state of human perfection and various forms of God's worship, and a better religion was evolved, the same as man was first evolved from the lower animals.

Sun and fire worship with the sacrifice of human beings gave way to the more refined Jewish rites of sacrificing the lower animals to a spiritual God.

This gave way in the beginning of the last third of the week of work, or the new dispensation, where a God dies for man to show that the greatest is not above the least, as Christ states when washing the feet of his disciples, that the greatest can be no greater in the kingdom of God than the least, in other words the greatest honor in being great is to serve those below.

The next change of dispensation will be the Millennium, or the Sunday of God's week; where Christ will establish his kingdom and reign for a thousand years perfecting it before turning it over to his father. Finishing his work on the seventh day the same as God was said to build the world in six days, laying his plan, and finished on the seventh, and rested reviewing the work he had done.

That we are in the last days—twenty-four hour days, or calendar years before Christ's second coming seems to be borne out by many fulfilled scriptural prophecies as well as many more that seem about to be fulfilled, and it is here that the great financial question takes its place.

As I have before stated, through the whole Scripture there is naught but governments talked of. The individual is lost sight of in the great plan of governments. The descendants of Abraham were chosen as a type, and after Moses led the people from Egyptian bondage, the people were generally well governed, mainly as a republic, until the reign of Saul.

From Joshua to the accension of Saul, 350 years, three-fourths of the time the people were at peace, and until the sons of Samuel who were judges but "forsook the ways of God and the ways of their father Samuel and turned aside after lucre," (see Samuel 8:3) the people were tolerably well satisfied. But now instead of calling for the punishment of the treasonable judges and placing honest ones in their place, they determined to have a king. God told them that the kings would rob them of their sons and daughters as well as their wealth, but they heeded him not (see the eighth chapter of Samuel). We have found that even the wise Solomon fell away from the ways of God and became extravagant with the people's wealth, and demonetized silver and brought rebellion among his people under Jeroboam. He was undoubtedly influenced by the selfish money loaning class:

"From Saul's reign to the dispersion of the Jews, except for a short period of the early part of Solomon's reign, the people were under the baneful influence or control of the moneyed classes. From the close of Solomon's reign, 976 B. C.,to Ezekiel's prophecies, 583 B. C., or 393 years, the people were in a continual turmoil and corruption."

Then God says to them in Ezekiel 22:3-5:

"Thou art become guilty in thy blood that thou hast shed; and hast defiled thyself in thine idols which thou hast made;"—"and thou hast caused thy days to draw near, and art come even unto thy years: therefore have I made thee a reproach unto the heathen, and a mocking to all countries."

Verse 10. "In thee have they discovered their fathers' nakedness: in thee have they humbled her that was set aside for pollution."

Verse 12-15. "In thee have they taken gifts to shed blood; thou hast taken usury and increase and thou hast greedily gained of thy neighbors by extortion and hast forgotten me, saith the Lord God.

"Behold, therefore I have smitten mine hand at thy dishonest gain which thou hast made, and at thy blood which hath been in the midst of thee.

"Can thine heart endure, or can thine hands be strong, in the days that I shall deal with thee? I, the Lord, have spoken it, and I will do it.

"And I will scatter thee among the heathen, and disperse thee in the countries, and will consume thy filthiness out of thee."

Then as now the poverty that the moneyed classes, through usury and selfish gain, caused the poorer classes to drop lower and lower in the scale of humanity, until both rich and poor put the harlots to shame, and accepted blood money for murder. That poverty will destroy civilization, is clearly stated in Proverbs 10:15:

"The destruction of the poor is their poverty."

The rich hope to buy their way to heaven, by robbing the poor through usury and monopoly, and then founding colleges, building monuments and churches, and supporting ministers that try to pray their souls into heaven.

"But Peter said unto him, Thy money perish with thee, because thou hast thought the gifts of God might be purchased with money."

Surely, this money changing must have been considered the essence of human selfishness by God, when he would take from the "children of Israel" that land that he had given them "for an everlasting inheritance." When we remember that the only time that Christ used force or sanctioned the use of force, was when with the scourge he drove the money changers from the temple. Is this typical of the great war that must yet come to scourge the money changers from the earth, and through the fire of tribulation, purify the temple of God, which is man? This we will find out as we proceed. But what a standing evidence of the truth of prophecy! The book of Ezekiel, written nearly six hundred years before the birth of Christ, tells us God said that he would scatter the Jews among the nations, and they would be scoffed at over the whole world, and here they are today a living testimony of the truth of biblical prophecy.

The year 450 B. C., or 128 years after Ezekiel, Nehemiah tried to reform the Jewish nation, and he cried out:

"I pray you, let us leave off this usury."—Neh. 5:10.

"Take thou no usury of him or increase," says Leviticus 25:36.

Neh. 5:5-7, says: "I rebuked the nobles and the rulers and said unto them, you exact usury every one of his brother, and I sat a great assembly against them."

Now I would ask the ministers of today if you "rebuked

the nobles and the rulers"? I will answer for you. "No; you have not." Many of your class have become as vultures, and your churches as "whited sepulchers"—too often used as a cloak to cover legal thieves. Under the guise of religion the selfish and unjust find a covering for their guilt, and ye rebuke them not. For six days do they deceive, steal and defraud, under laws they have had made for themselves, and on the seventh day they pose as christians, listening to your sanctimonious prayers; soothing their consciences preparatory to their next week's work of deception and fraud, and ye rebuke them not. Ye prefer to fatten upon the salary paid you from their ill-gotten gains.

"He that hath not given forth upon usury, neither hath taken any increase: that hath withdrawn his hand from iniquity, hath executed true judgement between man and man."—Ezek. 18:8.

"And if ye lend to them of whom ye hope to receive, what thanks have ye? for sinners also lend to sinners to receive as much again."--Luke 5:34.

Oh ye divines who read this, I beseech you turn upon this wrong of usury. Drive the usurers from your churches or their hypocrisy will block the doors of christianity, and if you refuse you certainly belong to that class of whom Christ spake when he said:

"Woe unto you scribes and pharisees, Hypocrites! for you shut up the kingdom of heaven against men: for ye neither go in yourselves, neither suffer ye them that are entering to go in. Woe unto you scribes and pharisees, hypocrites: for ye devour widows' houses, and for a pretense make long prayers, therefore, ye shall receive the greater damnation."

Let me say: "That ye deceive the poor; bidding them put all their hope in their future welfare, and while on their bended knees, with bowed heads, ye are robbing them for your temporal welfare. They feel the wrong you have done them. They see you are hypocrites; and they are following in your footsteps; ye are making devils of them—devils that will turn upon you with the furies of hell."

"Verily, verily, it is easier for a camel to pass the needle's eye than for a rich man to enter the kingdom of heaven."

Yet all things are possible with God. Riches is not the evil, but interest the curse.

Oh ye churches, ye are the harlots spoken of in Revelations 17. The Catholic church is the mother of harlots and the protestant churches are the daughters, and they are today drunken with the wine of their fornication, and wondering why they are preaching to empty benches. The old mother of harlots, "her flesh shall be devoured by the great red dragon—the money power—and the daughters, unless they repent, shall be overrun by the sea"—the people. And now I will take up the prophecies and prove my assertion.

The allegorical story of Adam and Eve eating the forbidden fruit because of the temptation of the old serpent, as I have before stated, was at the beginning of this week of God's work.

The serpent was the self will or the satisfying of one's own desires, instead of obeying God, and overcoming one's self. Hence God's kingdom was ignored, and man's determination to govern himself. Thus government are the basis of man's purpose here, knowledge the aim.

God's government is perfect; man's government soon runs to seed and becomes the embodiment of selfishness, hence is the old serpent condemned to crawl back to dust or destruction. And man was compelled amid thorns and trials to earn his bread by the sweat of his brow.

Of the serpent, God says: "And I will put an enmity between thee and the woman, and between thy seed and her seed: it shall bruise thy head, and thou shalt bruise his heel."

Now we shall find as we proceed that in prophecy the church is symbolized by woman, and governments as serpents and beasts.

Christ was the seed of the woman direct while the church was his bride. It was Old Pagan Rome that crucified Christ. The Jews had no government hence no power, except to call on the government over them to do it.

For 280 years; that is, from the day of Pentecost, A. D. 33, to 313 A. D., when Constantine established himself in Rome, Pagan Rome persecuted the church. Constantine to gain political power aided the church, and at length the church became prostituted to the kings and princes:

See Revelations 17:2: "And there came one of the seven angels which had the seven vials, and talked with me, saying unto me, Come hither; I will show unto thee the judgment of the great whore that sitteth upon many the waters."

The fifteenth verse says these waters are people, and nations, and the church has controlled many people and nations.

Second verse. "With whom the kings of the earth have committed fornication, and the inhabitants of the earth have been made drunk with the wine of her fornication,"—money getting—the sacrificing of love of God —of humanity of virtue, of all that is good for the great deceiver, Mammon, "love of money, the root of all evil."

The serpent, corrupt government, bruised the heel of the woman, the church, until he could make use of her then he married her—united church and state but she the church coqueted, played the harlot with other kings, and she has waxed very rich—look at the property held by the church, Chirst had no where to lay his head, but look at the great wealth of the church. I am not speaking against the good people of this church or any other church but I am giving prophecies as they appear.

A woman to become a prostitute must have been perfect to have fallen, and the perfection consisted in her unalloyed teaching of the love of Christ as he was the embodiment of purity, no selfishmess, no lustful desires after wordly gain or pleasures. He scourged the money changers from the temple.

The fathers of the Catholic church fought usury tooth and nail for ages. The old fathers recognized in the old Mosaic law the teaching of a horror of the crime of usury or loaning for increase. And the Scriptures are full of the commands against it.

St. Ambrose seemed to think that usury was confided to the Jews as an instrument of vengeance to be used against their enemies, and says. "take usury from him whom you may lawfully kill." This would class it with the crime of murder. Even the old Grecian philosophers opposed usury and Aristotle said, "that money being naturally barren, to make it breed money is preposterous and a monstrous perversion from the end of its institution, which was only to serve the purpose of exchange and not of increase."

Plato, when asked if he classed usury with murder replied by simply asking, "What is murder?"

St. Bazil in every way stirred his followers against usury, saying, "Sell thy cattle, sell thy plate, thy household stuff, thine apparel; sell anything rather than liberty; never fall under the slavery of that monster, usury." But at length the Popes were controlled by the kings and the church, and the kings prostituted her to the money changers, and as I have before stated in the thirteenth century the Pope's agents competed in England with the Jew money loaners and loaned money as high as 450 per cent. They then claimed that only unlawful interest was usury, making the crime geographical, like the great poet's stanza:

"When first we meet vice face to face
We first endure, then pity, then embrace."

So Pope Benedict XIV. in 1730 issued a bull declaring only unlawful interest usury. So the church finally plays the harlot with the kings and supports the money power, and the daughters of the old harlot are following in her footsteps and upholding the greatest of all evils, usury; and they are drunken with the wine of their fornication and wonder that the people are leaving them as they left the old harlot on account of corruption. But Christ, the seed of the woman, will come and establish his kingdom and gather his people, the just, and bruise the head of the serpent the "Great Red Dragon."

I wish to show that this Red Dragon is the money power in Lombard and Threadneedle streets, London, England, of which the Rothschilds are the head and that kings bow to them, they control the world even the great Bismark has been forced to bow to them.

In 1866 the Prussian government demanded an indemnity

of $25,000,000 from the city of Frankfort. The Rothschild sent word to Bismark that if any attempt was made to enforce the levy, they would break every bank in Berlin. Bismark knew this was no idle threat and he had to give way.

A few months ago Emperor William ordered some investigation in the affairs of the banks at Berlin, but he was ordered by them to desist and the matter was dropped. Of these Rothschild barons there are eleven, Nathanial, Alfred and Leopold are located in London and control the Bank of England.

Alphonse, Gustav, Edward, Adolph, and James are in Paris and in a great measure control the Bank of France. But the French people will not stand as much from them as other people, hence the recent attempt, with a bomb to blow up one of them. Nathanial is in Vienna and William in Frankfort.

The Belmonts are their relatives and agents in this country and their hand in our financial affairs go to show how completely they control this country. It is said their combined wealth is over $3,000,000,000, and all of the gold of the world does not exceed three billion eight hundred million. They can corner gold at will and enslave the world. No wonder they want a gold basis.

The founder of this great power was Mayers Anselem, in whose pawn shop bore the device a red shield, this in German is Rothschild—and *in prophecy, Red Dragon.* Hence the origin of the Rothschild's family name. Their motto is absolute secrecy in all dealings.

"A man will not tell what he has not heard."

"Gold never repeats what it sees."

In other words, bribery is all powerful.

These people control the world and out of wars and panics they wax rich hence do not hesitate to create them when for their interests, no matter at what cost, in blood and human suffering. This selfishness is the old serpent that deceived Mother Eve, and the church of which she was typical, and today controls kings, judges, pulpit, and the press.

God says of the old harlot:

"I will cast her into a bed." "And I will kill her children with death, and all the churches shall know that I am he who searches the reins and hearts."

Now I will go back and bring down the prophecies in farther proof of the conditions.

The prophecies are so arranged as to show several meanings. This is done that those who search the Scriptures, who like the ten wise virgins, may ever keep their lamps trimmed and burning.

Much more space should be devoted to the subject of the prophecies than I can spare here, as I must only refer to such prophecies as pertain to my subject.

God established his government on earth and men rebelled, and the rebellion has not been subdued.

God established the Jews in Palestine for an everlasting inheritance, again they rebelled and he cast them out. But he promised to bring them back.

Finally Christ came and was murdered at the command of the High Priests. This shows man he can not always depend on the priesthood, but to serve their own interests they will oppose the truth even to murdering God himself if possible.

Christ said he would return and establish his kingdom and reign for a thousand years and then turn it over to his father. All of this is foreshadowed in Daniel's visions, and landmarks are pointed out to guide the traveler down the stream of time, that the wise virgins or students may know where they are at.

The first of Daniel's prophecies are the answers to the dream of Nebuchadnezzer, king of Babylon, which is described in the second chapter of Daniel.

This describes an image with a head of gold, which he states was Babylon, "Thou art the head of gold," says Daniel.

But as this image could not illustrate all the conditions, the symbol of beasts were used for the purpose and Babylon was symbolized as a beast like a lion with eagle's wings.

Old Assyria was symbolized as a lion with eagles wings and sculptured lions with wings were found in the ruins of Ninevah. This was 677 B. C.

The breasts and arms of this image were of silver and were symbolized as a bear, with three ribs in its mouth, which were the spoils by conquest; representing three divisions, so divided for the better administration of public affairs. The bear also had two horns which represent it to have been formed of two kingdoms. The Medes and Persians known as the Medo-Persian kingdom. This was 539 B. C.

The belly and sides of this image: Daniel describes as being of brass. This has reference to "the brazen-coated Greeks." This is also symbolized by a leopard with four heads, and four wings like a fowl. Daniel 7:6.

The Medo-Persian empire was also described as a ram with two horns, one higher than the other. The higher one being Medea. This ram pushed north and south and west. But the third beast, or Greek power, was also described as a rough he goat. But let us quote Daniel 8:3-8, 20, 22:

"Then I lifted up mine eyes and saw, and, behold, there stood before the river a ram which had two horns; and the two horns were high: but one was higher than the other, and the higher came up last.

"I saw the ram pushing westward, northward, and southward; so that no beast might stand before him, neither was there any that could deliver out of his hands, but he did, according to his will, and became great.

"And as I was considering, behold, an he goat came from the west, on the face of the whole earth, and touched not the ground; and the he goat had a notable horn between his eyes.

"And he came to the ram that had two horns, which I had seen standing before the river, and ran unto him in the fury of his power.

"And I saw him come close unto the ram, and he was moved with choler against him, and smote the ram, and break his two horns, and there was no power in the ram to stand before him, but he cast him down to the ground, and stamped upon, and there was none that could deliver the ram out of his hand.

"Therefore the he goat waxed very great; and when he was strong, the great horn was broken: and for it came up four notable ones, toward the four winds of heaven.

"The ram which thou sawest having two horns are the kings of Media and Persia.

"And the rough goat is the king of Grecia; and the great horn that is between his eyes their first king.

"Now that being broken, whereas four stood up for it, four kingdoms shall stand up out of the nation, but not in his power."

Now this tells us who these powers were, and the description shows us at what time, for Alexander, the Great, came from the west with great rapidity, attacking Darius furiously, and nothing could stand before him, and after conquering the world in six short years, he died forsaken and alone in Babylon, and his kingdom did not go to his heirs, but was divided between four of his generals; Cassander in Macedonia, Ptolomy in Egypt, Seleucus in Syria, Lysimachus in Thrace.

It will be remembered that this prophecy took place hundreds of years before the scenes were enacted, and that secular history stands proof of this truth.

I will here quote an interesting anecdote from the history of "The World's Great Nations:"

"Alexander, after a protracted seige of the City of Gaza, marched on to Jerusalem, where, instead of meeting expected opposition, the priests and Levites in their robes came out to meet him, headed by Jaddua, the High Priest, in his beautiful raiment and the golden mitre on his head inscribed with these words, "Holiness unto the Lord." He had been commanded by God in a vision, and when Alexander beheld the sight he threw himself from his horse and adored the name on the mitre. He told his officers that before he set out from home, when considering his journey, just such a form as he now beheld had come and bidden him fear not for he should be led into the East, and all Persia should be delivered to him. The High Priest took him to the outer court of the Temple, and showed him the very prophecies of Daniel and Zachariah where his own conquests were foretold."

Now that we have been given a clue to understanding of prophecies. We must solve the rest for ourselves.

We were told that the head of gold of the image was Babylon, and we could plainly see the breast and arms of silver were Medo-Persia, and we are plainly told the belly and sides of brass was the Greek power under the Macedonian leader, Alexander. Now we come to the legs which were of iron, and feet of iron and clay. Daniel 2:31-32.

Then says Daniel in the 34th verse of the same chapter:

"Thou sowest till that a stone was cut out without hands, which smote the image upon his feet that were of iron and clay, and brake them to pieces."

"Then was the iron, the clay, the brass, the silver, and the gold broken to pieces together, and became like the chaff of the summer threshing floors: and the wind carried them away, that no place was found for them: and the stone that smote the image became a great mountain, and filled the whole earth."

Now in verses 39 to 46, Daniel interprets this dream, and shows us that the stone that broke this image to pieces is the kingdom of God to be set up at that time.

This of course is the spiritual kingdom of which Christ will have his throne at Jerusalem, which will fill the whole earth. But the United States of America is the power with which he enforces his will in the great war before Christ comes, and this will be largely spiritual by the example of a republic, which example will spread to all nations, and the forms of governments will be a adopted which will be to the consternation of the kings.

Now the Roman kingdom was divided into the Eastern and the Western empires, answering to the two iron legs, and between the years 357 and 483 A. D. the Roman Empire was divided into ten kingdoms, answering to the ten toes, viz:

1. The Huns, in Hungary, A. D. 357.
2. Ostrogoths, in Mysia, A. D. 377.
3. The Visigoths, in Pannonia, A. D. 378.
4. The Franks, in France, A. D. 407.
5. The Vandals, in Africa, A. D. 407.
6. The Sueves and Alani in Gascoigne and Spain, A. D. 407.

7. The Burgundians, in Burgundia, A. D. 407.

8. The Heruli, in Italy, A. D. 476.

9. The Saxons and Angles, in Britain, A. D 476.

10. The Lombards, on the Danube in Germany, A. D. 483.

These kingdoms "mingled among men," and were not stable like iron, but broke up and changed around somewhat, "as clay is not mixed with iron," yet in the days of these kingdoms shall God establish a kingdom which shall break them all to pieces, and these kingdoms are in existence today: Hungary, Naples, Belgium, France, Spain, England, Portugal, Sardinia, Lombardy and Bavaria.

Now we have found by this image the legs and feet is the Roman Empire; we will now find the nations symbolized by beasts.

Daniel 7:7-8.—"After this I saw in the night visions, and behold a fourth beast dreadful and terible and strong exceedingly: and it had great iron teeth: it devoured and brake to pieces and stamped the residue with the feet of it: and it was diverse from all other beasts that were before it: and it had ten horns.

"I considered the horns and behold there came up among them another little horn before whom there were three of the first horns plucked up by the roots: and behold, in this horn were eyes like the eyes of man and a mouth speaking great things."

Verse 21 - "I beheld and the same horn made war with the saints and prevailed against them."

Verse 25.—"And he shall speak great words against the Most High, and shall wear out the saints of the Most High, and think to change times and laws: and they shall be given unto his hand until a time and times and the dividing of time."

Now this Roman Empire did conquer the world and destroy what it did not want, or **"stamped on the residue."** I want the reader to take careful note of this, for we shall find the image of this beast as we go farther on.

I have shown what the ten horns meant in describing the ten toes of the image before spoken of. But the eleventh, or little horn with eyes, we must now consider.

Now Christ taught no creed or denomination, but "where two or three are gathered together in my name there I will be in the midst." Anything that forcibly disturbs the freedom of worship in his name was a persecution of the saints. The early christians, so long as they were being persecuted by the pagans, did not persecute those who might differ from them. But as soon as there was a uniting of church and state, oppression stepped in, therefore the Pope is this little horn that made war against the saints, and changed times by changing the Jewish seventh day Sunday to the first day; and spake great things, and within our own memory the Pope declared himself infallible.

Dr. Macknight, a writer on this subject, says:

"In process of time the bishops of of Rome having got possession of three of the kingdoms into which the western empore broken, which were signified by thee of the horns of Daniel's fourth beast being plucked up by the roots before the little horn, they called themselves the vicars of Christ, on pretence that Christ had transferred his whole authority to them * *
As the vicars of Christ they assumed the power of saving and damning men at their own pleasure, and altered the terms of salvation, making it depend, not on faith and holiness, but on the superstitious practices which they had established; and sold the pardon of sins past, and even the liberty of sinning in the future for money."

So we now find the little horn

spoken of represents the Pope.

A great deal of interesting testimony could be brought to bear to prove these prophecies true, but all that is intended in this work is to show and prove the present position of finance in prophecy.

I have shown that the dragon or serpent is deception and the imbodiment of selfishness. A government or great power is symbolized by a beast, and the church by a woman.

The United States has not yet appeared in prophecy. But we must now go to Revelations, for that. But as that comes in the last days before Christ's second coming, and the establishment of his kingdom, we must bring forward a few more facts to show we are in the last days, or the Saturday night of God's week of six thousand years.

Christ says when the fig tree putteth forth its buds, you say spring time is at hand.

I have pointed to the prophecy of the scattering of the Jews as a living evidence of the truth of prophecy; but their being gathered back to Jerusalem before Christ's second coming, stands as a sign or proof that the time is up, when we see them gathering back.

"Behold, the noise of the brute is come, and a great commotion out of the north country, to make the cities of Judah desolate and a den of dragons."—Jeremiah 10:22.

"Thy cities shall be laid waste without an inhabitant,

"The whole land shall be desolate."
—Jeremiah 4:7, 27.

History shows us that this has all taken place, and the whole land was uninhabitable, no rain falling, and the robbing, marauding Arab and the ferocious wild beast held sway.

"And I will bring again the captivity of my people Israel, and they shall build the waste cities and inhabit them; and they shall plant vineyards, and make gardens, and eat the fruit of them; and I will plant them upon their land, and they shall no more be pulled up out of their land which I have given them, saith the Lord."—Amos 9:14-15.

"And I scattered them among the heathen, and they were dispersed through the countries.

"And when they entered into the heathen, whither they went, they profaned my holy name (denied Christ).

"For I will take you from among the heathen, and gather you out of all the countries, and will bring you to your own land * and ye shall dwell in the land which I gave your fathers, and ye shall be my people and I will be your God. I will save you from your uncleanliness * * and I will multiply the fruit of the tree * * and the desolate land shall be tilled, where it lay desolate in the sight of all that passed by.

"But not for your sakes do I do this."—Ezekiel, Chap. 26.

There is a great deal more testimony of the gathering back of the Jews, but this is enough.

Less than forty years ago, it is said, there were not thirty Jews in Jerusalem. But five years ago it was reported in a letter written by a tourist of observation, there were over twenty thousand Jews in Jerusalem, and over a hundred thousand in Palestine. The hillsides that were barren, are now teeming with vegetation: rain is falling again as God promised it should, says this writer: Beyrout, a dirty little city of twenty thousand population, has leaped to a beautiful city of eighty thousand; her trading ships have increased from one hundred ships to four hundred steamers and three thousand five hundred sailing vessels, and at Joppa, the port of Jerusalem, still greater improvements are made. The orange trade alone amounts to eight or ten million. Interior towns show as marked a change

A fine new railroad runs to Joppa, and it is carrying the Jews back to their land very fast, and this is what the prophet saw when he said:

"The chariots shall rage in the streets, they shall jostle one against another in the broadways; they shall seem like torches, they shall run like lightnings."—Nahum 11:4.

Can any one describe our steam car and our electric car better that this? Look at an approaching engine with its great headlight, or the electric cars jostling each other in the broad ways (streets), and see if you can give a better description.

In the last days woman shall compass man (demand her rights; meet him on every plane in competition).

Is she not doing it?

Does she not compete with him in almost every line of business?

"But thou, O Daniel, shut up the words and seal the book, even to the end; many shall run to and fro, and knowledge shall be increased."—Daniel 12:9.

Not a hundred years ago the horse was the most rapid means of transit and Voltaire, the great infidel laughed and made sport of Sir Isaac Newton, the philosopher, because Newton said he thought prophecy would be fulfilled and we should yet travel in some way at the rate of fifty miles an hour, and he said the Bible had made a fool of Newton in his old age, but we now travel almost twice as fast at times.

Knowledge has increased wonderfully.

Less than four centuries ago illiteracy was so general that the English Parliament passed a law providing for those of its members who were unable to read. But now the telegraph and the telephone gather the news from the four corners of the globe, and the press and the rapid transit scatter it to the millions who read, and even the infants, the little tots at school, read and write, and in a spiritual sense, knowledge hath increased and people are no longer groping after truth, but are running to and fro gathering facts.

Another evidence of the last days is the growth of spiritualism and spiritual wonders performed.

"And it shall come to pass in the last days, saith God, I will pour out of my spirit upon all flesh: and your sons and your daughters shall prophecy, and your young men see visions, and your old men shall dream dreams.

"And on my servants and on my handmaidens I will pour out in these days of my spirit, and they shall prophecy."—Acts 11:17-18.

"For to one is given by the spirit the word of wisdom; to another the word of knowledge by the same spirit.

"To another the working of miracles; to another prophecy; to another discerning of spirits; to another diverse kinds of tongues; to another interpretation of tongues.

"To another faith by the same spirit; to another the gifts of healing by the laying on of hands."—Corinthians 12:8 9-10.

Christ said that greater wonders than he did should be done in these days.

But the soul of man is not changed at death, for it is said there shall be evil spirits in these days as well as in the days of Christ.

"Beloved, believe not every spirit, but try the spirits whether they are of God, because many false prophets are gone out into the world. Hereby know ye the Spirit of God; Every spirit that confesseth that Jesus Christ is come into the flesh is of God.

"And every spirit that confesseth not that Jesus Christ is come in the flesh is not of God."—John 4:1-2.

No one who has investigated psychic phenomena and latter day spiritualism can doubt these wonders.

One of the last acts of the drama, before God establishes his kingdom will be the driving of the Turk out of Europe.

"He shall plant the tabernacles of his palace between the seas in the glorious holy mountain; yet he shall come to his end, and none shall help him."—Daniel 11:45.

"At that time shall Michael stand up, the great prince which standeth for the children of thy people: and there shall be a time of trouble, such as never was since there was a nation delivered, every one that shall be even to that same time and at that time thy people shall be delivered, every one that shall be found written in the book."—Daniel 12:1.

October 11th, 1840, the Turkish Sultan surrendered his independence, to the great powers of Europe. From that day to this he has been known as the Sick Man, and only holds his position through the jealousies of the powers, which has seemed ready to heal at any moment and never so strongly as at present. Now the Turk seems to be left friendless today, if so he will be driven out of Europe and make his home at Jerusalem, but only for a short time. It matters not whether it be this year or next or in twenty years, but it cannot be long now. The Jews are being tormented out of other countries and must soon populate their own land thickly, when God's kingdom will be set up. We must see what this kingdom is.

The troubles spoken of as being such times as never was since there was a nation is the great wars that will be referred to farther on, and now we have reached

THE UNITED STATES IN PROPHECY.

We have described several

empires as beasts. Kingdoms were only described as horns. There is yet the beast spoken of by John in Revelations with seven heads and ten horns, but that is the old Roman beast. We still have another "with two horns like a lamb," which we shall find to be England. But the United States is a God worshipping people's government and was not made in the ordinary way, by conquest, but was built up without hands.

We find in Revelations 12:1

"And there appeared a great wonder in heaven; a woman clothed with the sun, and the moon under her feet, and upon her head a crown of twelve stars.

"And she being with child cried, travailing in birth, and pained to be delivered.

"And there appeared another wonder in heaven; and behold a great red dragon, having seven heads and ten horns, and seven crowns upon his head.

"And his tail drew the third part of the stars of heaven; and did cast them to the earth: and the dragon stood before the woman which was ready to be delivered, for to devour her child as soon as it was born.

"And she brought forth a man child, who was to rule all nations with a rod of iron: and her child was caught up unto God, and to his throne.

"And the woman fled into the wilderness, where she hath a place prepared of God, that they should feed her there a thousand two hundred and threescore days,

Possibly to to end of the millenuium. Fix the date of the woman's retreat to the wilderness, which would be about 1645, dividing the extreme time from first to last settlement of religious denominations in this country. Then add 1260 days (years) and you have 2905. Deduct the one day (Sunday), or millennium one thousand years and you have 1905, about the beginning of the millennium or God's Sunday.

"And there was war in heaven: Michael and his angels fought against the dragon; and the dragon fought and his angels.

"And prevailed not; neither was their place found any more in heaven.

"And the great dragon was cast out, that old serpent, called the Devil, and Satan, which deceiveth the whole world: he was cast out into the earth, and his angels were cast out with him."

This is the end of Daniel's prophecy and the beginning of John's prophecy or Revelations. We are at the feet of Nebuchadnezzer's image of iron and clay, and the stone that is cut out without hands is to be seen.

But before we proceed further we must state that John was prophesying of the last days. Of his vision, all pertained of things of the last days.

He knew nothing of America but was looking upon a picture, the perspective in the distance. Europe was the earth, all he knew of America was higher up in the heavens and was called the lower heavens, as he looked above to the higher or upper heavens. He described what he saw, not necessarily in consecutive line as he saw it. Hence we find things described at a later period which seem as if they should have been described first. But, as before stated, this is given purposely that we may be made to keep our eyes open and be on the alert all the time. As Christ is picking out only those who are to aid him in teaching and governing the world, it is not intended that all should understand but only those that will be watchful. See Mark 4:10.

"And when he was alone they that were about him with the twelve asked of him the parable.

"And he said unto them it is given to know the mystery of the kingdom of God: but unto them that are without, all these things are done in parables:

"That seeing they may see, and not perceive; and hearing they may hear, and not understand; lest at any time they should be converted, and their sins should be forgiven them."

This woman that John saw is the church, or in other words those that believe in Christ and wish to worship according to the dictates of their own conscience, it is the same woman that fled to the wilderness to escape the persecution of the Pagans. All who wish to be free from persecutions of any set form by others. The Catholic church had become a harlot and with the kings persecuted all who had ideas of their own. This stopped study and progress, or delving into the work of God for the truth.

"Where two or three are gathered togther in my name, there I will be in t e midst."

It did not matter what denominations these were, catholic or protestant, anybody who wished to worship as they pleased, so long as the faith was in Christ and the mind liberal. Hence we had the Puritans in New England, the Baptists in Rhode Island, the Dutch Calvinists in New York, the Huguenots in South Carolina; the German Moravians in Georgia; the Swedish Lutherans in New Jersey; the Scotch covenanters in North Carolina; the English Quakers in Pensylvania; the Episcopalians in Virginia; and the Catholic settle-ments in Nova Scotia and Canadian Province.

All of these came here to escape persecution. It was the woman who "cried travailing in birth, and pained to be delivered," that is, longed for a government of their own that would protect them in their rights.

The United States is truly a child of this woman.

The denominations persecuted each other. The Puritans even

publicly flogged Quakers in the streets of New England towns by court sanction. But God had prepared a place for this woman and she was beset by great dangers, from the savage and the wild beasts, so the sects were compelled to heal their differences and finally form a government of toleration towards all religious beliefs.

This woman was given two great wings (sails), and she fled to the wilderness, where God had prepared a place for her to be fed 1260 days (years). We do not know the exact date from whence this 1260 years starts but somewhere from 1605 to 1682, and will run to the end the of millennium, consequently we know the beginning of the millennium of a thousand years, or God's Sunday, mustbenear at hand. And when it begins the lovers of truth will have no more persecution in their search after divine truth. They will drink freely from the fountain head of the pure waters of everlasting life.

This woman is clothed with the sun and the moon under her feet.

Most of the colonies were settled by the English, the sun or most powerful nation on the face of the globe. France came next, and while there were a few Dutch and Spanish they never exerted any political influence in the formation of the new nation. Thus France was the moon under the feet.

These are the twelve stars that were on the woman's head:

French Catholics, Port Royal, Nova Scotia, and Quebec, 1605 and 1608.

By the protestants in Virginia 1607.

New York, 1613.
Massachusetts, 1620.
New Hampshire, 1623.
Connecticut, 1632.

Maryland, 1634,
Rhode Island, 1636,
Delaware, 1638,
New Jersey, 1664,
Carolina, 1670,
Pennsylvania, 1682.

See explanation of the fig, page 400 to 406.

Thus we find the mother church was the first to settle in this country after all, but did not join in producing the "man child." All of these settlements were in the seventeenth century, twelve of them. North Carolina was taken from South Carolina in the eighteenth century, in 1729, and Georgia not admitted until 1733; and many stars have been added to the woman's head since that time, or rather to the "man child." But the heirship left by the woman was the twelve stars, consequently Canada must yet come into the Union, as she was of the old mother church she could not be taken in at that time, for she would not be allowed to exercise the domineering principle of that church in shaping our government.

Georgia took the place of Canada and made up the twelve stars, and there were finally thirteen but the Carolinas were one.

The first starry banner offered to congress for adoption bore but twelve stars representing the twelve apostles, but instructions were given to put the thirteenth star on and a star was ordered for every new state thereafter.

England, as she always did lay claim to everything, laid claim to all of the colonies, and in 1688, after the last of the first twelve colonies were settled, she appointed twelve counselors to settle disputes among the colonies. This proves to us these were the twelve original stars on the woman's head.

It does not matter that one of the original stars did not come into the Union, as one of the twelve apostles was a traitor. Again, if Georgia came in at a later period so did the apostle Paul come into the apostleship at a much later period.

Because other stars came into the constellation after the nation was born has nothing to do with it, as these stars belonged to the "man child" and not to the woman.

Now that the "man child" was born with the advent of our nationality, which for the first time in the world's history there existed a government that granted full religious liberty. We must now find why God destined this country into existence, and why it shall rule the world with a rod of iron, before we discuss the "great red dragon" and his part with the "man child."

Many expositors have supposed this "man child Michael" to mean our Savior Jesus Christ. But it is not. Neither is this nation the kingdom that God sets up for Christ, as our Lord is to rule the world from his throne at Jerusalem and the United States will be the power he will use to subdue the world.

THE UNITED STATES IN GOD'S GREAT PLAN

is plain as we find the woman with the twelve stars so strangely typified. First the twelve princes of Ismael starts twelve as a prophetic number, Genesis 14:4 and 25:16. We then find the twelve sons of Jacob as the great starting point of the nation that constitutes the tribes of Israel. Let us remember one of these sons took a very peculiar part (Josoph) which was neither to stand to his credit or blame.

Now we find that Jacob prophesied that from the tribe of Judah, the lion of Judah (Christ) should spring, showing us the peculiar part that one of the tribes should take. We have also noticed that one of Christ's deciples took a very unpleasant part, as we find one of the twelve stars (settlements in Canada) taking a strange part.

As Judah was the means of selling his brother to the Egyptians, thus saving his life for a great purpose, and from the tribe of Judah comes the Savior of mankind, what may not even Canada do for the sisterhood of states yet?

After Israel settled in the holy land by God's order he says:

"He broke his staff in two; ten tribes rebeled and left their land and became lost sheep or lost ten tribes."

"But God would not let them fight." —See I King 12:24

The book of Esdras 11:10 says:

"Tell My people, that I will give them the kingdom of Jerusalem, which I would have given Israel."

The majority of people suppose Israel means the whole twelve tribes, or that the Jews are all of the twelve tribes that are left, or that in speaking of one necessarily means both; but God did not look at matters in that way. Though he scattered them all and drove them out of Jerusalem he said he would bring them back, but Judah he would bring back first, that Israel should not domineer over them.

The reader will ask, well what of all this? what has this to do with the United States?

Well the Anglo Saxons are the lost ten tribes. The United States being of the tribe of Mannasah, England is probably of the tribe of Ephraim.

The question will be asked how can the people of the United States be of the lost ten tribes; when we are made up of all nations!

All of the people need not be of the twelve lost tribes any more than all the people of

England should trace their ancestry back as they too were a mixture. Or re-incarnation would answer the question.

Dr. Yates, a writer on this subject says: "Saxon comes from the word Isaac. Drop the I and put on son and you have sacson"—Saxon.

"In Isaac shall thy seed be called."—Genesis 21:12.

"Neither because they are the seed of Abraham are they ALL children but in Isaac shall thy seed be called."—Romans 9:7.

This is very fair evidence in favor of the Anglo-Saxons being of the lost ten tribes.

The Lord said to Abraham:

"Get thee away from thy kindred and from thy father's house unto the Land that I will show thee, and I will make of thee a great nation, and in thee all families of the earth shall be blessed."—Genesis 12:1-3.

This is what God said to Abraham and surely he did not mean that little handful of roaming people that inhabited that little eight by ten country called Palestine, for he also said:

"Thy seed shall be as the dust and thou shalt spread abroad. I am with thee and I will not leave thee until I have done that which I have spoken to thee of."—Genesis 28:14-15.

You see he had a purpose in sticking to the descendants of Jacob called Israel, hence he repeated the last quotation to Jacob.

"The Lord shall call his servents by another name."—Isaiah 65:15.

The Jews, and Benjaminites that called themselves Jews still are called Jews but the ten tribes are lost by their names.

"With another tongue will He speak to this people."—Isaiah 28:11.

"I will turn to the people a pure language."—Zephaniah 3:9.

The English language is rapidly becoming the universal language. This is enough that the

Anglo-Saxon race is of the lost ten tribes, and the United States has been taken care of by the hand of God for a great purpose. That purpose is to subdue and teach the world:

"For it shall come to pass that as ye were a curse among the heathen. O House of Israel and House of Judah, so will I save you and ye shall be a blessing."—Zechariah 8.

"Through Thee will we push down our enemies; through Thy name will we tread them under, that rise up against us."—Psalms 44.

"And the Lord said unto me, Israel hath justified herself more than treacherous Judah. Return, thou blacksliding Israel; for I am married unto you."—Jeremiah 3:11-12-14.

Judah crucified Christ, the lion of the tribe, but the Anglo-Saxons are the truest and best christians and most civilized people of the world.

When Christ sets up his kingdom on earth it is to rule the whole world not a part of it, and his throne will be at Jerusalem; and the Jews and Israelites will be gathered back there.

What all the Jews and Anglo-Saxons back in that little bit of country? Not likely; but he has promised those who overcome shall help him rule the world from his throne, and that is very wise, for if a man can not overcome his own passions and rule himself he is hardly fit to assist in ruling the world.

I will now show that he is going to take both Jews and Israelites back to Jerusalem.

"And I will cause the captivity of Judah and the captivity of Israel to return, and will build them as at the first."—Jeremiah 33:7.

"For the children of Israel and the children of Judah have only done evil before me from their youth."—Jeremiah 32:30.

In the 37th chapter of Ezekiel God says he will bring Judah and Israel back and join them together, and they shall never be separated any more. There is a great deal of biblical evidence for this but my subject forbids my taking time and space to produce it.

If Christ is not going to establish his throne in Jerusalem what use is there of gathering his people back there?

"Blessed and holy is he that hath part in the first resurrection: on such the second death hath no power; but they shall be priests of God and of Christ, and shall reign with him a thousand years; but the rest of the dead live not again until the thousand years were finished."—Revelation 20: 5-6.

If the whole world is to be destroyed what need will there be for priests and teachers?

"I will take you one of a city, and two of a family, and I will bring you to Zion."—Jeremiah 3:14.

"Two shall be in the field; one shall be taken, and the other left. Two women shall be grinding at the mill; one shall be taken and the other left." —Matthew 24:40-41.

A small portion of the people will be gathered back to be priests and teachers with Christ to rule the world, but Michael, the "man child" will rule the world with a rod of iron. That is, Christ will use the United States to subdue the world.

"THE GREAT RED DRAGON"

"And the serpent cast out of his mouth water as a flood after the woman, that he might cause her to be carried away by the flood.

"And the earth helped the woman, and the earth opened her mouth and swallowed up the flood which the dragon cast out of his mouth." Revelations 12:15-16.

I have said that the great usurious money power was the "great red dragon" spoken of.

After the religious reformers had settled in the colonies, with the understanding that none should be sent to join them that were opposed to their peculiar faith, the money getting speculaters bought up large grants and flocded the colonies with criminals and paupers and anything they could get to come out here. This is the flood spoken off as people are symbolized as "a flood," "waters," "the sea," etc., etc. But the country being so large here there was room for all and it did little damage. In fact the broad scope gave all a chance to develop into better manhood.

"The dragon's tail drew the third part of the stars of heaven, and did cast them to the earth; and the dragon stood before the woman which was ready to be delivered, for to devour her child as soon as it was born."

Now when we take into consideration that the dragon money power of England had used and controlled the English government to further its East India Trading Company and other colonial speculations, it forced that heavy taxation that drove the colonies to rebellion. It was all grist to the moneyed men's mill, for the debt that must be created bound the English people into slavery, and the subdueing the colonies would enable them to lay heavy burdens upon the people here. Or if they failed they would soon get the new country into debt and so enslave the people here. The dragon, through the British government so nearly defeated the colonies that its tail, the British forces, cast down onethird of the stars; running over Georgia, Virginia, North and South Carolina, and held its headquarters in the City of New York. "And her child was caught up unto God and his throne."

It has always been claimed by believers in destiny that our

salvation was in the hands of God. Washington said:

"The hand of Providence has been so conspicuous in all, that he who lacked faith must have been worse than an infidel; and he more than wicked who had not gratitude to acknowledge his obligations."

O ye reformers of today have courage for the great Eternal God is with us.

Ours is a glorious land:

Daniel 11: In speaking of this great power in the last days says "he shall overflow and pass over many countries and he shall enter into the glorious land." In Daniel 8:9. In speaking of the "little horn" that it "waxed exceedingly great toward the south, and toward the east, and toward the pleasant land."

This couldn't mean Palestine as that was east and had been mentioned, and there was no glorious land lying west like our own loved America.

Surely this is the "man child caught up to the throne of God, the glorious land."

1. No nation ever existed whose foundations of government were laid so broad and deep in principles of justice, righteousness, and truth as ours.

2. No nation ever gave its people such protection in the freedom of worship according to the dictates of their own consciences.

3. No nation ever acquired so vast a territory in so quiet a manner.

4. No nation ever rose to such greatness by means so peaceable.

5. No nation that ever flung its banner to the breeze ever offered such an asylum to the oppressed of the world.

6. No nation ever possessed so many natural resources as this.

7. No nation in so short a time ever developed such unlimited resources.

8. No nation ever arose to such mighty power in so short a time.

9. No nation ever progressed in the arts and sciences in so short a time.

10. No nation ever produced such wonders in invention for war or peace, as ours.

11. No nation ever gave its people so many and so good homes, and so many political rights, as we possess.

12. God never did so much for any other nation as for this, in diversity of climate and in nature's gifts.

Let us praise the God and defend the land and its institutions, and the flag of which he gave us the first twelve stars, from the woman's head, and sustained us in acquiring the rest.

The flag is our flag. Let none usurp it or let no dirty rag take its place.

That the United States, the "man child," is the glorious country that is to develop a spirituality that will elevate mankind and free the world from commercial slavery, that degrades humanity, there is no doubt.

Our present spiritualistic movement, is, undoubtedly, the fertilizer of the spiritual movement to rend the veil between the physical and the unseen world. In this way we are led up to our destiny for:

"The kingdom of God cometh not with observation."—Luke 17:20.

But the spiritualist and all others who are seeking the truth earnestly must accept God, and acknowledge that Christ was manifest in the flesh.

William A. Redding, speaking upon the subject quotes from

an English writer who has been a great traveler in India and the whole eastern country who says:

"America is appointed for a much higher and nobler destiny than Americans now suspect. America is to produce the truly spiritual man. The conditions are all supplied, and the work has begun.

"What we English can not do, the Americans are soon to do. They are to produce a higher type of humanity. A grossly material people they can not remain. They are set in their present land to bring in the higher life, and if they fail or refuse, their corruption and decay will be ten-fold worse than the worst that is written of Greek or Rome.

"Thousand of years ago India raised and argued all the questions now being discussed in America about man and his relation to God, and the destiny of the soul.

"America is to argue these great questions once more and for the last time, for America will get the true light and the salvation that will fully satisfy the entire world."

Yes no doubt India and Budhism are relic of a former week of God's work and represents what our country will represent after the thousand years of millennium and man has once more forsaken God and fallen back to the seductive influence of selfish gain and usury and six thousand years of strife of the servival of the fittest must be gone through by all who do not overcome and are fitted to be raised to a higher sphere.

No wonder the dragon stood ready to devour the "Man Child," and plant his money getting systems here in the glorious land.

Our very first banking system established in 1781, was patterned after the dragon English system of finance, and Alexander Hamilton our first Secretary of the Treasury was an Englishman of this school of finance, and he recommended that system, and it was adopted and nearly ruined the country, and President Jackson began the fight against it, and the battle has been going on ever since and will not end until we are involved in war with nearly the whole of Europe.

This old dragon money power has destroyed American money to make room for their capital that has gone into every line of trade, which is crushing out the smaller business in every direction.

WHY IS THE ENGLISH MONEY POWER

called the "great red dragon?" when there are other money powers in nearly every country?

The reason is this: The prophecies, all the way down, have left us symbols and landmarks, that we might know the time to look for these things, if we are studious and watchful. We recognized certain governments by their symbols, in the peculiarity of certain beasts. The woman that fled to the wilderness was clothed with the sun which we recognize as the symbol of England, the moon as France under her feet, the stars on her head are the colonies. But in this instance we have a different description that there may be no mistaking what this *Great Red Dragon* is.

I have before called attention to the fact that in 1235 A. D., notwithstanding the early fathers of the Catholic church fought usury tooth and nail, the Pope sent his agents into England, calling themselves merchant strangers, and loaned money as high as four hundred and fifty per cent. And the bishop who opposed it was recalled. Thus it was at that time the dragon got his foothold in England and though he had his headquarters at Genoa and afterwards at Amsterdam, and did not take up permanent quarters in England until the latter part of the eighteenth century. It was from here his growth and power is recognized. It was here that the usurers formed an alliance with the English government and gave the government a per centage of the ill-gotten gains for the right to the practice usury.

But this does not answer the question of why he is called red.

Well to designate him from all others he is called red after the color of the banner of the country, which we shall hereafter have to refer to as the symbol of the clothing of the old harlot.

In the year 1244 A. D., just eleven years after the Popes establishing his usurious agents in England, King Henry III gave orders that the banner of the country or royal standard should be a

"A RED DRAGON

to be made in fashion of a standard, of red silk, sparkling all over with fine gold, the tongue of which should be made to resemble fire, and appear to be continually moving, and the eyes of sapphires, or other suitable stones."—Encyclopedia Britannica, under heading of flags.

We must remember that in olden times flags meant much more than they do now, as they were almost the language of a country.

Now we will find many symbols that so closely resemble this old serpent, called the devil, that we can not mistake it.

REASON NUMBER TWO.

There is no such beast as the dragon we see pictured, nor never was but in ancient times the great serpents were called dragons. Now we know a snake is a cold blooded reptile and money getting corporations have no souls and no feelings for suffering humanity.

REASON NUMBER THREE.

is the serpent charms its victim then, when in its power, crushes them. The money power charms the manufacturer with possible great profits, and when the poor creditor is helplessly in his power he closes down and crushes the life out of him.

REASON NUMBER FOUR,

The serpent coils upon a tree thus getting a purchase power and then when he gets his coils around a victim he has the strength of the stable tree to support him. The money power has always aimed to control the government wherever it hunts its game. For many years the money power has used England as a tree or a purchase power to sustain itself while robbing the weaker powers. It has also entwined itself around every other government wherever possible, by influence, by trickery, by bribery or intimidation.

REASON NUMBER FIVE.

The serpent does not roar like a lion, nor even steal upon its prey, but lies in wait in the locality where its victims must come for food or water.

The money power creates the conditions and then lets the people fall into its coils.

REASON NUMBER SIX.

The serpent has a great capacity for ingulfing everything.

THINGS THAT IT HAS SWALLOWED.

The control of the money systems of nearly the whole world.

All of the mining interest, and where gold is found in other countries, it forces England to lay claim to that territory, so common has this become that one of our great dailies, cartoons England, demanding a territory covering the golden paved streets of heaven.

The money power has gobbled every outlying island or section of country available and owns vast tracks of land in this country.

It owns the bulk of our railroads.

Great quantities of city property in all our cities.

It controls our import trade.

It controls our oil production.

Our wheat and grain trade.

Nearly all of the New England mills.

Our cotton trade.

The bulk of our breweries.

Our iron trade.

The live stock market.

Our dressed beef trade.

Our trade in hogs, pork and bacon, including our financial hogs.

It carries the mails of the world, even our South American mails must go through the London post offices.

It is rapidly getting control of our retail trade, establishing its department stores and driving out the small dealers.

REASON NUMBER SEVEN.

The serpent when once he gets a coil around its victim tightens a little more and more, and never loosens excepts to get more advantage.

The money power does the same. It gets hold of all lines of business in a country then tightens up on the money market, forcing people to sacrifice their goods; its agents then buy up the goods and bankrupt factories; then sell enough of the goods at ruinous prices to destroy the business of legitimate dealers, and to attract trade to its big department stores. The people begin to feel the depres sion by being thrown out of employment, the serpent loosens up a little on his money loaning coil, and when the people begin to get something ahead he tightens his toils again, now to give them courage he beslimes them with a little money, loaned at a high rate of interest. This gives encouragement and starts business, and the employer and employee begin to hope, when the dragon gives a mighty gulp and the victim is pretty near down. He repeats this a few times and the manufacturies of the community or of the nation are helplessly lost.

REASON NUMBER EIGHT.

The serpent was, from the first condemned to crawl on its belly; it hides in the grass. It was called the devil, the father **of** liars. The serpent is the symbol of this horrible money power, which is the very embodiment of selfishness. It causes more misery and suffering than all other evils put together. All business, to be successful, must be conducted upon its principles, which is fraud, falsehood and deception. With the press and the pulpit it deceives the people and crawls on its belly, by enforcing its agents to profess to be the owners of the big monopolies that its money controls.

Let me here quote from a book called the "Great Red Dragon," which I wish everybody could read. Says Mr. Woolfolk, its author:

"We believe that Com. Vanderbilt made $100,000,000, Jay Gould in ten years made $200,000,000, Rockefeller in ten years made $150,000,000, Armour in fifteen years $120,000,000.

"Jim Fisk, died and at his death it became evident that the firm of Fisk & Gould were not the owners of the Erie railroad but were only agents. Jay Gould's railroad system breaks down, and proves that he did not own the railroads he was believed to possess, but was only an agent, of the money kings. Commodore Vanderbilt dies, and only divides up three and one-half millions among his children."

"Where has the other ninety odd million, he was supposed to own, gone?"

"William H. Vanderbilt sells out the controling interest in the Vanderbilt system for $50,000,000, and places the money in a London bank and at his death he leaves his property so it can be easily controled by a single will.—A. T. Stewart dies, and it is proved that he was only an agent of the London money kings: These and many other similiar facts make it certain that these grand corporations in our country are the agencies of the London money power."

"During the ten years 1854 to 1864 the Rothcshild's furnished in loans to England $200,000,000, to Austria $50,000,000; to Prussia, $40,000,000; to France, $30,000,000; to Russia, $50,000,000; to Brazil, $12,000,000; and more to smallar states."

Since that time they have actually handled billions of money and my interest tables, before given, will show how rapidly they must be getting control of the wealth of the world.

It is natural that these Jew money loaners, with their native shrewdness, would control the press and who would they trust like their own kind?

The same author as quoted above says:

"That in Dresden, in a gathering of representatives of the press, twenty-nine out of forty-three were Jews.

"Of Berlin, out of twenty-three liberal and daily papers, there are only two which are not, in one way or another, under Jewish control.

"In Italy they control the Liberal press.

"The most influential paper in Spain is under Jewish control.

"It is well known that Jews have control of a great portion of the metropolitan press of the United States. They are always open to give the gloss to events, inspired by the money power."

He who runs may read and know that the great dailies of this country are forever in favor of the money power and bonding the government for their benefit; and lying and deceiving the public. They will not even give a true account of election news where the reform movement has gained any advantage.

The minister acts the lie when he refuses to preach against the greatest sin (usury, interest on money) spoken off in Scripture, because if he did he would lose his job.

The merchant, to hold his own in business, must continually act the lie, that he may make enough to pay the interest on his borrowed capital, and then ninety-five per cent fail sooner or latter.

The clerk must act the lie and put the best side out, or his sails will fall so low that his discharge is certain.

Even the laborer in the street must rest on his hoe handle, when the foreman is not looking, and husband his strength, for his meagre wages will not permit him to live as a man should.

The politician is a liar and a briber, and a bribe taker because he must make up what he paid for his office, and keep pace with the rest of the rotten social system. And so nearly every one has the mark of the old dragon in the forehead or in the right hand, and they can neither buy or sell without it. (See Revelations 13:15).

Revelations 20:2 calls the dragon Satan.

Sheitan is the Chaldæn word for Satan, rendered in Greek teitan (power) so the money power is the Satan spoken of in Revelations.

Christ said "ye are looking in the heavens for great wonders," rather than observing things around you. So you have been looking for a monster spiritual devil while it is a principle of wrong among you.

Many more proofs can be brought to bear on this subject but this is enough.

But this brings us to the discussion of the

THE OLD MOTHER OF HARLOTS AND THE BEAST RESTORED.

Now before I proceed to discuss this phase of the prophecies I wish to say a few words to my brothers and sisters of all denominations or unbelievers in anything. I am not writing this to quarrel with any denomination or to tear down or build up any sect or creed.

I myself belong to no church. I seldom go to church. Yet I believe in God and in Christ, the son of God and that Christ came manifest in the flesh, a blessing to the world. I pray to God daily and on the night of December 3rd, 1895, an angel visited me in my own bed room, in answer to a prayer. It was no dream, hallucination, or allegorical story. I saw the angel, accompanied by a spirit, with my own eyes, and in full possession of all my faculties. I also affirm I have received aid from unseen forces in writing this work.

So entirely unprejudiced am I against any religous body that I sanctioned the marriage of my daughter to a catholic, and I objected not to the burial, in a catholic cemetary, of my little grandson that I loved better than my own life. I care not what your religious creed may be but I hate selfishness, and wrong and will expose it in any creed, or organization. Now I know dear brothers and sisters if you desire the truth we shall not quarrel even though some things I write may touch a tender spot.

Now we will commence our story of the *Mother of harlots*.

I have, before, told you how God has favored republics and abhorred kingdoms. Well over four thousand years ago, one Nimrod, a grandson of Ham, and a mighty hunter, and his wife, who was a great whore founded old Babylon, and set up the God Moloch, or idol worshop. They formed a great secret society to rule the world.

We can trace usury no farther back than to this old city.

The founders of this great secret society well knew that the people believed in a god and wished to serve him so they took advantage of that and built a temple to their god of Baal or Bel and adopted many imposing forms to deceive the people. Chief among these forms was a college of pontiffs, numbering seventy members and from this no doubt arose their title of pagans. Over this body was one supreme pontiff, to whom all bowed their heads and bent their knees and even kissed his toe. He was considered infallible; he wore a mitre upon his head. That they might thoroughly understand the inner feelings and motives of the people they adopted a form of confessional, this gave them a tremendous hold of their subjects in case of rebellion. They made themselves images and gods of bread, Isaiah 44:15, and offered this bread-god up as a sacrifice. They had many ceremonies and fast days. God condemned the whole thing and warned the Israelites against them, and on account of the wickedness they wrought declare the destruction of Babylon and Ninevah.

In the days of Ancient Rome the society was revived and the keys to the secrets of the society was said to be received from "Peter-Roma." The society became very strong when our Savior, Jesus Christ, came and set the glorious example for the people to worship where they pleased, that a gaudy temple was not necessary. And our Savior was a preacher without a salary, without a church, and no place to lay his head, and that the people might know that no great society was necessary he said, "Where two or three are gathered in my name there will I be in the midst." Christ's deciples went preaching in this simple manner, neither calling for salaries or rich churches, and Christ said to Peter: "On this rock (simplicity, grace and truth) I build my church and the gates of hell shall not prevail against it."

Well, christianity grew and the pagans persecuted the christians, and the christians increased in numbers but the pagans decreased. Finally, in the year 325 Constantine, the Roman emperor, for political advantage espoused the cause of the church. In the year 592 the supremacy of the Pope was recognized by all nations.

The adoption of pagan customs and the use of images was growing, and finally caused discensions and strife, and the church split; a part went east and became the Greek church, and a part west and became the Latin church, and the church married to the state. This was in 755 when the Pope gained temporal power. Which one of these churches was right? Neither, because they united with the state to deceive and defraud the people.

THE ADOPTION BY THE CHURCH OF PAGAN CEREMONIES AND FORMS.

The use of holy water was not adopted until the year 109; penance 157; praying for the dead, 200; monastic orders, 325; Latin mass, 349: extreme unction not a dogma till 558; idea of purgatory adopted in 593; invocation to the virgin, Mary, 594; kissing the Pope's toe, 709; adoption of the crucifixion or images, 715; transubstantiation, 1,000; celibacy of the clergy ordered taught 1074; the sale of indulgences, 1109: express order of auricular confession as a religious duty, 1215.

Any interest on money was considered usury by the church, though, as I have shown, some Popes accepted great usury, but not until 1735 did the Popes openly declare for usury, then Pope Benedict XIV. openly declared that only unlawful interest was usury.

It was not until four hundred years after Christ that the Pope claimed to carry the keys of heaven.

Now my dear catholic brothers and sisters, you will notice the catholic church has a college of cardinals of the same number of the old Babylonion secret society and a supreme pontiff called pope.

The Pope claims authority from Peter and and his keys, so did the pagan Pope.

The kissing of the Pope's toe the same as the pagan.

The pontiff of Babylon was adored as being incapable of error (infallible) the same as the Roman Pope. The Roman Pope wears the mitre, so did the pagan Pope.

The Pope calls a piece of bread God or Christ, so did the pagan Pope.

The 25th of March is celebrated in the Church of Rome for the "Annunciation of the Virgin" or the miraculous conception of our Lord. The same day "was observed in pagan Rome in honor of Cybele, the mother of the Babylonian messiah."

Is it any wonder that Revelations 17:5, calls this old harlot the mother of harlots, when she is simply the Babylonian harlot over again?. Look in your catholic and protestant bibles, Matthew 23:9-10, and you will find this command, "call no man your father upon the earth," yet look at the fathers of the church.

Much has been said of the lasciviousness of Popes and priests of past ages. But that is nothing against the church as there are always some bad and some good men everywhere in all ages so the church can not be blamed for that. But God strictly prohibited the use of idols or adoption of the pagan customs. Because he abhored the old Babylonian harlot and customs as he knew they were only adopted to blind the eyes and deceive the people, and steal their liberties. It is for this the money kings of the world corrupted the early church and made it the mother of harlots, for the protestant churches are used for the same purpose and they are the daughters of the old harlot, upholding usury.

A friend writes from pagan, India to day and calls it "the land of palaces to the gods and mud huts for the people" and says four cents a day are the average wages and poverty and misery all over the land, they are slaves of the gold worshiping English money kings. And that is what these kings are trying to bring all countries to and the churches are used to that end.

A catholic friend of mine

says, "you are right" and says it is the rule of the church "a very rich man a pontifical high mass, a poor man a low mass, but a pauper no mass."

And so my good catholic brothers and sisters there is no mass for you if you have no money.

All of the churches are being built like palaces with grand pews for the rich Diveses but poor Lazaruses must enter with shame and hardly dare sit on the door step.

It is said that the bishop of Chicago holds in his own right over forty-two millions of dollars worth of property, and probably the same proportion is held in others cities; all of this is wrung, mainly, from the poorer classes. Nor would this matter so much if the poor were not kept in idleness, through the curse of usury which the church sanctions.

The churches might benefit the people and become a blessing but they favor usury and are aiding the money kings to rob the people.

The kings of the old world hate our republic as they know it means the destruction of their institutions and republican freedom there, so they have always tried to down us *and in January,* 1829 a great conspiracy was organized at Vienna, and their object was to show the helplessness of the catholic church without monarchy, and the vital necessity of the church to monarchy, as one could not long exist without the other and neither could live where equal rights and liberal opinions are tolerated.

All of the kings, monarchs and the Pope were present. Their secret society was called "the St. Leopold Foundation." The meeting was presided over by the Emperor of Austria who said:

"As long as I live I will oppose a WILL OF IRON to the progress of liberal opinions. The present generation is lost, but we must labor with zeal and earnestness to improve the spirit of that to come. It may require a hundred years. I am not unreasonable; I give you a whole age, but you must work without relaxation."

And these conspirators meet there once a year ever since.

You see this work should be done so gradually that the people would be lulled into a sleepy security, and when the fetters were so woven about them that resistance was useless they would be prepared, and how?

They impoverish us through the financial system; they control the government through corruption; they deceive you through the pulpit and press; they are forming military organizations in their churches besides civic organizations they expect to turn into military organizations at a moment's notice:

The Ancient Order of Hibernians, Irish American Society, Knights of St. Patrick, St. Patrick's Mutual Alliance, St. Patrick's Cadets; Apostles of Liberty, Benevolent Sons of the Emerald Isle, Knights of St. Peter. Knights of the Red Branch, Knights of Columskill, Knights of St. John. And the protestant churches have their military organizations as well.

And all these people are innocent, patriotic Americans who will be deceived to fight against their own liberties in the following manner:

As I have stated, through usury they will load us with bonded debt until the burden is unbearable and the people demand reform. The government and all its institutions will be in the hands of the enemy and that enemy will be unscrupulous. They will defraud the people, and when exposed, will call the people a crazy mob. They will claim the country and the flag, and these good people of the churches will be called upon and their patriotism and love of flag appealed to, and they will be deceived and called upon to fight against their own liberties.

The late Prof. Samuel F. B. Morse, the inventor of the American telegraph, while residing in Italy many years ago, got hold of information of this conspiracy, and upon investigation established proof of its existence. I am indebted for much of my information on the subject of this conspiracy to Mr. John D. Gill, secretary of the National Reform Association and author of a book entitled. "Timely Warning." I have been satisfied by events that such a conspiracy did exist and have before made note of the fact that in 1868, at 37 Mercer street. New York, a paper called "The Imperialist," advocating monarchy and treachery, was published, and I have watched the hands of the conspirators ever since and have been satisfied that the churches are being used to that end. Of course few of the church people, priests or laymen are aware of that fact and would rebel against it if they were not being deceived. But God is with the people and he has been calling you for eighteen hundred years to *"come out of her, my people, that ye be not partakers of her sins, and that ye receive not of her plagues.*—Rev. 18:4.

It is a well knows fact that foreign powers during our late civil war were all, except Russia, against us, and hoped our country would be divided, and even the Pope wrote a letter to Jefferson Davis promising assistance. Says Benjamin F. Butler, in his book, "England and France were in league to aid the South, and through treachery intended to betray us." But they feared Russia, and more, they feared the liberty loving people in their own country, and God was with us and their plans miscarried.

Now, brothers and sisters, I have shown you that usury is the greatest crime spoken of in the Scriptures, that is for a people or a nation. The individual must do as his surroundings compel him. But God said, the individual must not take these things to himself, for they were addressed to nations and kings."

Notice again what the new testament says:

"For we wrestle not against flesh and blood (the individual) but against principalities, against powers, against the rulers of darkness (selfishness) of this world; against spiritual wickedness in high places."—Eph. 4:12.

"Take thou no usury or increase," says God, but the Pope says, "only take what the law says you may, and the laws are made to screen the rich. "Ye have taken usury and greedily gained one of another, and ye shall be scattered among the countries and among the heathen," says God to the Israelites.

"The love of money is the root of all evil," says the Scriptures, yet your churches favor the rich against the poor. "Come out of them, my people," Ye have made my father's house a den of thieves," says Christ, and he scourged the money changers out of the temple.

"Ye strain at a gnat and swallow a camel," says Christ, and the churches are railing at the individual sin in low places and covering up the wickedness of the greatest sin of the world, usury and love of money.

Brothers and sisters, of all churches, call upon your ministers to persistently make war upon usury and monopoly, and if they refuse to purify the church, come out of them or you must suffer the consequences, for God says of the old harlot, "For her I will make a bed; the dragon shall eat her flesh, and her children (the protestant churches I will kill."

But I will tell you *now* they will heed you not, for they belong to the dragon money power and the dragon is corrupting them to deceive you.

We will now remember that the Roman Empire was symbolized by a beast exceedingly strong and terrible, with great iron jaws, with which he brake to pieces and devoured and stamped upon the residue.

The Roman Empire was divided and finally fell, but the ten horns, the ten kingdoms, continued to exist, and papal authority extended over them, until at last Napoleon I, who was admitted to be a man of destiny, kicked when being baptized by the priest at his birth, and kicked when he was crowned, and he took the crown from the Pope's hand and placed it on his own head. And finally took the Pope from Rome and brought him to Paris, and it was left to Napoleon III to withdraw the French soldiers, the last support from the Pope, and Victor Emanuel deprived him of his Imperial temporal power. Yet he exerts a wonderful influence that astonishes the world. He continually mourns and claims to be a prisoner in the Vatican. Thus this head of the beast received a deadly wound. The Pope here represents this head of the beast, and when the forced separation of church and state, the Pope mourns that he is a prisoner in the Vatican. He speaks for the church, which I stated is symbolized by a woman, and it is through him she cries for the restoration of the Pope to political power, which is about to take place. She says:

"I sit a queen and am no widow, and shall see no sorrow." - Rev. 18:7.

Now John saw this same beast coming out of the sea, (the restless people). Revelations, 13:1. But John describes it as he saw it in the last days. He describes it as having seven heads and ten horns, spotted like a leopard, (made up of various kingdoms).

The angel tells John the seven heads are seven kings; five of them had fallen at the time the woman with the twelve stars on her head had fled to the wilderness.

Head No. 1, Rome first ruled by kings.

Head No. 2, Rome ruled by two Consuls.

Head No. 3, Rome ruled by Decemvirs.

Head No. 4, Rome ruled by Dictators.

Head No. 5, Rome ruled by Triumvirs.

Head No. 6, Rome ruled by Emperors.

Head No. 7, Rome ruled by Popes.

Seven different forms of government. See American Encyclopedia.

But the Pope was the head that received the deadly wound which is to be healed and his power restored by "The Great Red Dragon," and even he will be the eighth, says John, and will be of the seven. So it is very clear this is the same old beast that Daniel saw and John saw at a later period and the money power is about to restore an empire out of the old one, under a little different conditions, an alliance, so that the temporal power of the Pope will be restored, so his head will be the eighth head yet of the seven, for he was the seventh head and the deathly wound will be healed:

"And the dragon gave him his power and his seat, and great authority."

"And they worshipped the dragon which gave power to the beast, and they worshipped the beast, saying, 'who is like unto the beast, who is able to make war with him.'"

Now it is very clear that England is not strong enough to enforce all of the claims of the money power, and especially in America, therefore the dragon wants more force at his command. Why not use the old "harlot?" (Again I say, let not my brothers and sisters of the churches suppose I am assailing their religion, so long as their sentiments are purely christian, for there are good christians in all churches. But the organizations have been used for base purposes, hence Revelations calls the Catholic church the mother of harlots and the Protestant churches the daughters).

Yes; why shouldn't the dragon use the old harlot. She has committed fornication with the kings before, and she and the Protestant churches, the daughters, sanction the taking of interest (usury) today, and they are all "drunken with the wine of their fornications." They are wondering at the falling off of the people.

That things are moving in the direction of the restoration of the temporal power of the Pope is plain to him who reads for such articles as the following, are often seen in the press of the day:

"THE FUTURE OF THE PAPACY."

Sunday News Tribune, Detroit, Sept 15, 1895.

"The papacy and its prospects for the future, immediate and remote, have recently been the subject of much thought and discussion among both the writers and statesmen in the highest circles of the old world. That, in spite of its loss of temporal power, it still clings to Rome and never by a word compromises its hope of recovering its ancient position as a temporal sovereignty, is a constant embarrassment to Italy and a puzzle, to not only the statesmen of that kingdom but to those of all Europe.

Its spiritual power and prestige have grown enormously since Rome was made the capital of Italy and the Pope was confined to the narrow limits of the Vatican gardens. Its influence upon the politics of every country in Europe has become more marked and there is scarcely one of them which can formulate a policy without reckoning with the position of its catholic subjects, whose action in public affairs was never before so completely controlled by the head of their church.

"The universal church has bowed submissively to the stupendous claims of the Vatican Council, and there is not a breath of schism or heresy anywhere on earth within the ranks of its followers. As a prisoner, which he is pleased to call himself, the Pope has more real power than he had formerly as a king.

"It might be possible to explain this growth by the changed conditions of the world which, in our time, have enabled all human activities to centralize and consolidate power, and to trace much of the facility with which the Roman church has done it to that very loss of temporal power, which she regards as a misfortune but which has freed the Roman See from the natural jealously which other catholic communities naturally felt toward her when her bishop was a king. It might not be unreasonable to hope, too, that the new condition would eventually be accepted by the papal court and become permanent But the persistence of the papacy in clinging to and constantly asserting its claims alarms statesmen and excites fears, that in the future wars of

Europe, the hiistory of the last quarter of a century might be reversed.

"This is the view which a recent writer in the Fortnightly Review, Capt. J. W. Gambur, of the British navy, takes of the situation. He predicts that in the coming struggle between the destructive agencies of European society—anarchism, socialism nihilism, etc.—the great powers will be compelled to call the papacy into alliance with them as the only conservative force which is equally strong among all their populations, and which can strengthen their hands by securing for them the faithful support of the catholic masses."

I do not want to offend any of my good catholic friends or turn them from the many good things in their faith, and I will say the Catholic church did fight usury nobly, but today it upholds usury and the rich oppressor as well as do the Protestant churches, and the Pope is longing and sighing for the flesh pots of temporal power; and one day in the near future, the money power will covet his influence to control the world and they will form an alliance, and if they cannot control the Pope they will seat one of their own making, and church and state will once more be united and the wound healed, and he will be the eighth head but of the seven.

I will have more to say of this beast further on, and of this Pope, but I must first explsin a little more of this "old harlot" spoken off in Revelations 17.

THE WOMAN SITTING ON THE BEAST

This woman John saw sitting upon a scarlet colored beast full of names of blasphemy; and the woman was arrayed in purple and scarlet. Now this not only gives us a clue as to who the woman is but what beast is referred to. First, the old Roman empire must be the beast and the scarlet flag denotes the color of the beast.

Away back in Ancient Greece the laboring classes adopted the blood red flag for their banner, as they said it was typical of the red blood that flowed in the veins of all mankind alike. And that is where our anarchists of today got their idea of a red rag for a banner.

The wealthy classes, feeling themselves of better blood than the lower classes, declared they had blue blood mixed in their veins, and so adopted the royal purple for their banner. As there was always strife among the classes the banners became dear to the followers of either side. When the new Roman Empire came up, it bid for the emigration of all classes and nationalities of people, something like the United States did some years ago; and in order to reconcile the two classes mingled the royal purple and the blood red and adopted a scarlet colored banner. Yet while Rome abandoned the blood red flag of the poor classes it not only carried the scarlet flag but maintained the royal purple, to satisfy the wealthy class. Thus while Rome's scarlet flag marking the beast as a scarlet colored beast, the church was made up of both classes of people she being the women clothed in scarlet and purple, and sitting upon the scarlet colored beast. This gives us another proof that Rome was the beast meant by both Daniel and John.

We will now find further proofs that the Catholic church is the woman "with whom the kings of the earth have committed fornication, and the inhabitants of the earth have been made drunk with the wine of her fornications." Verse 2.

This woman is decked with precious stones, and a golden cup in her hand full of abominations.

An emblem of the old Babylonian harlot or secret society was a woman holding a golden cup, and it is said that the Roman Pope, in the year 1825, had a medal struck off with his image on one side and a woman holding a golden cup on the reverse side.

The church is very rich and pays no taxes, and at one time sold indulgences, and has winked at many wrongdoings of the moneyed class, and though Christ and his deciples established a socialistic sytem, the church today would persecute, not only the socialist, but every class of reformers, to satisfy the moneyed classes, that do her bidding, and in forcing the people to keep her up and the Protestant churches do the same, hence they are the daughters, following in the footsteps of the old mother of harlots. Verse 5 says: "And upon her forehead was a name written, **Mystery, Babylon, The Great, The Mother of Harlots, and abominations of the earth.**"

John says he saw the woman drunken with the blood of the saints and of the martyrs of Jesus. Has there been any other woman church that has taken the lives of the worshippers of God, and lovers of Christ who saw fit to worship as they pleased?

"And he saith unto me, "the waters which thou hath sawest, where the whore sitteth are peoples, and multitudes, and nations and tongues."

Mystery, Babylon, confusion of tongues. The Catholic church does sit in almost every nation and numbers 190,000,000 souls. This should settle it as to what church is meant.

Thus the angel tells John who this woman is, and the angel tells John that the seven heads of the beast are seven mountains on which the woman sitteth.

The city of Rome sits upon **seven** hills, but mountains usually symbolize kings, and the angel says: "There are seven kings, five of them have fallen and one of them has not yet come." Now at the time John describes this vision is in the last days, or near the time of the woman that fled to the wilderness to be delivered of the "man child."

I have already shown the heads that had fallen, and called attention to the Pope's head that had been wounded but is to be restored by the money power that is the great dragon that the people worship, and today nearly every one is worshipping the mighty dollar. Now this is a fine chain of evidence.

The Pope the seventh head, which was wounded, and when restored by the dragon will be the eighth but of the seven, because he was the seventh, "and when he comes he must continue a short time."

Thus we have "the beast that was and is not, yet is." For we cannot say the beast now exists, yet the Pope still exerts his power, though he is not at the head of his former temporal power, so he is not, yet is.

This certainly must be the beast that Daniel saw, and the Romish church must be the old harlot spoken of by John.

Mr. Woolfolk, author of a book, called "Red Dragon," seems to think the seven headed beast meant seven empires starting back with Egypt and following down certain empires, ending with the image of the beast, which he thinks means a re-establishing of the Roman empire by an alliance of the powers with Germany at the head. This can't be possible, as it would not then be the beast that Daniel saw; and as the whole description is given merely as landmarks, it is not absolutely necessary that everything should be minutely described or it would become too easy and we would neglect to keep our lamps trimmed, (be watchful of events). Mr. Woolfolk does not attempt to explain everything of the old harlot. This may be because he is blinded on account of being a divine, or it is too sore a spot for him to touch. However, his work is an ably written work. Mr. Woolfolk, and all other expositors have made the mistake of supposing the dragon and the beast were one. But this is a great mistake as the beast has seven heads and ten horns and ten crowns upon his horns, while the dragon has seven heads and ten horns and seven crowns upon his heads. This makes a great difference and certainly can not be one and the same power, as in one case the crowns are upon the heads and the other upon the horns, and this shows us it is the same beast that Daniel saw but at a later period. The heads of the beast had fallen, passed away, but the heads of the dragon had not fallen.

As I have before stated, the prophecies all seem to have a double meaning. These heads may mean seven localities of power and the ten horns ten resting places. The money power certainly did control Babylon and its corruption destroyed Babylon. Then Medo Persian, headquarters at Ninevah; then Greece, headquarters at Athens. The money power was driven out of Athens and rested in Carthage, (where we first took up its history, as we have no history of finance of Babylon). It then established its headquarters in Rome and controlled the empire, but had not complete control of Carthage as

Hannibal impeached their judges and drove the money changers out. Thus Rome would be its fourth head. It now moved to Amsterdam, its fifth head; though after the destruction of the Roman empire it had a resting place first at Venice and then at Genoa. From Amsterdam it changed its headquarters to London. From London it must go to Rome as the English people will drive it out sooner or later. Thus we see the dragon's seven heads were as follows:

Head No. 1, Babylon:
Head No. 2, Medo-Persia.
Head No. 3, Greece.
Head No. 4, Rome.
Head No. 5, Amsterdam, Holland.
Head No. 6, England.
Head No. 7, Rome restored.
Horn No. 8, Carthage.
Horn No. 9, Venice.
Horn No. 10, Genoa.

Thus we have seven heads and ten horns of the dragon. And the above are historical facts without drawing upon the imagination or trying to make matters fit and it was under the golden head of Babylon that the Jews were reprimanded for taking usury or gain.

THE ABOVE FACTS I BELIEVE

to be correct, though we might take into consideration and watchfulness the fact that there are eleven Rothschilds, they are at the head of the money power of the world. They control at least five governing powers with controlling influence in several others. Let us suppose that one of them should die, and an alliance formed of the most of the European nations, with the Pope as arbitrator of the alliance, and the money power with seven great heads (crowns) controlling the seven governments, and the other three governing outlying interest you have seven heads and ten horns of the dragon.

Unless, perchance, the restored empire consisted of ten kingdoms, or ten powers, controlled by the ten horns of the dragon is meant; for the beast that John describes is certainly the same beast that Daniel saw, yet John saw it at a a later period, and then the angel told John the ten horns were ten kingdoms, not yet given; so by that we may suppose they were kingdoms yet to come with the restoration of the wounded head by the dragon.

THE IMAGE OF THE BEAST.

"And I beheld another beast coming up out of the earth; and he had two horns like a lamb, and he spake as a dragon.

"And exercised all the powers of the first beast before him and cause to the earth (Europe) and them that dwell thereon to worship the first beast whose deadly wound was healed." Rev. 13:11-12.

Now this is in no wise the first beast or the first beast restored. But what power is it that so closely resembles the old Roman Empire, spotted like a leopard, (made up of many peoples and tongues)? England, no other power. As Medo-Persia was made up of two kingdoms and symbolized by a ram so is England of two kingdoms (Scotland and England) representing the two horns.

Like old Rome, she devours and breaks to pieces and stamps on the residue. Her empire is made up of many peoples and tongues. She is "lamb like" See Revelations 8:2, professing a protectorate power for the purpose of Christianizing and better governing the poor savage souls, but really to rob them of their inheritance. And in this she speaks like a dragon.

Dealing with a double tongue,

laying claims of territory, or indemnities based upon rediculous claims. But enforcing it with her mighty navy, as in the case of the Nicaraugua, and other claims. She has always laid claim to the whole earth wherever she could get her old serpentine folds around, and then crushed the life out of the existing governments, and robbed the people under the pretence of governing them for their benefit. This is not the work of English people but the dragon money power that "has controlled England. She speaks like a dragon (double tongued, deceptive) even deceiving her own people saying: "See how rich we are?" But it is the riches of the money kings, the dragon, the people get little of it. When America casts off the yoke of the money power it will not be long before the noble English people will follow.

England is again like the old beast, because she is united church and state, and the church is becoming more like the Roman Catholic church every day. Thus she is a perfect image of the old beast.

She is to do wonders in the sight of the old beast, consequently the two are to exist at the same time. What these wonders are to be we must wait and watch for.

The following poem from the London Truth describes the selfishness of the image of the beast exactly:

THE FLAG OF ENGLAND.

"And the winds of the word made answer,
 North, south, and east, and west;
"Wherever there's wealth to covet,
 Or land that can be posess'd
Wherever are savage races
 To cozen, coerce and scare

Ye shall find the vaunted ensign:
  For the English flag is there!

"Aye, it waves o'er the blazing hovels
  Whence African victims fly,
To be shot by explosive bullets
  Or to wretchedly starve and die!
And where the beach-comber harries
  The isles of the Southern Sea,
At the peak of his hellish vessel,
  'Tis the English flag flies free.

"The Maori full oft hath cursed it,
  With his bitterest dying breath;
And the Arab has hissed his hatred
  As he spits at its folds in death.
The hapless fellah has feared it
  On Tel-el-Kebir's parched plain,
And the Zulu's blood has stained it
  With a deep indelible stain.

"It has floated o'er scenes of pilage,
  It has floated o'er deeds of shame,
It was waved o'er the fell marauder,
  As he ravished with sword and flame.
It has looked upon ruthless slaughter,
  And massacres dire and grim!
It has heard the shriek of the victims
  Drown even the Jingo hymn.

"Where is the flag of England?
  Seek the lands where the natives rot;
Where decay and assured extinction
  Must soon be the people's lot.
Go! search for the once glad islands,
  Where diseases and death are rife,
And the greed of callous commerce
  Now fattens on human life!

"Where is the flag of England?
  Go! sail where rich galleons come
With shoddy and 'loaded' cottons,
  And beer, and bibles, and rum!
Go, too, where brute force has triumphed,
  And hypocracy makes its lair:
And your question will find its answer,
  For the flag of England is there."

So closely allied to the dragon is the image of the beast that the

"Dragon has power to give life to the image of the beast, that the image of the beast should both speak and cause that as many as would not worship the image of the beast should be killed.

"And he causeth all, both great and small, rich and poor, free and bond, to receive a mark in their right hands or on their foreheads.

"And that no man might buy or sell save he that had the mark, or the name of the beast, or the number of his name."- Rev. 13: 15-16.

England slowly rose up to her mighty power, and it was the dragon, that had the power to give England this mighty growth, to place money everywhere under the name of English capital that controls the industries of the world; so that under the selfish, greed-begetting money system few can live who have not their mark of dishonesty in the forehead or in the hand, as I have before stated, or work directly for them, (ie.) have the number of the beast, not the image of the beast, must die. Unless ther names are already written in the book of life when God will find some means open for them to live.

It is thought by some expositors that this mark means the sign of the cross that is made on the forehead of all lay members of the Catholic church, and the right hand of priests at baptism, as that sign was also used by the Babylonian harlot, for all members why joined that secret organization. But it is more likely that it is as I have before described.

So closely allied are the dragon first beast and the image of the beast that we find the dragon has power to give life (strength and force) to the image of the beast and actually does restore life to the beast whose deadly wound was healed. He becomes the head of the beast power, hence the image forces the worship of the beast.

The money power will find England not strong enough to enforce its claims everywhere and the discontent of the robbed people of the nations will worry them so that an alliance of the nations: England, Germany Austria, Italy, Spain, Belgium, and some other small nations will be formed in this alliance.

The people of the United States will understand that this cry of "be honest and pay your obligations and save your credit" is like the cry of the thief of "stop thief, stop thief". It is only a deception and a means to rob the masses through fraudulent claims, and they will repudiate the whole debt; war will be made on us, first by England then backed by the allied forces. The great navies and armies of the all·ed forces will be no match for the inventive genius of Americans, through the help of God, and they will be driven out and through these wonderful inventions of destruction we will destroy our enemies. We will rule the turbulent American nations with a rod of iron, as we smote the image on the feet and it shall crumble, and our examble of a republic, with religious liberties will be adopted by all nations. Thus the stone cut out without hands fell upon the feet of Nebuchadnezzer's image "and it shall be broken to pieces altogether." This is done more by the example of a republican government, or a true system that other nations will demand.

The last act will be the great battle of Armagidon, near Jerusalem, between the allied forces of the beast, assisted by the troops of China and Japan on the one side, and Russia, Turkey and France on the other will take place. Then Michael, the great prince, (Christ) will stand up. So Michael, spoken of in Daniel 12:1, is not the stone spoken spoken of in Daniel 2:35 and in Revelations 12:7, as the word Michael is used in more than one sense.

These terrible wars will ruin all nations, hence the formation of new governments, republics under Christ, who will establish his throne at Jerusalem and there will be no more wars for a thousand years, then Satan will be loosed for a season.

This is the thousand years millennium, but before it comes such troublous times "as never was before or since there was a nation" must come. But, says God, I will shorten it for the elect's sake, lest there should be none left upon the earth.

What part will China and and Japan take? The Bible was not written to give a history of the world but to give instructions how to live and to mark the way of events. There is nothing said but we can see where they will be drawn in. Turkey being the little horn of the he goat or Grecia, must be annihilated. Russia, the king of the north, must be terribly rent asunder, but exists as a republic to the end to rule over her turbulent people, who will fear to make war and have little cause as Christ will see that all governments are just. France will only suffer the ordinary evils of a terrible war.

All governments will partake largely of socialistic forms though not to extremes. Individual rights will be protected as far as necessary. *Usury, interest, the great curse,* will be abolished altogether.

Under Christ's rule spirituality will be so wonderfully developed that no one will dare to think evil knowing that unseen individuals or his next friend will read his every thought. The spiritualists, clairvoyants, and investigators of psycical phenomena, today, all know how rapidly this wonderful spiritual gift is developing.

There are certain periods spoken of in Scripture, such as the 2,300 days, (years) spoken of in Daniel as giving the time of the end, whereby expositors try to fix the very year of Christ's coming; but as "no man knoweth the hour not even the angels in heaven," and as they cannot fix the point of starting for these given dates; and as I have before quoted "the kingdom of God does not come by observation" it is impossible for us to fix the exact time of Christ,s arrival but as the prophecies are nearly all fulfiled we know the time is very near. When Christ does come, life will be worth living for a thousand years, so continue to watch and pray: "Our Father who art in heaven, hallowed be Thy Name; Thy kingdom come."

As the peculiarity of my work does not call for an exhaustive treatise of the prophecies I had no intention of attempting to fix dates, nor shall I attempt it, as it is wrong for Christ said no man knoweth the hour, not even the angels in heaven. So it is useless to attempt to fix the exact date of Christ's coming. Yet there are certain dates that figure remarkably near our times.

First, let me say, however, that historical events lap each other, and a given historical event can hardly be said to take place on a given day, as things that lead up to it or follow it, should be taken into consideration as belonging to that event. It was the intention to veil the hour, which certainly must be the case or definite time would be given, then the starting and ending of these periods would be left partly hidden. There are four different times given, if we can be assured of a starting and finishing point (v.s.) Daniel 8:14, 2300 days; Daniel 12:2, 1290 days and Daniel 12:12, 1335 days and Revelations 12, 1260 days. Expositors all agree that these days mean, our vulgar or calendar years. This being the case we must get a starting point and ending for each period. We will then take the first period of 2300 days.

When Daniel's vision took place he stood on the banks of the river Ulai, at Shushan, and he saw the ram of Medo Persia pushing westward, northward and southward and he saw a rough he goat, with a notable horn, run into the ram and overthrow it. After a time the notable horn was broken and four horns came up instead and from one of these horns a little horn came up which grew very strong, nearly equaling the rest of the world which in part it conquered and trampled upon many of the kings and princes (stars) and finally a host was given him against the daily sacrifice and he cast the truth to the ground. Chapter 8:13. The angel tells another angel in Daniel's hearing that the period from the taking away the daily sacrifice and transgression of desolation to give both the sanctuary and the host to be trodden under foot.

That the starting point was to be far in the future, from Daniel's time was made clear, for the angel's said to Daniel: "Shut up the vision, for it shall be for many days," therefore it should be in the future.

We find in history, 636 A. D. that a part of Alexander's old Grecian empire did capture Jerusalem and clear away the old temple and build one to the Mohamedan God. And this agrees with the Scripture, and is the only time the daily sacrifice can be said to have been take away by a foreign power after the vision. As Daniel's vision mainly ends with events of about the time of the French Revolution, some expositors figure from the captivity of the Jews in 590 B. C. Two thousand three hundred days (years) from that time would bring us to 1710, which they claim would be the end of the great indignation and cleansing of the sanctuary, by the exodus of the Protestants from the old Roman church and the thorough establishment of the Protestant religions in America, and before another century closed the cry for republics struck France on the feet of the image, which idea is to grow and fill the whole world with republican forms of government, and thus it is the starting point.

Other expositors come to 426 B. C. as a starting point, which would bring us to 1874, but as nothing observable took place at that date we may naturally suppose them wrong.

Now if we take the capture of Jerusalem in 636 A. D., which is really the only time that accords with the scriptural description, the 2300 years would bring us to 2936. As Christ is to perfect his father's kingdom and then turn it over to him, of course the sanctuary will not be cleansed until the end of the millennium, or somwhere near 2936. Then if we take the one thousand years, or millennium, from the 2936 we have 1936, or thereabouts for its starting point, and as great events must take place before that starting point, in clearing the workshop, the rolling together of the nations, "the rolling together of the heavens as a scroll" and the "falling of the stars (kings, princes) of the heavens like a tree casting her untimely fruit, and the purifying by fire, heating as of an oven," the passions of men and great indignation of the people, which will result in universal war, as any one must see, is coming. Therefore it is quite likely this date is right.

Now the next date. Says Daniel 12:11: "And from the time the daily sacrifice is taken away, and the abomination that maketh desolate set up, there shall be a thousand, two hundred ,and ninety days." As I have shown nothing so desolates the world as usury and controlling money, by the selfish, unprincipled moneyed classes and what could be more abominable than uniting this power and the church, to deceive and control the people. Yet I have pointed out that is the aim and purpose of the alliance that is to be formed, if it is not already done but not yet made known. So if the 2300 years would bring us to the end of the millennium, and 1926 as the end of the horrors of universal war, we may see that from the point of starting, 636, we add the 1290 years, brings us to 1926, or allowing for lapping of historical events, it brings us to the same date as the 2300 years after deducting the 1000 years for the millennium.

The next is Daniel 12:12: "Blessed is he that waiteth and cometh to the thousand, three hundred and five and thirty days" (years).

What can we make out of this, but those who do not come on earth until that date, for they will escape the horrors of the cleaning up of God's workshop, as that date, figuring from 636, adding 1335 brings us to 1971, the wars will be over, the world cleansed and the curse of usury and monopoly bound for a thousand years; and those that do not come on earth until that time, are blessed by escaping the burning as an oven (of man's passions).

The next date is in Revelations 12:6.

"And the woman fled into the wilderness, where she hath a place prepared of God, that they should feed her a thousand, two hundred and three score days" —1260 years.

Now I have pointed out the woman—the religious colonies—fled to this country from 1605 to 1682. Now we cannot figure from either 1605 or 1682, but take the middle of the century, 1650, and add 1260 years, and it brings us to 2910. As the woman (church) is to be fed here 1260 days; of course this must be spiritual food, and as Christ is perfecting his kingdom, it is to be fed for the thousand year millennium, thus if we take off the 1000 years from 2910 we have 1910.

We see by all of this figuring these dates all converge to about one period. The universal war must begin somewhere not later than 1915, and extend not later 1971, but these events must take place probably much nearer than those extreme dates 1905 and 1971 given, but "as no man knoweth the hour" we can not get closer than that. But glorious is our country to be chosen for the place for the woman to be fed for 1260 days. We shall be the leaders in spiritual doctrines to the end of the millennium. But certainly all must admit that these dates figure very closely together, and where other expositors have failed I hope I have hit closer to the mark.

The dragon must remain an hour with the beast, and we may now look with assurance; that the alliance is about to be formed, and the money power (the dragon) will name the Pope and his decisions will always be in favor of the dragon, for he is the dragon head.

"*Here is wisdom. Let him that hath understanding count the number of the beast, for it is the number of a man, and his number is six hundered three score and six, 666.*"—Rev. 13.

Writers upon this subject explain this as follows: The Pope wears upon his pontificial crown in jeweled letters, this title: "*Vicarius Filii Dei*" (Vicegerent of the Son of God). The numerical value of the letters of this title is as follows:

V. stands for 5; I. for 1; C. 100; *a* and *r* not used as numerals; I. 1; U., anciently written as V., 5; *s* and *f* not used; I. 1; L. 50; I. 1; I. 1; D. 500; *e* not used; I. 1—666.

"The Pope, as the fountain of knowledge or head of the mysteries in the Church of Rome holds the same position as did Nimrod at the head of the Chaldean mysteries. Nimrod as God of the Chaldean mysteries, was known as *Saturn*. *Saturn* and *mystery* are both Chaldean words, and they are correlative terms. As *mystery* signifies the hidden system, so *Saturn* signifies the hidden God. To those who were initiated, God was revealed; to all else he was hidden. Now the name *Saturn* in Chaldea is pronounced *Satur* but consisted only of four letters, thus *stur*."

The numerals of these letters in the Hebrew or Chaldea alphabet are S 60; T 400; U 6; R 200; Six hundred and sixty-six. Each letter in the Hebrew alphabet has a numerical value.

The Pope, as the head of the mysteries of the Church of Rome, requires the services of the Church of Rome to be in the Latin language, and calls his church the Latin church.

Latin is from the Greek Lateinos, which is synvnomous with Saturn, and each belong to the "hidden one" or the god of "mystery." Apply the value of the letters in the Greek alphabet, which all have a numerical value and you have L 30; A 1; T 300; E 5; I 10; N 50; O 70; S 200, six hunded and sixty six

Sheitan is the Chaldean word for Satan, in Greek rendered *Teitan*. The Dragon is called Satan and as the Pope will no doubt represent the beast, his seat and power given him by the money power or dragon, or perhaps be one and the same person at the head of both; and as the numerals of the Greek alphabet for the letters in this word "Teitan" are T 300; E 5; I 10; T 300; A 1; N 50, thus six hundred and sixty-six.

So we see, using the old Roman legend, "all roads lead to Rome," these things tabulated would appear as follows:

VICARIUS FILII DEI	SATUR	LATEINOS	TEITAN
Roman	Hebrew	Greek	Greek
V 5	S 60	L 30	T 300
I 1	T 400	A 1	E 5
C 100	U 6	T 300	I 10
I 1	R 200	E 5	T 300
U (V) 5		I 10	A 1
I 1		N 50	N 50
L 50		O 70	
I 1		S 200	
I 1			
D 500			
I 1			
666	666	666	666

THE POPE IN ROME

Let not the protestants rejoice at this, for unless they repent and war against usury they must expect to suffer God's punishment, for he calls for the repentance of the churches or "come out of them my people."

THE END.

PART THREE.

WHAT IS COMING?

REPETITION FOR LECTURE PURPOSES.

Any person desiring to use this subject matter in the lectur feild may do so with my full consent.

The wide margin is left for the purpose of notation.

The object of summing up the matter in this book 16 years after its publication, is partly to bring the book down to the present time (1913) and partly to make it more comprehensive to the casual reader.

My book, "WHAT IS COMING," has done a great work in pointing out the dangers to our country and our flag, but many who were brought up to old orthodox ideas cannot understand the newer idea of creation, through evolution, and still recognize it as the hand of Divine power; nor do I wish to discuss it here except as a quickening to the understanding of our subject. Reject that part afterward if you want to.

CREATION.

All reason, all scientific research, go to show the earth has stood millions of years, and has been inhabited hundreds of thousands of years: that instead of a spontaneous creation, all things came through the law of evolution. This is well proven in my book, "Bible Astrology," $1.00, and in my litle booklet, "Cosmos," 25c.

Evolution does not deny the necessity of a master mind, in fact, goes to prove there is a master mind, and that this earth is a school house, or work shop, and that our lives from the first protoplasm to the finish was, is and will be under the guidance of a master mind, who like a good schoolmaster will punish, but make the cause for the punishment manifest and give the culprit a chance to take a lesson from the punishment; hence punishment, fear, folly, to be of any benefit to God or man must admit of improvement.

Any man, nation or creed that stands in the way of God's natural law must feel the weight of the punishment, sooner or later.

The child who burns his fingers is careful to avoid the fire thereafter. Every man, every animal, every bird and every insect is influenced by that law, and seems to be guided by an invisible power to some extent.

To make this consistent with a divine power, we must admit reincarnation is necessary to make the purpose of evolution complete.

Man tries to overcome all dangers by forming association and governments for self-protection against other organizations, and then proceeds to form parties, church societies and combinations within that government; to obtain privileges over his fellowman, in the same government.

All churches and societies are built from selfish motives and are inimical to a universal brotherhood. Aye, I am sorry to say, my experiences leads me to believe all organized charities, that are not of government, are little more than legalized graft.

Stop and think of the Good Samariton stooping to ask the wounded publican: "Are you a Catholic? Are you a Baptist? Are you a Mason? Are you an Oddfellow?

This of itself constitutes a danger to the general government. It is the first step toward revolution and d.solution.

If freedom is to be protected, it must be a freedom, so broad as to exclude all petty freedom, to form societies and combinations to obtain privileges from the government of the whole, and any one seeking such privileges, that does not emanate from a desire to collect pay, due for services already performed and overdue and neglected, should be considered treasonable and punished.

Any government that does not protect the rights of the least of its citizens as perfectly as it does the most powerful citizen, becomes the instrument of selfish men who are seeking to enslave their fellow-man, and is not worthy of the name of government, no matter what flag it flies.

GOVERNMENT GOD'S SPECIAL CARE.

The bulk of the Bible goes to show it refers to government far more than to individuals, especially the Old Testament.

The evidence of a guiding hand of nations is found all through the Bible, and it seems as if God had as hard a job of it to find an honest man as did Diogenes of Athens, who with a lantern, in the day time, was found seeking an honest man on the streets.

According to Bible history, Rebecca, a chosen woman and the mother of the 12 tribes of Israel, intrigued with her youngest son, Jacob, to steal the birthright of her eldest son, and, unless evolution is true, God made a mistake that he did not strangle Rebecca and Jacob right there.

Later we find Jacob intriguing to get even with a dishonest father-in-law.

Still later we find jealous sons selling a brother into slavery, who afterward saved the whole tribe by helping a selfish king monopolize the wheat trade.

Finally we find the 12 tribes of Jacob playing a trick on their masters, by borrowing all of their jewelry, and runing away to liberty with it. We read that God sanctioned the act, and even advised them to do it, and then helped them by drowning their pursuing masters in the Red Sea. This was probably as a lesson to the slaves of the twentieth century that the despoiling of robber masters is no sin. Or is it a precedent for the Socialists, in case they get in power, to show God favors their confiscation of the factories and means of transportation.

In fact the monied men themselves offered a fine precedent when ready to establish the National Bank system, they got the government to tax the old state banks out of existence.

So far as that is concerned the author of these line shas had property taken by law, from him, for public benefit and without adequate return, even to what one jury awarded.

Let us now return to our subject and trace God's plan down through the Jew to the Destiny of our country and our flag.

WHY THE JEWS WERE A CHOSEN PEOPLE.

The orthodox church people have forever been whooping it up that the Jews were a chosen people, with never a reason why.

If the God of the Universe, of which every man is a part, chose the Jews for a certain purpose, there must have been a reason for it.

I am not treating this matter so much from a Biblical standpoint as from a scientific standpoint, and sometimes I think it ought to be treated from the standpoint of a novel, or fiction based upon truth; yet truth is stranger than fiction, and the strange chain of evidence from historic and scientific research forms a better line of connected historic matter than is generally found in histories.

At the date of Biblical history, the Jews were certainly not the highest type of intelligence on the earth at that time; and as for reliability, it was of as low an order as of today. Consequently we will find the reason for God's taking especial charge of the Jews is the same as that of a loving parent taking especial care of a wayward child, and giving it more attention than to the rest of the family, because it needs more attention.

The Judges sold themselves for filthy lucre.—I Samuel, viii, 3-5-11-12-13. And the people cried, Give us a king, O Lord! "This will be the manner of king that shall reign over you; He will take your sons and your daughters and the best of all you have."

King Saul was especially favored and recommended by God, but luxury and opportunity caused his downfall.

King David was declared to be a man after God's own heart, and like all the rest in high life he became an old reprobate of the worst order, even ordering a battle where many must be slain, that one poor soldier should be killed in battle to take the stain of adultery off David's shoulders.

The twentieth century reprobates know a trick worth two of David's contemptible trick. They create wars to sell arms and lend money, no matter how many are slain; then they pose as the commercial giants of the age, and build colleges and libraries to educate their kind, and as monuments to themselves.

This class of world leaders turn heaven and earth to crush any evidence of intelligence of the plain people, while lauding to the skies the scions of the upper class.

Let any reader of history for one moment compare any character of history with the People's hero, Abraham Lincoln, and he will not have much respect left for nobility of history.

The Bible sings loudly of the wisdom of King Solomon, and then points out that he, by his extravagance, ruined his kingdom, to please the predatory class.

I. Kings, x., 27, shows he demonetized silver the same as our selfish class did.

Solomon reigned over Israel forty years, but gained nothing by experience and age.

When Solomon died and his son Rehoboam succeeded him all Israel cried out—II. Chronicles, x., 4—"Thy father made our yoke grievous; now, therefore, ease thou somewhat the grievous servitude of thy father, and his heavy yoke that he put upon us, and we will serve thee."

Rehoboam listened to the extravagant, fast young fools of his time just as the politicians are doing today, and he replied: "My little finger shall be thicker than my father's loins."

"My father made your yoke heavy; but I will add thereunto; my father chastized you with whips, I will chastize you with scorpions."

It is true Solomon said some good things, among which are:

"He that putteth not out his money to usury, nor taketh reward against the innocent. He that doeth these things shall never be moved."—Psalms, xv., 5

"The earth is the Lord's, and the fullness thereof."—Psalms, xxiv., 1.

"Take thou no usury or increase."—Lev., xxv., 36.

This shows us what constitutes usury.

The word interest was adopted because the word usury had become an unpleasant sound to the usurer, as the word thief is unpleasant to the thief. Yet I wish to say that the individual is not to blame for taking interest, for he must live as others live; but he is to blame for upholding a system that forces us all to become thieves, not for ourselves but for the big thief above us.

"He that withholdeth corn, the people shall curse him: but blessing shall be upon the head of him that selleth it."—Prov., xi., 26.

"The rich and the poor meet together: the Lord is the maker of them all. The rich ruleth over the poor, and the borrower is servant to the lender."—Prov., xxii., 2-7.

Solomon well knew right from wrong, but chose the path of oppression.

When oppression by the ruling class became unbearable and the people cried, "Give us a king, O Lord!" God said, "I will give you a king, but he will take your sons and your daughters, your lands and your vineyards, and the best of all you have, but I will give to my people a country and a language."

The country mentioned was not little 8x10 Palestine, which is not large enough for but a small number of God's people, nor was God's people to be confined to those known as the Jews, but to all seeking knowledge. Progress is God's purpose.

"Israel shall blossom and bud, and fill the world with fruit."—Isaiah, xxvii., 6.

That these shall not all appear to be Jews or Israelites is evident.

"For then will I turn to the people a pure language, that they may all call upon the name of the Lord, to serve him with one consent."—Zeph., iii., 9.

"For with stammering lips, and another tongue, he will speak to his people."—Isaiah, xxviii., 11.

"For the Lord God shall call his servants by another name."—Isaiah, 65-15.

When Daniel speaks of the little horn that came up and plucked up three small horns, and finally he says, "One of them came forth a little horn which waxed exceedingly great, toward the south and toward the east, and toward the pleasant land."—Daniel, viii., 9. That was the direction of America.

My object in speaking of the corruption of the ruling classes of those times is to show they were subject to the same rottenness in those days as we have today, and the Bible is nothing more or less than a history of nations in symbol, written by astrologers who were continuing the national lines into the future, and to show America is that country, the Pleasant Land to the west of the Holy Land

That there is a destiny ruling the affairs of men may be seen by paying a little attention to the Zodiac.

Any person who has noticed the effort of the orthodox church people, and that they are the handmaiden of the robber millionaire class, if they have paid just a little attention to the effect of the Zodiac on animal and vegetable life, will see proofs of the falsehood of the religious class. However, we will take up the subject with the Jews as a favored nation, who were punished for misdeeds and are to be finally rewarded for virtues.

By noticing the cut of the Zodiac below it will be seen to be divided into four quarters. This is the Great Zodiac through which the sun passes in his real motion, in twenty-six thousand years. This in reverse to his apparent annual motion, which is due to the real motion of the earth.

Each quarter of the Zodiac rules a race of people distinctly different from those of other races.

Thus, commencing at Capricornus and running down through Sagittarius, Scorpio and Libra, called the Commercial or reproducing quarter, and rules the yellow or Mongolian race which dominated the earth for six thousand years, and passed off from the zenith of their power over 16,000 years ago, but by retiring by

themselves have held their race habits and peculiarities better than have the other three-quarters of the globe. The great yellow or golden scales rules that quarter. Hence the yellow color.

Is 95,000,000 miles from earth, 1,300,000 times greater than earth and is 882,000 miles in diameter.

The Sun rules Leo. The majority of the people born in the sign Leo are very red-faced, and this quarter rules the red race, and they came onto the stage of action when the yellow race passed off. They dominated the earth up to ten thousand years ago, and they began to retrograde when the Caucasian race came on to the stage of action, though their power was felt longer into the Caucasion rule than the yellow race had extended into the rule of the red race. The quarter of wisdom, or maternal quarter.

Undoubtedly it was the wisdom and power of the red race that erected the greatest and most lasting stone structural work the world ever knew, the Pyramids, the Sphinx of Egypt, and structures found in ancient Peru all attesting to this idea.

The red man is as self-reliant as the Sun, which rules his race.

You can kill him, but you cannot make a slave of him.

The Caucasian, or white man, ruled by Venus, the goddess of beauty, is a licentious race, pretending virtue and never satisfied, yet struggling for a high order of virtue.

The black race, virtually without a ruler of high order, is easily broken up and enslaved.

The yellow race, the most numerous, are in that quarter where there are the most stars, in the sign of the Golden Scales, is a commercial race, shrewd and tricky.

VENUS-LOVE

Is 67,000,000 miles from sun and 7,700 miles in diameter.

The large and beautiful silver Venus rules the quarter of love, or so-called intellectual quarter, and rules the Caucasian race.

Why it should be called the intellectual quarter I cannot understand, unless it is because the people are determined to live on their wits rather than by the sweat of the brow, for of the four races none could have expressed more heartless selfishness than the white race has done, and covered it under the garb of religion.

This quarter runs from the first degree of Cancer back through Gemini, Taurus and Aries. (See Stowe's Bible Astrology.)

Through selfishness and shrewdness this quarter has extended its power through the first two thousand years of the serving quarter, though not without asissting the Ethopian race to liberty, from a foolish bondage, their selfishness and folly had placed them in.

URANUS.
Is 1,822,360,000 miles from the sun; 34,331 miles in diameter.

Uranus, the ruler of the serving quarter or quarter of labor. To being in opposition to the Sun p. uces the black man, or dark racesr

The serving quarter, or quarter of labor, runs through Pisces, Aquarius and Capricornus.

The sun entered Pisces two thousand year ago, or about Christ's time.

The Jews and Egyptians as well as the colored race properly belong to the Ethopian race. Of course I am treating of distinct races and not mixtures. The two extremes of this race have been held in bondage, and are yet favored, or under the guidance of heaven.

The Israelites were held in bondage in Egypt, by the Egyptians, and yet benefited, though unwillingly, by the Egyptians.

With all of the care God bestowed upon the Israelites, and the many warnings to take no usury, nor to oppress one another, yet they follow the promptings of the ruling class, and in Ezekiel xxii. He tells them: "Ye have taken usury and greedily gained one of another, and I have smitten my hand against thee and I will scatter thee among the countries and among the heathen until thy filthiness is consumed out of thee"; and they stand scattered today as an evidence of it.

There is not room in the Holy Land to shelter all of the descendants of Israel who are one end of the serving race. The necessity for God's care of the people of the serving quarter will be manifest in each of the four races as they pass off from and back on to the stage of action, to prevent them from becoming extinct.

The Jews were held in bondage by the Egyptians, and still, unwillingly, benefited by them.

A portion of the African colored race has been held in bondage in America, yet unwillingly benefited by the Americans, at a fearful cost in blood and money.

No race of people ever made such mighty strides in progress as the colored people have in fifty years in America, since the abolition of slavery, yet they would never have freed themselves.

The Jews were the real discoverers of America. The colored people unwillingly emigrated to America. Both have played a greater part in the history of our country than most people have any idea.

We know that as horrible as it was slavery was the real incentive to a paying quantity of cotton raising in this country, and finally a bone of contention that stirred the nation to untold active development.

But no matter what great part the Jews played in the destiny of this country, we must prove that it is the pleasant land lying west of the Holy Land.

The old astrologers who wrote the Bible saw the destiny of this country, and wrote it up in symbols.

God's people are those who wish to progress.

We must remember that the Jewish people were in bondage to the Babylonians at the time of Daniel's experiences, having been made prisoners by the Babllonian armq.

Daniel and several other of the captive boys became favorites of King Nebuchadnezzar, and he sent them to Chaldea to college for three years, to learn astrology and occult science. (See Daniel 1-5.)

Daniel became more favored than all others, considered ten times as good. The hypocritical priesthood did not like this, and did everything in their power to turn the king against Daniel.

The stories of the lion's den and fiery furnace are no doubt allegories treating of the trials Daniel had to undergo before these monsters in human form, the priesthood.

According to the story in Maccabees, Daniel had persuaded the king to believe the priests were a lot of hypocrites deceiving and robbing the people by inducing them to bring the best of all they had to the churches and leave it there, where, the priest told them, the spirits and the angels came in the night and carried it away.

Daniel told the king these priests lied about the matter, that it was they and their families who carried the stuff away.

The priests demanded Daniel's life, unless he proved his assertion, which he agreed to do if let be the last in the church at night and the first to enter in the morning.

The king insisted that this be granted Daniel, which was done, and when Daniel left the church he, by permission of the king, had the doors locked and sealed, and a guard placed at the door.

In the morning when the king and Daniel reached the guard the seals were unbroken, and the king was worried for Daniel, but Daniel exacted of the king the acknowledgment that if spirits and angels carried the goods away they would leave no tracks. However, the stuff was gone and the king was worried, for the king loved Daniel. But Daniel had done a little detective work that would have done credit to Sherlock Holmes. The hour that he was in the church alone he used to cover the aisles with ashes, and when the king observed the food had disappeared, Daniel called attention to the ashes he had placed upon the floor and asked the king who had made the foot marks in it? Daniel traced the foot marks to the wall and requested the king to order his workmen to tear down the wall and find the secret door. This so enraged the priests that from that day to this they have hated astrologers and astrology, and recently have carried their hatred so far and influence so great that they have prevailed on state legislatures in several states, 14 I understand, to violate the constitution of the United States.

When the church and the state unite to violate the constitution of a country, that country is in grave danger.

We have boasted of the freedom of every person to worship according to the dictates of the individual conscience.

The practices of astrology and clairvoyancy are religious forms and come under the rule of the constitution, which says, 1st amendment, 1st paragraph: "Congress shall make no laws respecting an establishment of religion, or prohibiting the free exercise thereof; or abridging the freedom of speech, or of the press; or the right of the people peaceably to assemble and to petition the government for a redress of grievances."

If the state and the church are in the act of rebellion, what may we not expect of the people at any time?

NEBUCHADNEZZAR'S VISION.

Nebuchadnezzar had a vision and it troubled him much because he had forgotten what it was. He sent for his wise men (astrologers), but none could relieve him. (Don't fail to read Daniel, there are only 12 chapters.) The priesthood and all that hated Daniel were ever on the watch to find something to enable them to turn the king against Daniel.

Daniel ii., 11: "And it is a rare thing that the king requireth; and there is none other that can shew it before the king, except the gods, whose dwelling is not with flesh" (i. e., spirits and mediumship).

So the priests and those who were not favored as was Daniel thought to get Daniel in trouble and they urged the calling in of Daniel.

Daniel says, "I will have to go and pray to my God first," and he went and returned and said, "Yes, I can tell you." The king promised Daniel great rewards.

Let Daniel describe this image. (See cut below Daniel 11-31.)

31. "Thou, O king, sawest, and behold a great image. This great image whose brightness was excellent, stood before thee, and the form thereof was terrible."

32. "This image's head was of fine gold, his breast and his arms of silver, his belly and his thighs of brass."

33. "His legs of iron, his feet part of iron and part of clay."

34. "Thou sawest till that a stone was cut out without hands, which smote the image upon his feet, that were of iron and clay, and break them to pieces."

35. "Then was the iron, the clay, the brass, the silver, and the gold, broken to pieces together, and became like the chaff of the summer threshing floors; and the wind carried them away, that no place was found for them; and the stone that smote the image became a great mountain, and filled the whole earth."

36. "That was the dream; and we will tell the interpretation thereof before the king."

Here notice we are going to get the interpretation; there is no guesswork about this; we shall find this image is the river of time. The image is just what it says; it is a succession of nations, and anyone who tries to twist the matter in a spiritual meaning is a false leader, an ignoramus or a deceiver.

37. "Thou, O king, are a king of kings (an emperor): for the God of heaven hath given thee a kingdom, power, and strength, and glory."

38. "Thou art this head of gold."

How can you make anything else out of that?

39. "And after thee shall arise another kingdom inferior to thee. * * *"

Astrology is the key to the prophecies, and history the testimony.

"The two arms of silver were the two kingdoms in one Medo Persia. * * * And another third kingdom of brass, which shall bear rule over all the earth."

Again history is testimony for Greecia as Macedonia under Alexander the Great, who with his army, with new arms of spears and brass helmets and brass armor, or belly of brass, defeated Darius of Persia, and subdued the whole world in six short years.

There is no room for guesswork about this. It is too clear for contradiction and says exactly what it means, and is testified to in history.

The fourth kingdom, or legs, is described as of iron and the feet and ten toes of iron and clay. There has been no end of attempting to give a spiritual meaning to this, which is the strongest kind of evidence of lameness or hyprocrisy.

The Roman empire was the power that finally broke up the old Macedonian empire. The Roman empire, or two legs, was a dual empire, or eastern and western Roman empire. The feet consisted of ten kingdoms representing the ten toes of iron and clay.

As iron is not mixed with clay, and it is on the feet of the image the stone strikes the image, these kingdoms are somewhat changed around.

To try to make this stone out to be Christ, or anything but a power that subdues all other powers, is ridiculous.

The stone is a different form of government, for God hated kingdoms and told his people what they might expect from them.

25th verse. Daniel tells the king the vision is certain and the interpretation sure.

DANIEL'S FIRST VISION.

Daniel vii.: Daniel saw a great sea or span of country.

3 v. "And four great beasts came up from the sea, diverse one from another."

4 v. "The first was like a lion, and had eagle's wings: I beheld till the wings thereof were plucked, and it was lifted up from the earth, and made stand upon the feet as a man, and a man's heart was given to it." (See cut.)

There is no more chance to blunder on Daniel's vision than on Belshazzar's vision, for the spirit tells him exactly what it means. In the 17th verse the angel says, "These great beasts, which are four, are four kings, which shall arise out of the earth."

We will follow this matter up and find these are the same kingdoms symbolized in another form.

Like England of today, Babylon was symbolized by a lion, except that it was a winged lion, which meant rapidity of motion, and up to that time when a nation was conquered every soul was put to the sword, except the fancy of a monarch kept a few for slaves.

After Babylon had built such mighty walled cities and great canals to be protected she ceased to be a nomadic tribe. (The wings were plucked.) She found it was more profitable to keep prisoners of war for commercial purposes than to slaughter them, and she restored the Jews to their own land. (was given the heart of a man and stood up among the nations as a humanitarian).

5 v. "* * * A second beast like to a bear, and it raised up itself on one side, and it had three ribs in the mouth of it between the teeth of it; and they said unto it, arise, devour much flesh." (See cut.)

The BEAR

This was Medo Persia. Persia was the last kingdom to come up and was the greater of the two—as a bear's hips are higher than his head. He raised up on his forefeet first, his hinder parts last.

Ribs do not talk, consequently these three ribs symbolized three powers. Persia took and held in their autonomy, for better form of government, these powers were Lydia, Egypt and Babylon. Thus the symbol is complete, and no room for a doubt.

LEOPARD Symbol of Greece.

6. "After this I beheld, and lo, another, like a leopard, which had upon the back of it four wings of a fowl; the beast had also four heads; and dominion was given to it." (See cut.)

This beast was meant for Medo Persia, spotted like a leopard, made up of many kingdoms. Four heads, four separate governments in one.

Daniel vii. 9. "And out of one of them came forth a little horn which waxed exceeding great, toward the south, and toward the east, and toward the pleasant land."

The east and the south were accounted for, and the sea lay on the north and the west, and in this direction was the pleasant land.

Now we must find the time is up by finding a succession of events.

The astrologers call Neptune the ancient of days, because he was the first satelite thrown off from the sun.

Daniel vii., 22. The saints, or progressive people came into possession of the kingdom. Neptune was rediscovered by M. Leverrier August, 1846, through mathematical calculation. I say rediscovered because there is little doubt the ancients knew all of astronomy that we do, if not more.

Daniel xii., 6. "* * * How long shall it be to the end of these wonders?"

The answer of a time, times and a half a time to the scattering of the holy people. This has been completely accomplished, and to the setting up of the abomination that maketh desolate 1290 days (years).

A person reading this interpretation should take the book of Daniel and read it carefully and compare with the interpretation, and he will find no room for a doubt.

In the seventh verse of the seventh chapter Daniel describes the Roman empire or fourth beast.

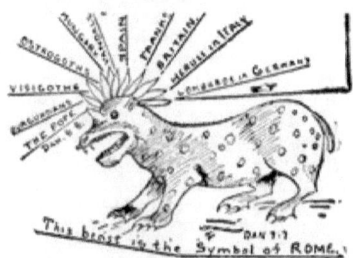

"After this I saw in the night visions, and, behold, a fourth beast, dreadful and terrible, and strong exceedingly; and it had great iron teeth; it devoured and brake in pieces, and stamped the residue with the feet of it; and it was diverse from all the beasts that were before it; and it had ten horns."

8 v. "I considered the horns, and, behold, there came up among them another little horn, before whom there were three of the first horns plucked by the roots; and, behold, in this horn were eyes like the eyes of man, and a mouth speaking great things."

(See cut.) There is no mistaking this beast, the Roman empire was meant and nothing else.

This beast, the Roman Empire, was made up of these ten-horns, or kingdoms: Lombards in Germany, Herul in Italy, Franks in France, these three constitute the beginnings of the western papal power, one of the legs of the image of Nebuchadnezzar.

The cut below was copied from the Standard dictionary showing the pope with his three crowns representing the three kingdoms or horns.

The other horns were the Bergundians, Visgoths, Ostrogaths, Hungary, Vandles, Spain and Britain.

This monster changed times and laws and made war on the saints.

Here I am compelled to use some latitude as to who are meant by the saints. I can conceive of no other saints than those who are trying to live a good square life, trying to progress and help others to progress. A man who would want his foot to honor his head and not give proper care to the foot will soon go lame.

A God who wants his poor weak mortals to continually bow in prayer to an unseen being without assisting their thinking faculties and benefiting them materially will soon find religion going to seed.

If there be a purpose in intelligent life, it must be to progress through certain plans.

If there be any place where the God of the universe is not there may as well be no God. If there be a God he must have something to do, there being nothing but Him, He must be laying plans. We could know nothing of pain or pleasure, bitter or sweet, if we never thought of the opposites. We must learn by experience. Thus these lives are a school. The saints those who wish to progress.

Creeds are inimical to progress, because you are tied to one line of thought. All the human liberty that man ever lost has been lost through the church, and through the selfishness of the ruling classes who have used the church to deceive mankind, while they have their hands in the people's pockets.

Every step of progress has been opposed by the church.

Galileo was imprisoned because he tried to prove the earth revolved on its axis.

Printing was opposed and you have the hell box and printer's devil as a remembrance of the opposition. The idea of the circulation of the blood was ridiculed, free schools were opposed, and afterward the school house closed to the discussion of necessity of railroads and other improvements. Today we see their opposition to moving picture shows and every other form of amusement of the people, instead of guiding and directing everything they seek to prohibit.

If the God of the universe did not want beer, wine, whisky and tobacco used he would not have made it possible to use it. Poisons are not prohibited, yet we seldom see them abused. Why should we prohibit the use of liquors? No reason why only the silly fanatic wants to rule on the one hand and the millionaire robber wants the attention attracted from himself on another, and the church the handmaid of the trust conspirators, wants to appear that they are doing something for God's sake. They have made wars and murdered untold millions for God's sake, and the pope, the little horn, spake great things and he made war on the saints. If you dared to believe anything, the church said you should not believe, you were burned at the stake or otherwise tortured, and he changed times and laws, our day of worship from Saturday, the last day of the week, to Sunday, the first day of the week.

That evolution is a truth and progress God's law, we may see the evidence before us every day.

All matter is divided into atoms and molecules and every atom is a thinking entity.

The law of the universe permits of periods of labor and periods of rest. The condition of mind, before it enters activity of a plan, might be termed perfect rest. The head of the universe that lays his plans offers a premium of greater enjoyment to the greater knowledge, or experience, we know this is so, for see what we old soldiers paid for our experiences, yet where will you find one who would sell that experience, if he could? In fact, we could know nothing without experience, hence the atoms of intelligence leave the place of rest and rush in to nature's workshop and through the law of evolution permit themselves to be used as matter and then gradually through evolution and reincarnation form new organic bodies, thus progressing.

The elementary state is a period of rest before starting, the spirit state, a rest between incarnated lives, just as the night is a rest to the activity of the day, the winter a rest to the summer. The author's meaning of "More rejoicing over the one sinner returned than over the ninety and nine who never went astray, is nothing more nor less than the reward of experience.

Agitation is the incentive to progress. That was the meaning of the sacred writer when he said there was no virtue in the pool of Siloam until agitated by the angel.

The ground must be agitated before the crops will grow.

The grass grows best that feels the sharp tooth rake.

The tree that feels the pruning hook returns its reward in beauty and fruit.

The steel can only be polished by the application of friction.

The human mind is brightened by experience.

Deprive a man of the opportunity of getting drunk and there is no virtue in his sobriety.

The intolerant church would shut off all progress and help the vilest class in Christendom by attacking everything, but the crime most condemned by the book he accepts as his guide book.

"THE LOVE OF MONEY IS THE ROOT OF ALL EVIL."—I. Tim. 6:10.

"TAKE THOU NO USURY OR INCREASE.—Lev. xxv., 36.

During agitation the tendency of all things is upwards. The vine crawls up to heat and light, the fungus in the cave spreads upward. Even stones work up to the surface. Many wild animals and birds seek the inhabited portions of the globe. The domestic animal will leave its kind to follow the master and man seeks to get nearer to his God, and he measures his God by his own capacity of understanding.

The little horn, the papal power, was that fourth beast with great iron claws and teeth, and a mouth speaking great things. "The infallibility of the Pope."

Daniel vii., 9. "I beheld till the thrones were cast down, and the Ancient of days did sit."

Who is this ancient of days?"

The astronomer makes Neptune, the oldest of the Sun's satelites, and the astrologer calls him the ancient of days, with the rediscovery of Neptune, these kingdoms underwent a great change, "were cast down."

NEPTUNE.

Is 2,745,998,000 miles from sun
Diameter, 38,000 miles.

"The beast was slain." The papal temporal power was destined to fall. But the dragon, the money power, is to restore the papal power for an hour and the United States is to be the place of his restoration.

When you see the sign of man appear in the heavens, you may know the time is near.

The water bearer is the sign of man in the Zodiac. The Sun has just entered the sign, and the great unrest and progressive movement is the result.

Uranus, "One like the son of man, came with the clouds, entered the sign with the sun for the first time in 26,000 years.

I shall prove that the stone that smote the image on the feet is the United States of America, but I must first take up Republican form of government when perfected, on a Socialistic plan. But we must now take up the subject of

DANIEL'S SECOND VISION.

Dan. viii. Daniel describes a ram pushing westward, northward and southward. Nothing could stand before him.

The angel told Daniel this was Medo Persia, the two horns, the two kings. There can be no guess work about this. (See cut.)

Daniel then saw a rough he goat; he had a notable horn between the eyes. Nothing could stand before him. He overthrew the ram, and then the big horn was broken and in its place came up four small horns, and out of one of these little horns came another little horn and he waxed very great, to the rest of the earth. (See cut.)

THE ROUGH HE GOAT WAS MACEDONIA, ALAXANDER THE FIRST KING. THE SMALL HORNS—POTOLMY IN EGYPT. SELEUS IN SYRA. CASSANDER IN MASSEDONA, LYSIMACHUS IN THRACE. THE OTHER LITTL EHORN·MOHOMIT.

When Daniel asked the angel the meaning of these things the angel told him the rough he goat was Greecia, the large horn meant the first king. This was Alexander the Great, who built up the Macedonian empire in six short years and then died alone in Babylon.

The angel said the four small horns meant that his country did not go to his heirs, but went to strangers, and that is just what did occur.

When Alexander lay sick, he was asked, "Who will you leave your and structures found in ancient ePru kingdom to?" Alexander replied, "To the strongest."

It went to his four generals, Potolomy in Egypt, Celeus in Syria, Cassandra in Macedonia and Lysimachus in Thrace.

Out of Celeus in Syria came the Mohammedan power, and in 636 he too Jerusalem and cleared away the debris of Solomon's temple where the Jews were still performing the daily sacrifice and built a temple to the Calphia that stands there to this day.

As the angel, or spirit, told Daniel.

There is no room for a doubt here, for every point is proven. The feet of the image brought us down in the river of time until the stone cut out without hands, or republican form of government, strikes empires on the feet and topples them over, does not strike them on the head and crush them out.

We must now prove that the stone is the United States Republic.

If the United States is the promised land, it is the stone cut out without hands.

THE UNITED STATES—THE STONE CUT OUT WITHOUT HANDS.

If the United States is the stone cut out without hands, it is also the man child, born of the woman who fled to the wilderness. See Revelations xii. As these books are astrological and had to be written in symbols to prevent the enemies of truth from destroying them, it is not an easy thing to unravel them and place them in a connected form as we desire evidence placed today. As John takes the story up where Daniel left off, we are compelled to prove our position every step of the way.

The universe is God's work shop, or school house. Progress his aim and purpose. Happy results his rewards. Period of examination and graduation mile stones between plains of progress. The sun in the great Zodiac, the school teacher that forms in classes God's children from the atom to the strongest organic body in God's work shop.

I have shown that the villain in the play is just as necessary to a well written play as is the hero.

I have shown the reason why nations and people were God's especial care.

I have shown the reason why God hated kingdoms and empires and just as the least atom will through the law of carma rise, through mineral, then vegetable, then insect, then reptillian, then the lower animal life, finally to man, thence to planets and to suns, finally the very least may reach the apex of the universe, thence to go down to give the next a chance. (See cut.) Thus the selfishness of empire frequently turns back civilization and becomes the fertilizer of the next stronger civilization that arises over the ruins of the past.

The Israelites had been warned, and punished time and time again, through the decay of their power, just as civilization and nation after nation had gone down, finally different lands under different conditions were necessary. So here we will point out the hand of God and the instrumentality of the Jews in the discovery and the establishment of the American government. To do this so as to make it the most powerful, I quote the following from an article furnished me by a Jewish gentleman. The introductory shows where he got it.

JEWS' PLACE IN NATION'S HISTORY.

Have Been in the Van When the Need Was the Greatest.

Discovery of America Due to the Aid Given by Jew.

Tribute Paid to Race at Meeting of Daughers of American Revolution.

One of the most interesting meetings of the Daughters of the American Revolution held this year was on Tuesday last at the home of Mrs. S. M. Perry. The paper of the day was read by Mrs. Samuel Nathan, an historical review of what the Jewish people did in the war of the American revolution. Mrs. Nathan's paper is reproduced here because of its general interest and because it is replete with facts that are not commonly known. Her information was gathered entirely from Gentile sources. She said:

"It is the opinion of most people that the Jew is narrow-minded, prejudiced and unpatriotic, that he is so wrapped up in heaping dollars, so deeply engrossed in the mad rush for wealth, that he has time for naught else. However, such opinions are formed by those who have mingled with the uneducated and lower type of Jews, but are strictly erroneous, when applied to the higher class. So far the Jew has been unjustly dealt with. Little or no credit has been accorded him for glorious deeds achieved. He is ever pushed to the background. No school child is taught that the Jews had anything to do with the finding of the new world, no one sees a Jewish name in the history of the United States, where, as I will state, with the best of authority to substantiate my utterances, that had it not been for Jewish interest, Jewish brains, Jewish energy and Jewish financial backing American might not have been discovered by Columbus in 1492.

"It was in August of that year that he arrived in Spain disheartened by failures in his own country, weary in mind and body. He gained admittance to court and laid his plans before Ferdinand and Isabella of finding a westerly route to India (with which country they had much commercial intercourse at that time), and begged them for assistance; they thought the man a crank, a madman, and would not pay any attention to his wild ravings. But two Jewish men heard him and became interested; they knew that he did not rave, that his plans were possible, because for many years the Jews had been savants, scholars and explorers. These two men, Louis De Santangel, comptroller and counsellor of Aragon (a great favorite at court), and his brother-in-law, Gabriel Sanchez, treasurer of Aragon, promised to further his plans for, being patriotic men, they knew that such a discovery would add riches to the crown of Spain. They placed the ideas of Columbus before their sovereigns couched in such vivid and glowing language that their rulers became immediately enthused.

Made Possible His Journey Over the Sea to America.

"They woud lend a kindly ear to his pleadings, they said, and would become his patrons, but he needed money; they had none; even the crown jewels were already pawned in order to secure funds with which to carry on the internal wars (then tearing their country to pieces). 'Fear not,' said Santagel, 'I will furnish the money from my own personal funds.' He thereupon made over to Columbus 1,700 ducats, or $20,000, with which to undertake the voyage that terminated in the finding of America. Nor was this all; the maps that Columbus used were drawn up by Jafunda Cresques, a Portuguese Jew. The nautical tables, from which he derived untold benefit, were the work of another Jew, Abraham Zecutobut. As they were in Hebrew, the nephew of Jecuao and Joseph Vecincho translated them into Latin and Spanish and presented them to Columbus. The first man to sight the new world was Rodriques De Triarina, a Jew sailor. The first man to set foot on American soil was Torres, the interpreter, a Jew.

The Surgeon of the Ship Was a Jew.

"The Jews began to arrive in New Amsterdam as early as 1654. However, Stuyvesant, the dictatorial and narrow-minded governor of the colony, tried to stop the Jewish settlers from coming there, but when he wrote to this effect to the West Indian company, the reply was that the Jews were directors and shareholders in the company, much of their revenue came from them, and they must be given the same rights and privileges as others.

"Lord Bellamont reported to England in 1700 that he had much trouble in paying the soldiers their weekly sustenance, that they would not pay any money on his orders, and that were it not for one Dutch merchant and three or four Jews who gave financial help he would have been undone. Though small in number at this period, the Jews were an influential class of people. Hayman Levy of the same colony at this period traded early with the Indians in furs. An historian of that day declared that Mr. Levy was fairly worshipped by the red men. John Jacob Astor was his clerk and received $1.00 a day for beating furs. Nicholas Low, an ancestor of Seth Low, late president of Columbia College, was also a clerk of Mr. Levy's and laid the foundation of his goodly fortune in a hogshead of rum purchased from his former employer. A hero of the revolution was Mr. Comez of New York. When companies were being formed he applied to the continental congress to raise one. The member addressed said: 'Mr. Gomez, you are too old for active service (he then being 68 years of age). His answer was, 'But I can stop a ball as well as a younger man.' He was allowed to raise his company and did good service in battle.

Bearer of Many Important Messages Across the Water.

"Col. Isaac Frank, of New York, contributed £3000 sterling to the colonial treasury. He was aide de camp to Gen. Arnold, but however guilty Arnold was found to be, Col. Frank was held perfectly blameless. He was the bearer of very important messages to Jay and Franklin in Europe. He was held in high esteem as a brave, wise and tactful man. It was through him that the Spanish minister loaned a large sum of money to the United States. After the war Col. Frank was one of the incorporators of the Bank of New York.

"During the rule of Stuyvesant many Jews left New York and settled the beautiful seaport town of Newport. Its Jewish citizens were noted for their matchless enterprise, eminent respectability, wonderful sense of mercantile honor and great benevolence to all mankind. Longfellow made the ancient Jewish cemetery the subject of a lovely poem.

"The Jews of Philadelphia were noted as patriots during the revolution. Haym Soloman, who died in 1785, first came into public notice in 1778, when he was commanded by Gen. Washington to burn the British fleets and storehouses, which he was doing when taken prisoner by the enemy. Luckily he escaped in two days and returned home, where he was welcomed with much enthusiasm. It was he who executed the loans and grants made by the generous monarch of France to further the cause of freedom. Haym Soloman made many and considerable advances from his own personal fortune, none of which was ever paid back. Among those that he helped in time of greatest need were Robert Morris in the congress of declaration, 1776; Gen. Miflin, Gen. St. Clair, Gen. Steuben, Maj. McPherson, Maj. Franks and many others. He also helped the cause of freedom by making gifts of money to the noted Virginia delegates, Lee, Randolph, Bland and Mercer. James Madison said of him, 'that when even pecuniary aid, both public and private, were cut off, recourse was made to Mr. Soloman, who was always found extending a welcome hand and met their current expenses.' After the struggle was over and Mr. Soloman had passed away, his youngest son said, upon coming of age, 'that nothing was left of his father's vast fortune except the grateful remembrance of a just and generous republic.' Mr. Soloman was a trader in foreign countries.

"There were many other Jewish patriots made of the same true stuff. Isaac Moses, of Philadelphia, in 1777 contributed $15,000 to the colonial treasury. Herman Levy of the same city advanced a large amount of money for the support of the armies in the field. In the non-importation act in 1869 the first organized movement that led to independence, **there were nine Jews who signed the resolutions.** This original document is still to be seen in Carpenter's hall, Philadelphia. Among the signers of the bills of credit in the continental congress in 1776 were Benjamin Levy of Philadelphia, Benjamin Jacobs of New York, Isaac Morris and others.

"The first people who settled in Oglethorp colony were very unthrifty and a worthless class, constantly quarreling among themselves, and had it not been for the timely arrival of some Jews whom Oglethorpe welcomed with open arms, his colony would have been anything but a success.

Introduced Important Plants Into the New Colonies of America.

"The Jewish settlers were people of thrift and industry, coupled with intelligence. One early Jewish settler, Abraham De Dyon, was a noted horticulturist and the first man to introduce useful foreign plants into this country. Moredcai Sheftal of Savannah, Ga., was chairman of the rebel parochial committee organized to regulate the affairs of the colony, which was composed of patriots who were opposed to the royal rule. In July, 1777, he was appointed commissary general to the troops of Georgia. He was afterwards on the staff of the continental troops and when Savannah was attacked by the British his name was foremost among the defenders of the city and as one who advanced large sums of money to the cause for which they fought. He was made prisoner on the enemy's ship because he would not fight under their standard. In 1780, when the British passed the disqualification act, his name was near the head of the list, together with the most prominent patriots of Georgia.

"At the departure of Oglethorpe from Georgia, many Jews left and went to Charleston, S. C. At the breaking out of the revolution a company of soldiers composed almost altogether of Jews, comamnded by Col. Lushington, fought under Gen. Moultrie and did noble work at Beaufort, S. C.

"Manual Mordecai Noah of South Carolina not only served on Washington's staff and likewise with Marion, but he gave $100,000 to the support of the colonial troops Maj. Benjamin Moses was also a brave and illustrious patriot. He came to the colonies from France in 1777, served on the staff of Lafayette and again with Washington, fought in almost every action which took place in the Carolinas, became major of a legion of 400 men attached to De Kalb's command, and when De Kalb was killed in the battle of Camden, Maj. Nones, Capt. Jacob de la Molta and Capt. de Lelon, all Jews, bore their brave commander from the field. Maj. Nones did great service in many other ways to his adopted country.

"Rodriques Marquis was a member of the West India company. His grandson, Samuel Mendez Marquis, owned vessels which plied between

New York and Charleston, S. C., during the revolution. He set his ships aside for the use of his country. His son, Isaac Marquis, was a brave soldier fighting in Van Reusselaer's company, Schurmerhorn's regiment.

"Philip Russel also deserves special mention. He enlisted as surgeon's mate to Surgeon Norman under Gen. Lee. After the British occupied Philadelphia in September, 1777, he became surgeon of the Second Virginia regiment and went into winter quarters in Valley Forge when, through illness brought on by the severe winter and poor quarters, he became deaf and blind, which forced him to resign. Gen. Washington wrote a letter commending him for his assiduous and faithful attention to the sick and wounded. Moses Bloomfield of New Jersey was another faithful surgeon and hospital physician, enlisting Aug. 14, 1780. Michael Gratz, father of Rebecca Gratz, known as the heroine of 'Ivanhoe,' was noted for his active patriotism.

Constantly Promoted Because of Valor and a Noble Mind.

"A lover of his country was Aaron Benjamin of Connecticut. He enlisted in the Eighth Connecticut regiment Jan. 1, 1777, and saw active service for thirty-eight years. He was constantly promoted, going in as ensign, and when he resigned was lieutenant of the Thirty-eighth United States Infantry. A patriotic man was Jacob Hertz of Maryland. He loaned Lafayette £2,000 with which to procure shirts and shoes and overalls for the ill-clad soldiers. Though only coming to the colonies from Germany in 1775, he became instantly imbued with a love for his adopted country.

"The marking of the first battlefield of the revolution was made possible by a Jew, one noted for his patriotism and philanthropy — Judah Touro. When Amos Laurence, of Boston, announced that he would give $10,000 with which to mark the battlefield of Bunker Hill if anyone else would give a like amount, Touro immediately wrote out a check for the desired amount.

"Enough has been said to show that the Jew has heart and soul, that he gives with a lavish hand when the needs of his country, the good of humanity and the cause of liberty is at stake; that he makes a pretty good citizen and that he most assuredly deserves to hold a place in the history of that country he has so zealously helped to make; that his lifeblood flowed freely and stained many battlefields where he fought side by side with his brother of other creeds; that he always has and always will be found ready to guard our nation's flag and hold aloft that beloved and starry banner that floats over the greatest and most glorious country in the known world."

Let me add that in the war of '61 to '65 there were more Jews in the Northern army than Washington had soldiers in the revolutionary army, and were among our most trusted spies; while I can never remember of having seen one among rebel soldiers.

WHY WAS THE UNITED STATES CALLED THE MAN CHILD?

We find all the other powers called beasts of prey, because they were forever taking by conquest and giving little or no personal liberty. This was under the rule of the so-called better classes.

The people to get any freedom from the bondage of these better classes have had to fight over every inch of ground, while their rights, their powers, their money have been used to keep them in bondage.

The ruling classes have not hesitated to create wars, sometimes over so silly a pretext as a broken teapot, or an individual insult of a glass of wine thrown by one intoxicated noble into the face of another. Sometimes it was to get possession of a woman, or to attract the attention of the people from a liason (as in David's case).

In more recent ages it was to get possession of a territory held by another power. More times of late it has been to run nations into bonded debt, to make room for a paying investment for idle money, or to sell arms, or something of that sort.

There have been few justifiable wars like most of the wars of the United States.

More generally were these wars for the purpose of devouring territory belonging to a weaker power. Thus it is very clear the other nations were beasts of prey.

The United States gave the first ray of light to personal freedom. We have paid for the land we took.

When we whipped Mexico, and could have annexed the whole country, with the consent of the Mexican people, we paid her a war indemnity instead, by the purchase of California, New Mexico and Arizona, and gave her fifteen million dollars.

The United States gave Spain thirteen million for Florida. We gave France eighteen million for Louisiana territory extending to Oregon. We gave Russia seven million five hundred thousand for Alaska. After whipping Spain in 1898, and could have taken all of her colonies, we gave her twenty millions for the territory we took. Thus the United States is the man child. Is magnanimous. And through her mistaken kindness she has let foreign capital come in and shape our laws and rob us of our natural resources.

This is why the United States is called the Man Child and other nations Beasts of Prey.

FLAGS.

Let us now prove by the Flag the United States is the "Man Child."

From the most remote period of the world's history all animated life has learned there is strength in union, hence signals to attract each other are used, even among the lower order of being, the insect and reptilion life, the bird and the beast, all have their rallying signals. This is sometimes immitated, hence a silent signal was sought by Man. This originated in families, and a well-kown family garment hoisted on a spear handle became a recognized rallying standard.

Men in general demand something more than abstract ideas and principles, hence symbols were adopted to the more forcefully express an idea. This is why the bible was so profusely expressed in symbols.

Language may change, but the sun, moon and stars, rocks, rivers and mountains are eternal.

Fixed rallying standards were first discovered in Egypt. Then we find the tribes of Israel all had their special standards, these were divided into four divisions.

That of Reuben was a man.

This denotes intelligence, the first division.

That of Dan an eagle, a corps or division of observation.

That of Judah, a lion, great power.

That o Ephraim, a steer.

The division protecting the supplies of the army.

These were the four divisions of the tribes.

The standard of the Athenian was an owl, of the Thebins a Spinx.

The standard of Romulus was a bundle of hay tied to a spear, afterward a human hand.

Eagles have always been a favorite emblem; why, no one seems to know. They were formerly made of silver with thunderbolts of gold, in Julius Caesar's time they were all gold.

Formerly standards were extensively carved objects, very expensive. In ancient Greece the struggle between the rich and the poor, standards were necesary, and the working people being too poor to afford expensive carved objects selected a red rag as their standard, and said it typified the blood that flows in all men's veins alike, rich or poor. Thus the red flag is the oldest flag.

This flag became very popular and the children of the rich could not be kept from it. This necessitated a flag for the rich, and they said the blood in their veins was not red, but blue, as their delicate white hands, unstained with honest toil, showed the blue veins through the white skin. Hence, they chose the Royal purple flag.

When the young Roman Empire came up it bid for the working classes, and so adopted or carried the red flag. They soon sought to invite the rich, and so carried also the Royal Purple flag.

There was a Jewish carpenter who was an astrologer and a reformer, advocating labor interests under new religious principles, always at war with the rich. He established Socialism, though he frankly told his followers it was too soon. But, he said, "When you see the sign of man in the heavens, then you may know the time is near."

The Sun's now passing into Aquarius, the sign of man, or water bearer, which is now in the heavens, or sun just entering the sign.

It was the high priests, under the favor of the rich men who crucified Christ, and then pretended to follow him.

The old Pagan church of Babylon, established by a harlot, was losing ground in Rome, and under the sharp politician Constantins, the Pagan church pretended to become Christianized, and became very popular, taking in rich and poor.

As a mixture of red and purple makes scarlet, Rome adopted a scarlet flag as the national standard. Thus the church is always symbolized as a woman. (Christ speaks of the church as his bride), became the (mother of harlots and abominations (as the Catholic church is the mother of all other churches), clothed in scarlet and purple, and sitting on a scarlet colored beast, thus the flag of labor was abandoned, and instead of Christianizing the Pagan church it was the young Christian church which ws Paganized. I have elsewhere shown that the feeling against the rich was so bitter that for 1500 years after Christ no one dared openly advocate interest on money, none but the Jews being permitted to lend money, in England, at interest until the Pope sent his agents into England and loaned money for 450 per cent; this was in 636, and all churches now favor . interest.

The people became angry and the Bishop sent the agents back to Rome, the Pope now in turn became angered and then sent the agents back to England and gave the King of England 10 per cent of his ill-gotten gains to leave them there, thus committing fornication with the kings and princes. Sometime after this the King of England issued an edict that the royal standard of England should be a dragon on red silk, sprinkled with gold, eyes of saphire, tongue resembling fire and continually moving. This is the Great Red Dragon of Revelations.

I have before shown this is God,s country and the part the Jews have played in its discovery.

Now, remember, there were twelve colonies from 1605 to 1682, and notwithstanding some were settled by the Dutch, some by the French, England claimed them all, and sent twelve privy councils to settle the affairs of the twelve colonies.

Little Rhode Island struggled for her independence, and did not come into the Union until after the war began, that making the thirteen colonies.

England had changed her flag several times and at that time carried the cross of St. George.

Several of the colonies wished to show their loyalty, and go back to the mother country if treated properly, hence they wished to continue in some way to carry the English flag, slightly modified.

Long before there was a war thought of between the colonies and the mother country there was a flag known as the American flag. A company of shippers in Connecticut styled "The Williams Importing and Exporting Trading Co.," who carried a flag on their ships, made up of twelve alternate stripes of red and white, this was, and now is, the basis of the American flag.

France owned and claimed the Louisiana territory extending to Oregon. This was granted to the East India trading company under John Law, a Scotchman, who was the financier of France. The name of this company was changed to the West India Trading Company, and consolidated with the Williams Trading Company of Connecticut, and the flag of alternate stripes used. This flag was known as an American flag for years before the war began.

In the absence of art and things of mechanical beauty in this wilderness it was little wonder this beautiful flag of colors should become a favorite with the people.

Poverty is a great impelling power to induce men to risk suffering and privation in a new country, so it was only poor men who came to the wilderness, and it is little wonder the red flag of labor was a favorite flag with them also. When the Colonial army began to gather at Cambridge all sorts of banners were adopted. Red cutting the strongest figure.

The flag that Putman flung to the breeze at Prospect Hill, July 6th, 1775, was a red flag bearing the motto —"An Appeal to Heaven."

At Bunker Hill, the troops carried a red flag, with a pine tree painted on it. When Pulaski was raising a body of men, the nuns of Bethlehem presented him with a red flag, with emblems worked on it with their own hands.

The Army had adopted a red flag, and the Navy a white flag, with a red border.

The variety of flags used by the Colonial troops are too numerous to mention here, but suffice it to say the majority of them had red or the beautiful flag of stripes for a basis.

Some years ago when aristocracy was trying to make out that a coat of arms of the Washington family, back in England, was the basis of the American flag, Benson J. Lossing, the historian, scouted the idea and said if anything suggested the basis of the flag, it was the flag of the East India Trading Co..

The fact that Washington himself suggested several ideas for the flag, but never his coat of arms, is strong evidence against the silly aristocratic coat of arms idea.

When Dr. Benjamin Franklin, Mr. Lynch, and Mr. Harrison were selected as a committee on flags, they repaired to the army, then 9000 strong, at Cambridge. The taste of the army was divided between the red flag of labor and a flag of seven alternate stripes of red and white with the cross of St. George and St. Andrew joined together.

Although labor comprises 80 per cent of the population, it shows its weakness by selling out at the ballot, or at least never hanging together, so the red flag was falling into disgrace, and has long been held as the auctioneer's emblem. Consequently, the flag adopted by the committee January 1st, 1776, was the striped flag of alternate red and white stripes, with the crosses of St. George and St. Andrew joined. This was known as "The Great Union Flag." This flag was used nearly two years before the adoption of the stars and blue field on the background of stripes. By that time the cross of St. George had become so obnoxious that it was determined to abandon it altogether.

Here is said to be an exact cut of the flag John Paul Jones fought his first sea fight under as a privateers man. He received his commission on the same day of the birth of the flag, June 16, 1777, and hoisted the stars and stripes on the Ranger on the same day.

"Don't tread on me" became quite popular, several organizations adopting it. South Carolina adopted this flag with the addition of a crescent in one corner, and the snake cut into twelve parts and the added words, "Unite or Die."

The committee was urged to adopt this flag, and on seeing the device painted on a drum-head, Mr. Franklin said he thought it very appropriate, as the stripes united the Army and Navy flags, and the white stood for purity, the red for the red flag of labor, and the stripes stood for the stripes the vigilant must wear.

The serpent was considered the emblem of wisdom by the ancients, and with his tail in his mouth represented eternal, or continuous, life.

The rattlesnake is peculiarly symbolic of America, as it is found no where else but in America. As eternal vigilance is the price of liberty, he represents that vigilance, as his eyes are very bright and he never closes them because he has no eyelids. Again, he never begins a fight and never surrenders. He may be misrepresented and have to stand for the crimes of the silent massasauga or moccasin, but he never strikes a foe without warning, again he cannot strike until he coils and springs his alarm. His weapons of defense are his poison necessary to the digestion of his food, but deadly as a weapon.

Last, but not least, his rattles are never more than twelve and a button, these are like the states, independent, yet so connected they cannot be separated without breaking to pieces.

Books were few, and the Bible was the library, school book and family dictionary, and the story of the serpent in the Garden of Eden was too familiar in the minds of the people to permit of their acceptance of a snake as an emblem on their flag.

Another Richmond had now come on the field demanding recognition.

Little Rhode Island, extremely religious, as well as patriotic, had adopted a flag, the beauty of which at once attracted the attention of all.

THIS WAS A BLUE FEILD WITH TWELVE WHITE STARS.

This blue field was taken from the blue flag of the Scotch covenant, a religious society. The white stars, while twelve in number, representing the twelve apostles, the idea was to typify the constellation of Lyra, a northern constellation on the meridian, northwest of Aquilla. Vega, or Alpha, is its only star of the first magnitude, and is 100 times greater than our sun, his present light to us about 40,000 of our sun, because of his great distance.

At that time our Solar system was supposed to revolve around Vega. Fourteen thousand years ago Vega was the North Pole star, and will be again in about 11,000 years. Now over 50 degrees from the pole.

This constellation has one star of the first magnitude, one of the third, five of the fourth and eight of the fifth magnitude, making fifteen altogether.

Rhode Island insisted that her flag be recognized in the national colors. On this being taken into consideration it brought the number of States from twelve to thirteen, the religious people said this would give them a star for each of the apostles and one for Christ. However, it was decided that the States would represent a new constellation. But a ready explanation of the situation was, Vega, the largest star, represented the mighty territory, while the smallest star would represent the District of Columbia and the thirteen stars for the thirteen States.

THE ABOVE REPRESENTS A FLAG MUCH IN FAVOR WITH THE ECOLONEST.

We will trace the flag back to Genesis through the number twelve, which is a prophetic number.

The Zodiac is a circle of 360 degrees, divided into twelve signs of thirty degrees each, divided into minutes and seconds.

The Zodiac has been the basis for fixing time as far back as history.

There are twelve constellations from which these signs are named.

There are twelve months of the year.

Twelve hours of the day.

Twelve hours of the night.

The hour is divided into five parts of twelve each.

The prophetic number so often used in the Bible as time, times and a half a time, or 1260 years, is a Zodiacal period time 360 days, or year, a year representing a siderial day, times 720, a half a time 180.

Now remember there were twelve sons of Ishmael, representing twelve princes, or cities.

Twelve sons of Jacob, representing the twelve tribes of Israel.

There were twelve apostles.

When the judges sold themselves for filthy lucure, and the people cried "Give us a King, Oh Lord."

God said, "I will give you a King, but he will take your sons, and your daughters, and the best of all you have, but I will give to my people a country and a language."

And remember the woman who fled to the wilderness, the church had twelve stars upon her head, representing the twelve colonies England acknowledged, and before Rhode Island came in to the Union.

BETSEY ROSS AT WORK NO THE FLAG.

We have found twelve playing an important part all the way through, though the twelve is sometimes slightly broken, but when chained closely to events the prophetic twelve may be easily traced.

THE FLAG THAT BETSEY MADE,

Thus there were really twelve stars or states when the war began.

In 1812 our, second struggle, there was twenty-four states.

In 1861 to '65, with the Great Rebellion, there was thirty-six States, and eleven of them seceeded, and the South claimed the twelve. Kentucky played, too, the part of Judas Iscariot, At least it was a great honor to Kentucky to help to save the Union.

now there will be one great attempt
Now we have forty-eight stars and to first establish a King and then the Pope, but it will finally fail and the people will rule in some way more completely than ever before.

The starry banner, with its beautiful stripes and blue field, was adopted by resolution of Congress June 14th, 1777.

In 1792, on the admission of Vermont and Kentucky, a resolution was passed to add one star and a stripe for each new State, this was found to be impracticable, so far as the stripes were concerned, so May 1st, 1795, by another resolution, the stripes were fixed at thirteen and an additional star for every State. This has never been changed.

Some over-zealous church people have put a cross above the stars and stripes. This should never be permitted, and there is no authority for it, besides if a religious flag is desired there can be nothing equals the starry banner that the whole world must respect and nearly everybody love.

OLD GLORY.

As a sonnet must exhaust the subject in just fourteen lines, it is claimed a sonnet could not be properly written, to the flag, but I have accomplished that literary feat, and here it is.

A SONNET TO THE FLAG.

OUR HEAVEN BORN BANNER

When Freedom sought an emblem true,
  A banner from the God of Right,
She tore from out the azure blue
  A raiment from the robes of night,
As if her cap from heaven's store
  Was set with glorious stars of white.

"Eternal Vigilance" 'tis said
  "The price of Liberty" was given.
The stripes the vigilant must wear
  Were also symbolized in heaven.

The red was found in crimson glow
  Between the sun set and the night,
While purity of white we know
  Is found at dawn of early light.

THE END OF THE WORLD.

As far back as we have history we have records of the people looking for the end of the world, while Ecclesiastes says the earth abideth forever.

The people draw their ideas from the astrologers' talk of the end of an old dispensation, or from the fact that every time the sun, in the great Zodiac, passes from one sign to another it brings a change of dispensation, or worldly conditions, and surely brings an end of the world to many, as it causes earthquakes, tidal waves, wars, pestilence and famine. It invariably brings a new religious wave and new kinds of religion and a new religious leader, a wave of corruption and a counter wave of conscious desire to overthrow corrupt methods, and a consequent clash of arms.

Many people really thought the year 1900 would bring the end of the world; most of these are Bible students, and they think they quote scripture to prove it. They are terribly in error. In their anxiety to have the world destroyed, and a few snatched up to heaven, they have overlooked plain statements and facts. They have interpreted those things as having a spiritual meaning, which really have but a material meaning. Especialy is this so of the book of Daniel and the book of Revelations.

It is from the taking away of the daily sacrifice that all figures for the future date should be made, and Daniel xii is the only place where it tells us who took afaw the daily sacrifice, but we now know it was the Mohammedan power, and that it was taken in the year 636.

Daniel now asked, when will all this take place? The Angel replied: "From the taking away of the daily sacrifice Jerusalem shall be trod down time, times and a half a time." How shall we define this period? Astrology is the key, History the testimony.

God puts his clock in the heavens, the circle of the Zodiac is 360 degrees and the circle is divided into degrees, minutes and seconds; thus it is God's clock dial. In casting a horoscope Astrologers use a day for a year. The Bible prophecies use a day for a year. Daniel was placed at the head of Astrologers.

The Bible is an astrological work. 360 days is an astronomical year, the solar year of 365 days, or the lunar year of 354 days are man's system of counting. Taking the astronomical year, 360 days, and counting a year for a day, a time would be 360 years, times 720 years, and a half a time 180 years; add these together and you have 1,260 years; 1,260 is a prophetic number much used. Then if Jerusalem is to be trod down 1,260 years from the taking away of the daily sacrifice, which occurred in 636, we will add 636 to 1,260 and you have 1,896. What occurred in 1896? Nothing; but we must remember we are counting solar time; we must take away five and one-fourth days to the year: this we find amounts to 17 years; taken 17 years from 1896 and you have 1879. What happened in 1879? A Jewish Society, under Rabbi Gaster, of London, England, and Dr. Hazel, of Vienna, Austria, are at the head of the movement. They purchased the Holy Land off the Turk, and when the Turk was persecuting Christians in Armenia and Persia you did not hear of it in the Holy Land, for the Turk respected his sale.

This, then, is evidence No. 1 for the proof of my interpretation.

We shall find further on why God scattered the Jews, and that He said He would return them. Now this Jewish Society is to raise $10,000,000, which is nearly raised, and then the taking of the Jews back to Jerusalem under a true Socialistic Republic will commence in earnest. I have shown in my book, "What Is Coming," the wonderful strides made in repopulating Jerusalem in the past few years. This is evidence No. 2.

This does not mean that every Israelite will go back, but one tribe, the tribe of Juda, was called Jews.

Daniel asked the Angel, "How long before all of this vision is fulfilled?" The Angel answered: "From the taking away of the daily sacrifice, 636, to the cleansing of the Sanctuary will be 2,300 days (years). This, then, would bring us to the year 2936. What! for Christ's coming? Oh, no! For the signs for Christ's coming show He is close at hand. But Christ is to remain 1,000 years perfecting His Father's Kingdom, and during this time Satan is to be bound for a thousand years and then to be loosed to deceive the nations. So the world is not to be destroyed at Christ's coming because there would be no nations to deceive. Then we will take off a thousand years for the millennium, and that brings you to 1936. Now subtract 5¼ days from 1,300 years, add 646 to the remainder, and you have 1918 for Christ's coming. Daniel wanted more evidence, and the angel told him such troublous times as never existed would occur, and at this time Michael shall stand up and deliver his people; this is Daniel, 12th and 1st. In the same chapter he tells him, many shall run to and fro and knowledge shall increase.

Now we know the past century has developed more knowledge than the balance of a thousand years, and people travel around the globe in less than 80 days. Other passages in the Scriptures tell us that the signs of the times in the last days, "Your sons and your daughters shall see visions, your old men dream dreams; some shall be interpreters of prophecies and some shall prophesy and some heal by the laying on of hands, and some shall be discerners of spirits."

In the book Nahum, 11th chapter, 4th verse, says: "The chariots shall rage in the streets; they shall jostle one against another in the broadways; they shall seem like torches; they shall run like the lightnings."

I would ask the reader to picture

the electric cars and automobiles in as few words if he can.

Daniel 11th chapter describes the Turk and says: "He shall plant the tabernacles of his palace between the seas in the glorious holy mount; yet he shall come to his end, and none shall help him." The driving out has recently taken place.

Daniel asked for still more evidence, and the angel told him: "From the taking away of the daily sacrifice to the setting up of the abomination that maketh desolate, would be 1,290 years. Add 636, the period of taking away of the daily sacrifice, and you have 1,926; add five days to the year for the difference in Solar and Astronomical or Bible time, and you have 1908 for the setting up of the Abomination.

What is the Abomination? It will be a uniting of the crowned heads against republics, and freedom of thought; it will produce such wars and tribulations as never was before known, but it is promised to be of short duration. The angel then tells Daniel that "Blessed is he who waiteth, and cometh to the thousand three hundred and five and thirty days."

What does that mean? It means that reincarnation is a fact, and he who does not come on earth until after the tribulation is past will escape the trouble, as all would have settled down to the peace and harmony of the Sunday morning of God's Sunday or millennium, for remember, "a thousand years is as a day with the Lord."

When God told Adam, "The day thou eatest thereof thou shalt surely die," God was speaking of his thousand-year day, and no man ever lived a thousand years. Then it was two thousand years to the flood and a change of dispensation, two thousand years from the flood to Christ and a change of dispensation. It is now two thousand years again, making six thousand years, or six of God's working days, and we are about to enter on the seventh or God's Sunday. That is another proof that the world is not to be destroyed, but Christ reigns a thousand years. Now 1335 and 636 makes 1971; deduct the five and one-four days for 1,335 years and add the remainder to the 636, and you have the true beginning of the millennium of Sunday morning starting about 1951.

1951, or 1908 to 1951 for preparation, as the abomination was set off in 1908.

This is the fourth count in figures to prove the interpretation.

The Book of Revelation.

The greater part of the book of Revelations is a sealed book until Christ's coming. But there is a great deal of it that is as plain or even more plain than the book of Daniel.

Many Bible students have supposed John was reiterating the very things that Daniel wrote of. But there was no necessity, for it were superfluous for him to do so. He did, however, take up the subject where Daniel left off.

Remember Daniel's prophecies, though they cover the whole period to the end of the millennium or cleansing of the Sanctuary, they treat mostly of a period down to the French revolution, or the feet of the image.

John, in the 12th chapter of Revelations, says, "And there appeared a great wonder in the heavens, a woman clothed with the Sun, and the Moon under her feet, and upon her head a crown of twelve stars."

2. And she being with child, cried travailing in birth, and pained to be delivered.

And there appeared another wonder in the heavens: and behold a great red dragon having seven heads and ten horns and seven crowns upon his heads.

4. And his tail drew a third part of the stars of heaven, and did cast them to the earth; and the dragon stood before the woman, which was ready to be delivered, for to devour her child as soon as it was born.

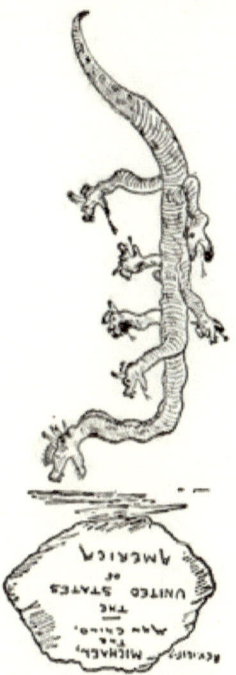

5. And she brought forth a man child, who was to rule the nations with a rod of iron; and her child was caught up unto God and to his throne.

And the woman fled into the wilderness where she hath a place prepared of God, that they should feed her. A thousand two hundred and three score days! 1,260 years.

What is the interpretation of this?

As the Bible has been much mutilated and many books that it speaks of lost, it washows it was necessary to write in symbols; besides as language changes meaning or definitions are liable to change, so those important parts were written insymbols. The church was symbolized by a woman, as Christ speaks of his bride the church. Very well then, what church, and what church was it that fled to the wolderness? Remember the Papal power offended God and the little horn blasphemed and made war on the Saints. Now it is not necesasry to blame all Catholics or the church for all time because of the errors of some leaders. But this power did put a stop to liberty of thought, and as we are here to develop a character, God's plan was being interfered with and it did not alone affect the Protestants but many conscientious Catholics were longing for the privilege of broader views.

All intellectual people could see if there had been no controversy there would have been no advancement, for all would have been barbarians or fire worshipers. There would have been no Catholic religion even, and even Christ was crucified for opinion's sake.

Very well, then; many people were crying to be delivered from the bondage of opinion by the Romish Church; they had new ideas, they wanted a government where they could worship as they pleased, hence were crying with labor pains to be "delivered." Now, as this represented a number of religious denominations, including Catholic reformers, what was meant?

Christ took no cognizance of creeds, but said, "Where two or three are gathered together in my name there am I in the midst of them." He did not say two or three Catholics, two or three Methodists, or two or three of any denomination; therefore it meant any one who was conscientiously seeking the truth.

So the woman that fled to the wilderness was the 12 religious denominations forming the 12 colonies, who fled to this country during that century from 1602 to 1685, and this included the reform Catholics. The 12 colonies were the 12 stars on the woman's head. This is more fully dealt with farther on. The two great wings that were given to the woman were the fore and aft sails of that period, which very much resembled two great wings. (See cut.)

She was clothed with the Sun, England the foremost nation, who claimed all of the colonies, notwithstanding some were settled by the Dutch and some by the French, and in 1688 she appointed 12 privy councils to settle the affairs of the 12 colonies.

The Moon under the woman's feet meant France, who supported the woman, the colonies, when the man child, the new system of government, was formed.

This woman is to be fed 1,260 years. This woman was certainly a symbol, and as it could mean nothing else but a church, how could it be fed except by liberal enlightenment, and all churches, including the Catholics, have been growing more and more liberal. But what about the 1,260 years? Events which cover a number of years could not be fixed at a given period except approximately, therefore from 1602 to 1685, dividing the period at about 1640 and adding 1,260, brings you up to 2,900, taking one thousand off for the millennium during which Christ and his 144,000 teachers are to feed, teach the rest of the world, and it brings you to the present time.

This mathematical calculation is problem No. 5, in proof of this interpretation of Christ's second coming about 1918.

We find here a proof that a time, times and a half a time is 1,260 years, for it is already stated that the woman was to be fed in the wilderness a thousand two hundred and three score days—Revelations xii and 6th; and the same chapter, 14th verse, says time, times and a half a time; so we know John's and Daniel's dates agree and are astrological years.

Now what or who is the red dragon? We have found so far the symbols all refer to earthly things; now this red dragon must be looked for as an earthly institution; and as it is pictured as a great evil we must ask ourselves: what is the greatest evil spoken of in Scripture?

1. "The love of money is the root of all evil."

2. God gave the Holy Land to Abraham and his seed for an everlasting inheritance.

If you wish to punish a child, you take away a cherished gift.

In the 22nd chapter of Ezekiel, God says to the Jews: "Ye have taken usury and greedily gained one of another, and I have smitten mine hand against you and ye shall be scattered among the heathen and among the countries until thy filthiness is consumed out of thee." And they stand scattered today as an evidence of the prophecies. But God said he would bring them back for his word's sake, and I have shown they are already assembling back.

This does not mean that every Israelite shall go back, but the Jews as a nation shall be established there.

The Scriptures say, "Take thou no usury or increase."

The only time that Christ used force was when with the scourge he drove the money changers from the temple. Then the greatest evil spoken of in Scripture is the misuse of money, and this is the great red dragon (a money power).

That the church and the woman are one and the same may be easily determined by reading Revelations carefully.

The Scriptures charge the woman, the church, with committing fornication with the kings and the princes, and as we found historical parallels for everything so far we must find a historical parallel for this and a historical name for the red dragon. Murry on Usury says that up to 1235 the church taught that usury or interest on money was a crime and some philosophers and priests classed it with murder. In England up to 1235 none but the Jews were permitted to loan money on interest. But during that year the Pope sent his agents into England and loaned money for four hundred and fifty per cent, says Murry on Usury. The people became very indignant at the idea of the church doing such a thing, and the bishop, a very worthy and honorable gentleman, sent the agents back to Rome. The Pope became angry and recalled the bishop and sent the agents back into England. He then gave the King of England 10 per cent of his ill-gitten gains to leave the agents there, thus committing fornication with the kings and princes. Encyclopedia Britannica under the head of flags says that in 1244, eleven years late, the same kinw issued an edict that the royal standard of England should be a dragon on red silk, sprinkled with gold, eyes of sapphire, tongue of fire and continually moving. So here we have the parallel and the red dragon. A dragon in the ancient language was a serpent. From this time forward interest on money became popular, though the church did not publicly recognize it until 1730, when Pope Benedict XIV. declared only unlawful interest was usury, where the Scriptures say, "Take no usury or increase." Thus the Catholic church became the mother of harlots and the Protestant churches the daughters, as all uphold interest on money. But God says, "Unless they repent I will make a bed for the mother of harlots, but her children I will kill with death." This, then, is evidence enough of what constitutes the red dragon.

The money power, the red dragon, was established and is rapidly binding the world in bonded indebtedness and all will soon be slaves to the few bondholders.

All of this trouble could be overcome by the government loaning money to the people at mere clerical expenses, or as no one but a government can make money, let the government issue paper money and start public works and pay it out to labor, until there is not a forced idle man in the land. Then let the government take the average price of one thousand of the most staple articles, and stop issuing. A few of these articles might fluctuate from year to year, but as a whole they would only rise and fall in proportion to the volume of money in circulation; thus if they rose above that fixed sea level we would know hoarded money was coming out or the metals flowing in as a substitute, and the surplus should be taken in by taxation. If on the other hand prices were falling below that fixed sea level we would know money was becoming scarce and the government should again start public works and pay it out to labor; thus we could always keep a stable currency and never have a panic or enforced idleness, and we should remember enforced idleness is the devil's workshop. But while the government, under the control of the dragon's agents, will come to the rescue of the bankers and money loaners, as several of the secretaries of the treasury have done, they will never come to the people's rescue in the same manner. The money loaning and privileged classes would rather plunge the country into war and issue more bonds to enslave the people, and under a pretense of civilizing the weaker nations, than to elevate their people in a peaceful manner.

It is true a nation should grow, or in other words eat or be eaten, under the present systems, and so far our government has been wisely conducted in that matter, even by the present money man's government, with the exception of the wrongful issue of bonds instead of non-interest bearing legal tender paper money. In this respect we need a balance wheel, and I can give no better illustration than by quoting history in the following manner. It is a historical fact that as wealth concentrates in the hands of the few, nations decay. Goldsmith sings:

"Ill fares the land, to hastening ills a prey,

Where wealth accumulates and men decay."

When old Egypt died, four per cent of the people owned all the wealth.

When Babylon died three per cent of the people owned all the wealth.

When old Persia died two per cent owned all of the wealth.

When Greecia died, one-half of one per cent owned all of the wealth.

When Rome died, two thousand people owned the civilized world, and then followed the dark ages from which we did not recover until wealth was scattered or destroyed by continual wars.

I have shown that republics are God's chosen form of government, and that England's attack on the Boer Republic and what it cost her prove to the world her decay, and here we may note this—

A LESSON IN HISTORY

Oh! England, 'tis thy boasted freedom
 Comes down from an old ancient cry,
It is mine! The world I must conquer,
 It is yours to yield or to die.

While under the broad cloak of freedom
 All banners must needs be unfurled;
Great nations have died like a tyrant
 Attempting to conquer the world.

Old Egypt, the foremost of nations,
 Whose army was great and was brave,
Succumbed to her privileged classes
 And wealth made her labor a slave.

Great Babylon in all of her glory,
 In majesty, grandeur and pride,
Ignored both God and her people,
 In sin and corruption she died.

'Twas Carthage in all of her splendor
 Who gave to her Hannibal fame,
Let greed run away with her reason,
 Leaving only in history a name.

It was Media and Persia united
 Who fattened on Babylon's fall,
Then died when the people had nothing
 When privilege had gathered it all.

When Grecia came on to the carpet
 Under Alexander the Great,
She traded her national glory
 For merely expansion of state.

Then Rome in the pride of her power
 Ruled all in her own bloody way,
She yielded to wealth and corruption
 And finally went into decay.

Oh England, thy hour approaches,
 No matter whatever you do,
Thou hast followed the footsteps of others
 To the brink of your own Waterloo.

American statesmen, take warning,
 If heeding your own country's weal,
Beware of both greed and expansion
 By attaching a good balance wheel.

John told us the dragon hated the woman and poured a stream from his mouth and tried to drown her, and he stood ready to devour the man child the moment it was born.

By 1602 the money power was fully established and wealthy church dignitaries were its leaders, and they became land owners here in America. They wanted settlers, and as the reformers were crying to be delivered, wanting a government of their own, these land owners said to them: "Go over and settle on our lands; we will pay all expenses and you can pay us back in a percentage of your products, and you can make such laws as you please, and we won't send anyone to your colonies but those who believe as you do." Under this promise the people came, but the money lords soon found the country was greater than they supposed, and there was not enough of these people, so they tried to send others over. But the colonies objected and would not let them in. The money lords now became very angry and the dragon opened his mouth and poured a stream of water and tried to drown the woman. The people are always symbolized as water, the mouth of the money power (dragon) was almshouse and prison house doors, and the money power created hard times in the old world and filled almshouses and prisons, and then told these poor creatures, if you want your freedom, go over and settle on our lands and you can go free, and they tried to make this country penal colonies, as they afterward made Australia. But when they sent this stream of people over here, as John says, "The earth opened its mouth and helped the woman." Colonists who were organized said to these people, "You cannot settle with us." "Very well," said the people, "we will go into the forest deeper and hew ourselves out homes, and we wont's have to pay the money lords anything." So as there was no profit for them they ceased to send any more, so the earth had opened its mouth and helped the woman.

The dragon stood ready to devour the man child the moment it was born. I have shown God hated kingdoms, and Alexander Hamilton, whom the money lords extol today, urged Washington to accept kingship, and Hamilton established the English system of finance here, which is rapidly devouring this country with bonded indebtedness.

The symbol of the money power as a serpent is very complete, as he charms his prey, as he tells the nations they should bond the country to build navies and armies so they could capture the weaker ones. And he gets the business man to borrow, then tightens his folds and causes him to borrow more money, and when he has beslimed him enough he swallows him.

It is a statistical fact that 95 per cent of all business is done on credit and that 95 per cent of all business men fail sooner or later.

We know that a real serpent uses a tree for a fulcrum to crush its prey, so the dragon or money power used England for a tree, and the English army which overrun four of the states which were the stars on the woman's head; thus it was the tail of the serpent which drew a third part of the stars after it, but remember in the war where the dragon and his angels fought with Michael and his generals, Michael overcame the dragon; and the Americans overcame the English army, with the assistance of the moon, France, who was under the woman's feet, assisted the woman when the man child was born.

Now John saw another wonder in the heavens, and he saw a great beast, which he describes to be like the beast that Daniel saw having a head with ten horns; but this beast had, besides the head of ten horns, seven heads, all hanging down but the one that was wounded unto death; if this meant the Roman empire, we must find what forms of government Rome had, for we found heads means governments, as horns means kingdoms. So Rome was first governed by kings, second by council, third by Decemvirs, fourth Dictators, fifth Triumvirs, sixth Emperors, seventh Popes, and he is to be restored by the dragon power and then "Even he will be the eighth head but of the seventh."

When was this head wounded? When Napoleon the First took the Pope a prisoner to Paris in 1810 and after returning him to Rome he left a guard of French soldiers, thus destroying his temporal power. In 1870 Napoleon III. withdrew the soldiers and Victor Emmanuel shut him up in the Vatican, and he says, "I am still emperor but a prisoner in the Vatican," and the Scriptures say the woman(church) he represents says, "I sit queen and am no widow and shall suffer no violence."

Why and in what way is this wounded head to be restored?

John saw another wonder in the heavens and he saw an image of the beast coming up out of the earth.

This image was lamb-like in appearance, having two horns; but he speaks with the tongue of a dragon who has power to give life to the image of the beast.

And he causeth all, both small and great, to receive a mark on the forehead or the right hand, that no man might buy or sell save he had the mark or the name of the beast or the number of his name. Now his name is six hundred three score and six (666); I have explained what that is in the second part of the book. But what was this image of the beast?

I have shown that nations are symbolized as beasts of prey; what nation so resembled the old Roman Empire and was built up so quickly? None but the English Empire that the dragon power built up, "gave life to," and used as a tree to hang from and a fulcrum to crush its prey. It caused fire to come down out of the heavens to astonish men. When Benjamin Franklin drew lightning from the heavens he was a British subject.

The dressing of servants in uniform and putting a number on the hat, the building up of great corporations, trusts, and even labor societies including grips, signs and boycott, are the result of the great money trust of England, and are the marks in the forehead and the right hand. Besides, England has church and state, an image of the beast.

The two horns, England and Scotland, have both ruled, like Media and Persia; Ireland never; she speaks with the tongue of a dragon; establishing a suzerainty here and a protectorate there, and advancing Christianity, but always where there is a gold mine.

Telling her own people how rich they are, when it is only the riches of the dragon money power, while the people are under a yoke of bonded slavery. See Hazard circular, the Panic Bulletin and Bank circular. She never makes a treaty that she doesn't break if it is for her interest to do so. Now this is nothing against the English people but citing history and Bible prophecies.

England is not a big enough tree for the money power, therefore with its influences it will form an alliance of European powers against republics and all freedom of thought and speech; England at first will be with that alliance and aid in forcing the worship of the beast, to get the influence of the Catholic church, the Pope will be made spiritual adviser and arbitrator of their differences; now remember in Daniel's vision there was no crowns upon the horns, but in this case there are crowns upon **the horns, showing it is** but an alliance; thus the wounded head is restored, but not exactly as before, because in this case he is the eighth head but of the seven.

I have a book in which I published this matter in 1900, and I there stated that if my interpretation is right, the King of England will form an alliance with the powers, apparently against Germany, but in reality against human liberty, and that he would do some unreasonable thing to curry favor with the Pope.

I have a newspaper clipping showing that in 1908 King Edward formed such an alliance, and that, notwithstanding when he takes his oath of office, he takes his oath he will never enter a Catholic church. But, in November, 1908, he violated his own oath and entered a Catholic church; thus setting up the abomination that maketh desolate.

Think of a King violating his oath. Indeed it must be a powerful incentive that leads a King to do that, if that clipping is true, and we are told that the present King refused to take the oath of office until the oath was modified.

I have no war with the Catholic, or any other religion, nor was it a crime for the King to enter a Catholic church, but to violate his oath is a different thing, and it shows the money power, or Red Dragon is about to restore the wounded head to power, and that he intends to restore it here.

Mark Hanna said nothing but the Catholic church could defeat Socialism and control labor.

The recent rebellion of the Swiss guards show the Pope is preparing to move.

It has been claimed that the vast sums of money of the Catholic Hierarchy have been invested in this country, and that the late railroad magnates, Harriman and J. Pierpont Morgan, were the agents of the Catholic Hierarchy.

The powers seem to be groping for a pretext for a falling out with us, in the matter of tolls in the Panama Canal, and have refused to be present at the San Francisco Exposition, and it is claimed England is preparing for a naval station in Bermuda, which she denies. But these are straws, it is well to watch.

Farther on, the illustrations of your present flying machines, were taken from a book I published in 1884. These go to show the accuracy of my predictions.

Good and wise Catholics have told me they expected this was about the time for the appearance of the anti-Christ they look for and that he would be a Pope.

Arnold de Vion, a Benedictine monk, who was an astrologer in the year 1595, made this prediction describing a hundred and eleven Popes: He describes Pope Leo XIII. as "Lumen in coelo," a light in heaven. But he describes the Pope following him as "Ignis ardens," "a burning fire." "Religio depopulatar," "religion laid waste."

Rev. 13:1.

This prophet says there will be but eight Popes after Leo, seven to follow the living fire. The last will be a Roman Peter, who will raise his scourged church from under the lash brought upon it by the burning fire, and he presides under many tribulations until Christ takes the reins of the church. This was certainly a remarkable astrological prediction, which seems to add testimony to the nearness of Christ's coming.

This alliance, then, is the setting up of the abomination that maketh desolate. What is more desolating than the money power that monopolizes all the gifts of God or nature, and what greater abomination than joining that usurious dragon with the church who has played the harlot with the money kings, and the Protestant churches the daughters of the harlot doing the same thing: for fifty Methodist bishops who went down to tell McKinley, the money power's candidate of 1896, that their people would vote for him. All committing fornication with the money lords. That we may know this is the woman and Papal power, John describes another wonder in the heavens; this is the same seven-headed beast, but he is scarlet in color and has a woman seated upon him clothed in scarlet and purple.

"And I saw a woman sit upon a scarlet colored beast, full of names of blasphemy, noving seven heads and ten horns.—Rev. xvii, 3.

The struggles of capital and labor caused the people of old Greecia to choose a blood red banner, because red signified the blood that runs in all men's veins. The wealthy classes said they had blue blood in their veins and they selected royal purple for their banner. When the young Roman Empire came up it wanted emigrants of the wealthy for their enterprise and wealth and it wanted the poorer classes for their labor; therefore, to make harmony, they amalgamated the two colors, blood red and royal purple, and adopted a scarlet flag. But while she abandoned the blood red flag, her standard-bearers always carried the royal purple flag to please the wealthy classes, so when the young Christian church came up it was composed of both rich and poor, thus the woman, the church, was sitting on the scarlet beast, for scarlet was the avowed color of Rome. But the woman was clothed in scarlet and purple, for the common people had no other than the Roman flag while the wealthy classes had their royal purple.

See the Jew in history of the U. S.; also our Flag in Prophecy.

PART FOUR

THE POLITICAL HISTORY OF OUR COUNTRY

As the financial question is closely connected with the political history, and somewhat with the religous history, I concluded to give a brief revew of both the political and religious history, each by its self.

THE HISTORY OF OUR POLITICAL PARTIES.

All things, from a solar system to a blade of grass, are built up by accretion and pass away by erosion. Political parties are no exception to this law.

Political parties are originated to force some political issue to the front, which other parties in existence will not do for fear of losing power.

As soon as a party gets into power, with a showing of stability, dishonest men rush to it, like flies to a molasses barrel.

You can never purify a party that has once become rotten; as well try to restore a rotten egg. When bad men get hold of the machinery of a party, every move they make takes it deeper into the mire, and the people had better abandon the party and organize a new party with sound principles, than to waste time with a rotten old party.

New parties carry out the principles for which they were organized. But after that, the leaders seem to think the party belongs to them, and they use it to serve selfish ends.

The colonies formed into a confederacy to repel the oppressive old mother country. On account of petty jealousies, they distracted each other from the first, and so were held, loosely, together, and governed by a Continental Congress, who selected the following Presidents:

First Congress, Sept. 5, 1774.

1st Pres., PEYTON RANDOLPH,

of Virginia. Born in Virginia, 1723, died in Philadelphia, October 22, 1785. Second Congress, May 10, 1775. Peyton Randolph, president, resigned May 24, 1775.

2nd Pres., JOHN HANCOCK,

of Massachusetts, elected Randolph's successor; born in Quincy, Massachusetts, 1737, died October 3, 1793. President of Congress until October, 1777.

3rd Pres., HENRY LAURINES,

of South Carolina, president from November 1, 1777 to December, 1778; born at Charlestown, South Carolina, 1724, died in South Carolina, December, 1792.

4th Pres., JOHN JAY,

of New York. President from December 10, 1778, to September 27, 1779. Born in New York

City, December 12, 1745, died at New York, May 17, 1829.

5th Pres., SAMUEL HUNTINGTON

of Connecticut, president from September 28, 1779, until July 10, 1781. Born in Connecticut in 1732, died 1796.

6th Pres., THOMAS McKEAN,

of Pennsylvania, president from July 1781, until November 5, 1781. Born in Pennsylvania, March 19, 1734, died at Philadelphia, June 24, 1817.

7th Pres., JOHN HANSAN,

of Maryland, president from November 5, 1781, to November 4, 1782.

8th Pres., ELIAS BEAUDINOT,

of New Jersey, president from November 4, 1782, until February 4, 1783. He was born at Philadelphia, May 2, 1740, died 1824.

9th Pres., THOMAS MIFFLIN,

of Pensylvania, president from February 4, 1783, to November 30, 1784. Born in Philadelphia, 1744, died in same city, January 21, 1800.

10th Pres., RICHARD HENRY LEE

of Virginia, president from November 30, 1784, to November 23, 1785. Born in Virginia, 1732, died in 1794.

11th Pres., JOHN HANCOCK,

of Massachusetts, president from November 23, 1785, to June 6, 1786.

12th Pres., NATHANIEL GORHAM

of Massachusetts, president from June 6, 1786 to February 2, 1787. Born at Charlestown, Massachusetts, in 1738, died June 11, 1796.

13th Pres., ARTHUR St. CLAIR,

of Pennsylvania, president from February 2, 1787, to January

28, 1788; born in Edinburg, Scotland, ——, died in 1818.

14th Pres. CYRUS GRIFFIN,

of Virginia, president from January 28, 1788 to the end of the Congress under the Confederation, March 30, 1789. He was born in England in 1748 and died in Virginia in 1810.

After the adoption of the Constitution presidents were elected by the Electoral College, and for a term of four years. The person receiving the highest number of votes was declared president; the one receiving the next highest number of votes was declared vice-president. This, of course, was before candidates were put up as figure heads for parties.

During the Revolutionary war there were two parties, the Whigs and the Tories. The Whigs were the war party, the Tories favored the mother country; but, of course, at the close of the war a reconstruction of the parties on new lines became necessary. Two new parties were formed, Federalist and anti-Federalist. The Federalists favored a compact government, the anti-Federalists favored state sovereignty, the right of states to secede at will; though the parties died out and the question slept for a season, the question was finally settled with the settlement of the slave question by the crushing of the great rebellion of 1861 to 1865.

Under the constitution the

1st Pres., GEORGE WASINGTON,

of Virginia, inaugurated April 30, 1789; second term, March 4, 1793; born in Virginia, February 22, 1782, died at Mt. Vernon, Virginia, December 14, 1799. Vice-President, John Adams of Massachusetts; born October 19, 1735, died July 4, 1826.

The people were happy under

Washington's administration. He refused a third term as a precedent inimical to our republican system of government. His farewell address will ever be cherished as an affectionate missive of a kind and careful father to an appreciative and loving family.

The anti-Federalists somewhat modified their views, and adopted the name of Democratic-Republican.

The prime mover in the Federalist party was Alexander Hamilton. It would have been better for our country had this man been strangled in his cradle. He was a born aristocrat and a monarchist. He was the first Secretary of the Treasury and established the English system of finance in this country. His influence has led to sly treason to our republican institutions.

The great leader of democracy was Thomas Jefferson, who does and should, stand in the honor of his country not one whit below our loved and honored president, George Washington. The

2nd Pres., JOHN ADAMS,

of Massachusetts, was inaugurated March 4, 1797.

Vice-Pres., THOMAS JEFFERSON

of Virginia; born in Virginia, April 13, 1743, died at Montecello Virginia, July 4, 1826.

3rd Pres, THOMAS JEFFERSON,

of Virginia, inaugurated March 4, 1801.

Vice-Pres., ARON BURR,

of New York; born at Newark, New Jersey, February 6, 1756, died at Staten Island, New York, September 14, 1836.

The currency question was a burning issue at this time, and found Jefferson, Calhoun and other great leaders of their class with the people, in favor of a government, absolute, paper money. Alexander Hamilton, and his class of aristocratic monarchists, opposed it.

The monarchists opposed Jefferson very bitterly, and the contest rose so high that there was no choice by the Electoral College, and the election went to the House of Representatives where Jefferson was declared elected.

Jefferson's second inaugural occurred March 4, 1805, his

Vice-Pres. GEORGE W. CLINTON,

of New York; born in Ulster county, New York, 1739, died in Washington, D. C., April 20, 1812.

Though Jefferson's administration of eight years was a quiet one, a number of events of great national importance took place. The territory of Louisiana was purchased from France, the post road to Ohio was also determined upon, and the first breath of secession of some of the states from the Union was made public.

Jefferson, like the noble Washington, refused to accept a third term.

4th Pres., JAMES MADISON,

of Virginia, was inaugurated March 4, 1809; born in Prince George county, Virginia, March 16, 1751, died at Mt. Pelier, Virginia, June 2, 1836.

Vice-Pres., GEORGE W. CLINTON

Madison's second inaugural occurred March 4, 1813.

ELDRIDGE GERRY,

of Massachusetts, his second Vice-President, was born at Marblehead Massachusetts, July 17, 1744, died at Washington, D. C.

Madison, like Jefferson was a republican, the name democrat not being much used, as it was hooted at by the aristocracy, the same as the name of the Greenback or People's party is hooted at by them today and the same as they always will hoot at any party name that belongs to the party of the masses.

During this administration, in 1811, the charter of the old United States Bank expired. In 1812 the war broke out with England and peace was declared in the winter of 1814. This war gave an opportunity for the money kings to corrupt the party, and in 1816 they re-chartered the United States Bank for seventeen years.

Now, to attract the attention of the people from the vital issue, or money question, they set up the tarrif question. It is true the tarrif question was of more importance then than now, as our infant industries required protection. But the cry of the opposers of protection has ever since been a bug-a-boo over *taxation, taxation. All fools from that day to this, who try to frighten the people with the cry of oppressive taxation, either because they know no better, or for the purpose of deception, fail to notify the people that ever so small a tax to unemployed people is oppressive, but ten times the tax they ever paid would not be oppressive to a well paid and employed people.*

The money power had now got things fixed for seventeen years. Our foreign relations were pleasant. Both parties were in the hands of the moneyed classes, so there were no political issues other than that one party was in power and the other would like to get there, for the spoils of office only.

5th Pres., JAMES MONROE,

of Virginia, inaugurated March 4, 1817; born in Westmoreland county, Virginia, 1759, died in New York, July 4, 1831.

Vice-Pres., DANIEL D. TOMPKINS

of New York; was born at Fox Meadows, New York, June 21, 1774, died at Staten Island, New York June 11, 1825.

James Monroe was inaugurated for his second term, March 4, 1821; Daniel Tompkins, Vice-President.

During this very quiet administration we got the Monroe Doctrine, we hear so much about of late.

The slavery question was a bone of contenton, even among the colonies, and was hotly discussed at the adoption of the Constitution, but had never risen to a political issue. But during this administration the admission of Missouri as a slave state brought the question squarely into politics and the *Missouri Compromise* forbidding slavery north of latitude 36 degrees 30 minutes, was passed. To balance Missouri Maine was admitted as a free state.

8th Pres., JOHN QUINCY ADAMS

of Massachusetts; born at Quincy, Massachusetts, July 11, 1767, died in Washington, D. C., February 23, 1848; inaugurated March 4, 1825

Vice.Pres., JOHN C. CALHOUN,

of South Carolina; born in Abbeville district, South Carolina, March 18, 1782, died in Washington March 31, 1850.

This election could not be decided by the electoral college and went to the House. Andrew Jackson received the electoral votes of seven states, 99 votes; Adams received the votes or thirteen states, 84 votes; the balance scattering to Henry Clay and H. C. Crawford. Adams was declared elected by the House of Representatives.

Jackson was defeated through an alliance of the friends of Adams and Clay. Clay being made secretary of State. The whig party was now formed from the old Federal party and what they could draw from the Republican party who hoped for greater powers with the new party. The Republican party now dropped the name Republican and took the fore part of their name and called their party the Democratic party.

7th Pres., ANDREW JACKSON,

of Tennesee; born in Mecklenburg county North Carolina, March, 1767, died at the Hermitage, Tennessee, June 8, 1845, inaugurated March 4, 1829. John C. Calhoun Vice-President.

Jackson was inaugurated for his second term March 4, 1833.

Vice-Pres., MARTIN VAN BUREN,

of New York; born at Kinderhook, New York, December 5, 1782, died in New York in 1862,

Jackson was the right man in the right place. The tariff question, as it must always be a question of sectional more than national importance, it assumed a sectional phase at this time, and was the means of again bringing forward the question of states rights. John C. Calhoun threatened to take South Carolina out of the Union, but President Jackson said, "John C. Calhoun, you go home and behave yourself or I will hang you higher than Haman, and he hung seventy-nine feet in the air."

Calhoun was a good man and a statesman but in this threat he made the mistake of his life. South Carolina, in 1832, did go so far as to pass the Nullifycation Act, which was to proclaim the state's right to declare null and void the acts of Corgress intorfering with the affairs of the individual states.

Jackson immediately sent a naval force into Charlestown harbor and the incipient rebellion was squelched. Jackson declared: "Our Federal Union it must and shall be preserved." It is said he afterwards regretted he did not hang John C. Calhoun.

The second charter of the United States Bank was to expire in 1836, the currency question became the great issue and the usurious money lords were driven together into the Whig party But Jackson swept everything before him in his second election, and the old piratical bank system was driven to the jungle, where it remained until our late war gave opportunity for it to come out with all of its whelps, as the national banking system.

The money power sought to divide the Democratic party by organizing other small parties to attract the attention of the people, consequently Jackson had the following opposition at his second election: Henry Clay, National Republican; John Floyd, Nullifycation and William West, Anti-Masonic. This last was brought about through the great excitement of the disappearance of one Morgan, who had threatened to expose some of the secret workings of the fraternal order of Masonry.

The Anti-Slavery Society was formed in 1833. Discussion ran high and Congress declared it would listen to no petitions pro or con on the question of slavery, but Jackson being from the slave states it was natural that his sympathies would be with the slave holders, and he requested that the sending of abolition documents through the mails be prohibited. This was refused by the Senate and the question so hotly debated that it finally ended in the assassination of Lovejoy.

8th Pres., MARTIN VAN BUREN,

of New York, inaugurated March 4, 1837.

Vice-Pres., R. M. JOHNSON,

of Kentucky; born 1780, died November 19, 1850.

Nothing of note transpired during this administration except the great financial panic of 1837, treated of in the body of this work.

Though the Whig party had its origin under Adam's administration it assumed no great proportion until its election of the

9th Pres., WM. HENRY HARRISON

of Ohio; born in Barkeley county, Virginia, February 9, 1773, inaugurated March 4, 1841, died just one month later, April 4, 1841. He was elected out of respect and gratitude for his service and military genius.

10th Pres., JOHN TYLER,

of Virginia; born at Charles city, Virginia, April, 1890, was made president by the death of Harrison. Took the oath of office April 6, 1841. The popular vote for Harrison was 1,274,783 against 1,128,702. The Democratic party was the popular party and in the absence of a great issue, so great a turning over showed the desire of the people to extend their respect and gratitude to General Harrison.

The slave question was now assuming sharp political proportions and the Abolition party ran a ticket and cast 7609 votes. They were undoubtedly told they were losing their votes, but men who vote for principle know their votes can never be lost, and some of these voters lived to see slavery abolished. The poor, cowardly sneak, who is afraid to vote for principle for fear he will not be on the popular side, is unworthy the name of citizen, and he is the man that loses his vote.

The Democratic party was now controlled, mainly, by leaders from the South, and at their convention at Baltimore offered resolutions to the effect that Congress had no power to interfere with or control the domestic institutions of the several states. They also offered a resolution aimed at the know-nothing tendency, then just appearing. The Know-nothing party was one of those small parties pushed forward to attract the attention of the people from the great issues; like the Prohibition party, the Socialist party, the Land or Single Taxers, and other similar small reform, or so-called reform movements of today.

The discussion of the admission of Texas territory and Oregon arose and entered into the campaign for the

11th Pres., JAMES K. POLK,

of Tennessee; born in Mecklenburg county, North Carolina, November 7, 1795, died at Nashville, Tennessee, June 15, 1849. Inaugurated March 4, 1845.

Vice-Pres., GEORGE M. DALLHS,

of Pennsylvania; born in Philadelphia, July 10, 1792.

The new administration favored the admission of Texas, which finally ended in the war with Mexico, and the accession of New Mexico, including California and the Sierras, a vast and rich territory. There was an attempt here made, called the *Wilmot Proviso*, which was intended to prohibit the extension of slavery into free territory. Texas, however, was admitted as slave territory and Oregon as free territory. The campaign of 1848 was quite a political upheaval. Neither the Democratic or Whig party would touch the slave question and tried to attract the attention of the people from it by eulogizing the soldiers of the Mexican war, urging the tariff and other questions of no importance. Just as the Democratic and Republican parties did to attract the attention of the people from the great financial question, for the past twenty years.

The Liberty party had increased its vote from the Abolition party of 7,609 to 62,290 votes for James G. Birney, under the name of Liberty party.

Many of the Democratic party favored the abolition of slavery but thought it beneath them to go to the Liberty party, therefore, split off from the Democratic party and at first called themselves "Barnburners" or Liberals. At Utica, New York, they adopted a platform of abolition tendencies and nominated Martin Van Buren. The Liberty party or Abolitionists being the true patriotic reformers, who sought any measure to carry out reform, at once withdrew their candidates, John P. Hale and Leicester King, and supported the Free Soil ticket. In the election that followed Taylor received 1,362,031 votes, Cass, of Michigan, 1,222,445, while the Abolitionists, under the name of Free Soilers, increased their vote to 291,455. Our cowards of today would say they were throwing their votes away, but they knew better. This was the election of the

12th Pres., ZACHARY TAYLOR,

of Lousiana, Inaugurated March 4, 1849, born in Virginia, 1784, died in Washington City, July 9, 1850.

Vice-Pres., MILLARD FILLMORE,

of New York, born in Locke township, Cuyahoga county, New York, January 7, 1800, died March 8, 1874.

Though Taylor was not an abolitionist he opposed the extension of slavery into free territory, and the red hot abolition shot poured into the public ear by Philips, Garrison, Whittier and many others, was stirring up the country from one end to the other. Polititions were afraid of this great issue, as we know them to be a cowardly lot never touching a new issue until crowded into it. The able and eloquent politician, Henry Clay, introduced a series of eight resolutions, which brought out a debate running four months and the resolutions increased to no less than thirty, and finally ended in the compromise of 1850, which admitted of the organization of New Mexico and Utah as territories without mentioning the subject of slavery, then admitting California as a free state and abolishing slavery in the District of Columbia.

At the death of Taylor the Vice-President took the oath of office, July 10, and became the

13th Pres., MILLARD FILLMORE,

The slave power now pushed forward the American or Know-nothing party, which had been talked of before. The issue they offered was a fight againts foreign born citizens; and it was a side issue, only intended to attract attention from the vital issue. It never amounted to much.

The campaign of 1852 now came on. The Whig and Democratic parties both determined to ignore the slave question at the same time offering sops to deceive the abolitionists; the same as the Republican and

Democratic parties deceive the finance reformers of today.

The democrats put up Franklin Pierce; the Whigs, who had lost power terribly, sought to gain it back through the gratitude of the people to General Scott, the hero of the Mexican war. This move did increase the Whig vote and reduce the Free Soil vote, and, of course, some declared the slave question was dying out as a political issue just as they now declare the finance question is dying out of politics, but like Banquo's ghost it would not down. Or, as Lincoln said of the rebellion, it was like an old dry cowhide, if you pushed it down in one place it bulged up in another.

The democrats were successful and elected for the

14th Pres., FRANKLIN PIERCE,

of New Hampshire; born at Hillsboro, New Hampshire November 23, 1804, inaugurated March 5, 1853, died in 1870.

Vice-Pres., WILLIAM R. KING,

of Alabama; born in North Carolina, April 7, 1786, died at Cahawba, Alabama, April 18, 1853.

The slave question now so far overshadowed all side issues that the parties could not keep out of the fight. The last election fairly killed the Whig party but the slave power decided to keep it alive, if possible, to hold its followers from going to the Abolition party, just as the money power today keep the rotten old Democratic party up to deceive the people.

In the campaign of 1856 the Republican party was formed from the Free Soil party as a nucleus and drawing heavily from the old parties, for the people began to see their rottenness. The new party put up John C. Fremont, "The Pathfinder," for its candidate. The remnant of the Whig party joined the Know nothing party, styling themselves the "Silver Greys," and put up Fillmore for their standard bearer. The democrats put up James Buchanan; thus we reach the election of the

15th Pres., JAMES BUCHANAN.

of Pennsylvania; born at Stony Batter, Franklin county, Pennsylvania, April 22, 1791, inaugurated March 4, 1857, died June 1, 1868.

Vice-Pres., J. C. BRECKENRIDGE

of Kentucky; born near Lexington, Kentucky, Jan. 21, 1820.

Buchanan was a man of no force of character. The slave power emboldened by its success and maddened by the growing power of the abolitionists they determined to force matters to please themselves. The slave power was the arrogant money power of the country; it controlled the press, the pulpit and the bench, as does the money power of today. But abolitionists with their pamphleteering did wonders as do the financial reformers of today, in educating the people by the same means.

Kansas became a terrible battle ground, overt acts were continually being perpetrated by the tools of the slave power and as quickly resented by the people.

Chief Justice Taney declared the compromise of 1850 unconstitutional. He declared that a negro was a chattel, that a slave owner might settle with his property where he pleased, in any territory. This set the whole country on fire; and John Brown's raid, and his capture and death, filled the South with fierce hate and the North with pity for the slave. The southern leaders saw they would be defeated sooner or later and so determined to bring matters to a crisis, by letting the coming election go by default, as it were, and they allowed the Democratic party to split up in the following campaign in 1860. Rule or ruin was their policy. They did just what the money power will do when they see their power slipping away from them, they will plunge the whole world into war. Revelations clearly pictures this same thing.

In the campaign in 1860 the "Constitutional Union Party" met in Baltimore. Its only demand was: "The constitution of the country, the union of the states and the enforcements of the laws." This party put up John Bell of Tennessee.

The party here split and a straight Democratic ticket was put up, its platform re-affirming the Cincinnati platform of 1856. They selected for their standard bearer, John C. Breckenridge of Kentucky.

At a convention held at Charleston, South Carolina, the Democratic party again split and one faction supported Breckenridge, another adopted a platform favoring the acquisition of Cuba and declaring that the state legislatures, which interfered with the enforcement of the fugitive slave law, were revolutionary and subversive of the Constitution, and re-affirmed the Cincinnati platform of 1856. They chose for their standard bearer, Stephen A. Douglas, of Illinois.

All the reform parties united under the Republican banner, and at a convention held in Chicago adopted a platform denouncing the threats of disunion made by the southern leaders in Congress and their avowal of contemplated treason. They declared the re-opening of the slave trade to be a crime, advocated the maintenance of the territories in freedom from slavery, and the passing of a complete and satisfactory homestead law, and that duties should be adjusted so as to encourage the development of the industrial interests of the whole country, and that the rights of citizenship, native or naturalized, should be protected at home and abroad. The party chose for its standard bearer Abraham Lincoln, of Illinois. This broad platform was evidently adopted to draw together the many diverging factions, but it shows us how all minor issues are quickly overshadowed by the great issue when the crisis arrives. There could be but one outcome to such a state of affairs and at the election that followed the choice was made for the

16th Pres., ABRAHAM LINCOLN,

of Illinois; born in Hardin county, Kentucky First inaugural, March 4, 1861; second inaugural March 4, 1865. Assassinated April 14, at Ford's theatre, Washington, by John Wilkes Booth, who was undoubtedly an unknowing tool of a conspiracy of moneyed men, who feared Lincoln would stand in the way of the successful working of their plots against the government.

Vice-Pres., HANNIBAL HAMLIN,

of Maine; born in Oxford county, Maine, August 27, 1809. The second Vice-President Andrew Johnson, of Tennessee; born in Raleigh, North Carolina, 1809; died July 31, 1875

On December 20, 1860, South Carolina declared that the Union was dissolved, and a secession resolution was adopted. Every preparation was now made for war by the South; armories were stripped, the treasury looted, and everything subverted to the itnerests of the South that they could control. Oh, for a President Jackson at this time. But Buchanan, if he did not sympathize with the rebellion, had not force of character enough to attempt any stringent measures to hinder the conflagration.

When Mr. Lincoln took his seat he had a war on his hands, and promptly called for 75,000 three months volunteers to put down the rebellion. This was soon followed by a call for 300,000 three years volunteers, and before the war ended both sides employed millions of men at an expense to the government of a million dollars a day. The English money kings did all they could to help the South and to prolong the war in aid of a conspiracy that is fully shown up in the body of this work.

Politics were now lost sight of in the great struggle for the union or dis-union of the states, and the outgrowth of this struggle was the emancipation proclamation of President Lincoln, January 1, 1863.

The government successfully putting down this gigantic rebellion and ended the right of chattel slavery and the right of states to seecssion forever. But while the people's attention was drawn in this direction a conspiracy of moneyed men were weaving the meshes of a commercial slavery around the whole people through a bonded indebtedness which was procured by the most gigantic fraud ever perpetrated upon a confiding people.

Upon the death of Mr. Lincoln Mr. Johnson took the oath of office and became the

17th Pres., ANDREW JOHNSON,
of Tennessee.

Mr. Johnson soon got into trouble with his cabinet over

the reconstruction of the slave states, and the proper safeguarding of the rights of the newly freed slaves. Mr. Johnson attempted to remove a cabinet officer, Stanton, Secretary of War, without just cause or reason. This brought about an attempt to impeach Mr. Johnson, which was defeated by barely one vote. Mr. Johnson was unjustly charged with connivance with J. Wilkes Booth in the plot against Mr. Lincoln, but there was no evidence for this cruel and false charge.

The money power was shaping everything to suit themselves and they wanted a man they could easily handle on either ticket, so for the campaign of 1868 the democrats put up Horatio Seymour, of New York.

August Belmont, a great bondholder and special agent of the Rothschild's, was chairman of the Democratic National Committee. It was asserted that he had received instructions from Baron James Rothschild to see to it that a plank be gotten into the Democratic platform favorable to the paying of the bonds in gold, as it was clearly understood they should be paid with greenbacks, the same kind of money with which they were bought. This was called the "Government Credit Strengthening Act." Belmont, undoubtedly, supposed he would have no trouble to get this into the Democratic platform. The convention was called in New York but when it came to adopting a platform containing a plank of such barefaced fraud it was more than most of the delegates could stand, and a substitude was offered in favor of paying the bonds with the same kind of money that paid the musket holder and the plow holder, and the cry went up.

"Read it again! read it again!" The platform with the substitute was adopted, and it nearly split the convention, as Mr. Belmont and his friends left in anger. Horatio Seymour and Frank Blair were nominated.

It was afterwards charged, and never successfully contradicted, that at a dinner, where Mr. Belmont, chairman of the Democratic National Committee, and Mr. Schenk, Chairman of the Republican National Committee, were present, that matter was cooked up and fixed so as to go into the republican platform. The charge added that Mr. Belmont, to make assurance doubly sure that this measure should be carried, gave his interest, worth $60,000, to Manton Marble, editor of the New York World, to cry down the democratic candidates as being too heavy a load for the party to carry. Of course if he did so it was rank treason to his party and to his country, and whether he did so or not that plank went into the Republican party platform.

The Republican party put up General Grant.

The country was then too intoxicated over the success of the war and the prosperity of the country, brought about through the large volume of money the war caused to be put in circulation, to pay any attention to the great conspiracy, then in operation, to rob the country and enslave the people. Their gratitude went out to General Grant who was, through force of circumstances, a very successful general though a much overrated man. With all of this in their favor the republicans elected the

18th Pres., ULYSSES S. GRANT,

of Illinois, inaugurated March 4, 1869; born at Mt. Pleasant,

Ohio, April 27, 1822, died July 23, 1883.

Vice-Pres., SCHUYLER COLFAX born in New York city, March 23, 1823.

Grant's second inaugural took place March 4, 1873.

It has been shown that if Grant was a great soldier, he was certainly a poor business man. Whether he was a poor statesman or a scoundrel makes little difference now, but one thing is certain, there were more frauds perpetrated under his administration than during any administration since the republic existed. The first great fraud was the "Government Credit Strengthening Act," which robbed the country of at least six hundred million dollars. Then vast tracts of land were given to railroad companies and funds loaned to them to build roads where the government had better have built the roads. The "Credit Mobellier" swindle and the great whisky ring came under his administration. Then last, but not least, was the dishonest passage of the silver bill of 1873, demonetizing silver.

In 1872 the finance question was talked of a little, but in 1876 the first ticket was put in the field, headed by Cooper and Carey.

The democrats put up Samuel J. Tilden, of New York. The republicans put up Rutherford B. Hayes, of Ohio. Neither party dared to touch the financial question.

The greenbackers, though polling a light vote, only 81,740. aroused the country and the education of the masses has been steadily going on ever since.

Tilden was undoubtedly elected, the popular vote standing 4,284,885 against 4,033,950. But fraud was declared in some of the states and the matter was finally settled by a commission which gave the election to Hayes, 8 to 7, notwithstanding the governors elected in the disputed states were democratic. The money power, undoubtedly, desired the democrats to resist, that they might call on Grant and make him dictator. Such, at least was thought and charged at the time, at any rate the

19th Pres., R. B. HAYES,

of Ohio, was inaugurated March 4, 1877. William A. Wheeler, Vice President.

During this administration the great Pittsburg railroad riots took place; the Bland silver bill was passed and vetoed by Hayes, and then passed over his head.

In the campaign of 1880 the tariff was made the leading issue. The Democratic ticket was headed by General Winfield Scott Hancock of New York; the Greenback ticket by General James B. Weaver of Iowa; the Republican ticket by General James A. Garfield of Ohio.

20th Pres., JAMES A. GARFIELD

of Ohio, inaugurated March 4, 1881. Vice-President, Chester A. Arthur of New York.

The assassination of Garfield is treated of in the body of this book, so it will not be farther mentioned here. Upon the death of Mr. Garfield the

21st Pres., CHESTER A. ARTHUR

took his seat and was President until 1885.

The two old parties, like the old parties in the days of the agitation of the slave question, were trying to crowd on the same ground as in the campaign of 1884, though pretending to make an issue on the tariff. The democrats put up Grover Cleveland of New York; the republicans nominated James G. Blaine, of Maine, greenback candidate Benjamin F. Butler of Massachusetts; the Prohibition party J. P. St. John of Kansas.

This campaign was marked by fraud at the polls all over the country. There is little doubt that the Butler vote in New York, was counted for Cleveland, thus retaliating on the republicans for counting Tilden out.

22d Pres., GROVER CLEVELAND

inaugurated March 4, 1885.

No one observant of these matters doubted but what Mr. Cleveland would be a pliant tool of the money kings. There was nothing worthy of note transpired during his administration except that labor agitations ran high and several innocent men were condemned, convicted and hung in Chicago for the alleged throwing of a bomb, killing several policemen; but it was shown by many powerful writers, that these men were convicted through prejudice and wrong, and many will always believe it was all brought about by a conspiracy of the money kings to intimidate reform agitation all over the country. It is claimed that persecution was the seed of the church, and it is one thing sure this affair never stopped the growth of reform movements.

The campaign of 1888 the democrats again put up Cleveland; the republicans nominated Benjamin W. Harrison, of Indiana; the greenbackers now became the Union Labor Party and selected A. W. Streeter for its standard bearer. The republicans elected the

23rd Pres., BENJ. W. HARISON.

Inaugurated March 4, 1889. The republicans were enabled to carry through a measure of high tariff, known as the "McKinley Bill," which seemed to make better times, but the better times were really brought about by the increase of currency, by Sherman's trick bill, which was really for the purpose of getting rid of the Bland Bill and which Sherman voted afterwards, in 1893, to repeal.

In 1882, the democrats again ran Cleveland and Harrison ran for second term on the Republican ticket, and Wing represented the Socialist Labor party and Bidwill, the Prohibition party.

The finance reformers now came up under the name of the People's party, headed by James B. Weaver, of Iowa.

While Harrison had, in a measure, seemed to favor the money loaning classes, his administration was the cleanest since Lincoln's; he refused to favor the issuing more bonds, and, probably, refused to enter the conspiracy against silver, so the shylocks did not like him and determined to re-elect Cleveland, which they did; and Mr. Cleveland has issued their bonds without authority from Congress and he is doing all he can for their silver conspiracy. It really seems as though no well posted man could ever think that Cleveland was anything else but a downright fool or a treasonable knave. Besides working right in the interest of the money loaning scoundrels of the world and using the army to help capital crush out labor, he lets slip the opportunity to acquire the Hawaii Islands, the key to our western coast, and Cuba, the key to the gulf of Mexico.

Of these productive islands one is ready come to us for the taking the other at little cost. They should be taken and made the Gibraltars of the extremes of our American continent. A statesman would do it. A fool would let it slip for fear, and a knave, to favor the enemies of his country.

THE POLITICAL OUTLOOK.

The two old parties, are in indentically the same position of the Whig and Democratic parties on the slave question.

The Whig party was a corpse held up by the slave power until it fell to pieces of its rottenness.

The Democratic party has been a stinking corpse for over twenty years but it has been held up by the money power, to hinder the formation of new parties on new lines. But since Cleveland stultified himself and his party on the silver question, it is doubtedful whether they can hold it together much longer. The Republican party, though honey combed with corruption is not yet as rotten as the Democratic party.

The people are scattered in factions, led by the secret work of the moneyed kings to advocate many supposed reforms. This is done to lead them away from the finance question. But the silver question is the entering wedge that is to consolidate the factions on the finance question, the same as the Republican party consolidated the opposing reform factions in 1860. If so, it will place the new party where the Republican party was in 1856. Thus the two old parties will be driven together, and even if they carry the election, the money power can't help but see it is their last chance, consequently, they, like the old devil spoken of in Revelations, knowing its time is near at hand, become enraged. The same as the slave power did in 1860, and will therefore resort to any measures, even to destroying the government, if possible, though it die with it. Therefore it is quite possible the following program has been marked out:

In whatever way parties may be divided, let corruption have such sway as to disgust everybody and then urge an uprising of the people. The republic will be declared a failure, a temporary dictatorship set up before forming a monarchy. If the powers that be are not strong enough to put down the people, the enemies of the country have already provided for that by calling on England and Spain, whose navies and armies have been brought to our doors, apparently for other purposes. Thus the secret alliance of Europe, under the dragon and Pope, spoken of elsewhere, will be made public to the world. Whether this takes place at this election or in the future, it is sure to take place soon. But they will never succeed for God has destined different.

OUR POLITICAL INSTITUTIONS.

and form of government should be somewhat changed. The President should be elected by popular vote and the Electoral College abolished, as the present system is cumbersome and liable to be productive of much evil, thwarting the wishes of the people.

The Senate should also be abolished, and the House reduced in numbers, and none of them hold over two years, and the newly elected representatives should take their seats immediately. In this way the whole legislative assembly could be changed once in two years and not, as now, the sentiments of the people ignored year, after year, beyond the time of expression.

All great questions should be voted upon by the people, thus the referendum system should be adopted.

No representative should hold office more than eight years, unless returned by over two-thirds vote of his constituents, and then never more than twelve years.

If the President veto a bill the measure should at once be referred to the people. If Congress is sustained the President should step down and out and his place filled by the Vice-President, if not available, by one elected by the House from the representatives, until the close of the term.

THE POLITICAL HISTORY OF

OUR COUNTRY CONTINUED.

It will be noitced that this work was published in 1895, just prior to the McKinley-Bryan campaign of 1896. It was published for a speaker's text book, and that is why the shape was long and slim to fit the side pocket and partly because the matter had appeared in the columns of a newspaper and so were utilized without resetting the type.

I have elsewhere stated that the two old parties had been on every side of every question and their platforms had promised much, but carried out little for the benefit of the people, while the plans of the conspirators were made to keep steady pace with conditions.

Nobody doubted but the 7 to 8 commission that seated Hays over Tilden was a genuine political fraud, or that the Democrats stole Butler votes in New York to carry New York for Cleveland in 1892.

In 1896 the Democratic party was badly split over the money question. The predatory class had determined to carry their schemes of enslaving the people to a final finish. (See Hazard Circular.)

The people were rapidly losing confidence in the old parties, and the people's party was growing rapidly.

It was necessary to do something to break up this growing independent party, so once again the Democratic party posed as the people's savior. They held their convention in Chicago and William Jennings Bryan, a young attorney, became the people's champion and in an eloquent address to the convention, wound up his oration with these words:

"You shall not press upon the brow of labor this crown of thorns; you shall not crucify it upon a cross of gold.".

This won the hearts of the people and carried an overwhelming majority of votes to Mr. Bryan.

"Hold on," says the reader. "Have you not made a mistake? I thought McKinley and Hobart were elected."

Well, maybe they were, but there was much evidence that went to show stupendous fraud that I sometimes forget myself.

The people's party met in St. Louis and put up a ticket with Bryan at the head. This would catch the votes that would otherwise go back to the Republican party, and the bulk of the floating votes would go to Bryan.

Mark Hanna, the chairman of the Republican National Committee, had openly boasted that the right way to get an election was to get it. Evidently the Republican Party went in to get it.

The year before, Ohio, in a state election, had got out every available vote, yet in 1896 it was charged she would have had to increase her population two million souls to have cast the increased vote cast, and Ohio, an old and finished state, while Texas, the largest state in the union, and a new state, had met with hardly a perceptible change in population that horrible, dull year.

The corrupting influences of this awful political crime was felt in the state of Ohio for years, and whole townships were thrown out and illegal voters prosecuted many years after the '96 election.

General Benj. Harrison, republican candidate for President, had carried Indiana by a majority of 50,000 votes in 1888. It was claimed Bryan cast 50,000 more votes than Harrison, and then was beaten by 80,000 votes.

Whole counties in Iowa and in California and other localities were said to have been thrown out or fraudulently counted.

I well remember, in the city of Detroit, my son-in-law and I went down town to hear the returns read or see them thrown up on the screens with limelight. We noticed supposed returns thrown up of western districts several hours before the polls could have closed in those localities and these figures were not changed, and while circulating among the crowd we overheard wealthy politicians chuckling with glee, and asserting to each other the assurance that the people would find they could not have things their own way, even if they had the numbers.

I must say that at no time during my three years' service in the war did I ever feel so much like shooting traitors.

I never felt so sad and yet so ugly in my life, and the next morning many people expressed themselves to me in the same way.

For all of this Mr. McKinley made a good president.

The ruling classes saw the temper the people were getting into, and an inflation of currency was resorted to at once; meantime there was a general rush to the gold mines, and business started up everywhere.

A little war with Spain in 1897-98 helped to circulate money and start the wheels of business. Annexation of new territory and taking in of the Hawaiian Islands all went to create new sentiment and take the minds of the people from their old troubles.

But just the same, the forging of the fetters of slavery have been going steadily on. Every possible excuse for creating a bonded debt for every state, county, municipality and town has steadily gone on, and the public domain steadily swallowed up by the few.

Mr. McKinley had made so good a president that the people readily supported him for a second term; again against Mr. Bryan, who swallowed the gold bug wing of the Democratic party who deserted him and the people four years before. He pretended to see no necessity for the money question, which had never been settled.

President McKinley was assassinated by a crazy man, and every American citizen, including the crazy man himself, was sorry for it. Of course the Vice President, Theodore Roosevelt, was sworn in to fill the balance of the term. This opened the way for Roosevelt, who was elected over Judge Parker, Democrat, in 1904. By this time the people had no confidence in the Democratic party, and it was a walkaway for Roosevelt. Besides, he carried out some reforms and apparently made big efforts in other directions; half the people believed him to be in earnest and others thought it was political gush. Roosevelt's name will live in history as one of the great Presidents and his name linked with the greatest canal building episode of the world's history.

It matters not twho ran agains Roosevelt in 1904; there was not enough opposition to bother him much.

Roosevelt declined the nomination in 1908 and Taft was elected over Bryan for a third run.

Though Taft did some good work and nothing more to his discredit than any other of the moneyed men's presidents, if we take a close under-view we will find that it was an anti-Catholic expression, together with the high cost of living, and unreasonable salaries continually voted to office holders and general corruption everywhere which caused unrest and a change of politics.

At no time had the moneyed men let up on their purpose to rivet the chains of slavery on the people, and while they had frequently blamed the people for agitating the money question, yet a bill known as the Aldrich bill, which was really the old fight for a central bank they had waged back in Jackson's time, has been continually pressed to the front.

I must not forget to state right here that, notwithstanding the Bible says "The earth is the oLrd's and the fullness thereof. The love of money is the root of all evil. Take thou no usury or increase," and the Jews were driven from their native land for taking interest on money, and stand scattered today as an evidence of it, the only time Christ ever used force or sanctioned the use of force was when with the scourge he drove the money changers from the temple. Yet we find the churches with the money changers and eighty of their preachers went to Cleveland in 1896 to tell Mr. McKinley, the money lenders' president, that they would support him.

Money is a creation of law, and law belongs to the whole people, and he who would monopolize law for selfish gain, where it is not justly due him, is no better than a thief and a robber.

The government should furnish money to the people so cheap it would not be profitable; that is, so low that the money loaners could not find it profitable to lend money at interest. (See part first of "What Is Coming," pages 253 to 263.)

There is no reason, at least, why the government should not lend money to the state, city and town at one-half of 1 per cent, as well as to lend it to the banker for that.

Notwithstanding Mr. Wilson and Bryan are great church men, the recent bill of Mr. Wilson's favors the money loaner more than it does the people, and Mr. Bryan, who in 1896 so earnestly declared, "You shall not press upon the brow of, labor this crown of thorns. You shall not crucify it upon a cross of gold," now says, "The business interests will, I think, welcome this bill as an unalloyed blessing." He should have said bankers, instead of business men.

I must not forget to mention that in 1907 the moneyed men brought on a little financial panic, but the people were not in a temper to be troubled much along this line, though much sad distress was caused by the crime.

It has been found that Socialism has been spreading all over the world. Some think that it was not so much to defeat his own party and a love of reform that led Mr. Roosevelt to run independently as it was to catch the dissatisfied vote and prevent it from going to the Socialist party. As far as I am concerned, I do not wish to impugn Mr. Roosevelt's motives, but his part in the campaign of 1912 acted in accord with the plans of the political tricksters of all times past.

That we may quickly grasp the situation as to what is coming, let us take the matter up from another standpoint.

INTEREST ON MONEY.

As you have seen, money is a creation of law, pure and simple, therefore an ideal thing. Ten mills make one cent, yet no person ever saw a mill. Therefore, the tool called money is a thing of specific value, measured by the ideal, a law of man; but its exchange, comparative value is measured by the law of supply and demand, a natural law, which may be controlled by man's manipulation of the supply and demand end, and whoever controls this is a privileged class.

It takes the whole people to make money, so none but the whole people, their Congress, should be interested in its creation and its volume and especial benefits. This was thoroughly understood by our forefathers, when they penned the constitution of the United States. Article I, Section 7, paragraph 5, says: "To coin money, regulate the value thereof, and of foreign coin, and fix the standards of weights and measures." Also Section X, paragraph 1: "No state shall enter into any treaty, alliance or confederation; grant letters of marque and reprisal; coin money; emit bills of credit; make anything but gold and silver coin a tender in payment of debts; pass any bill of attainder, expost facto law or impairing the obligation of contracts, or grant any title of nobility."

Thus it is seen how jealously they guarded the people's rights. Later the Third Congress of the United States, Dec. 23, 1793, passed the following resolution:

"Any person holding any office or any stock in any institution in the nature of a bank for issuing or discounting bills or notes payable to bearer, on order, cannot be a member of the house whilst he holds such office or stock."

This resolution was signed by President Washington.

This shows how carefully the rights of the whole people were to be guarded against encroachment of states, sections, parties or classes.

Right here let me add that after months of preparing and gathering evidence for my revised "What Is Coming," the work was so great and seemingly so impossible that men would be so cruelly selfish, I was compelled to divide my work into two parts—one of science and fact, and the other a novel based upon facts, so this work stands revised and brought down to the present date, and the balance will appear as a novel.

I here simply call attention to evidence already published in this work, showing their purposes to cary out the designs expressed in the Hazzard Circular, found on page 119; President Lincoln's Warning, found on page 139; the Bank Circular, on page 147; the Bankers' Rebellion, on page 158, and the Panic Bulletin, page 180; all pointing to a terrible conspiracy of the upper class against the people, to enslave the masses—a conspiracy that is as terrible and merciless as it is cunning and devilish.

The process has ben to get control of the bulk of all wealth, and so control prices, and thereby keep the masses with their noses to the grindstone, so they will have no time to think, except as the small manufacturer or the middle class would be ground by the interest power on the one hand and crushed labor on the other, as the crushing of labor by the middle class would be a necessity of self-preservation.

How they are succeeding may be seen by their own statements, namely that five per cent of the people own ninety-five per cent of the wealth of the country.

Second. That the estimated value of property in this country at an inflated price is $140,000,000,000, while debts public and corporate, leaving out private debts and open accounts, is $85,000,000,000—more than on half, and we know values often shrin one-half in times of panic.

As they are monopolizing the functions of government, and get the government to let them have money at one-half of one per cent; but the government will not give the people, the states and cities money at the same rate.

In our own city of Detroit the average daily balance of the city for 1912 were $3,483,000. On this vast sum we can only get two per cent, while at the present time, September, 1913, the banks refused to take our bonds at four per cent and a private citizen takes one million of them at that rate.

This is supposed to be a saving to our city of $34,830 annually.

With so much money collected by taxes it is strange the city cannot do business on a cash basis.

Now suppose Mr. Ford is one of the schemers and he wants a place for his money. He encourages building up our city, and invites every ruff-scuff of creation here. He then gets the papers to advocate much needed improvements we could do without. The unsuspicious people permit themselves to be chained in bonded debt. What does Mr. Ford make out of it personally?

First he is highly honored as a patriotic and public-spirited citizen. But what are his financial gains for the use of one million dollars for thirty years?

The annual interest on one million dollars at four per cent is forty thousand dollars, or in thirty years one million two hundred thousand. In other words he has got his money back twice over and two hundred thousand besides.

Now supposing each year he tricks the city into unnecessary improvements to make a place for his $40,000. The interest at four per cent on $40,000 is $1,600. In thirty years he can double his money again.

We must suppose Mr. Ford is a perfect gentleman, merely taking advantage of a false system, which he is sincere in his belief is the best system possible. But what about the people that permit such a system?

I just received a letter from the city of Boston, from a friend who sends me an authentic document showing the city of Boston paid for interest alone last year $6,010,289.96.

Is it any wonder that Christ scourged the money changers from the temple, or that God drove the Jews from their native land for taking usury?

It was interest on money that caused the destruction of Sodom, Gomorrah, Tyre, Sidon, Thebes, Nineveh, Jerusalem, Babylon, Carthage and Rome, and is about to engulf us in the horible wars spoken of in Daniel and Revelations.

Can you not see the signs?

"When the sign of Man is seen in the heavens then you may know the time is at hand."

What is the sign of man?

It is the sun which has just passed into Aquarius the water bearer.

This is the sign of Man, in the top of the celestial head, or spirituality.

The people will wake up.

I have seen a whole town suddenly rise up in a mob as one man, apparently without cause.

I have seen a regiment of men suddenly refuse to cheer a general, and no two had spoken together on the subject.

History is replete with evidence of the hand of Destiny in the affairs of men.

If we are to believe the Bible, God used a lying spirit in the mouth of Ahab to deceive the enemy. And he said, I will go out, and be a lying spirit in the mouth of all his prophets. And the Lord said, Thou shalt entice him, thou shalt also prevail: go out and do even so.—II. Chron.-XVII.-21.

We are told that with the help of God, Moses marshalled 600,000 men and their families, and led them through a wilderness for 40 years. Even God acted as quartermaster, supplying water and food for the host, and then punished Moses and Aaron for taking the honors upon themselves.

We are told God even went so far as to stop the motion of the Sun, Moon and Stars while Joshua fought a battle.

As it is presumption to deny holy writ, we will simply say the hand of destiny was recognized in those marvelous victories, and the form of interference given tangible shape for the benefit of weak minds. Let us take a glance at the hand of destiny farther down in the pages of history.

Alexander, the Great, with his small army conquered the Persian hosts and destroyed Darius of Persia and his army.

We attribute the victory of Alexander to his new arms and brass armour, but was that his?

History tells us that after the terrible seige of Gaza, Alexander moved on to Jerusalem, expecting another stubborn siege, but instead he met the Jewish people coming forth in Holiday array, lead by the priests carrying their miters, while singing joyous songs.

They escorted Alexander and his generals through the gates and showed him inscriptions on the inner walls, where it had been prophesied he was the man to free Jerusalem.

Though Alexander was a prince, he had been a plain, modest man, until puffed up by the sycophants who prevailed on him to erect his statue in the public squares of Athens, to be worshiped as one of the Gods, and then his star went down and he died alone in Babylon.

The mighty Hannibal of Carthage saw the rising power of Rome, marshalled his armies from among the barbarians and held Rome in check for thirty years. He did not recognize the hand of destiny, but grew proud of his own powers, and after the battle of Canna, where 60,000 dead Romans lay stretched upon the field, Maharrable, his chief of cavalry, cried out, "Now, Hannibal, let me on to Rome before they know that I am coming."

Hannibal, in his moment of pride, flushed with victory, proudly replied to Maharrable, "I can take Rome when I want it."

Maharrable indignantly answered: "Hannibal, I see the Gods do not give all of the attributes to one man. You, Hannibal, understand the secret of winning battles, but you do not know how to take advantage of them."

When Hannibal found the fruits of his thirty years' war were lost, through the selfishness of the wealth gatherers at Carthage, he commented sorrowfully: "Once I had the opportunity to take Rome, but lacked the desire; now I have the desire to take Rome, but lack the opportunity."

Not only was Hannibal punished for his self-glorification, but the Grafters of Carthage were humbled also.

Hannibal was forced back to Carthage, and when Scipio was thundering at the gates of Carthage, then those selfish rich men saw their stolen wealth would soon be lost to them, they called a council of war.

Hannibal, with contempt and sorrow, stood with folded arms when a wealthy senator, Mahitibal, by name, said vehemently, "Hannibal smiles, and his country is in danger."

"Yes," replied Hannibal, "the smile of contempt for him who feels his country's loss, only when his own interests are threatened, is sorrow for Carthage."

While pride and greed of the rich in all ages has been the downfall of nations, yet fate seems to be the nemesis that follows on to punish greed and pride.

Napoleon, the son of poverty from the Isle of Corsica, at the close of his military education, without a sou, was on his way to the Seine to commit suicide, but fate had a different course for him, and he met an actor who wormed out of him his purpose, and he gave Napoleon funds and encouragement. Two months later he won undying fame at the battle of Austerlitz, and started on his ascent to the Empire.

Napoleon had shaken the earth to its foundations, and though a momentary defeat had caused his capture and confinement on the Isle of Elba, he had escaped and marshalled his army to meet the world.

Just before his final defeat at Waterloo, he had called a council of war, and at its close an under-general meekly suggested "Emperor, had we not better take circumstances into consideration."

Forgetting he had been the target of expert riflemen, forgetting the fates would not let him commit suicide, but hoisted him from the ranks of the lowly to the throne of his Empire, and then back to a fugitive, and again to the throne and the head of his army. He turned upon the modest general, who had suggested that it would be well to take circumstances into consideration, and hotly hissed forth, "I make circumstances."

Then turning to his right hand man, Marshall Ney, who had never failed him he said, "Yonder lies the black forest through which Blucher must pass to go to the assistance of Wellington. Overtake him at Quarterbrass and destroy his army."

Marshall Ney succeeded in overtaking Blucher and defeating him, but, like Hannibal, flushed with the pride of his victory, he sat down and let Blucher escape. This was circumstances No. 1 for the men who made circumstances.

There came up a rainstorm which made the roads impassable, and he could not get his artillery, his favorite arm of service, on the field.

That was circumstance No. 2 for the man who made circumstances.

Napoleon's engineers failed to notify him of a sunken road he was unable to pass until filled with his own dead men. Circustance No. 3 for the man who made circumstances.

Upon learning of Marshall Ney's failure to destroy Blucher, he sent Grouchy, the only general he had taken from the ranks of the nobility, to intercept Blucher and detain him, and Grouchy sold his country for British gold, and that was circumstance No. 4 for the man who made circumstances.

If it is true that God Almighty led the Jews out of Egypt and favored them at various times, and that he said he would give his people a country, and a language, we may as well give him credit for establishing a republic in this land, for I have shown how Columbus could not have succeeded only for the help of those Jewish gentlemen.

It may well be said here that these Jewish gentlemen were also acting under Divine influence, since God hated Kingdoms and Empires, and had promised his people a Kingdom and a language, and on the very day that Columbus sailed their humanity for their race was quickened, by the fact that Spain which had long been a friend to the Jew, had suddenly turned against them, and as if to disgrace the very name of Christianity the Holy Catholic Church caused 60,000 Jews to be driven out and left without a home, and without a land. This alone should be enough to put that institution in disgrace forever.

Let us now trace the hand of destiny through our own country.

There are many things that would lead one to believe in an intelligent hand of destiny. Let us trace them.

1st. The Papal power was pointed out by prophesy as a dispoiler.

2nd. We have found, in history, when religion ran rampant, the most blood-thirsty and most bloody period of history.

3d. The church was forever and is undoubtedly the friend of the moneyed men and power.

4th. Christ was the friend of the poor man, always found with the poor, and he said: "Where two or three are gathered together in my name, there am I in the midst of them," and he had no church or place to lay his head.

5th. To all appearance this country was discovered by the hand of fate, was settled by the hand of fate, and we will now prove it has been sustained by the hand of fate.

6th. "And his number is 666, the number of the Papal power, and we find the yellow flag and the double Eagle playing an important part with the Papal power.

7th. We find the meeting in Vienna, Austria, that Prof. Morse speaks of gives one hundred years to destroy this Republic, and the Papal power was powerful there.

8th. We find the Papal power nearly driven out of Europe.

9th. We find it was undoubtedly European money that helped newspaper agitation to bring on the great war between the North and South.

10th. We find for many years the great buildings at Baltimore, Md., had excited comments that it was for the purpose of sheltering the Papal power.

11th. We find the Pope was the only European power that openly recognized the beligerancy of the south, though the other powers did so covertly.

12th. We find Father Chineque in his 50 Years in the Roman Church points to powerful evidence of the hand of the Catholic church as in the assassination of President Lincoln.

13th. We find where the Catholic rule is strongest the most backward tendency in civilization. As for instance, in Mexico, the first place where the printing press was set up, though a strong Catholic country, is the farthest back in civilization of any in America.

14th. Every instance of importance points to the United States being the man-child or place established for the maintanance of freedom of speech and freedom of the press.

15th. The hand of destiny seems traceable in a vast number of events, some of which follows:

I will leave to history that part of the hand of destiny in shaping the affairs of our country down to the opening of the great war between the North and South.

16th. Says James G. Blaine in his "Thirty Years in Congress:" "No one expected the War of the Rebellion would last but a few months. Representative men of both sides thought the war would end with the first big battle, and both sides expected to win that battle.

Not without a long war would slavery be abolished.

Had the North won a decisive victory at the first battle of Bull's Run, the South would have given up if she could have been left her cherished institution of slavery, so a victory was necessary to give her the confidence of Europe and funds to carry on a long war.

Had the South won a decisive victory, she would have come back in the Union and dictated terms of slavery to the North. It was not to be. The unforseen influence made a drawn battle, with a doubtful victory which gave her the prestige necessary to carry on a long war.

An apparent victory for the South that did not take the capital, yet threatened it, was just what was necessary to awake the prodigious energies of the North and fit her for a great sacrifice in a long war necessray to final victory and the abolition of slavery.

The European powers were every one anxious for the destruction of our republic, but they were jealous of each other, and so none but the Pope recognized the South, which proves he was not in favor of the poor and down-trodden slaves, but with their slave-masters, and he went farther than any other power dared to go. Though all of the other powers stood ready to take advantage of any one to recognize the South.

17th. The sea monster of war of today could take on board an old wooden war vessel of that period and make a toy of it. Iron and steel sides to vessels were unknown, and Mother Shipton's prophesy—

"That iron in water yet will float
As easy as a wooden boat,"

was laughed at. But when the Merrimac was nearly ready for sea, Europe rejoiced at the prospects of her bombarding Northern ports. But that unseen fate that rules the affairs of men brought from the unknown some where that little Yankee cheese box called the Monitor, and right in the flush of the Merrimac's victory plucked her laurels from her and sent her like a wounded panther back to her lair, never to come forth again. The powers were driven to wait a better time and a better excuse.

18th. All remember the Mason and Slidel affair, and that England was preparing to attack us, but the Russian fleet was in our waters, and England held off.

19th. McClellan's defeat on the Peninsula was nearly enough to give the powers their desired excuse, but to make it perfect Lee was to invade the North, which he did, but his defeat at Antietam destroyed that opportunity.

20th. Still hoping for an excuse for interference, when Hooker had succeeded Burnside and performed a masterly piece of strategy in succeeding in getting in Lee's rear, and then lost his head, and in his pride forgetting his God, his generals and his army, boastfully said, "Now let Mr. Lee slip by me (the big I) and I will be after him." Hooker was then seized with an unaccountable impulse, and contrary to the wishes of his council of war, withdrew his forces from an impregnable position into the wilderness, where he could not handle them, and then Stonewall Jackson, Lee's right hand man, marched his forces directly over that ground. Hooker had vacated and attacked his right, and all he wanted was another day to finish his work. But Destiny removed Jackson that night and restored Hooker to himself and a successful withdrawal of his troops to safety.

21st. Once again Europe awaited Lee's success in the North, but destiny was with the Northern forces, and the defeat of Lee at Gettysburg and Pemberton at Vicksburg deprived them of another much hoped for excuse to recognize the South and aid her.

In tracing the hand of destiny in reform we must not forget the North needed much punishment before they would even admit of the abolition of slavery, and very much experience before they would admit of the abolition of interest on money, another form of slavery, so the war must be prolonged.

The mighty army of the Potomac had fought the great battles of the Wilderness, Spottsylvania, North Ann, and the first day's battle of Cold Harbor, and Grant sent his dispatch to President Lincoln:

"I have fought a bitter battle, and lost 10,000 men, but I will take Cold Harbor, if it costs the life of every man in my command."

The ground had been fought over for two years, and the blood of tens of thousands of men were crying up from the ground, "Boys, don't go in there to be slaughtered."

That beautiful June morning Grant marshalled his mighty army aginst that impregnable position. The bugles sounded "Forward." But not a man moved, not a general could give an order.

The blood of the dead was crying out to the souls of the living, "Don't go in there, don't go in there." The living heard the appeal and refused to go.

22d. Defeat and victory must fluctuate, and Rosecrans' Army of the Tennessee had met with a terrible check and lay at the point of starvation at Chattanooga.

Bragg's forces were jubilant, gazing down from Lookout Mountain, whose sides seemed to offer resistant steeps that no man could scale, much less an army. Hooker and Sherman had come to the aid of the rested Army of the Tennessee, and Grant ordered an attack with strict orders that his men must not go beyond a given point, but those men, all fit to be generals, saw the impossibility of remaining where they were, and so received their orders from the spirit of the air, climbing the supposed impregnable position and moved on, on, up, up, that supposed impassible barrier, and to victory, and the powers lost another opoprtunity.

23d. The blockading of Southern ports had never been quite perfect, and the depredations of an English-built blockade runner called for stringent measures, and the Kearsarge was sent to camp on the trail of the Alabama until she was destroyed.

The professed neutrality of the powers did not prevent them from giving to the Alabama all the news possible, and aid and comfort as well.

The Kearsarge found the Alabama in a French port, and challenged her out to battle, and when she came out the Kearsarge apparently turned tail and ran. This was to draw the Alabama far enough from land to prevent her rescue if crippled.

The first shot fired by the Alabama struck the Kearsarge in the stren post, and may be seen in the post in the Naval Museum in Washington to-day. Had the shell exploded the Kearsarge would have gone to the bottom, and even that victory would have been seized upon as an excuse to demand the raising of the blockade. But! Destiny ruled otherwise, and within one hour the Alabama went to the bottom.

24th. The last hope. The confederacy was crumbling and Mobile Bay, where Benjamin F. Butler says he defeated the plans of England and France from carrying out a plan to recognize and assist the South, was still a comparatively safe harbor for blockade runners, and that harbor was well laid with torpedoes and held several powerful Southern iron-clads.

Faragut had asembled a powerful fleet and attacked the stronghold.

There was but one narrow channel of approach, and one of our vessels was crippled and shut up the channel. The flag ship must pass by it, and to do so was almost certain destruction if the torpedoes exploded. There was no time for thought; this was a time for action. The admiral took the lives of himself and command in his hands and moved on to probable destruction, but fate held her hand over the torpedoes and their tin cases rattled harmlessly over the bottom of the Hartford, and the last hope of the war to the Confederates and their sympathizers was gone forever.

Remember, President Lincoln said the war had enthroned a class of unprincipled wealthy men he feared more than he feared the foe in the field.

I have pointed out that Harriman and Morgan have been charged as financial agents of the Catholic Hierarchy, as an evidence of it, that though Morgan was not a Catholic, the largest candle ever burned in the vatican was burned in his honor. Why?

The Dragon power I have pointed out is to restore the power of the wounded head of the old Roman power, that means establish it here in this country, and remain with it for one hour. Astrologically, that is 15 years, and then both of them will be consumed by the wrath of the people as pictured in Daniel's time of trouble, and that time spoken of in Revelations as the heat of a fiery furnace, and if you do not wish to partake of the plagues of the churches—

"Come out of them, Oh, my people." Revelation xviii-4.

Christ established a socialistic system among his followers, and according to VI. Chapter of Revelations, "A measure of wheat for a penny, and three measures of barely for a penny; and see thou hurt not the oil and the wine." Means when the demand of usury is taken off from the price of necessities of life that price will drop and the fallacy of prohibition and false reforms will cease, and if men wish to cultivate temperance they will be encouraged to it, but not forced against their natures to follow the dictates of fanatics.

The souls of the oppressed of the thousands of years are crying to the living, "Don't stand this legal robbery system any longer."

All nature is helping the oppressed people to throw off the yoke of mammon, and the people are beginning to heed the cry. The promised signs are here; see Nahum, 1-4.

"The chariots shall rage in the streets, they shall jostle against one another in the broad ways, they shall seem like torches, they hsall run like the lightning."

Describe the automobile better if you can.

I am an astrologer, these prophecies are astrological. The Bible was written by astrologers.

The spirit told Daniel: "Shut up the words and seal the book, evn to the time of the end. Many shall run to and fro and knowledge shall be increased." Daniel, 12-4.

How few grown people could read and write, in my boyhood days, and the tinder box and tallow dip took the place of the electric light and lucipher match of today. The street car and the telephone were unknown, and a thousand and one things to elevate the mind we now have wer yet in the womb of the future.

"And he shall plant the tabernacle of his palaces between the seas in the glorious holy mountain and yet he shall come to his end, and none shall help him." Daniel, 11-45.

This is the Turk who was just driven out of Europe, and none of the powers remain to help him.

Now look at ll Timothy lll, 1-6:

1. This know also, that in the last days perilous times shall come.

2. For men shall be lovers of their own selves, covetous, boasters, proud, blasphemers, disobedient to parents, unthankful, unholy.

The covitousness is certainly manifest where there are so many millionaires and the masses with nothing. They boast of 8,000,000 of bank depositors and say nothing of over 80,-000,000 with nothing in the banks.

"Traitors, heady, high-minded, lovers of pleasure more than lovers of God."

The churches are symbolized by a woman, and as the Catholic church is the mother of harlots, because "the love of money is the root of all evil," yet the churches will not say one word against interest on money, the greatest of all crimes. But forever harping against the slums they have made, and making war on food and drink and the films of moving pictures, but never on the great sin of greed and creed.

Revelations, 11-22-23: "Behold, I will cast her into a bed, and them that comit adultery, with her, into great tribulation, except they repent of their deeds.

"And I will kill her children with death; and all the churches shall know that I am he which searcheth the reins and hearts; and I will give unto every one of you according to your works."

That the above is true is shown in Revelations, 11-3: "And will give power unto my two witnesses and they shall prophecy a thousand two hundred, and three score years clothed in sackcloth."

This is Helio and Geo systems of astrology, which the church has been 1260 years persecuting and trying to stamp out.

See, I have explained that the mother of harlots is the Catholic church, the seven heads, the seven forms of government of the Roman Empire. (1) Kings, (2) Consuls, (3) Decemvirs, (4) Dictators, (5) Trumpers, (6) Emperors, (7) Popes. The seven hills on which the woman sitteth are the seven hills the Roman city is built on.

In Revelations 18 and 1st to 5th, it shows plainly it is the churches that is meant and calls the people out of them.

4th verse: "And I heard another voice from heaven saying, 'Come out of her, my people, that ye may not partake of her sins, and that ye receive not of her plagues."

We are told that God hardened the heart of Pharo, which caused him to follow the Israelites to his own destruction.

The hatred that is rising against the millionaires of today they do not see because they have no care for the people and they are paving the way for their own destruction.

"The stars of the heavens shall fall to the earth, like a tree casting its untimely fruit, shaken by a mighty wind."

These are not the stars that it has taken three millions of years for their light to reach us, and of which our earth would not be a drop in the bucket. What then? Just what it says—kings, princes and money lords.

"And the heavens departed as a scroll when it is rolled together; and every mountain and island were moved out of their places."

This does not mean the Alps, the Rockies, the Blue Ridge, the Andes and all mountains, but is a symbol of governments.

"And the kings of the earth, and the great men, and the chief captains, and the mighty men, and every bond man and every free man hid themselves in the dens and in the rocks of the mountains."

Mountains and islands are governments. Rocks and dens, state and municipal governments, that everybody will want to get into as quickly as possible after the great uprising, for as sure as Christ established Socialism so sure will Socialism rule the world whether we want it or not, and everybody will want a job with the government, for no one can make a living outside of it.

The Socialists make one terrible mistake that they do not make interest on money the point of attack, for interest is the supply train of their enemies, and they are likened to a foolish general, that wastes his army against an impregnable position, where a few men could attack and capture the supply train and force the enemies out of their stronghold.

In a recent street railway controversy, in an article of defense, the company showed that nearly 5 per cent of the receipts went for interest on bonded debts. They then go on to show what goes out for a hundred and one articles that go into the construction of and repairs of the cars and road-bed. It would look like this:

Interest on bonded debt for road, 5 per cent.

To pay dividends, which is interest, 5 per cent.

Interest on debts of mining company, 5 per cent.

Interest on money invested in rolling mills, 5 per cent.

Interest on lumbering enterprise, 5 per cent.

Interest on mills to saw the logs, 5 per cent.

Interest in factories in leather industry, 5 per cent.

Interest in paint industry, 5 per cent.

Interest in glass industry, 5 per cent.

Interest in tool industry, 5 per cent.

Now this is only ten of the hundred and one articles: now look at the ramifications. Each one of these industries has its special wants, all calculate their returns must cover not only the interest on the debts they owe, but on the money invested at their own estimated value.

CUT

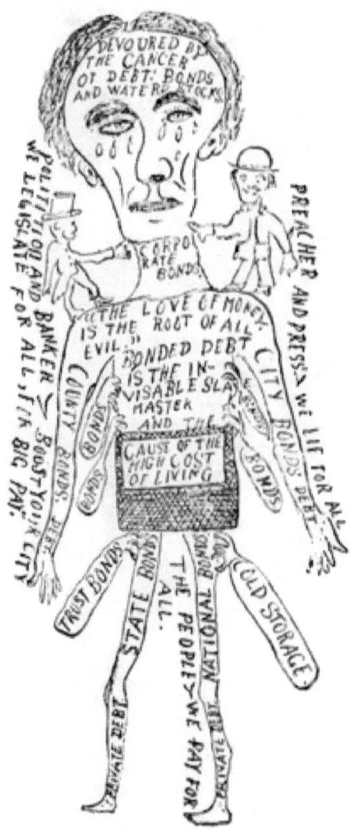

The illustration above shows how the

cancer saps the vital forces, exactly as does a cancer.

The nature of a cancer is to eat, eat, eat, until it has devoured everything around it, until it kills the patient, and after the man is in his grave, it eats the body until there is nothing left, and then it devours itself.

When Egypt died four per cent of the people owned all of the wealth; when Babylon died three per cent owned all of the wealth.

When Greece died less than two per cent owned all of the wealth.

When Rome died less than two thousand people virtually owned the world.

Less than five per cent of the people in the U. S. own 95 per cent of all of the wealth, and now the cancer has begun eating itself, and great failures are likely to occur, and then the unprincipled creatures that have brought on the disaster will charge it to the unrest of the people, and if they do, it should be hurled back in their teeth with such force that it will make them swallow their own lies.

With the vast number idle and cost of living out of sight, they may be thankful if the people do not repeat the French uprising of 1798.

Is it any wonder there is but little left for labor, and then the laboring man must pay interest on the ramifications of factors that create what he consumes, so if labor strikes at interest on money he strikes at the most vital stronghold of mammon, his oppressor.

The working man is given a chance to get a few cents interest as a bate to keep him voting for interest bondage.

Mammon is the only devil, the bruitish deceivers, the church has twisted into a spiritual devil to further deceive man for the benefit of the rich usurer.

The kings, princes and money lords know that, and also know the cancer must soon begin to eat itself so the middle class will be, yes, are being, ground between the upper and nether millstones, and then there will be uprisings, for men will not starve and see their families starve. Already selfishness is on the increase, and the break is near at hand; they know and are preparing for it.

In 1900 I stated that if my interpretation was correct, from the taking away of the Jewish daily sacrifice, 1260 years would be up in 1908 and that King Edward of England would form an alliance of seven kingdoms, representing the seven crowns on the dragon's head, apparently against Germany, but in reality against freedom, when the oppressed people arise against his satanic majesty mammon, and that he would do some outlandish thing to curry favor with the pope. It is now history. He formed such an alliance and we all know that when an English king takes his throne he takes his oath he will never enter a Catholic church. But—In November, 1908, King Edward violated his own oath and entered a Catholic church and had a mass said, thus setting up "the abomination that maketh desolate."

Now begins the cleansing of the sanctuary.

Aquarius, the sign of man, is in the heavens.

The dragon has power to give life to the image of the beast and to restore the wounded head.

What is more desolating than the robbery system that has converted all of the natural wealth from the hands of the public to the hands of a few selfish, grasping men?

What is a greater abomination than joining that horror to a church to deceive the people and keep their heads bowed in prayer while being robbed by the legal thieves?

"And now we are to have a king. His name is Prince Robert of Bavaria, deslendant of the Stuarts."

THIS IS THE PICTURE OF THE MAN THEY WOULD MAKE KING

"Boston, Mass., Nov. 1, 1900.—A proof will soon be given that the axiom 'Westward the course of empire takes its way,' is no more an empty phrase her in the United States. A band of cavaliers, casting the cherished sentiments of democracy to the winds, will, on April 19 next, plant the royal standard of the Stuarts in the very heart of the old mother of states.

"These enthusiasts, who take themselves very seriously, glory in the name of the 'Aryan Order of St. George and of his Holy Roman Empire.'"

Mark this: Holy Roman Church

The papal power has virtually been driven out of Europe. He has lost his temporal power. Mammon, who controls the power by force of his money, has power to restore the wounded head, the powers who hate republics are willing to establish the papacy here, but all Christendom would oppose it, yet would not say so much against a king, hence the preparation to establish a king here first.

THIS IS THEIR KING'S COAT OF ARMS.

Where open treason is talked you may depend upon it it is backed up by men of power in high places.

The following was openly published in the rounds of the press in November, 1900, and here is the picture of the intended king, his flag and his coat of arms:

The above is but one of many evidences of a drift to monarchy.

J. Gould said he would give a million dollars toward establishing a monarchy.

Wm. Vanderbilt said "The public be damned."

In 1869 a paper called the "Imperialist" was published at 37 Mercer street, New York. Its editorial said it came unannounced, but not undesired. It was supported by many big capitalists, but deemed too early as there were too many old soldiers at that time.

Some years later, in 1876, a similar paper was published in New Orleans.

In 1905 a lot of army officers at a banquet in New York expressed themselves in favor of monarchy as a necssity for the army.

In 1896, the Des Moines, Iowa, Globe came out in strong terms in favor of monarchy. At the same time Senator Jones said, "The principal issue is imperialism."

I have a great deal of such matter that has appeared in the press from time to time.

Many men of note in Europe and America have expressed themselves in very strong terms in favor of monarchy.

In 1901 a prominent official and well known public man by the name of Biglow, a man of sufficient influence to cause the press of England and America to note what he said, expressed himself in favor of monarchy as being preferrable to a republic and said:

"In Washington I found a cynical contempt for the United States' constitution. Of course I should not think of reflecting on such men as Secretary Hay and Judge Taft, but if Hay were the archangel Gabriel and Taft St. Peter returned to earth, they could not stop the complex and far-reaching system of thievery that prevails in the public service."

Of course the masses would not be told the plans of the great plotters, for of course they are not fools. Nor would many of the effects of their scheems be directly their work, but would be the effects of their infernal plots.

The schemes of such men would naturally be to get possession of the land and producing factories. I have shown you that by their own confession this they have done.

We know who has got the loot and that is sufficient evidence who the thieves are in common court, then if they wage war to steel the government to protect their stolen property, why should the people divide to shoot each other to sustain thieves and traitors?

The continual raise of official salaries is to prepare the people for the blow.

Not only to tire the people of our present government but to prepare them for a political aristocracy.

The people should frown down all attempts to rais political salaries, as the work of traiters, and vote down every form of bonds, as bonded debt is a form of slavery,

It has been claimed that Harriman, Morgan, and certain oil companies wer backed by money of the Catholic hiarchy, and the burning of the largest candle ever known, in the vatican at Rome, in honor of Mr. Pierpont Morgan, would lead one to that belief.

The apparent preparation of years for the pope at Baltimore adds to that evidence. At any rate, the powers and mammon are prepared for that even, and own everything, and all of the armies and according to the prophecy will seat a king and then the pope, and dwell with him for an hour 15 years and then Socialism, whether we want it or not. Unless we rally and defeat mammon, it will be slavery of the worst aspects.

THIS IS THE FLAG OF TREASON—THE GUDGEON A YELLOW RAG WITH A DOUBLE EAGLE.

"Eternal vigilance is the price of liberty." HA, HA, HA! Yet, who is exerting vigilance?

Remember that preceding the fall of Rome and the establishing of the papal power, a Bavarian prince made his flag familiar to the people through secret societies. Apparently as the colors of innocent trading societies. During the month of September, 1913, here in Detroit the trators' flag has been flaunted in the faces of the people, where not a single color or starry banner could be found. Hereafter when you see a yellow rag with this design upon it you may know traitors who favor monarchy or papacy are around you.

I have showed you they would naturally encourage political corruption just to make the people dissatisfied. The high cost of living is one of the desired ends of thes traitors. Though this is partly due to three causes:

First, the cold storage, and the means of holding up products until spoiled, for the purpose of higher prices.

2. The natural increased demand because of the great increase of population and lack of time to settle to raising necesistics of life. Also through ease with which it can be shipped abroad.

3. Because of high cost of transportation charges, necessary to pay interest on money and watered stock, as well as to pay interest on the thousand and one investments, along the line of creation, and this forces combines among the commercial element.

It may all be traced back to interest on money, as shown in the accompanying cut.

The time is near at hand when it is impossible to make two ends meet, and then crime will increase tenfold, and the people will rise up in rebellion.

The moment they have brought on a panic, they try to make the people believe it is their restless demands that have caused the business failures. When they do this, the people should demand that the government sieze every railroad, factory and public utility, and run them for the public benefit; and issue good full legal tender to pay all dues, and furnish employment for all idle people.

NOW, PATRIOTS OF AMERICA, LOVERS OF FREEDOM, I APPEAL TO YOU.

Show this book to your friends and form patroic societs ,anb spred the news.

THE END.

www.ingramcontent.com/pod-product-compliance
Lightning Source LLC
Chambersburg PA
CBHW051236300426
44114CB00011B/767